# ON THE EDGE

## The Road to Rome

### R. E. Anderson

The Path we have chosen, while not correct in all things, is the path we are on. Some will be left behind. Some will excel. Corporations saved will rise and fall. The big question is will this country retain its soul.

Title: On the Edge: The Road to Rome
Author: Ronald E. Anderson

©Copyright 2013 by Ronald E. Anderson

This is the second book in my series, starting with *Transitions 1941*. It is the continuing fulfillment of my education and life experiences, my years of work at Rio Hondo College (in Whittier, CA) and the California Polytechnic University (in Pomona, California). My major was Political Science, Public Administration. These years of education and work experience have helped add depth to this continuing fulfillment of my life's work.

David H. Anderson

James A. Rae

Margaret Moor

David and Shannon Perez and family

C. Mahoney

Thank you...

...for supporting my efforts in putting this book together.
...for investing in my ideas.
...for the feedback and input in the writing of this book.

# TABLE OF CONTENTS

1. G. K. GALBRAITH
2. WAY BACK WHEN
3. JOHN STEWART MILL
4. TRANSITION
5. ON ALAN GREENSPAN
6. CREATIVE DESTRUCTION
7. IRATIONAL EXUBERANCE
8. GREENSPAN'S SPEECH
9. WINDS OF CHANGE
10. THE FINANCIAL SERVICES MODERNIZATION ACT
11. SURPLUS/RECESSION
12. A 2012 TIME WARP
13. THE AMERICAN MYTH
14. SOCIAL DARWINISM
15. JOHN D. ROCKEFELLER
16. IN CONCLUSION
17. BUSH TAX CUTS 2001
18. A TIME LEADING TO WAR
19. NATIVE AMERICAN CULTURAL MYTHOLOGY
20. CALIFORNIA POLITICS:  February 19, 1967
21. July 16, 1967
22. November 3, 1968
23. December 30, 1968
24. January 3, 1969
25. REAGAN'S MENTAL HEALTH PROGRAN:  January 21, 1969
26. FLOODING: January 30, 1969
27. THE WELFARE ISSUE:  January 14, 1970
28. MULTIPLE PARTIES
29. INTRANSIGENCE: May 28, 1969
30. REAGAN'S THREE YEAR TAX PLAN:  June 11, 1969
31. THE LEGISLATION THAT CHANGED IT ALL:  June 12, 1969
32. DEATH PENALTY

33. BUDGET WAR: June 20, 1969
34. FLOOD REPAIR: September 8, 1969
35. January 14, 1970
36. THE MORATORIUM: January 29, 1971
37. THE FISCAL CRISIS: February 3, 1971
38. BEFORE THE AXE: December 11, 2009
39. CALPERS: January 15, 2010
40. GIFTS
41. CALIFORNIA SECLUSION RADICAL THOUGHT: February 26, 2010
42. STATE SELLS SURPLUS BUILDINGS
43. February 26, 2010
44. THE INSURANCE INDUSTRY
45. COASTAL CONFLICT
46. LET THE RACE BEGIN: May 1, 2010
47. EVEN IN VERNON: March 4, 2010
48. IT REQUIRES A LICENSE: May 8, 2010
49. TAX FREE BONDS: March 9, 2010
50. WHITMAN'S PORTFOLIO: March 11, 2010
51. STEVE POIZNER
52. THE TORTOISE AND THE HARE: March 11, 2010
53. THE DOODAH PARADE: March 11, 2010
54. MORE ON WHITMAN: March 24, 2010
55. AB 32
56. HEMET
57. WHITMAN ON HEALTH CARE: March 31, 2010
58. NURSING HOME ABUSE: March 31, 2012
59. ACORN: April 5, 2010
60. STATISTICS, STATISTICS, STATISTICS: April 5, 2010
61. LEGALIZE MARIJUANA? April 8, 2010
62. NATURAL GAS: April 9, 2010
63. RED LIGHT CAMERAS: April 23, 2010
64. STATE PROPERTY (continued): April 28, 2010
65. CALPERS FRAUD: May 6, 2010
66. CALPERS FRAUD: May 7, 2010
67. WHO'S RUNNING THEIR RECORDS
68. CALIFORNIA'S SENATE CANDIDATES
69. November 4, 1970
70. FUND RAISING
71. PENSIONS AND THE LEGISLATURE

72. POLITICAL CHANGE THE EARLY YEARS
73. THE OPEN PRIMARY
74. CONFLICT OF INTEREST
75. CALIFORNIA 1968
76. CALIFORNIA POLITICAL SOCIAL INFLUENCE
77. ELECTIONS
78. EMINENT DOMAIN
79. THE NATIONAL SCENE
80. TRANSPORTATION
81. TACTICS
82. MAGIC
83. STYLE
84. CALIFORNIA SCENE 1976
85. THE 9/11 AFFECT
86. THE NATIONAL SCENE
87. A HOME INVASION
88. THE WEST COAT
89. AN EYEWITNESS
90. THE FLIGHT OF HEROES 93
91. A PEOPLE'S CALLTO WAR
92. VILLAIN UNVAILED
93. THE AIR DOWN TOWN
94. WHY THE TOWERS WERE STRUCK?
95. THE SUSPECTS
96. AMERICA ASKS FOR SUPPORT
97. BUSH ACTION/ECONOMIC REALITY
98. BIOLOGICAL CHEMICAL WARFARE
99. FORCES THAT UNIFY: September 22, 2001
100. HOLLYWOOD ADJUSTS
101. HISTORIC FIGURES
102. THE FAVORITE SON CAMPAIGN
103. NORTH ATLANTIC TREATY ORGANIZATION
104. ON SOCIALISM
105. ON GEOGRAPHY
106. RELATIVE MILITARY STRENGTH
107. EUROPEAN POLITICS
108. SHAPE
109. NEW NATO AND CYPRUS
110. THE COMMUNIST QUESTION

111. U.S. PRESENCE
112. THE IRANIAN REVOLUTION
113. RONALD W. REAGAN
114. GOVERNOR JERRY BROWN
115. PRESIDENT JIMMY CARTER 1977
116. 1978
117. September 12
118. 2013 (part two)
119. THE FIRE SEASON DOWN UNDER
120. ON POLITICS: January 22, 2009
121. THE MIDDLE EAST
122. ON THE PRESIDENT
123. BACK TO THE MIDDLE EAST
124. ON APPOINTMENTS
125. OBAMA ON EXECUTIVE COMPENSATION
126. BLAGOJEVICH
127. CORPORATE LAYOFFS
128. JUST HOW COLD IS IT (January 29-30, 2009)
129. IRAQ AND POTENTIAL ELECTIONS
130. THE STIMULUS PACKAGE
131. THE EMPLOYMENT ISSUE: February 2, 2009
132. THE MORTGAGE ISSUE
133. BACK TO THE MIDDLE EAST: February 4, 2009
134. CRITICISM
135. DEFAULT
136. MORE ON JOB LOSS
137. OBITUARIES
138. THE MIDDLE EAST
139. JOB LOSS UPDATE
140. THE REPUBLICANS
141. ON THE HEALTH ISSUE
142. SRI LANKA
143. ON THE LIGHTER SIDE
144. FOREIGN POLICY
145. THE TALE OF ANGEL ISLAND
146. THE INTERNATIONAL DRUG TRADE: February 13, 2009
147. PAKISTAN
148. A SEASON FOR GIVING
149. THE WEIRD EXPERIMENT

150. THE WORLD ECONOMIC CONDITION
151. SIDE-EFFECTS: February 14, 2009
152. THE BREAK-DOWN
153. February 21, 2009
154. MEDICAL FRONT
155. THE JUDICIARY
156. IN THE OOPS COLUMN
157. ON HEALTH CARE
158. THE DRUG WAR
159. THE ECONOMY: February 1, 1996
160. THE Y2K AND NEW ZEALAND
161. ROLLING BLACK-OUTS September 13, 2000
162. THE BLAIR WITCH PROJECT March 20, 2001
163. THE E BUSINESS April 2, 2001
164. FANTASY GAMES April 2, 2001
165. THE ENERGY CRISIS
166. LINUX-MICROSOFT
167. THE CONSORTIUM CONCEPT: April 2, 2001
168. STOCK MARKET
169. EMPLOYEE EVALUATIONS: April 8, 2001
170. QUALITY TIME
171. THE LANDLORD CONCEPT
172. DEREGULATION: May 6, 2001
173. THE EDISON COMPLEX
174. EDISON TIME LINE
175. May 12, 2001
176. THE URBAN RETAIL REACH
177. THE CENCUS EFFECT
178. THE ENERGY ISSUE: May 15, 2001
179. May 23, 2001
180. May 25, 2001
181. THE JOB SCENE
182. ENERGY SOLUTION: June 19, 2001
183. FIBER OPTICS
184. THE MEDIA
185. IT'S A PLASTIC WORLD
186. GROSS DOMESTIC PRODUCT: July 28, 2001
187. NOW THE REAL DAMAGE: September 28, 2001
188. THE LIABILITY OF 9/11: September 28, 2001

189. THE AIR MARSHAL PROGRAM: September 28, 2001
190. NEW JERSEY
191. THE CHRISTMAS DILEMMA: October 22, 2001
192. FEDS CUTS RATES
193. PAKISTAN
194. TOO BIG TO FAIL: March 13, 2009
195. AMERICAN ISLAM
196. JUSTICE
197. PERSUASION
198. THE NASTY EGG HUNT
199. THE WINDS OF CHANGE
200. SOCIETY ADJUSTS: March 7, 2009
201. THE MONTAGE: March 18, 2009
202. March 23, 2009
203. March 7, 2009
204. CONVICTED
205. ENERGY
206. ASTRONOMY
207. EARTH MATTERS
208. March 22, 2009
209. THE VOTING RIGHTS ACT
210. THE TIMES THEY ARE A GHANGING
211. ON THE WORLD
212. U.S. POLITICAL STRATEGY: March 29, 2009
213. HOME FRONT
214. CHANGE AND WORLD ELEMENTS
215. CHINA: March 31, 2009
216. ECONOMIC ISSUES
217. FOREIGN LANDS
218. NATIONAL DEBATE
219. INTRIGUE AND CHANGE
220. OBITUARIES
221. A WORLD APART
222. SCIENCE
223. A QUESTION OF INTENT
224. DETAINEES
225. A NEW DIRECTION
226. OBITUARIES
227. ECONOMIES OF SCALE: April 7, 2009

228. BACK IN THE USA
229. DISCLOSURE: April 17, 2009
230. CALIFORNIA
231. THE BATTLE OF SAN JACINTO
232. CHANGE
233. ONWARD
234. ON CIVIC RESPONSIBILITY
235. THE PROGRESSIVES
236. CONSPIRACY
237. THE CHANGE ELEMENTS
238. SPECIAL CIRCUMSTANCES
239. H1N1
240. AMERICANS AS TARGETS
241. POLITICS IN THE AMERICA'S
242. CARTEL WARS
243. April 29, 2009
244. SOCIAL PRESSURES AND CURES
245. SCIENCE, TECHNOLOGY, AND POLITICAL CHANGE
246. POLITICS
247. OBITUARY
248. OBAMA'S 100 DAYS
249. WEST COAST SYNDROME
250. THE DRUG SOCIETY
251. MORE ON THE 100 DAYS
252. H1N1 (continued)
253. AMERICAN FOREIGN POLICY
254. BANKING INDUSTRY
255. OBITUARY
256. ECONOMY
257. PEST CONTROL
258. SOCIAL AND HEALTH ISSUES
259. THE UNION ISSUE
260. OUR FRIENDS OVERSEAS
261. FAST FOOD: April 30, 2009
262. TREASURY BONDS
263. GROSS DOMESTIC PRODUCT SHRINKAGE
264. CREDIT CARD BILL
265. REVOLUTIONARY LAW: May 20, 2009
266. OBITUARIES

267. INDIA
268. CALIFORNIA AND THE NATION
269. IDENTITY THEFT
270. WASHINGTON
271. May 5, 2009
272. OBITUARY
273. PRIVATE THOUGHTS
274. ON THE LIGHTER SIDE
275. HEALTH CARE
276. ASTRONOMY
277. END OF A DYNASTY
278. RELIGIOUS DIALOGUE
279. AFRICA/RUSSIA
280. THE HEART OF DOGMA
281. ECONOMIC FORCES
282. May 16, 2009
283. CULTURAL INFLUENCE
284. THE PROPOSITIONS
285. WHAT POLICE DO
286. LEGISLATORS AND THE WAR
287. MILITARY TRIBUNALS
288. SHUTTLE PROGRAM
289. ON THE SUPREME COURT
290. OBITUARY
291. PEOPLE IN THE NEWS
292. BRITISH PORK
293. GUANTANAMO
294. JUSTICE?
295. CORRUPTION
296. END TIMES
297. LOS ANGELES POLITIC'S
298. THE SUPREME COURT: May 28, 2009
299. A WORLD APART
300. IRAN
301. MEXICO
302. ISRAEL
303. PAKISTAN
304. OBITUARIES
305. THE CORPORATE MENTALITY

306. STOCK MARKET PLUNGE 1987
307. CORPORATE POLUTION:  November 25, 1989
308. CONTINENTAL AIRLINES BANKRUPTCY:  December 4, 1990
309. IDM BANKRUPTCY:  November 20, 1992
310. SECURITY PACIFIC: November 24, 1992
311. MARTIN MARIETA
312. COMMUNICATIONS TECH:  December 14, 1992
313. RETAIL GIANTS:  January 14, 1994
314. AIRLINE PRICE FIXING:  March 18, 1994
315. NORTHROP GRUMMAN:  April 5, 1994
316. April 6, 1994
317. THE SOURCE OF THE G M BAIL-OUT:  May 12, 1994
318. THE EGG WENT SPLAT
319. CLASS ACTION LAWSUIT:  January 19, 1993
320. THE ORANGE COUNTY BANKRUPTCY:  December 14, 1994
321. THE FLOW OF COMMERCE
322. THE INFLUENCE GAME
323. WORLD TRADE:  May 20, 1993
324. DETROIT:  February 7, 1995
325. ANTI-TRUST ISSUES: February 15, 1995
326. CORPORATE NOMAD'S:  March 17, 1995
327. WESTING HOUSE CORPORATION:  August 2, 1995
328. DISNEY TO BUY ABC:  August 1, 1995
329. BOEING MCDONALD DOUGLAS MERGER:  November 17, 1995
330. R. J. R. TOBACCO:  March 20, 2001
331. JAHWA A. CHINESE SUCCESS:  April 2, 2001
332. THE FORTUNE 500
333. PG&E THE BONUS ISSUE:  April 8, 2001
334. SOUTHERN CALIFORNIA EDISON:  May 8, 2001
335. EARTHLINK:  May 11, 2001
336. AOL:  June 19, 2001
337. FORD MOTOR COMPANY
338. TECH MERGERS:  September 5, 2001
339. CHINA:  September 26, 2001
340. ENRON ON TRIAL:  February 1, 2006
341. *THE TIMES* OF LONDON:  May 7, 2004
342. IN KIND OIL CONTRACTS:  September 17, 2009
343. THE TARP ISSUE
344. NORTHROP GRUMONN

345. FINANCIAL RED LINING
346. FILM MAKERS:  December 10, 2009
347. GENERAL MOTORS:  December 2, 2009
348. COMCAST:  December 3, 2009
349. BANK OF AMERICA:  September 15, 2009
350. THE BANKS:  June 10, 2009
351. THE TANGLED WEB
352. THE HEALTH CARE ISSUE
353. HOUSING PRICES FALL
354. THE CATFISH ISSUE
355. A TRIP TO THE MOON:  June 27, 2009
356. FLAT TV SCREEN:  June 29, 2009
357. GOVERNMENT STIMULUS RECESSION ENDS:  July 17, 2009
358. PUBLIC SECTOR JOB LOSS:  July 18, 2009
359. THE NATIONAL HEALTH PLAN:  August 1, 2009
360. THE FORTH OF JULY:  June 29, 2009
361. THE COUNTY FAIR CONCEPT:  September 11, 2009
362. THE AUTO INDUSTRY:  October 2, 2009
363. U.S. INVESTMENT ABROAD: October 4, 2009
364. MANSIONS
365. THE LOCAL CORNER STORE:  October 12, 2009
366. THE POP-UP STORE:  October 17, 2009
367. BANK OF AMERICA
368. COMMERCIAL TRANSPORTATION:  October 23, 2009
369. HOLLYWOOD PROPS
370. THE TIMBER INDUSTRY:  October 28, 2009
371. FEDERAL HOUSING ADMINISTRATION:  December 3, 2009
372. OLD TECHNOLOGY STATE EFFICENCY:  December 9, 2009
373. ASSESMENTS FOR THE BENEFITS OF CREDITORS:  January 23, 2011
374. ALL IN THE NAME OF SECURITY: January 14, 2010
375. FREIGHT BY RAIL:  January 14, 2010
376. HOME SALES:  February 27, 2010
377. FORECLOSURE DILEMMA
378. SMALL BUSINESS RISING:  March 1, 2010
379. THE PAYDAY LOAN
380. THE YEAR OF THE PINKSLIP:  March 2, 2010
381. AMERCAN DREAM VALUE DILEMMA
382. THE TECH STARTS UP:  March 5, 2010
383. TOYOTA'S RECALL:  February 25, 2010

384. BORDERS LIQUIDATION: February 21, 2011
385. THE DOUBLE DIP? February 23, 2011
386. SMALL BUSINESS AND THE TAX CODE: February 28, 2011
387. VIRTUAL SHOPPING:
388. TARP
389. ETHANOL: March 3, 2011
390. PUBLIC EMPLYEE UNIONS: March 12, 2011
391. FARM WORKER UNION REFORM: April 1, 2011
392. AMERICAN APPAREL INDUSTRY
393. WHAT AFFECT A SHUT-DOWN
394. JOB GROWTH
395. THE ANTI-UNION PUSH
396. WHAT ABOUT GOLD: April 5, 2010
397. THE GOLDMAN SACH'S HEARINGS: April 30, 2010
398. THE BUSH HOUSING TAX CREDIT
399. JOBLESS BENEFITS END
400. PRISONS AND THE ECONOMY: May 3, 2010
401. THE MIXED RECOVERY: May 4, 2010
402. THE DAY THE DOW DROPPED: May 7, 2010
403. SPAIN'S ECONOMIC TROUBLES
404. RETAIL STEADY AND SLOW
405. THE AIRLINES: May 8, 2010
406. THE BUS SYSTEM: May 11, 2010
407. MICROSOFT: May 12, 2010
408. THE BOEING STRIKE
409. THE DEEP HORIZON AFTERMATH: May 18, 2010
410. PUTTING THE BRAKES ON RENTAL DECLINE: April 7, 2011
411. AMERICAN ENTERPRIZE: April 23, 2010
412. OIL MONEY/THE SUDAN: May 18, 2010
413. BUFFETT
414. FED FORECAST
415. PROPOSED HOSPITAL UNION MEMBERSHIP
416. RETIREMENT LIVING WITH STYLE
417. HOT MONEY: May 27, 2010
418. SMALL FIRMS AND HEALTH INSURANCE
419. HEALTH RISKS AND STAFFING LEVELS
420. GIFT CARDS/ SMALL BUSINESS: June 7, 2010
421. SO YOU WANT TO START A RESTAURANT
422. SMALL BANKS: June 10, 2010

423. BANKS AND SAVINGS:  June 12, 2010
424. ON THE ISSUE OF POT
425. FORECLOSURE UPDATE:  May 12, 2011
426. THE CRISIS DEPARTMENT
427. MEXICAN DRAFT BEER
428. THE LENDERS TWO TRACK FORECLOSURE:  April 15, 2011
429. FEDERAL CUTS:  April 12, 2011
430. MORE ACQUISITIONS
431. CONCERNING BEYOND PETROLEUM:  March 4, 2010
432. THE STERILIZATION:  February 26, 2010
433. DEEP WATER HORIZON:  April 30, 2010
434. THE WILDLIFE EFFECT
435. WASHINGTON DEBATES HOW BAD IT WAS
436. OIL DISPERSANTS
437. TOURISMS WET BLANKET
438. THE SCHEDULE
439. THE BIG BOX
440. ALASKA
441. A SMALL BOX
442. May 7, 2010
443. COAST INVADED
444. TOP KILL:  May 25 2010
445. OIL ILLNESS:  May 26, 2010
446. MORE DATA
447. THE TRUTH COMES OUT
448. TOP KILL (continued):  May 27, 2010
449. IT DIDN'T WORK:  June 4, 2010
450. REVIEWING THE BAN:  June 6, 2010
451. THE BRITS REACT:  June 12, 2010
452. LOOSE FIGURES:  June 16, 2010
453. THE PUSH FOR ALTERNATIVE ENERGY
454. SB 1070
455. THE STORM
456. THE POLITICAL OIL STORM:  July 21, 2010
457. BRITISH PETROLEUM SELLS ASSETTS
458. THE WELL IS CAPPED
459. THE 100 DAY MARK:  July 29, 2010
460. THE MOMENT ARRIVES:  July 30, 2010
461. PRESIDENT BARAK OBAMA:  June 16, 2009

462. FOREIGN POLICY/ IRAN:  June 23, 2009
463. THE CLIMATE BILL:  June 29, 2009
464. THE SUPREME COURT:  July 12, 2009
465. THE IRANIAN PROTEST
466. GOVERNMENT LIFTS OIL DRILLING BAN:  July 17, 2009
467. NAACP
468. THE DETAINEES
469. HEALTH CARE BATTLE
470. THE TRANSPERANCY WARS
471. PROFILING AN A TEACHABLE MOMENT
472. THE METEL OF FREEDOM
473. LIBERAL REVOLT
474. GEORGE H. W. BUSH HONORED:  August 10, 2009
475. COMMUNITY OUTREACH
476. ON EDUCATION:  September 8, 2009
477. THE BATTLE FOR THE HEALTH PLAN
478. September 11, 2009
479. ABORTION ISSUE
480. THE SPECIAL EXPERIMENT:  September 12, 2009
481. THE DOCTORS:  September 15, 2009
482. THE RACE ISSUE
483. ON CONSUMER PROTECTION:  October 4, 2009
484. ON FOREIGN WARS:  October 10, 2009
485. THE CLEAN ENERGY ARGUMENT:  October 28, 2009
486. HOW TO BREIF A PRESIDENT:  October 31, 2009
487. A MILLION JOBS CREATED OR PRESERVED
488. 30,000 MORE TROOPS
489. December 10, 2009: JOBS:
490. THE MORE THINGS CHANGE THE MORE THEY STAY THE SAME: January 21, 2010
491. GOING IT ALONE:  February 26, 2010
492. ON EDUCATION:  March 2, 2010
493. HEALTH CARE GROUND ZERO
494. March 9, 2010
495. March 11, 2010
496. ON ISRAEL:  March 24, 2010
497. OBAMAS CORPORATE CZAR
498. HE DID IT:  March 28, 2010
499. ON AFGHANISTAN:  March 31, 2010
500. THE NUCLEAR AGENDA:  April 5, 2010

501. THE NEW ECONOMY VERSES THE OLD ECONOMY: April 8, 2010
502. ARMS REDUCTION: April 9, 2010
503. THE KARZAI ISSUE: April 10, 2010
504. FEDERAL REACTION TO THE ARIZONA LAW
505. DISASTER IN THE GULF: May 3, 2010
506. CALDERON, OBAMA, AND THE ARIZONA LAW: May 20, 2010
507. May 26, 2010
508. THE POLITICS OF OIL: May 27, 2010
509. THE BLOOD LIBEL ISSUE: January 13, 2011
510. BEFORE IT WAS OFFICIAL: April 15, 2011
511. ROMNEY'S HEALTH PLAN: May 12, 2011
512. THE ISRAELI POLICY: May 22, 2011
513. THE INTELLECTUAL TWINGE: May 29, 2011
514. PALIN AS A DISTRACTION
515. ON ROMNEY AND HUNTSMAN: June 4, 2011
516. SANITORUM: June 7, 2011
517. HERMAN CAIN
518. THE FIRST REPUBLICAN PRESIDENTIAL DEBATE June 14, 2011
519. JON HUNTSMAN BEGINS:
520. BACHMANN FEDERAL AID: June 26, 2011
521. MIXED MESSAGES: July 5, 2011
522. ARIZONA'S CLEAN ELECTION LAW
523. RICK PERRY'S RISE: August 4, 2011
524. THE STRAW POLL DINNER: August 15, 2011
525. THE THREE WAY RACE: August 16, 2011
526. TEXAS
527. August 29, 2011
528. September 1, 2011
529. THE DEMOCRATS: September 2, 2011
530. THE SECOND DEBATE: September 8, 2011
531. THE IMMIGRATION ISSUE: September 27, 2011
532. CAIN'S TROUBLES: November 3, 2011
533. THE OCCUPY WALL STREET MOVEMENT RISES: October 7, 2011
534. ON FOREIGN POLICY: October 28, 2011
535. NEVADA: October 17 2011
536. HEALTH CARE WAR: October 18, 2011
537. THE 999 TAX PLAN: October 19, 2011
538. THE VEGAS DEBATE
539. THE IOWA TRAIL: October 21, 2011

540. CALIFORNIA: October 28, 2011
541. CAIN ECLIPSED
542. THE FLORIDA VOTING ISSUE
543. THE CAIN EXPLANATION: November 1, 2011
544. THE FORUM
545. ROMNEY ON CUTS
546. CAIN ON RACE
547. CAINS FALL: November 9, 2011
548. QUANDARIES: November 10, 2011
549. CHANGING STATUS: November 17, 2011
550. ON CHILD LABOR: November 26, 2011
551. BANK OF AMARICA: November 2, 2011
552. CANDIDATES SKIP IOWA FORUM
553. THE EUROPEAN EFFECT: November 3, 2011
554. CAIN LINKS ISSUE TO RACE: November 5, 2011
555. ROMNEY IN IOWA
556. ROMNEY CUTS/CHANGES
557. THE TIDE WAS TURNING
558. ON ROMNEY: December 3, 2011
559. ROMNEY'S CAMPAIGN
560. A SYRIA REFLECTION
561. THE RON PAUL AFFECT
562. THE LATIN VOTE: January 30, 2012
563. TO BE A EXECUTIVE AND A PRESIDENT THAT IS THE QUESTION
564. THE CONCEPT OF WEALTH: February 1, 2012
565. REGIONAL VICTORIES
566. THE RON PAUL AFFECT
567. THE RACE NARROWS
568. THE BATTLE FOR MICHIGAN: February 21, 2012
569. THE BATTLE FOR DELEGATES
570. TACTICS
571. THE LATIN VOTE: April 27, 2012
572. CALIFORNIA'S OPEN PRIMARY: May 14, 2012
573. A SHIFT TO THE CENTER: January 27, 2011
574. A TIME OF UNITY: January 26, 2011
575. THE REPUBLICAN RESPONSE
576. HOW DO THINGS STACK UP: January 27, 2011
577. SMALL BUSINESS: February 23, 2011
578. LIBYA AND U.S. PRESSURE: March 12, 2011

579. ACCOUNTABLE CARE ORGANIZATION: April 1, 2011
580. THE QUESTION OF LIBYA: April 2, 2011
581. OBAMA'S EDGE
582. THE DEFICIT: April 12, 2011
583. SB 1070
584. ENDING THE WAR IN IRAQ: April 14, 2011
585. AN UNPLANED ROAD TRIP: April 30, 2011
586. ON BIN LADIN: May 2, 2011
587. THE JOINT CHEIFS OF STAFF: May 29, 2011
588. THE SECOND EUROPEAN TOUR
589. NATIONAL SECURITY: May 31, 2011
590. THE ORWELLIAN HEALTH PLAN: June 3, 2011
591. THE ROUGH ROAD: June 4, 2011
592. MORE ON THE LATIN VOTE: June 15, 2011
593. THE DRAW DOWN
594. CAMPAIGN MONEY: June 25, 2011
595. THE INOVATOR: June 29, 2011
596. THE PENTAGON FACTOR: August 4, 2011
597. OUR CREDIT PROBLEM
598. ENOUGH NOT ENOUGH: August 18, 2011
599. August 19, 2011
600. ENTERING THE RING
601. KATRINA THE AFFECT: August 29, 2011
602. A TIME FOR ACTION: August 30, 2011
603. September 1, 2011
604. September 8, 2011
605. THE FAA: September 17, 2011
606. THE SOLINDRA ISSUE
607. THE NEW PATENT LAW
608. THE CONCEPT OF THE BEAR
609. BEING ROME
610. ON EDUCATION: September 29, 2011
611. WHAT IS JUSTICE?
612. JOBS ACT PRESSURE: October 7, 2011
613. FAST AND FURIOUS UNRSOLVED
614. SOLYNDRA: October 8, 2011
615. LATIN VOTERS WANTED: October 19, 2011
616. TRANSPERANT GOVERNMENT: October 31, 2011
617. TRANS-CANADA PIPELINE: November 7, 2011

618. THE LOW PROFILE:  November 9, 2011
619. ASIAN CONFERENCE:  November 12, 2011
620. THE PALESTINIAN STATEHOOD ISSUE
621. THE CAMPAIGN TRAIL
622. ASIAN CONFERENCE (continued):  November 14, 2011
623. THE BALANCING ACT:  November 30, 2011
624. THE PAYROLE TAX-CUT FIGHT
625. MEANWHILE IN EUROPE
626. THE JAW BONING AFFECT December 1, 2011
627. ONE WAR ENDS:  December 13, 2011
628. MEANWHILE BACK IN BRITAIN
629. THE CANNONS ARE SOUNDING OFF:  January 24, 2012
630. THE STATE OF THE UNION
631. HOUSING:  January 26, 2012
632. ARIZONA'S GOVERNOR
633. THE PRESIDENTIAL MANUFACTURING PLANTHE NATION 2012
634. SYRIA:  March 7, 2012
635. MORE ON SYRIA
636. ON RUSSIA
637. LAGOS NIGERIA
638. THE KOREAN SUMMIT:  March 24, 2012
639. HEALTH CARE ISSUE AS A TAX
640. IRAN'S PRESSURE:  February 29, 2012
641. THE KEYSTONE PROJECT:  March 23, 2012
642. THE TRAYVON MARTIN CASE:  March 24, 2012
643. THE PRESIDENT'S TAX ISSUE:  April 14, 2012
644. THE ELECTORAL COLLEGE
645. THE FINAL STATEMENT

# PROLOGUE

*On the Edge: The Road to Rome* is the second in the series of compendium-style books that I have been privileged to write. The first volume, *Transitions 1941* (available online at Amazon.com), the story of the rise of Corporate America was written in pretty much the same style.

I have also written a volume of poetry, prose, and plays, written for performance in what is called "black stage" production, that is, very few props, putting the onus on the actors. Also in the book is commentary dialogues written by yours truly. It is called *Patterns with a Twist* (published through Xlibris). The book itself is a chat-style variety, subject-oriented experience that challenges the mind. To read this book, go to the table of contents and follow the subject you want to research, and it leads you by date from 1967, the source of my earliest material, to the year 2013.

It can be a guide into the minds of Galbraith to Greenspan. I cover the economy both in general and the corporate structure itself. Other areas are political-historical, as in early modern California history and how it affects us today. I cover some of our presidents, as I did in the first volume. I look at the nations of the world as we relate to them, even those we consider hostile to us. The 2012 election is covered from both the Democratic and Republican side, and I take it as far as the ending of the primary process, leaving you with projected analysis, leading to the day of the election, which is when President Obama was re-elected.

It is always good to keep one's opening statement short and sweet in order to encourage the reader to explore new vistas. This book is two years in the making, and a labor of love. I hope it will inform and entertain. Enjoy the read.

# 1. G. K. GALBRAITH

We are about to enter a world of growth of man's dreams as he scratches his way into the modern era. We are about to enter the Affluent Society.

During the time known as World War Two, price controls and rationing were applied to the domestic economy, which were credited with keeping the economy and business on track during the war years.

Economic prophets were sought to give the economy and business a direction. It is here that the corporate mentality has its seed.

In Europe, Germany in particular, the economic trusts were dismantled, giving way to the American model of the newly rising conservative movement that dates to 1948. This leads to the concept of anti-bureaucratic, market-driven economic growth. The corporations were just starting out.

It is here that the concept of eliminating the farm subsidy program began. We all know where that led. (Corporate farms) The Eisenhower Administration did not act on the elimination of subsidies like the farm subsidy, because it realized the arguments were just conjecture not meant to be acted upon. The Administration declared it was Keynesian, philosophy and policy.

The Keynesian theory on economic expansion consisted of social spending without raising taxes and a reduction in spending as the economy improved. It was also referred to as the Soft Policy on public spending: commitment to Keynes's philosophy was subject to selective scrutiny. The States' policies would grow subordinate to the market. This was acceptable to the conservative mind. The increase in social spending went hand in hand with increased taxation.

There is an accepted need to balance public and private expenditure for the public good. An allegory goes like this: A man leaning against an unsure door would give the appearance of violence. It could also be an unsure door.

That the idea ad men tell us our desires and needs is part of that affluence we rely on for production. Too bad we are buying it from our competitors, and not producing it ourselves.

Galbraith basically states the degree that we don't understand our affluent society, can and will endanger that society. Now think of our burgeoning trade imbalance with China, and how our dollar is held hostage through our debt to them.

On the other end of the stick, it is equally undesirable where only the necessities are gotten in such a bare bones world, there would be no demand for anything. The bottom line on the consumption society lies in being worth your labor and to enjoy the fruits of it.

Galbraith states in his book The Affluent Society, Second Edition: "Speakers before the Chamber of Commerce rarely denigrate the business man as an economic force. Familiarity is a necessity when studying social behavior, especially economic behavior."

People have a tendency to follow people like Donald Trump, and they read his words as if they see the Bible. The argument lies in the ivory tower discussion or discourse. Knowledge in and of itself is useless. The application of what you hear to the world lies between the learning and the learned.

The social compact and conventional wisdom propels the common man, who gets power in a corporation or head of state to explain his or her concepts of conventional wisdom. This is sophistry. Galbraith cites General Motors and US Steel Corporation of America as examples. Remember when this book was written, he did not take into account when they no longer listen to their consuming audience and start initiating change from the top. Changing the bottom line is not solely in profit, but service and employment.

Galbraith does acknowledge a transition from exponent and a wise man to old fogey (who can't see their own shoelaces) and gives golden parachutes only to the chosen, bringing everything up to 2010. Bonuses to CEOs whose corporations have taken government money and still continue their old ways.

Voltaire observed, "It is only because the English have become merchants and traders that London has surpassed Paris in extent and in number of its citizens, that the English can place 200 warships on the seas and subsidize allies."

Think about it. Is not that what the United States did and does? This has been from the end of World War Two to this present day. The rise of the need for services, according to Galbraith, set in motion the setting aside of classical liberalism and the rise of what we call Socialism (Social Security). The rise of the trade unions, social insurance, and the softened corporations changed the world and brought about a new reality.

President Hoover's time line in the early thirties, related to the demand for goods and responsible management to avoid deflation. Now think about Wal-Mart. Foreign goods and blue light specials. Now back to his logic. A balanced budget was, in his terms, paramount: "Absolutely necessary. Most essential factor, to economic recovery." He referred to it as an "imperative immediate step."

The interesting side to all of this perceived conventional wisdom is as if biblical: The high will be made low. The good life of the socially elect shields him from annoyance (poverty) and dissent which comes with age. The strong and the soft position is exchanged for what Galbraith would call a weak one in the future. Let me translate my translation into the language of the common man. When you hit a certain age you become a liability (unless you can join the elite structure), and if not, you are denigrated to the factory, if there is one, or the unemployment line and total disappearance from the statistics of the employable. You are too rigid. The truth is, you are over 40 and have acquired a few limitations. You are an old car. What do you do with an old car? This is the corporate mentality I keep referring to, regardless of the language employed by the establishment. If these businesses can control the social costs, you just fell through the safety net. This is my spin on what Galbraith has inferred.

## 2. WAY BACK WHEN

From 1380 to 1510 CE, artisans enjoyed good return for their efforts. I suggest the mercantile movement, and subsidies from the landed class were part of this growth. By the 16th century, there was a decline that continues to the modern era of industrialization generated by civil war. Technology became the standard, and man followed. The factory replaced the household, and the ancient feudal wars that were so devastating were replaced by world wars. After the aftermath of the first and second World Wars, both sides have recovered and flourished. The interesting thing is that corporatism overcame Communism, which was just another form of corporatism, similar to National Socialism.

Historically speaking, Adam Smith, in 1790 was the first to follow central economic tradition. He envisioned an advancing national community. He wrote an article inquiring into nature and the causes of the wealth of nations. Competition and markets are the wheels that move the system, not the power of the state. Merchants, manufacturers and landlords on one hand and the working masses on the other. Relative bargaining strength is the key. The sad thing is, the mass of the labor force has lost this hand of poker, and the employer seems to be redefining the rules of the game.

David Richardo (1722–1823) and Thomas Robert Mathus (1766–1834) form the trinity of economics in the English-speaking countries. When mankind first looked at modern economic structure, the factors were determining prices of rents, wages and profits. These principles have served economists ever since, Marxist or Capitalist. They were called Respectable Professors of Dismissive Science.

To Mathus, food and population were linked. Lack of food (starvation), along with famine and death, stabilize supply and the growing and expanding population. Also, add where they live, such as a swamp, New Orleans, or a sandbar in Bangladesh, Sri Lanka, and you can have some stark realities. The number is limited by those who endure.

Today we talk about who is allowed to live, and in what state. How you will live is directly related to you economic stability, and that today is largely controlled by corporate interests. In the Omen series, upon the death of Ambassador Thorn, Damien Thorn, his son, went to his brother, the owner of Thorn Enterprises. His eventual rise in the corporation, and the death of the brother, also, and how the corporation bought up farm land and went into famine control, well, this abstraction is what the corporate farm is, fantasy and reality mixed.

Richardo had population as his dependent variable: "Regulates itself by funds which are to employ it and therefore always increases or diminishes with the increase or diminution of capital." The argument is that advanced wealth brings more population. The down side is, they do not bring more land to feed this population. Add water usage to that, as well as housing and other social uses. These are the scarce resource products, and wages are in direct conflict and considered flat to the rest of the product.

The increase in profit means a lowering of wages. Being equal means a reduction in profits. Every rise in profits is favorable to the accumulation of capital, and to further population, and therefore, in all probability, ultimately leads to the increase of rent.

As the population expands, with increasing capital product, profit and goods, as the product expands, the population will increase. Food requirements of the population will press on availability and land supply, and force up rents, to the advantage of the land owner. Translated, capitalists must prosper if there is to be progress. The children of this inescapable misfortune are the people at large. They can- not reap the fruits of their labor. The flip side to it, as I see it is they get unlimited access to established family interests, and when their usefulness diminishes, they are shut out.

Labor, like all other things which are purchased and sold, and which May be increased or diminished in quality, has its natural and its market price. It is the natural price of labor, which is necessary to enable laborers, one with another to subsist and perpetuate their race without increase or diminution. This was what was referred to as the iron law of wages.

In an improving society market, wages might be above the natural wage for an indefinite period. The condition that ruled the iron wage has been sliding into history since the 19th century.

What replaced this model was an artificial, legally regulated wage to labor: importance linked to the value society puts on a thing. All of this is related to who produces it, food, or other consumption product like a hard good that requires a skilled work force to prop up that society. Here is where the perks come in. The unskilled need certain things to make their lives tolerable. Remember, the farmer, as long as he is not heavily taxed, and given autonomy, will stay where he is. The dependent worker needs services, or deviation occurs.

## 3. JOHN STEWART MILL

This man refined and organized ideas of the past. His formula centered on life being regulated by the market, not the State. On the continent of Europe, men talked of socialism. The Anglo-Saxon tradition took the market as an automatic functioning mechanism. The result was they didn't think about it. Don't we do that today, and take our corporate goal-oriented economy and think it will automatically function in our best interests?

## 4. TRANSITION

Richardo sets the basis for Marx and the Capitalist State. Both Richardo and Marx emphasized the underlying peril of hopelessness. Richardo's system survives, not because it serves the citizen, but because there is no viable alternative. Vladimir Putin makes a statement on how the United States was becoming communistic. He was referring to the level of alienation of the old who have been cast aside in this economic recession by our major industrial and service sectors, the only exception being working at McDonald's.

An idea surfaced under Mill about paying the employee less than his value, leaving the higher wage offer to his competitor.

In times when companies consume companies (your competitor), it puts the working class in a box. Wages themselves are confined to child production and nothing more. Note the split between the entrepreneurs, who invests to make money, as opposed to working for it. He is allotted his due reward, and the other is just part of the mix. The inequality of resulting monopoly is the inherent flaw in the system, and this has proven to be correct. The rule is the bottom line (efficiency/profit). Those companies that are not efficient fail. Those that control the market and meet the bottom line live. It is a bit like the original meaning of God. Capital and labor are spread along the same rules.

The mark of the twentieth century is imbedded in competition, and failure to compete in this idealized model was and is bankruptcy. Now look at the twenty-first century and look at General Motors, Chrysler, Pontiac, AIG, Goldman Sacks, Solutia, and Anderson. Note the concept revolving around holding companies that produce nothing and regulate everything. Note the need for government intervention, bailout packages, and extended social nets. All of this, in a sea of red ink. Could Vladimir be right? Have the American people slipped into that market maintenance, price-structured matrix that could be called Communism, Fascism, in the economic sense of the word?

The bad luck of the employer whose products don't sell inadvertently reflects on the loyal servant. Even in modern Russia and China there is unemployment, and an unwanted work force. These are inherent tendencies of the time in 2010.

Note the concept of protectionism in the model is potentially viewed as a flaw. This is my catfish argument. Vietnam has a different breed of catfish: the eyes are in a different place, and they are bigger and more aggressive. They can walk on the land, and eat other species. They don't see the difference between their and our catfish industry that is corn-fed and raised in more sanitary ponds. They are fed scraps. They want to trade with us, but their catfish can, and are destroying our catfish industry. Do people go for the cheaper, unregulated product? Is it a natural cycle of economic development, or do we use protectionism? That in itself is a weakness.

In the 19th century the means of production seemed to be passing into fewer hands at a progressive rate. Marx argued that this development heralded the system's doom. The conflict became the Firm against Organized Labor as a mandatory concept. Unfortunately, with the idea of power sharing, the unions basically enforced company policy at the expense of their electorate. All the water flows to a logical base.

## 5. ON ALAN GREENSPAN

During the time of World War Two, governments felt that economies needed to be managed. Central Planning was widespread in the developing and developed world. It was not till the mid-seventies and the meeting of the economic policy committee meetings that you see a shift. The name of the organization was called the Organization for Economic Cooperation and Development (OECD). Keynes had been replaced by Adam Smith as a result of the 1830's Depression. The concept of central planning had not risen to the point of price controls. This meant voluntary compliance.

At the founding of the International Monetary Fund in 1944, the world was enamored with Keynes and his policy that natural market forces didn't always meet the social need, so government intervention was necessary for the public good. That was the Macro Economic concept.

Econometrics was born out of the desire for structural reality in decision making. The more real and detailed the plan as to the direction of the economy, the better the forecast. The down side is that like a picture taken by a photographer, if the subject moves, the image is distorted. You can't pull and economic model out of a pre-imagination.

To the emerging corporate structure it was not important to forecast general economic direction, as to the decline of U.S. Steel in 1958, as it was to evaluate individual current markets. An example: suit sales versus general clothing sales. Where do you put your short term assets for long term gain? The broad theories concerning the public good did not interest them.
Ian Rand, the founder of objectivism, was based on the Aristotelian concept of purpose. The idea that government must tax for the collective good is not a denial of responsibility, but necessary for the common good. In 1968 Greenspan joined the Council of Economic Advisors being formed under the Nixon Administration. It was Ian Rand that convinced Greenspan to look at the human reaction to economic events, and how they fit into the puzzle.

After the Cuban Missile Crisis of 1962 the economy was sluggish. Kennedy was convinced to sign into law a tax cut at or larger than all three tax cuts initiated by President George W. Bush, and according to the CEA's annual report, the economy was growing at a six percent rate. Economists all considered themselves Keynesians. They thought they had the road map to the future. Then the Vietnam Was came, and the GDP dropped and we were in trouble again. This success was due to Macro Economic Theory, and the initial success was claimed by Walter Heller, who was head of the Fed at the time.

President Nixon was elected, and he retained President Johnson's 10% surtax that funded the Vietnam War. There was a thing called the discomfort index that was roughly 10%. The unemployment rate was 5.6%. The economy was, at best, erratic. Greenspan had been appointed to the Council of Economic Advisors, who was working on ways to fund an all-volunteer army. This led to the elimination of the draft. The worry over the fluctuations in the economy led Nixon, on August 13, 1971, to apply wage and price controls, something that Arthur Burns, who was now head of the Fed probably had to grit his teeth to do, for he was a free market economist. The effect of the 10% surcharge Johnson era, 10% discomfort index, and the 5.6% unemployment rate, and rising inflation led to the price freeze on the economy, and when it was removed some six month later, everybody in the business world made up for lost ground.

President Nixon resigned, and his Vice President took his place (Gerald R. Ford). The economy was still erratic, but Ford seemed to be a level-headed man to counter Nixon. Ford would eventually accept a policy of voluntary price freeze. It had limited success. Greenspan pointed out that small business men do not operate on slim profit margins, and you can't control the basic means of production at the cost level. This was something on the compulsory level under the rules of polemics, and it didn't work.
The economy eventually readjusted only after Ford was defeated for re-election by Carter.

The concept of scientific regulation was discarded by Ford in favor of deregulation in 1975. To give you the depth of this change, imagine railroads and airlines as the first to deregulate despite the pressure from unions to maintain those regulations. All sections of the economy were targeted for deregulation. In Chicago 1975 Ford stated, "Take all the shackles off the American business man, and get the federal government as far out of your business, out of your lives and pocket books, and get out of your hair as I possibly can."

You would think bombings were the subject of the late twentieth century, but in 1920 a horse-drawn delivery wagon was pulled up in front of a bank. It was loaded up with dynamite and shrapnel. The explosion killed dozens of people. The bombing was attributed to anarchists, and the crime was never solved.

Early on, J. P. Morgan Co. ran on a Meritocracy. Greenspan sites Denis Weatherstone, who became CEO in the 1980's. He started out at a polytechnic school as a trader at Morgan's London branch. It could be argued that he hardly had the social connections for the job. Greenspan was actually awed by the historical company. In Greenspan's mind it was a splendid opportunity to learn after the Ford White House.

This business does not operate on forecasting. How it makes its money is by collecting the money between the spread and the bid. It does not matter which way the pendulum moves. If there is a big drop in the market, they make money or the other way around.

People who invest in business like J. P. Morgan, Chase Manhattan, Mellon, and Bankers Trust are not necessarily the most informed people on how the economy works, but they are in key industry and places. Suleiman Olayan was an entrepreneur who drove trucks in the oil fields of Saudi Arabia. He also delivered water and whatever they needed. He made a one per cent investment in the above holding companies. He is on their board of directors.

President Carter inherited Ford's period of economic growth. But due to conflicting goals, the economy stalled. A 6.8% inflation rate rose to 12%. He tried to lower unemployment, cut inflation, and reduce the deficit. He wanted to be the man for all seasons. He had no fewer than seven economic remedies.

Internationally, he was viewed as weak, as in negotiating with the Russians, and the fall of the Shah of Iran, one of our key allies at the time. He also did not understand the nature of European Communists, who were the bane of the Soviet Union. He was a president in training.

The Federal Reserve under Bill Miller had trouble finding a middle ground between job stimulation and deficit cutting. (This problem is endemic in the Obama White House in 2012.) The economy was going flat, and a recession seemed possible, especially with the new oil crisis and labor troubles within the United States. What this says to us today is, don't promise a dynamic economy with good job growth if you're trying to cut the deficit, or (control inflation). Especially don't do it, from the center.

Bill Miller, as head of the Fed faced the argument that even if the rate of inflation were 6% per year, the economy could be indexed to inflation. The nation of Brazil was cited by both left and right. Brazil's inflation started at 12%, and collapsed when it reached 5000%.

What especially did the Carter administration in was the fall of the Shah of Iran and the Iraqi war with that country. Our supplies just became scarce. There has always been enough oil, but when the cushion gets thin, people panic and prices rise. They call that speculation. It seems historical, or should I say, hysterical for those of us who were alive at the time to remember the odd-even system and the long lines. Gas stations did run out of gas. It actually had a lot to do with our refining capacity at the time.

When Paul Volcker headed the IMF, the Mexican debt crisis was world stage and in danger of default. The interest rate for 10 year treasury notes was 11% by October 23 of that year. He masterminded the strategy that no longer would there be short-term micro management. His policy revolved around how much money was in the economy. The money supply was measured by a statistic called M1. It consisted of money in circulation and demand deposits, like checking accounts. The problem comes when you have too many dollars chasing too few goods.

It was Milton Friedman's long consistent argument, "Until you tame the money supply, you have not tamed inflation." The down side to this argument was the policy to do this was extremely harsh. The interest rate would have to rise till the interest rate was cut off. The result of such a policy was more unemployment, and a deep recession. (Now consider France and its election of a Socialist president, and the reaction of Greece to its austerity measures and how the two economic realities are linked.) It must have been extremely unpopular, and took a great deal of courage. To his credit, President Carter backed Volcker in his capacity as Fed chairman in 1980. He declared inflation was the number one problem.

Edward Kennedy, who was running against Carter, thought that Carter was not paying enough attention to the poor or tax cuts. (Another irony. Look at the Republicans, who argue smaller government with tax cuts. That means less, services. On the flip side is Obama and his social agenda, and an increase in the taxes of those with over $100,000 annual income. Notice I have not even mentioned the concept of the deficit.) The lion just did not get it. As the election drew near, Carter blinked and started arguing for tax cuts against Fed policy. By the 1980 election, interest rates rose to 20%. The result: cars and other big-ticket items went unsold.

It was because of this situation that Greenspan got involved in Reagan's second attempt at the White House. What attracted Greenspan to Reagan was his conservative attitude. Reagan stated, "The government exists to protect us from each other. Where Government has gone beyond its limits is in deciding to protect us from ourselves."

According to Greenspan, Regan's view was not to let them eat cake, but it was not Government's roll to ease social pressures on the poor due to economic cycles. It was Government's job to optimize the opportunities for raising oneself. Note the extension of unemployment benefits or the expansion of the health safety net as it relates to the health of the economy. I do believe they call that Social Darwinism.

David Stockman, a 34 year old congressman from Michigan helped to initially set the tone of the Reagan administration. His system based on front loading and no tag-ons to bills. The legislature, on both sides of the aisle could not live without their pork. Spending was dictated by the Lapher Curve that had the effect of forcing states to initiate programs and then reach Washington. Constitutionally, that was the correct position. The down side to that would be, governors would have to be the innovators of change, not the presidential candidates. Another thing, change would not be based on the party structure. According to Greenspan, Stockman and Donald Regan were concerned about the deficit and any potential tax reductions. They were not allowed to participate, just observe. Greenspan had a direct voice while they fumed in the corner. When the cuts from the congress did not come, Stockman got the axe and Regan remained, and eventually, through creative math, the deficit did appear to go down on paper, but in reality it continued to grow. Reagan got his tax cuts. The people got what they wanted, and today Reagan is idealized. It was Paul Volker who managed to get positive results from his position as head of the Treasury Department, essentially balancing both ends against the middle.

Alan Greenspan had been named head of the Federal Reserve, and Greenspan headed up a commission. A bipartisan commission was set up from power brokers in both the House and Senate. Four points were raised: 1) Separating Social Security from the Medicare issue. Handling both together would sink both. 2) Get everyone to agree on the math. It was so important to have them not treat their opinions as facts. 3) Everybody had to be in the loop on the decision-making process. This meant both Reagan and O'Neil. 4) Once a compromise had been reached, no member of the committee would allow revision of the plan.

The Social Security system was amended and signed into law in 1983 by President Reagan, and it caused pain and higher costs to employers and higher taxes to employees.

The Fed chairman's job is not what you might think. He is Chairman of the Board of Governors, and is but one vote on the Board. He operates on the basis of consensus. He was not automatically chairman of the Federal Open Market Committee. That body is the primary lever of US monetary policy. It is commonly known by the initials FOMC. The Board of Governors controls the discount rate. These funds are lent to what is called Depository Institutions. This rate moves simultaneously with the allocation of federal funds.

What led to Black Monday was a series of steps. The Fed was attempting to rein in inflation by making money more expensive to borrow. It was intended to tame the fervor, as Greenspan put it, of the investors, and direct them to bonds and securities. Greenspan was heading for a meeting in Switzerland of the IMF. That day, stocks dipped and prime lenders moved in the same motion of the Fed.

The stock market engaged in speculative bets. This was causing a weakening of the dollar and putting pressure on a card game where the players thought their bets would not pay off. The worst loss occurred on Friday, April 16th, with a drop of 108 points. A half trillion dollars in paper wealth had just gone "poof." This also extended to losses in currency and other markets. According to The Wall Street Journal, it was called the Wall Street October Massacre.

The stock market opened up weak on Monday morning, but it was agreed that Greenspan should go to the IMF conference to show the Fed was not in a panic. The stock market had dropped 200 points by the time he left the ground. There was no cell phone communication while in the air. When he landed, he found the stock market had dropped 22.5%, or 508 points. It was bigger than the crash of 1929.

The reason for the Great Depression was at the time of the crash the banks pulled back, taking the liquidity out of the market. (Think about 9/11 and the banks pulling back on financing venture capital and insurance companies refusing to authorize events. Now draw parallels.) It was imperative that the Fed make sure that banks continue to lend and take risks. The Fed backed the banks though inflation did rise. It also leveled off. (Note the fact.) The economy did not stall, and the economy did recover. (Note we are recovering but only in certain sectors in 2012.)

The Federal Reserve System is not like a cabinet post, though the Fed Chairman is appointed by the president. The Fed is independent of the president, and makes its money by selling treasury bonds and securities. George H. W. Bush had been riding on Reagan's economic bubble that was about to burst. He warned the Fed not to interfere with the growth of jobs and prosperity. It is 1988 and the Fed is raising interest rates to head off another meltdown. The economy tanks, as it is supposed to and George got the blame. William Machesney, who was Fed chairman in the 1950's and 60's stated that the role of the Fed was to "order the punch-bowl removed before the party warmed up."

Now what happened on 9/11 was not a natural cycle, and 2,746 souls left this earth, but the downturn in the economy could have been avoided by, 1) Not going into Afghanistan as we did, but push for a UN action. Yes, I know Russia and China would have vetoed the measure, but look at the economic grief, coupled with our system refusing to allow normal activity. The economic upswing would have been faster, and George would have been branded as indecisive. 2) Instituted reforms that would have stopped the corporate abuses of the time and stimulated small business instead. 3) Institutions similar to what we have today would have to be put into place. We probably would have done something to punish Al-Qaida, and we would still fight a war on terror, but just Maybe this idea of pre-emptive war coupled with a down economy May not have gotten as deep as it did. Yes, Saddam would still be in control of Iraq, and there could have been another Kurdish slaughter. The point is we had just had our Peloponnesian War, and after over ten years, we are still just economically coming out of it.

President George H. W. Bush became the victim of the economic cycle. The life of the Reagan prosperity was coming to an end. Production was pretty much full tilt. Employment was high relative to population. Bush, in 1987 when he was nominated to run for president, said he would hold the Fed in check and made a pledge of no new taxes. It was after his election and the pending collapse of the Reagan period. The Fed was raising rates, including the prime rate. Bush was forced to break his pledge. The 1991 Gulf War happened, and our deficit began to rise. We did not have the surtax that was used to pay for the Vietnam War. When the next election cycle came, William J. Clinton came up with "It's the economy, stupid, " and George was defeated. A similar tactic was waged against George W. Bush's proxy, Senator John McCain in 2008. The muddy attacks partially stuck to Senator McCain and Barak H. Obama became our president. Now what Barak was president, the Republican members of the legislature used the same tactics in the governing of this country that were used in the election of 2008. In all fairness, Obama had taken the Republican positions and turned them around, so the Republicans denounced their own positions. The politicians have been playing volleyball for a little over three years. The economy is slowly improving in certain sectors. Internationally, we are outing ourselves from our problems (Afghanistan and Iraq). We have improved our image, but the world is about to change again. But we still have our same old economic principles we don't understand and blame others for.

Charles Keating popped into the headlines. He played with the balance sheets and cost a lot of people their life savings. Fortunately, he was sentenced to prison for his efforts, but he gave brokerage houses a bad name. He almost ruined five senators and the reputation of the Fed for trusting him. After the mess, the taxpayers were on the hook for 3.4 billion dollars.

Two years before the fall of the Berlin Wall and the Soviet Bloc in general, Greenspan was at their Spaso House, which was the equivalent of their Federal Reserve in the Soviet Union. He was there to explain the Fed's version of the Fed and its functions, and how the private economy worked. He was surprised at their questions and the extensive notes they took.

Greenspan dealt with Leaned Abalkin, who was the Deputy Prime Minister in charge of reform. He had been in Gorbachev's kitchen cabinet. The Soviet Government had just been asked to ban strikes, Perestroika. The fact was Gorbachev's four-year plan was just about to collapse. Abalkin described the States' plan to fight inflation by indexing wages to prices as a way of fighting inflation. Greenspan stated that it would work in the short term, but have long-term consequences. This fact did not seem to surprise him, though he continued to defend the qualities of the system.

Vast changes had begun to occur. Poland had just completed free elections, and elected the Solidarity Movement, and Leff Walensa as its president. The Soviets accepted their decision. East Germany was starting to dissolve, and immigration to the west was occurring, though not sanctioned. Hungary's Communist Party had just renounced Marxism in favor of Democratic Socialism.

In the Brezhnev era corruption was rampant, but they had oil to keep the economy going. With the collapse of oil and out-of-control inflation caused by the Reagan era and the Strategic Defense Initiative, which Greenspan carefully did not mention, coupled with the failure of their agri-business sector. Greenspan witnessed jewelry for bread, and the lines that went with it.

Gorbachev was described as a man of two minds struggling to liberalize a system bound to another era. The events of his time had the effect of changing his beliefs. This was a fact, despite the fact also that he was very much a product of Stalin and Khrushchev. The Gorbachev vision was a Soviet Union participating in a capitalist free market, though he did not understand its principles.

Leontief Gosplan had perfected the theory of Polemics to the umpteenth degree. His theory was any economy, by mapping the flow of materials and labor through it, done thoroughly, the economic model would be the ideal instrument panel. Greenspan raised the concept of dynamic change and he shrugged his shoulders as if it were not part of the equation.

In all of this that I have described let's not get too cocky. Remember how corporations deliberately cut costs and labor to the point where the product is not viable to would-be customers. It is not all that different when you see what the Soviets were doing with their economy. Could we, if we don't pay attention to the warning signs, have a similar fate? Just look at Obama's too big to fail, and how it has impacted government and the economic incentives of those who have gotten too big for their own britches. (In all fairness, some of those who took the stimulus have paid back the money with interest, but they still primarily operate overseas.)

You recall me talking about that point below which no price can fall, how corporations manipulated the basic cost of seed farmers buy. There is an anecdote: A man on a street corner was selling hammers for two dollars apiece. A customer, admiring his ingenuity asked how much her hammers cost. The man said two dollars. The customer said, "You can't make any money that way." The man responded, "yes, but it beats farming."

If you don't allow the price of seed to go where it will in the cycle like Nixon, who, when he tried to freeze prices found that there was a shortage of supply of the raw material which could mean the existence of the American independent farmer (it has been said that the American family farm is hone), the corporation should be able to absorb the lessoning cost of seed for its margins will grow with volume, or collapse into the dust from which they came. The same logic applies to financial instruments. They should not be above loss. Risk determines profit, and mistakes are punished.

In 1989, when Solidarity was popularly elected in Poland, the economy was about to tank completely. A western economics professor from central Poland by the name of Balcerowicz had a conversation with Greenspan and told him on January 1, 1990 all price controls were removed. His logic was that incremental change was doomed to failure due to adjustment in the status quo. Initially prices went through the roof and then they started to come down and stabilize. The first to fall was the price of eggs. You can't be afraid of a price rising or falling below its expected point. The labor cost of producing something in China is cheaper than that in the United States, and the profit margin using U.S. labor lowers the profit by 50%. Wages in China are rising and the advantage for corporations is less with more hassle. This message to corporations like Apple and Google Services: America is home. Let's build her up.

Vaclav Klaus, an economics minister of Czechoslovakia took the experiment of a free market economy dramatically further. The Czech currency was in the toilet in the early 1990's. All property was state-owned: industrial, agricultural, and the retail sector. They gave each citizen a certain sector of land that they could sell, cultivate, or incorporate as they wished. There was even a mechanism for the transfer of the lands. This became the basis for their stock exchange.

The Soviets, when they were forced overnight into their open market experiment did so without the blessing of common law and property right protection (Natural Law). Without property rights and guaranteed protection under law, two things happened. Russian currency lost half of its value, plus a black market rose, not a free market. A class of nouveau riche oligarchs was created.

The first effect was that the people's wealth evaporated overnight. It was like the dreams we all have when we think we are accomplishing something and expect what we did to be there when we wake up. We sadly find that is not the case. Your average Russian did not think much of capitalism at this point. Goods did appear, but in the black market. There was a competition of sorts, but no regulation to back it up. Property grants were given to the people and were stolen by unscrupulous business men who became as oligarchs. Think of Cuba today and what is called Revolutionary Law. Let's say their system collapsed and the above steps were taken without the backing of what we call common law. A totally different hybrid system would emerge. Cuba could get lucky and follow the example of the Eastern European model or the Russian mode. It was not until the actual fall of the Berlin Wall that we actually saw the concept of free market operation in what we knew as the Soviet Union.

Let's not boast too much about our system. Remember, we have been drifting towards socialism and a police state. As now Russia moves toward capitalism and corporatism and freedom of speech reluctantly, we even had people like Keating. It is fortunate that Keating and those like him were prosecuted, but many others have simply gotten away with it. Many of our citizens have lost their homes and savings to unscrupulous brokerage houses that make their money win or lose between the margins. Some of our greatest landmarks sit as useless pieces of real estate.

When William J. Clinton became president he sought the advice of Greenspan on world leaders he had not met. He impressed Greenspan as being one of the two smartest presidents, the other being Richard M. Nixon, whom Greenspan regarded as erratic in temperament.

The economy was improving on its own as a result of the bush administration, but the Clinton program for job creation had to be put on hold to fight the burgeoning deficit (260 billion dollars), which was 50 billion higher than expected. He also had to abandon his plans for the middle class tax cut for the same reason.

His appointments were all economic centrists: Treasury Secretary Lloyd Bentson, Senate Finance Committee Rodger Altman, Budget Director Leon Penette, his deputy Alice Rivlen. Robert Ruben of Goldman Sachs would be the economic equivalent of National Security Advisor. He was following the Kennedy model, adopting some familiar Republican traits, not that of the tax and spend liberal. This was according to Greenspan.

The first Clinton budget offended everybody: 277 Democratic congressmen and the 177 Republican congressmen, largely because of the lack of pork that the legislative body could take home to their constituents.

The friction was also within the White House for a policy less friendly to Wall Street. James Carvill made one of his famous wise cracks, "I used to think there was reincarnation. I wanted to come back as the president or the Pope or a .400 baseball hitter, but now I want to come back as a bond market."

President Clinton's popularity rating was at 28%. Greenspan met him on June 9th. Gergen, who saw the need for this meeting had been in the Nixon, Ford and Regan White House. Now he was in the service of President Clinton, who chose him because he was level-headed. Greenspan's advice to Clinton was that long-term rates were always trending down, and his admission that the deficit had to be tackled showed his insight as to the seriousness of the problem. He was urged to stick to his budget, for it was the best long-term solution for the country.

The other big battle that faced the Clinton presidency was the issue of NAFTA.

The treaty was negotiated under the auspices of the Bush administration. The treaty itself phased out tariffs and trade barriers between the U.S., Canada and Mexico. Labor unions, along with most democrats, hated the treaty. Greenspan urged the Clinton administration to stick to its guns because you can't stop the world from turning, and America, with its financial interests was increasingly interdependent on other kindred systems that compose the international economy. It was agreed that trade and competition would create prosperity, and you need a free market to do that. After two months the treaty was approved.

Greenspan took the position that the distinction between domestic competition and cross-border competition has no economic meaning. If you are in a Dubuque, Iowa, plant, it makes no difference whether you're competing with someone in Santa Fe or across the border.

I have observed an effect with the transfer of labor and/or production of goods that are sold back to us as finished products. Unless there is an even exchange at some level of society, we are going to get a segment of society that would be a permanent underclass which could lead to social unrest. Look at Allen Toffler's Future Shock. How do you explain the anti-Wall Street movement that is sweeping this country in 2012?

Clinton's tech bubble was showing signs of stress. At the Fed there was discussion on waiting till the bubble actually bursts or to raise the rates modestly till things averaged at 5.5%, which it did in the end. Initially, when Clinton was confronted with potential Fed action, he favored modest raising of the rates. Unfortunately, Congress was not of the same opinion. Senator Paul Sarbanes, a frequent critic of the Fed implied that you might think that you should destroy a farm house because the villain inflation is inside, but in actuality there is nothing but a happy family appreciating the restoration of economic growth.

The brakes were applied throughout 1994 and the economy still grew at 4% with a job growth of 3.5 million new jobs. The productivity increased, and business profit rose. The most important thing was that inflation did not rise. It had been under 3% for three years running. To tell of the short-sightedness of some in business, they were trying to increase prices but having a hard time making those increases stick. Greenspan was not sympathetic with them. Now think back to the real intention of some businesses, and it is not in the public interest.

There was political change in America. The Republicans won seats in the House and Senate. Newt Gingrich and Dick Army had promoted the Contract With America, and Bill Clinton's healthcare initiative had gone down in defeat. (President Barak H. Obama would succeed where Bill failed, and it is still being contested.) The big push was for tax cuts, welfare reform and a balanced budget. (Note the deficit was missing.) It sounds very much like what is happening today.

The storm was coming from south of the border. Mexico was about to default on its short-term debt after a period of prosperity. In this country there were two camps: those who would like to see Mexico fall and those who realized that the domino effect on the economies of the region. Mexico's leaders asked for help with their downward spiral. They had 6 billion dollars in reserves and 25 billion due. To the uninformed, had Mexico defaulted, we would have had triple the immigration rate of undocumented aliens. We know how we all feel about that. What happened next was one of those miracles of Christmas. Newt Gingrich and Bob Dole, now the majority leaders, got together with the Clinton administration and the Fed through the Treasury Department and, backed by the IMF enacted a stimulus package that allowed Mexico to pay its short-term debts and stabilize itself. Their economy did recover and they did pay back the loan. (A similar thing happened with President Obama's stimulus package and the TARP program.)

What is so remarkable about this compromise is that it came on the heels of the NAFTA debate. Today we are facing a presidential election in 2012. Originally, a host of candidates were seeking the Republican nomination. What I call the Libertarian Right (Ron Paul) advocates the elimination of the Federal Reserve. This is a dangerous thought even in this integrated international economy.

## 6. CREATIVE DESTRUCTION

Here's something the yet-to-be-nominated, but presumptive nominee of the Republican Party should be familiar with: starting in 1991, technology was shaping the future of what was regarded as the traditional manufacturing industry. Companies like General Motors wee investing in companies like Google. The office staff and what was considered blue collar workers was becoming a relic of the twentieth century. If you will excuse my analogy, it was a form of Social Darwinism. The Silicon Valley seemed to be defying the future. The need to know now replaced the concept of holding on to employees as back-up plans. One hundred million jobs were lost in the process. It is argued that one hundred and fifty million jobs were created. The displaced worker became useless fodder from the year 1996 to the year 2000.

Companies caught up with the internet experience and the concept of fiber optics, and hired employees and bought technology that in the end did not benefit them. That is to say, they did not gain market share. They overinvested in innovative technology, putting themselves at odds with the workforce.

In 2012 the economy is slowly growing and the Green energy businesses seem to be leading the way. The unemployment figure stands at 8.1%. That figure is deceptive, for many have fallen off the rolls and through the safety net. This last quarter, 15,000 new jobs were created. This does not balance with the new workers entering the economy.

It is known that one million citizens leave their jobs yearly. This statistic has held true going back to the seventies/eighties. It was projected that people would have as many as 20 jobs in different fields in the $20^{th}$ and $21^{st}$ centuries. What was not projected was the dislocation of the workforce and technology- and age-related matters.

A new term was born: Non-accelerating rate of unemployment (NAIRU). According to Greenspan, this was a neo-Keynesian concept that operated on the concept that if the unemployment rate dropped below 5.6%, it would have an inflationary impact on wages. As the unemployment rate dipped in 1994 to close at 4%,1 the fed felt it had to put the brakes on the economy.

In 1995 Clinton's advisors felt he was getting carried away with the new technology elements, so they brought in a man by the name of Summers who felt a need for tightening the labor market. Clinton flatly disagreed with him. He felt there was no limit to this growth. Most politicians look to satisfying their constituents. Job loss is not a popular thing. Remember what happened to George H. W. Bush.

## 7. IRRATIONAL EXUBERANCE

When does risk taking turn into folly? How do you judge what price is too high for a stock that will adjust back to the appropriate price? These were the questions asked in the Clinton era. It must be noted that George H. W. Bush, who was the victim of being at the end of a cycle got the blame for being a bad manager of the economy, and Clinton got the benefit of what became the tech bubble that burst of George W. Bush's watch.

The idea of spending money on new equipment as long as it increased the efficiency of the factory and its output was center to the investment in that equipment. This led to the wealth effect that spurred the economy in luxury and hard goods for those who were able to train for and benefit from it. There was a parallel thought that could be traced to 1959 (American Statistical Association). The price of newly produced plant equipment on the physical plant and the price it fetches on the stock market. Greenspan wrote an article entitled "Stock Prices and Capital Evaluation." The article suggested a link between technology and the expanding market that linked itself to the price of a given stock.

Companies invest in each other as a hedge against failure. General Motors, at a time when they announced plans to lay off 30,000 employees and close 12 plants was investing its resources in Silicon Valley capital venture firms between 2005 and 2008. Areas like building factories to create future work forces that bring with them pension issues and health benefits would actually be a drag on the economy in comparison to wealth creation. The net effect of this was that Google stock was 11 times that of General Motors. That is a good example of how irrational exuberance leads to creative destruction.

This issue is like a two-sided coin. On one hand, without advanced technology a work force is employed, but that same work force only existed because employers had a lag time about what they needed to know and when they knew it. This meant that those employees were not producing income for the firm. With technology, a smaller work force was linked, from the trucker, the factory, or import house where he gets his goods, and the retail store that places the order. The argument was this gives better service. It also cuts down on labor needs and creates more leisure time so the work force can do more useful things. Might I suggest the beach?

The statistics say that between 1994 and the year 2000 the unemployment rate was lowered from 6% to 4%. In the Clinton tech boom it was argued that 16 million new jobs were created to replace those that were lost. There was an analogy made to the telegraph operators of the old west. This was the thing the Indians called whistling death because it came in conjunction with the railroads and ended a way of life. Is there a connection to the older and entry work force of our age? Some jobs did go the way of the dinosaur: drafting jobs, architecture, not to mention automotive and industrial design. The issue of what was called the blue collar worker started to become an issue in 1990 and accelerated into the Y2K question. In those of that general field, 46% were living in fear of a layoff as of 1996, which was the start of rapid tech growth.

There is an economic argument that when the economy and the official unemployment rate drops below 4% you set off an inflation cycle due to an overheated economy. Several things had changed. The globalization of the economy and the tech factor had apparently lowered the threat of inflation with the spreading of risk. The cycle was still there, but the scale was much larger (worldwide). This, some argue, could have an impact of what is perceived to be our national debt.

There was a side to this expanding economic argument that centered on Japan and the collapse of its real estate market in 1990. It was noted that the economy at the household level and businesses in general were exposing themselves to equity risks. Both the treasury and the Fed sat down informally on what to do if the bubble bursts. This concern about the stock market had several layers and reasons not to go into them. 1) "There is no way to know for certain when a market is over or under valued." 2) "You can't fight the market forces, so talking about it won't do any good." 3) "Anything you say is likely to backfire and hurt your credibility. People will realize you don't know any more than anybody else." Greenspan's problem was that he felt he had a truth that had to be addressed. He was just trying to figure out how to do it.

It was for Greenspan the perfect audience: The American Enterprise Institute. He draped his concerns in history (Alexander Hamilton and William Jennings Brian). He worked his case study from the past cases till the present, and the possible future. It was only at the end of his speech that twelve lines were inferred with irrational exuberance being part of that structure. The phrase stuck out of the document like it was in red. The following is that section of the speech that raised the hackles of a nation and touched a nerve.

## 8. GREENSPAN'S SPEECH

"The Congress willing we will remain as the guardians of the purchasing power of the dollar. But one factor will continue to complicate the task of the increasing difficulty of pinning down the notion of what constitutes a stable price level.

Where do we draw the line on what prices matter? Certainly the price of goods and services now being produced—our basic measures of inflation—matter. But what about future prices Or more importantly the price of claims on future goods, and services. Is stability of these prices essential to the stability of the economy?

But how do we know when irrational exuberance has unduly escalated asset values (Here is where the audience woke up.) which then become the subject of unexpected and prolonged contractions as they have in Japan over the past decade? And how do we factor that assessment into monetary policy? We as central bankers need not be concerned if the collapsing financial asset does not threaten to impair the real economy, its production, jobs and price stability. Indeed the sharp stock market break of 1987 had few negative consequences for the economy, but we should not underestimate, or become complacent about the complexity of interactions of asset markets and the economy."

The reaction to this speech prompted headlines in the Philadelphia Inquirer, "A buried message loudly heard." The *New York Times* also proclaimed the term in headlines. The initial reaction was felt all around the world with a drop in stock prices. The New York Stock Exchange dropped 150 points but recovered the following day. By year's end stocks in general were up 20 points.

The Dow Jones industrial average had reached 7,000 when the FOMC met in 1997. It was the view of many governors and bank presidents that they were worried about what they referred to as a potential stock bubble. The Fed started to consider reining in the bull. They were thinking about some kind of a preemptive move. Greenspan stated, "We need above all to make certain that we keep inflation low, risk premiums low, and the cost of capital low. If we are talking about long term equilibrium, high market values are better than low market values. What we are trying to avoid is bubbles that break, volatility and the like." There was a 0.25 increase to 5.5 and the market dropped 7%. That was 500 point. It rebounded in a matter of weeks. If you included all the losses, there was a gain of 10%. What the Fed was witnessing was thought to be the stock market itself saying you're wrong. Paper wealth increased for three more years and the Fed was trying to figure out how to deal with a potential bubble in what those in the industry were calling the New Economy.

## 9. THE WINDS OF CHANGE

This segment is about the rise of millennium fever: the long made short, the fear that the computer systems would revert to 1900 and throw the world economy into a panic.

There was fear of foreign competition that was not with us prior to 1980. Those that we had fought had now recovered and were starting to kick our economic butt. The fact that we were a super power really had no relevance in this new rising corporate world. Larry Summers stated of our economic rivals Germany, a newly Unified Europe and a reconstructed Japan, "Were more investment-oriented, more manufacturing –oriented, had fewer lawyers and more scientists, and more discipline than we."

Japan was a true conglomerate corporate culture (Zaibatsu). We had lost our steel industry to them, and they were in contact with mainland China that was starting to rise with economic agreements between them, The area of consumer electronics was Japanese. Just look at the TV sets we were buying (Sony, Panasonic and Hitachi). In terms of what we felt we could produce we were feeling extremely insecure.

Where the American advantage lay was in our heads. U.S. information technology was on the rise. We now had derivatives which were a form of credit protection that allowed businesses to take risks. We were modernizing our economy and starting to invest heavily in technology to gain the advantage. We had gone through two decades of deregulation and downsizing. Both Europe and Japan had peaked and were in a slide.

We were starting to create a surplus as of 1997. Tax collection was 50 billion dollars ahead of projection. The Office of Management and Budget, along with the Federal Reserve were at a loss on this matter. It was thought that this was an aftereffect of the stock market surge. There was an increase in household income related to stock options, grants, and capital gains. Here's an oddball thing: the deficit as of 1997 was 22 billion dollars. The federal budget was 1.6 trillion, and the GDP was 10 trillion. The Congressional Budget Office, as of 19987 saw a surplus of 660 billion dollars over ten years.

On the political end, the Republicans, who did not vote for the 1993 deficit reduction budget, were claiming credit to the effect that it was their policies in the Congress (controlling spending and less government and tax relief) that brought the nation to this point.

President Clinton, who was the recipient of this rising tech economy, took credit for the recovery and chastised the Republicans, who were not at the celebration and not invited for voting against the reason they were there. It's all politics.

Bob Ruben, head of the Treasury Department, felt that this surplus should be used to pay down the national debt that totaled at this time 3.7 trillion dollars. Here's a historical note: the last time up to this point that we had a surplus was 1969. Who was President at that time? Nixon.

The problem seemed to be political will. The simple argument was that as long as Congress did not pass legislation creating spending bills, any funds that flowed into government coffers would automatically pay down the debt. This would only happen if the legislature could resist raiding that designated cash box. A quote from the Senate Budget Committee that the government could happily whittle down that deficit for years: "It will not harm the economy in any way of which I am aware to allow the surplus to run for quite a long period of time before you touch them. If the surpluses are evolving, let's not look at them as though they are a threat to the economy. They are surely not."

The solution that availed itself was simple and politically expedient. In Clinton's 1998 State of the Union address he proposed linking the surplus funds to Social Security. The following is that excerpt on that subject.

"What should we do with this projected surplus? We have a simple four word answer. Save Social Security first. Tonight I propose that we reserve 100% of the surplus until we have taken all the necessary measures to strengthen the Social Security System for the 21st century."

The solution that came from the Clinton White House was commented on by a White House staffer, Gene Sperling: "You've found the way to make debt reduction politically attractive."

The whole idea worked admirably. In 1998 the surplus was 70 billion. In 1999 the surplus was 124 billion. In the year of Y2K, the year 2000, the surplus was 237 billion. Now, you have to ask yourself what went wrong. The Republicans in the year 1999 proposed tax cuts amounting to over 800 billion dollars over the next ten years. Greenspan was called before the Senate Banking Committee and he disapproved of the idea of the proposed tax cuts at that time. He told the committee that while the projection of the surplus was up to 3 trillion dollars, the uncertainty of the economic future with those big numbers was in doubt. He told the committee that things could easily go the other direction, and they did. He also stated that the stimulus of a tax cut could cause the economy to overheat. Being the diplomat he was, he stated that there was no reason why the tax cut could not be delayed.

The loyal opposition, being what it is, passed the tax cut, which was vetoed by President Clinton. The president stated, "At a time when America is moving in the right direction, this bill would turn us back to failed policies." Ironically, the politics of the Obama years would be strangely reminiscent of this time, but for flip side reasons.

In the Clinton years the world wanted to piggyback on our economic progress, and our business men, egalitarians that they are, wanted to increase their rate of return. The developing nations sought safe haven by fixing/tying their exchange rate to the U.S. dollar. What that essentially meant was the United States and foreign investors could consider their investments protected from exchange rate risk. This would be true at least in the short term. The borrowers of the dollar would convert the domestic currency and make loans within the developing country at the prevailing high interest rates. By such actions they were playing table stakes that when the loan was repaid they would be able to convert the money back into dollars at the fixed exchange rate and repay their own dollar borrowing with no exchange rate loss. The result was that it did not work, and the developing countries ran out of their reserve dollars. This came to be known as the Asian contagion. The first to fall was the Thai Baht along with the Malaysian Ringgit. This happened in the summer of 1997. This disease also hit Hong Kong, the Philippines, and Singapore after it caused a recession in Thailand and Malaysia. In the country of Indonesia, the Rupiah imploded affecting 200,000,000 people. There was a collapse of their stock market. Riots ensued and President Suharto fell. Japan informed the Fed and treasury that South Korea was about to default. It turns out they had cooked their books, still listing dollars that were already spoken for. The funny thing about Korea was that they were now considered a developed nation. It looked as though they were sitting on $25,000,000,000 in reserves.

Korea lucked out and got a 55 billion dollar bailout from the International Monetary Fund. The Fed and Treasury talked to the world's banks, asking them not to call in Korea's loans. Newly elected President Kim Dae Jung had to agree to reform and austerity measures. The dilemma of the lenders in such cases was referred to by the insurance industry as a moral hazar4d. Default would have been worse, for it would have sent shock waves across Asia and the world.

Now let us look at ourselves and our federal deficit. There are those that say default would be good for it would force us to live within our means. That is the argument that the Republicans gave last time around when the issue of raising the debt ceiling came in, and the fight went right to the wire. That issue was to come up again. Think of the consequences if we were to default.

Now ask the question, what if Russia defaulted? Well it did, in 1988, and Yeltsin's economic experiment was in deep trouble. Russia was in a black market economy. The central planning system had collapsed. The oligarchs were in control of the ball. The people of Russia were viewing capitalism as a dirty word, for their savings had vanished. It became diamonds for bread.

The reason Russia faltered was the drop in the price of oil to eleven dollars a barrel. The industry had been nationalized and was paying the bills of the country. Their marketing strategy for oil and gas was faulty as in charging lower than average prices to their customers in Europe. They did not repair their equipment to a proper standard and it often broke down. It all broke down to a selective enforcement of laws enacted and limited property rights that were selectively enforced. A 23 billion dollar support package was offered by the IMF, and they got it, but the Duma, Russia's Parliament, refused to go along with the austerity measures, and the rest of the contract was withdrawn.

The Russian default was the beginning of the end for us. That big economic boom we were experiencing and all the politicians were arguing about was about to end. The Dow dropped 1000 points or 12% of its value. The bond market was affected, and investors fled to treasuries. Banks pulled back on their lending. This is strangely reminiscent of what happened on September 11, 2001, and the reason our economy stalled and took its sweet time to recover. Going back to Russia's default, they handled their nukes a lot better than their economy.

Our economic wakeup call was not related to us running out of steam. It had its roots in 1996 with the start of the tech boom, and the imbalance it caused in what became the new economy. We became too tied-in to what was happening overseas. Our corporate entities, in seeking greater returns, were just now discovering the greater risks.

Greenspan stated, "It is not credible that the United States can remain an oasis of prosperity unaffected by the world that is experiencing greatly increased stress." He points out that we as a country can- not have full benefits of the technology revolution unless all the nations of the world share in that growth.

When Greenspan spoke certain phases leapt out at his audience and the nation as a whole. He was speaking at Berkley on the Russian Crisis, and how it had prompted him to do a major bit of rethinking. Our obsession with domestic inflation had become antiquated in his mind, and how e had better pay attention to the signs of international economic breakdown. It was this part of his speech that the media heard and broadcast, and as if in a fairy tale, Wall Street was listening. The FOMC was poised to lower interest rates. The G7 nations play an important part in all of this. In a behind-the-scenes effort, Greenspan at the Fed and Bob Ruben at Treasury were contacting the Central Banks of those nations in order to coordinate a response.

The organization known as LCTM dealt in speculative investments (ulcerative arbitrage U.S., Japanese and European bonds). They were located in Greenwich, Connecticut. Their earnings were out of this world. Imagine a 125 billion dollar portfolio for wealthy clients. Among these were two Nobel laureate economists, Myron Scholes and Robert Merton. Merton was famous for his mathematical models. Econometrics, what he did, was the firm's money machine, according to Greenspan. It was found that for every thirty-five dollars of the firm, one dollar was actually invested. I believe they called that buying on the margin, and it was once of the causes of the Great Depression.

The dissolution of LCTM, as opposes to selling of its assets in a bankruptcy, saved a shock wave that would have hit Wall Street in a big way. It was done in legendary style by a man by the name of Bill McDonough. I agree with Greenspan that this is the stuff of legends. He gathered 16 representatives of the world's most powerful banks in one room, fed them coffee and sandwiches provided by the Fed, and stated that if they really understood the losses they would face in a fire sale of LCTM assets, they would work it out. The result was an infusion of 3.5 billion dollars that allowed LCTM to dissolve in an orderly way. Greenspan and McDonough were called before the House Banking Committee and asked why it was necessary to use Fed resources to save a millionaires' club. As I said, it was pointed out they only supplied coffee and sandwiches. Were these part of the fabled Builder berg Group?

Congressman Michael Castle half-joked "Mutual funds and real estate weren't doing so well, but no one is helping me out." Congressman Bruce Vinto, Democrat from Minnesota, stated, "There are two rules: one for Main Street, and one for Wall Street." Greenspan pointed out that a lot of little people would have been hurt had it gone the other way.

## 10. THE FINANCIAL SERVICES MODERNIZATION ACT

Up to this time the law that governed banks and other financial institutions was known as the Glass Seagull Act. It had been in force since the 1930's. It had the effect of limiting the ability of investment firms, banks and insurance companies from entering into each other's territory.

With the enactment of the Financial Services Modernization Act there still was an area of disagreement, i. e., who controlled what. The Congress had wrangled for months on what the Fed would do and what Treasury would do. The solution was to lock Greenspan of the Fed in a room with Larry Summers of Treasury and let them fight it out. Seriously, both gentlemen did meet and hashed out an agreement by listening on who could do what more effectively. Our banks were hamstrung in ways universal banks were not, and they both agreed that needed changing. Treasury, through the Office of the Comptroller of Currency was responsible for supervising all nationally chartered banks. The Federal Reserve looked over bank holding companies and state chartered institutions that chose to be regulated by the Fed. The differences described were worked out point by point in an hour or two, and a bill was able to become law.

The stock market party was continuing in the NASDAQ, for it had almost doubled. The Fed did not take the punch bowl away. The politicians were relieved that the Fed did not act for at least a while. The Fed did tighten up interest rates between 1999 and the year 2000 and raised the points from 4.75 to 6.5. They took back liquidity from the market as a safeguard relating to the international crisis. Bill McDonough tightened the labor market to avoid overheating the economy. They were setting the economy up for a soft landing when the economy turned.

Now in the year 2000, George W. Bush becomes President. The economy is cooling and guess who is being blamed for that? It was December 18, 2000 in a meeting with President George W. Bush and His father, George H. W. Bush, and Vice President Cheney. He informed the President that the Clinton boom was coming to an end. The outlook for the year ahead was not good. The NASDAQ lost 50% between March and the end of the year 2000. The S and P 500 was down 14% and the Dow was down by 3%. He told them the losses were miniscule compared to the paper market they had brought into existence. It was stated that for much of the year the nation had entered a mild cyclical slowdown. Inventories were high, and there was an increase in unemployment claims. Earlier in the year 2000 oil prices had spiked to $30 a barrel. Natural gas prices were also up. All Christmas shopping had this season pegged as a bummer of a year. The odd fact was that the Federal Government was running a surplus for the fourth straight year. Now your average Joe Public would say that the government is hoarding money and not helping the little guy. This was the worry that the Bush administration had as to its perception in the public eye. Add to that the perception that he stole the election, and you have a definite kettle of fish. G. W. told the press, as he had told Greenspan, that he had full confidence in the Fed and their decision-making principles.

To his credit, Al Gore, in his concession speech stated, "Almost a century and a half ago Senator Stephen Douglas told Abraham Lincoln, who had just defeated him for the Presidency: 'Partisan feelings must yield to Patriotism. I'm with you, Mr.

President, and God bless you.' Well, in that same spirit I say to President-elect Bush that what remains of partisan rancor must be put aside, and May God bless his stewardship of this country."

George W. Bush drew from the well of the Ford administration. The staff that Ford had was exceptional. Donald Rumsfeld was Ford's first Chief of Staff, and had been appointed as Ambassador to NATO at the time of his appointment as Chief of Staff. He is the one responsible for organizing the Ford White House. With the defeat of Ford by Carter he became a key figure in restoring G. D. Searle, an international pharmaceutical company, back to solid ground. Paul O'Neill was Ford's head of the Office of Management and Budget. This was a mid-level appointment that was utilized as one of the inner circle. At the conclusion of the Ford administration he became CEO of ALCOA. Greenspan was on the board of directors that appointed him. Bush wanted him for the position of Treasury Secretary. O'Neill was undecided, and the Vice President asked if he, Greenspan, could talk to him. He said the same words that influenced Greenspan to say yes. "We really need you down here." Of course he said yes.

One of Greenspan's motives in pursuing Mr. O'Neill was that President Clinton had reappointed Greenspan in the year 2000, and he had three years to go on his term as Chairman of the Fed. V P Cheney wanted to establish a task force on energy policy. Greenspan gave him his input on the oil and gas industry, including liquefied natural gas. Remember the Bush family was an oil industry family.

Looking back to look ahead, Social Security would be raising its head with a projected problem in the year 2010. It is fortunately stable until the year 2035 with little fixes along the way to keep it so. The problem is the declining workforce and the retirement of those born around 1949 and later who would be coming of age to retire. The problem would become, how do you fund the needs of the recipients with the present and future work force?

## 11. SURPLUS/RECESSION

Have you ever seen it rain on a sunny day right where you were standing? That was the feeling that George W. Bush had when he took office. The Clinton tech bubble was coming to an end, but the economy was still rising at a slower rate. It was argued that the economy was like a dam bursting. Bob McTeer, who was head of the Federal Reserve Bank in Dallas stated, "The R word is used openly about everywhere." The released committee statement said, "The committee will continue to monitor closely the evolving economic situation... The risks are weighed mainly toward conditions that May generate economic weakness in the foreseeable future." Companies were raking in the dough and at the same time ridding themselves of unproductive employees. They worked themselves out of a job.

`By January 3, 2001, the economy had been in a slide for two weeks. The Fed, by conference call lowered the federal funds rate by half of a percent to 6.0. It was hinted that reductions would possibly have to occur at a faster rate. This would be according to the cyclical adjustment. The other strange anomaly was the potential disappearance of the national debt if the surpluses continued as they were doing. There had been nearly a decade of rising productivity. The restraint of not spending in excess of your revenues had put the federal government in a solid position. This was basically not giving tax cuts as advocated by the Republican side, and not spending on social programs that would have depleted the surplus. The Congressional Budget Office was at this time projecting a 5.6 trillion dollar surplus into 2011. The long made short, the technology revolution had changed the rules of the game, and the economy was on autopilot (minus the benefit to the people). Only a small sector of the economy was benefiting.

If things were to continue as they were, the Federal Reserve would have to re-evaluate where it made its money. The Fed's fundamental lever for making money was and to this date still is the selling of Uncle Sam's IOU's, treasury securities. But with the debt going down, the Federal Reserve would have to find other ways to make money to sustain its agency. There was a 380 page study done that showed how, but these new instruments would have less liquidity. It could consist of municipal bonds issued by foreign governments, mortgage-backed securities, auctioned discount window credits, plus other debt instruments. These would entail greater risk and, as I said, would have less liquidity. As you well know, later in the year, on September 11, 2001, our house of cards would come crashing down, but the sad thing is, we did it to ourselves.

Paul O'Neill, head of Treasury at the time, had a solution. He split the 5.6 trillion in two with 3.1 trillion that would be deemed untouchable, and 2.5 trillion that would be guarded as usable funds. He set himself apart from his father according to Greenspan by sticking to his pledge of not only no new taxes, but to return what he viewed was the people's money in the form of a tax cut. This was the fundamental point that separated Bush and Gore in the campaign. Gore wanted to apply the funds to social programs and pay down the debt. The bush quote goes like this: "My opponent thinks the surplus is the government's money. What I think, I think it's the hard-working people of America's money."

The Gore position was that the debt, which at that time stood at 3.4 trillion to the Public could be paid down by the 2.5 trillion, reducing the overall effect of our national debt. Our irreducible debt included and includes savings bonds and other securities. These would be considered assets by those who hold them, and they would decline to sell.

He touched on the one trillion dollars that was needed in 2001 of additional funds that would be a down payment on Medicare. He argued that the national government and its people had not even begun to deal with the ballooning costs of the program. As far as Social Security was concerned, the projection of ten years down the road was like counting on un-hatched chickens.

The concept of triggers was introduced. If the surplus lessened or disappeared there had to be a capping mechanism on spending.  Balancing the budget had been the law of the land in at least two of the previous administrations.  If you proposed a program, you'd better have a way to pay for it.  The trouble as I see it is our irrational extending and enhancing of programs beyond justifiable boundaries.  This puts you in trouble like that which exists in Greece today, and the potential consequences as of 2012.  As of 2001 we were operating on the pay-as-you-go rules.  Despite our passion on 9/11 we should put ourselves in check, and maybe taken a different path.

Some of the wrong path ideology came in part from a hurried program.  The Bush administration had six, as opposed to ten weeks to prepare for the inauguration.  Remember the promises broken by both Reagan and Clinton on taxes.  Their reason was sound: as things change, so do your policies.  Bush did not feel that way.  It was as if he were trying to prove something in the face of reality.  Cheney was in the way the band leader in all of this.  Remember Halliburton.  There were certain expenses that a tax cut helped cover up.  Vice President Cheney, on a Sunday morning TV interview stated, "As President-Elect, Bush made it very clear.  He ran on a particular platform that was carefully developed.  It's his program and his agenda, and we have no intention at all of backing off it."

You can go back to Nixon and Reagan and Clinton and find that some promises did not survive one weekend of the actual presidency.  In a way, Bush was trying to prove he was different by listening to the music from rainbow stew.  An actual hard fact statement would be that most of the decisions were made by the White House staff.

The issue of the surplus caused Greenspan to appear before the Senate Budget Committee, and at that time, certain things were said that did not come to pass.  In recent years he had always simply stated, pay off the debt.  This time around these burgeoning surpluses were like tantalizing candy that politician's dream of.  The statisticians had projected exponential growth (too bad it wasn't in job creation).  Under current policy it was stated that in 2001, 281 billion would be the surplus.  By 2002, it was projected to be 313 billion, and by 2003, 359 billion.  It was estimated that half a trillion in assets would flow into Uncle Sam's Treasury each year for the foreseeable future.  It is just bad that all that cool cash evaporated like some magician's trick.  Greenspan viewed excessive surpluses and special committees designed to invest such funds as flawed in application.  He cited the Nixon and Johnson administrations on that one.  He preferred a gradual glide path to lowering those surpluses through a combination of tax cuts and Social Security reform.  There was a 1.6 trillion dollar tax cut on the table via the Bush administration.  The bill itself was introduced by Senators Phil Graham and Zell Miller.  Tom Daschle had a more modest 700 billion dollar plan.  Both plans, in Greenspan's mind would do what needed to be done.  As a note of caution, he urged that all tax cuts should be conditional.

Greenspan thought he was striking a balance when he stated, "With today's euphoria surrounding the surpluses, it is difficult to imagine hard-earned fiscal restraint developed in recent years could rapidly be dissipating.  We need to resist those policies that could resurrect the deficits of the past fiscal imbalances that followed in their wake." This testimony was often told in advance to avoid affecting complex financial markets. To Greenspan's surprise, he was called into Democratic Senator Kent Conrad of North Dakota. He was concerned about the revitalization of the Bush tax cuts. The Senator came straight to the point. "You're going to create a feeding frenzy. Why are you backing the Bush tax cut?"he felt, and this later turned out to be correct, for the congress started not to care about the deficit and fiscal discipline, and it was not until early 2003 that Bush would stand up to the congress and take the issue of deficits and fiscal restraint seriously again after we had succeeded in digging a bigger hole. Part of the problem had become the wars and the divisive attitudes on each side.

## 12. A 2012 TIME WARP

I now bring you to the pages of the *L.A. Times* that I w2as reading last night, and I am starting to see some disturbing parallels. Christopher Whalen, who, as of this date in 2012 is Senior Managing Director of Tangent Capital Partners in New York, stated concerning what Greenspan would call irrational exuberance at best on the part of the banking systems, stated, "We have to understand that these losses are not rare. These are recurring events that have to do with the fact that banks won't lend money. They want to trade opaque, illiquid securities that are not well understood, and I am not sure banks should be doing that." What he was referring to was and is those back-room deals where those who manage and invest our money are engaging in over-the-counter synthetic derivatives and credit default swaps. For the layman, the bad debt that corporations have is being treated as an asset to be bet against in hedge funds that were originally used to back up underwater mortgages. Here is the scary part: J. P. Morgan Chase and Company have recently lost 2 billion dollars in bad investments. This is four years after their collapse in 2008.

A little history lesson comes with the ending of the Glass Seagull Act that dates back to the depression era that Greenspan called archaic. It was replaced by the Banking Reform Act in 1999 in anticipation of the Y2K situation, in anticipation of the changing economy. It in essence allowed banks to cross into the areas where insurance companies operated, and allowed those institutions to cross into the banking arena. To put Greenspan's irrational exuberance into the back room even when only a small portion of the traders were involved, the propensity for flipping bad debt like they flipped houses, causing the collapse of the housing market could impact the economy in the year 2013, or as late as 2014 when our troops come home. That could impact the job market in a negative way and cause the economy to go flat (no growth or minimal growth).

Remember Econometrics, those mathematical formulas that cover a variety of economic scenarios? Today they are referred to as quantitative analysts and through various formulas guide investor to exotic positions. We now have hedge funds that are not hedge funds. The banks have turned the traditional hedge fund that was intended as insurance against loss into this morphed version with refractions on the wrong side. They are gambling with the public's money. There will be more on this later. The source article was dated May 30, 2012.

Now to history. There was a panic in 1907 that left the economy flat. Now think of World War One and our potential reasons for entering that war. Time passes, and courtesy of margin buying and the crash of the stock market in 1929, the Great Depression followed. Then think of World War Two and the way we entered that war. It is all rather interesting and ironic.

In this early time we did have innovation. Our auto industry was born out of deprivation and we forged our American myth that took on a life of its own. This is inherent in all cultures, especially the Great Experiment that was this country. It got to be expected when the word "panic" was replaced by "depression," then rolling readjustment (1953 through 1954). The term "rolling readjustment" fell into disfavor. The analogy of a fire sale was used by Galbraith. We look to the bargain advantage, to our own disadvantage.

## 13. THE AMERICAN MYTH

On the American economic myths we draw from: Smith, Richardo, Mill and Marshall as source of water to draw from. On land values and perceived wealth, the landlord class seems to be lucky, for they reap benefits in good times and in bad. The economic value of the land, independent of its actual worth never goes down in terms of rent. This is unrealistic, and creates displaced population.

The theory of the leisure class (Thorstern Veblem), of the fraud of competition, and the inherent nature of economics, to overproduce a thing to obsolescence. The other side of the mindset, of the worker that runs, counter to Family and Church. The worker has the caste mark of inferiority, and little idle time, to the rich, what was called immoral idleness, they are advertisements of success in the pecuniary culture. I guess you could call it Pop Culture.
Again, for the worker and his mark of inferiority lies the tradition accorded the glory of Honest Toil. Even this is denied. Veblem thought evolving society was destroying the greater choice. This includes all civilization as well. This was the voice of the frontier world of America. Veblem's ideas never entered the textbooks of Central American economic thought.

## 14. SOCIAL DARWINISM

This theory was the brain child of Herbert Spencer (1820–1903). The principle runs along the lines of those who contest the market and win are rewarded and perpetuate themselves. Those who fail in their attempt to adapt fall and are forgotten as the dust of the earth. Their kind ceases to exist. This is the principle of corporate merger where the man who produces the Edsel dies and the corporate entity that produces the electric car that can get 130 miles to the gallon takes off.

All things public were abhorred, for they create dependency right down to the post office, education, and sanitation. All should be run on the basis of private enterprise. Ignorance and consequence were his byline. Spencer states, "What can be more extreme absurdity than the proposing to improve social life by breaking the fundamental law of social life."

The year was 1904, and a Supreme Court decision was made: the ten hour day for breaks of bread. The dissenting opinion of Justice Holmes, "The Fourteenth Amendment does not enact me Herbert Spencer's social statistics." The backdrop to Social Darwinism in the United States and the meteoric rise in the economy was done on the backs of women and child labor. All wished to be rich, so they did not complain. Migrants kept leaving Europe, providing a cheap labor pool, which fed the American economy. Abstractly now, think of today's migrant labor and corporate farms, and the prices we have in our stores. The down side is we, as Americans become unemployable. Foreign skilled and unskilled labor will work for less. We just get the finished product.

## 15. JOHN D. ROCKEFELLER

This man once put forth this idea to a Sunday school class: "The growth of large business is merely the survival of the fittest. The American Beauty rose can be produced in the splendor and fragrance which brings cheer to the beholder by sacrificing the early buds which grow around it."

In 1956 the National Association of Manufacturing called solemnly in Herbert Spencer's name, "Before we can build a glorious future, this is another unsound part of our structure which we'll have to get rid of, even though it causes severe pain to us business men to forgo the federal crutches we have been leaning on." He was referring to union representation and social issues. Not a business man or union member acted on his statements.

## 16. IN CONCLUSION

We have come through the maze of social evolution to our present day: from the bad old days when life was nasty, short and brutish, and all the theories that evolved from the beginning of time to this time of special awareness and public need. We still have to keep in mind the limits of economic systems.

## 17. BUSH TAX CUT 2001

It all started innocently enough: Greenspan had explained to the Dakota Senator what he meant, and it was now the second day of his grilling before the Senate panel. Senator Conrad addressed Greenspan by thanking him for his balanced approach. Senator Conrad then said, "As I hear you testifying, you're proposing we don't abandon fiscal discipline." Greenspan's response was in the affirmative. He then outlined and expanded on the point. The questions followed along party lines, and each side had its own plan. Senator Phil Graham of Texas (Republican): "I think we pretty well know where we're going. The sooner we write the budget, the better, and get on with it." The Democratic reaction was that taking action on the tax cut issue, we were going to be starting a stampede. South Carolina Senator Paul Sarbanes flatly stated, "It wouldn't be far off the mark for the press to carry the story 'Greenspan Takes Lid Off Punch Bowl.'" West Virginia Senator Bob Byrd stated, "Now I am a Baptist. We have a hymnal. We have a song in our hymnal, 'The Anchor That Holds,' and I've looked at and through this economic expansion period, and I've considered you to be a great portion of the anchor. I have listened to you over the last several years that we need to pay down the debt. That is a basic need. I believe that you were right then, and I am somewhat stunned by the fact that the anchor is wavering today." In all this Greenspan hoped that his message on excessive surpluses and a glide path with a trigger was heard by the Senate. To top all this off, President Bush told reporters that very evening that what Greenspan said was, "Measured, and just right."

The press weighed in and viewed the matter of tax cuts as a political juggling game. The *Financial Times* of New York stated, "Tax cuts are inevitable, and it makes sense for Mr. Greenspan to avoid disagreeing with the new administration at this early stage."

He spoke of things in retrospect of how he had Clinton's back at the start of his administration when it came to the issue of the deficit back in 1993. He also saw this time around his words were becoming the base for the biggest tax cut (Republican sponsored) since the Reagan administration.

The House was being irresponsible, and Greenspan, in February and March of 2001 was urging the Congress, and specifically the House of Representatives, "It is crucial that we develop budgetary strategies that deal with any disappointments that could occur." There was a group of five Republicans and six Democrats prepared to press on the trigger concept, but there was no political will to carry if forward. When Greenspan pressed the White House, Ari Fleischer declared, "We need to make it the permanent law of the land." Karl Rowe called any trigger dead as far as the Bush administration was concerned. The thing that confounds me on this point is that we are about to go to war, and we are already shooting ourselves in the foot. The Bush tax cut was 1.35 TRILLION DOLLARS, and it is about to expire again. Let it die.

## 18. A TIME LEADING TO WAR

George W. Bush was doing his best with the perception problem he had. Under the Bush administration, there were seven cuts in the interest rate that were necessary due to the dot-com bust, and after we were attacked, there were four more in that same rate. We also had a series of corporate scandals in 2002. By the month of October 2002, the interest rate was 1.25%. This was the interest rate during the Eisenhower Administration. The market forces, it seemed, were conspiring to hold down wages and prices. It was called a disinflationary spiral. Ten year Treasuries saw a drop in yield from 7% to 3.5%. What was causing this effect? Globalization and our flat currency were feeling the brunt of it. The economy did grow by 1.6% in 2002 (GDP). The corporate structure was not doing well. Holding companies like Aetna, and SBC Communications had weak profits and were laying off people. The unemployment rate was now 6%. Those planes that hit the Twin Towers and took the wind out of our sails as if we were passing through the Sargasso Sea were finally starting to kick up and the stock market was showing signs of recovery. It was this atmosphere that brought about the sub-prime loans to create a bubble of economic growth.

## 19. NATIVE AMERICAN CULTURAL MYTHOLOGY

America has lost its way. When we bought into the corporate world of consolidation for its own sake, we actually violated some very basic rights that we fought the Red Man for on this continent. Now we willfully give it away for a little security that isn't.

We regard the land as secondary to the concept of profit. This follows even if we give up economic rights that are rightfully ours by conquest. As a matter of fact, aside from certain groups like the Amish, Mormons, and those in the Native American culture that control their own interests, we have become but a flash in the pan.

What backs up this tradition of self-reliance is the mythology of the people and how strongly they believe it. Black Elk, one of the last surviving medicine men of his time, before his death gave an account of an abstracted history of his people.

The American Indian tradition is steeped in vision. The following is an anthology of sorts of the history of Black Elk's people as told in a series of dreams. Six figures, north, east, west, and south, Earth images, appeared as men. These are referred to as thunder beings. They took Black Elk on a high and lonely center on the Earth so that you see the place where the sun continually shines. "I give you the power to make life and it's yours."

The second grandfather: "Take courage, younger brother. On earth a nation you shall make live. To yours shall be the power, to yours shall be the power of the white giant wings, the cleansing wings. This was followed by the singing of a song:

> They are appearing May you behold
> They are appearing May you behold
> The thunder nation is appearing behold
> They are appearing May you behold
> They are appearing May you behold
> The white geese nation is appearing behold

The third grandfather spoke: "Take courage, my brother, for across the earth they will take you (pointing to the stars). From them you shall have power. From them who have awakened all beings of the earth with roots, legs and wings (He held up the peace pipe of the spotted eagle). With this pipe you shall walk upon the earth, and whatever sickens there you shall make well." The old man then turned into a bison and galloped to the sorrel horses of the East.

The fourth grandfather spoke: "Younger brother, with the power of four quarters you shall walk a relative distance. Behold the living center of the nation I shall give you and with it you shall save a tree sprouted with many branches." And birds began to sing.

There was talk of bloodshed and great war. A cup of water brought back by the black horse rider with the writing and the sacred herb. There was a sorrel horse with a holy pipe and buckskins with a flowering stick.

Black Elk recounts a journey into a green land that was getting steeper, and a vision occurred to him. A voice said to him, "Behold your nation and remember what your six grandfathers gave you, for thence your people will walk in difficulties." Looking down, Black Elk saw his people breaking and following their own visions. They were like winds of war and fighting beasts.

He remarks at this point, "I think we are near that place now, and I am afraid something bad is going to happen all over the world. The holy tree which was the center of his story seemed dying, and all the birds were gone.

The people changed from animals to humans. The Holy Tree was gone, and the horses, as the people, were as if they were skin and bone.

The sacred man went into the center of the people, lay down and rolled around. He was a huge, fat bison. On the spot where he was, a tree sprang up with four blossoms on one branch, blue, white, scarlet and yellow. These rays flashed to the heavens. All seemed better when the herb had grown and bloomed. He was still the spotted eagle, and in the fourth ascent, the world beneath him was wailing with dark clouds and conflicting winds. Women and children were crying and like horses screaming all over the world.

## 20. CALIFORNIA POLITICS
### February 19, 1967

California, in the years Regan was governor was a regular battleground, especially in the area of higher education. Universities asked 264 million for their annual budget. The figure of 255 million was proposed. It was argued that the first sum would enable the system to admit 10,000 more students that year.

Assembly Speaker Jesse Unruh contended that the Board of Regents"...were in for one hell of a fight, especially after all the beating around the mulberry bush, which they did before coming to grips with the problem Thursday. The short term and long term goals are at the point of demoralization."

Board Chairman Theodore R. Meyers sated, "The Regents are not prepared to settle for 255 million. The universities live on faith. We created the new campuses on faith (Irvine, Santa Cruz, and San Diego). We live on faith every year. We have faith in the legislative process, and the people of the state. We think we have an excellent case for our budget of 264 million, which would enable us to take on an additional 9,000 to 10,000 students."

The other big issue in California was the death penalty. Assemblyman Lester A. McMillan, Los Angeles Democrat, and Democratic Senator George R. Moscone, San Francisco had proposed legislation on the elimination of the death penalty, and the bill that proposed a moratorium on the same penalty. It was also recognized that then Governor Reagan would veto such a bill. You would have thought Governor Edmond G. Brown would have had that honor. There were placed before the legislature 20 bills to eliminate the death penalty since 1933. The last person to be executed was in 1963. None of the aforementioned ever hit the governor's desk.

Have you ever heard of the National Student Association? Well, they were at the heart of the controversy concerning the Central Intelligence Agency. It seemed that the CIA planted agents in the organization.

They demanded an apology for the previous 13 years where they were dupes of the CIA. They wanted then President L. B. Johnson to declare all student associations off-limits to the CIA. They made this declaration on the White House lawn.

### 21. July 16, 1967

Inglewood's Assemblyman, who was speaker of the house, Jesse N. Unruh was going to introduce legislation that would eliminate eight positions from the Board of Regents and the Board of Trustees of the California colleges. Unruh called it, "An attempt to return the discussion of public higher education to an objective, nonpartisan basis." Those on the board as it stood were the Governor, Lieutenant Governor, Superintendent of Public Instruction, and all elected officials that made the board partisan. Other members that would be excluded would be president of the Mechanics Institute of San Francisco, president of the University Alumni Association, president of the University, president of the State Board of Agriculture, and other gubernatorial appointees. The removal of all political types would, in Unruh's mind, created an apolitical board that would do the right thing. Remember, any appointment would be for 14 years, so when a candidate would be officially appointed, you have to look at his age.

Unruh's view could be summarized by his statement, "As long as we continue to place partisan office holders on these bodies as active participants in the day-to-day operation of campuses, this widely held impression will continue." He argued they only attended meetings that would be of benefit to them, not the day-to-day operation, but instead, he contended, "In that event, politicians feel obliged to attend and use the Board of Regents or the Board of Trustees as a platform for making their particular views on the issue known. Both the governor and the Speaker of the Assembly have ample opportunity to make their views known, and affect statewide policy on higher education."

I can, for devil's advocate position, come up with something to counter that. These guys were elected to represent the public interest and education, and its best interest is served by the informed.

Eugene J. McCarthy was challenging Vice President Hubert Horatio Humphrey for the presidential nomination of the Democratic Party. Humphrey's campaign was best described as loose and disorganized. The vice president only at this late date had pulled his act together and was punching hard.

The Nixon campaign for the Republican nomination was organized and well-oiled. Nixon was also in his home state, with a definite advantage.

## 22. November 3, 1968

This was the year of change. Several leading figures were leaving the political arena. Charles Meyers, Democrat of San Francisco, Edward Eliot, Democrat of Los Angeles, and Stewart Hinkley, Republican of Redlands was not seeking re-election. In all, 80 seats were up for grabs, and the heat was on. Of the 13 targeted districts, Milton Marks of San Francisco, Republican, and Nicolas Petris, Democrat of Oakland was vulnerable districts. Third parties did not seem to be much of a factor.

Under newly-created measures, a public transit system, the old Red Line was now history, and essentially there were no buses. A 2.5 billion dollar bond issue was up before the voters. There was a Proposition 9 in 1968, but it pertained to a proposition 13 type of formula which would come later. It limited property taxes to assessed value and financing through other programs would come from other sources. The alternative, which was Proposition 1A, provided a $750 tax credit to home owners. There was a school construction bond (250 million dollars) for the University of California and run-down schools, called Proposition 3.

Jesse Unruh complained about false negative ads in the form of posters that invited assassinations and something akin to the Watts riots. He was being linked to the Black Panther leader, Eldridge Cleaver. Dr. Verreege stated, "Blows it all out of proportion to what it should be. There are always self-appointed groups that do something outlandish in every campaign." That is true especially today. When Santorum attacked Romney in 2012, he forced him right into a position that would backfire on Republicans in the general election of 2012.

Alan Cranston was leading Rafferty in the polls, but he told his supporters in a speech at Roy Campanula Park not to rest on their keisters.

### 23. December 30, 1968

The inappropriate use of power had become an important issue. Unruh lost his bid for the Senate, but retained his position as head of the Democratic lower chamber. His bill basically disallows a member of the legislature to hold a committee chair in the area he owns in excess of one tenth of one percent of a business interest that would come before the state. He stated, "In addition to guarding against impropriety, this legislation is needed if we are to restore public confidence in the process of government in California. The sad fact of life today is that public faith in government is at an, extremely low ebb." Jesse Unruh could be considered a populist. Today he is head of a foundation centered on research and the public trust.

### 24. January 3, 1969

The location was Los Angeles, and the first day of filing for all public offices. Mayor Sam Yorty signaled his desire to run for a fourth term. Those running against him were former Police Chief and Councilman Tom Bradley, Robert J. Wilkinson, and an attorney, Laurence Schulner. Positions open on the city council and boards numbered eight of fifteen seats on the city council, seven seats on the Board of Education, and all seven seats that were created for the new Junior College Board.

This particular election got dirty, and when the contest boiled down to Bradley against Yorty, the race card was played, but Tom Bradley won.

### 25. REAGAN'S MENTAL HEALTH PROGRAM
### January 21, 1969

Reagan was known as a micro-manager. He had a tendency to get bogged down in the details. Here was his proposed budget for mental health.

1. An increase of 22.8 million in the years 1968 through 1969.
2. An increase in the presently authorized level of care in mental hospitals by retention of 559 nurses and rehabilitation therapists which would have been laid off with the decreasing number of patients.

3. An additional 175 hospital workers' positions.
4. An additional 63 psychiatric technicians' positions.
5. An additional 100 maintenance positions, such as plumbers, painters and electricians.
6. An 18 month phase-out of Modesto State Hospital, with the future of 3.5 million in annual savings in operating expenses after it is closed.
7. An additional $750,000 over and above the cost of living increase for operating expenses, such as purchase of diapers, towels and bedding, and other similar items.
8. Establishment of 11 additional coordinator's positions at the hospitals at a cost of $164,000.
9. Completion of the preliminary architectural plans for the new Langly Porter Neuropsychiatric Institute in San Francisco.

In a way, it is unfair when critics stated that he shut down the mental health system. You see, he did fund it.

## 26. FLOODING
### January 30, 1969

At this point in our history 25 of the 58 counties were affected by flood waters due to the heavy rains that occurred two weeks earlier. Assemblyman Ken McDonald, a Democrat of Ventura reflected his constituency that was damaged severely by the flooding. He proposed a once cent increase in the gasoline tax for six months to pay for the rebuilding of the roads damaged by the flooding.

Governor Reagan's position was that the once cent tax on petrol would be a considered item, and felt that the repairs to the affected counties could be done within the existing budget. It must be remembered that Reagan promised no tax increases.

Funding for private property would not be covered. It was suggested that those on private roads could, with community effort, rebuild those bridges and repair asphalt.

## 27. THE WELFARE ISSUE
January 14, 1970

Regan was always an individualist and couldn't understand failure. The issue of welfare and the need for it eluded him. He stated, "The agency that prescribes a service should be paying for it." Dorn, Regan's spokesman, stated, "The level of care is being reduced and the cost of care is increasing. That is ridiculous. The whole program is the most colossal flop in the history of local government." He continued, "The 31% increase in county welfare costs expected for the 1970-71 budgets for the fiscal year starting July 1 is almost entirely due to the continuing increase in the recipients.

"Despite the additional money being spent on the program, thousands of individuals and families will still be receiving help below the minimum considered necessary for properly maintaining life, according to the State's own standards."

Some who got on welfare, especially leaders of the movement, came into question. Mrs. Alisia Escalante, leader of the Welfare Rights organization of East Los Angeles, at the December 18th meeting of the Board of Supervisors, was asked how she could justify her welfare check being forwarded to her when she was traveling all over the world. The answer was direct and simple: The trip was sponsored by the Presbyterian Church that paid all expenses for her and others that were on a fact-finding tour that lasted seven weeks. The topic was nutrition and hunger. Why do officials pick the wrong people to attack when they are trying to make their point? Shouldn't they do their research first?

## 28. MULTIPLE PARTIES

The Prohibition Party was the last legal third party and that was back in the fifties. The political climate as it was in 1968 fostered an abundance of challengers. The American Independent Party had George C. Wallace, a famous segregationist at this time. He would later recant that belief. There was the Peace and Freedom Party, who had as its candidate Eldrige Cleaver of Black Panther fame.

The McCarthy for President Campaign had legal difficulty. His running mate, Peggy Terry, was not a legal match on the ballot. George Wallace's running mate was General Curtis LaMay, but on the ballot it was Governor Marvin Griffin of Georgia. Eldrige Cleaver would not appear on the ballot, but Peggy Terry would. Any altering of the ballot would disqualify it.

Under write-ins, Dick Gregory had thrown his name in under the Socialist Labor Party. Henning A. Bloman and George S. Taylor were listed as Independents. James P. Powers was running under the Berkley Defense Group. The Communist Party even made it. Their slate was Charlene Mitchell and Michael Zageral. You could not say the presidential choices were limited.

The U. S. Senate race had three candidates: Former State Controller Alan Cranston, Democrat, State Superintendent of Public Instruction Max Raferty, Republican, and Paul Jacobs of the Peace and Freedom Party. The Cranston-Raferty contest proved to be bitter, and the way things go today have not changed that much.

Sam Yorty was Mayor of Los Angeles at this time. He came to office in 1961. There was a law set in motion that all contracts had to be brought before the board for approval. There would be no back-room deals. Well, there was a company, Umetoto-Perkinson, who contracted to build a fifty-four hole golf course in the Sepulveda Basin. They were paid $59,099 for the preliminary work. The problem was, they had no business license, and no business office at the time. The contract was cancelled. This was one of four questionable contracts. Mayor Sam blamed it on the bureaucracy.

### 29. INTRANSIGENCE
May 28, 1969

Here was the beginning of the fiscal battle. Reagan had a 6.2 billion dollar budget, which was 2.4 million dollars higher than originally submitted by then Assemblyman Frank Lanterman, Republican of Pasadena, who was chairman of the Ways and Means Committee. It was a key vote, so that the budget could take effect on July first of that year. The Democrats were holding out for a shifting economy and increased school aid. The Democratic members of the legislature blocked the budget.

### 30. REAGAN'S THREE YEAR TAX PLAN
June 11, 1969

The year is 1969, and Reagan views himself as the Great Reformer of the budget. He put forth a three point plan. 1) Property tax relief: 1) Better source of income for school support and a revised distribution formula to erase the disparity that now exists between the wealthy and the poor districts, and 3) No increased taxes.

## 31. THE LEGISLATION THAT CHANGED IT ALL
### June 12, 1969

To start off, there was legislation in the works in 1969 that stated that anyone stopped for suspected drunk driving had to submit to chemical tests, and if he refused, his license would be suspended for six months, even if he was later found by the court not to be under the influence. The new proposed legislation was passed in the Senate by a margin of 34 to 1. The California Assembly had passed similar legislation under traffic safety legislation by a margin of 45 to 21.

The bill that declares that anyone with a blood alcohol level of 0.10% was legally drunk, and if the level was 0.06% he would be sober. This bill changed the premise of the law from being innocent until proven guilty to the other way around. The guy in the Senate that had to guts to oppose this legislation was Senator Ralph C. Dills. He stated, "This is not going to solve the problem. There isn't a man in this room who seriously thinks this bill will make a damn bit of difference to the guy who wants a drink." He added to his comments by stating that 0.10% levels would clog the court system and increase the need for judges. He added this law makes one guilty automatically. There was no presumption of innocence.

The scientific approach was used, assuming a man 180 pounds could drink up to 8.8 ounces of 80 proof liquor in 60 to 90 minutes before hitting the 0.10 mark or higher. The statistic used was that 50% of adult drivers that met their end in California traffic accidents had been drinking. This was the way it was described back then, and since then the blood alcohol level was lowered to 0.8%.

Since then people have been trapped by checkpoints and have blown into the breathalyzer guns multiple times as directed by the officer without his recalibrating the gun in order to obtain a conviction. This is common practice, and the denials on the art of law enforcement abound. The system justifies itself.

## 32. DEATH PENALTY

Those who kill the police in the process of an altercation found themselves, courtesy of the California State Senate in the position of a death penalty charge. The vote was 23 to 8. The author of the bill was California State Senator H. L. Richardson, Republican, Arcadia. The reason for the bill was the increase in the statistical killing of police officers. Prior to the passage of this law, the sentence was either life in prison or the death penalty.

It is always refreshing to hear the other point of view. Senator Anthony Bellenson, Democrat of Beverly Hills: "Why is it worse to murder a police officer than a defenseless woman or a child?" The rebuttal from Richardson was, "Because the police officer is a symbol of law enforcement." He added that a convict who murders a guard is executed.

My take on the argument is that the field of law enforcement is an inherently dangerous profession. At times they exceed their authority. Sometimes they die as a result of conflict. If you choose a profession, you accept the odds. Therefore, it should rest upon the burden of proof, and not an automatic bias. Oh, yes, dogs are not police officers, they're trained dogs. What about when the police officer unjustly kills the civilian? There is a bias in his favor. Should not the playing field be even?

### 33. BUDGET WAR
June 20, 1969

The state budget as proposed by Governor Ronald W. Reagan was subjected to the political storms of the legislature. Reagan's 6.22 billion dollar budget was trimmed by 27.2 million in the Senate. It now totaled 6.19 billion. This was after intensive hearings were held on the subject. A Senate quote stated, "The committee was pretty hardnosed on capital outlay, and agreed to move ahead only when bonds are available." The Senate Finance Committee had approval and sent the budget to the full Senate Thursday, the spending blueprint for the fiscal year 1969-1970. Because of the two-thirds rule, the Democratic minority in the Assembly would have to be accommodated. By the way, that is the reason for the two-thirds rule: so the minority party's rights are protected.

### 34. FLOOD REPAIR
September 8, 1969

Remember the one cent increase in the gas tax to cover the flood damaged roads?

Governor Reagan stated, "Tax reform should not be an excuse for a tax increase. It is impossible to have compulsory withholding without getting some additional revenue that the people are not now paying. This in effect constitutes a tax increase whether you change the rates or not." Here we see the starts of intransigence.

Assemblyman William T. Bagley, Republican, San Raphael, who was chairman of the Revenue and Taxation Committee put forward the idea that a compulsory withholding was necessary. He put it this way, "If we do not have total withholding, we don't have a chance of putting this through the legislature." This sentiment was only magnified by Assembly Speaker Robert T. Monagan, Republican representing Tracy, and the Senate President Pro Tem Howard Way, Republican, representing Exeter made the point that mandatory withholding May be vital if any major tax reform was to happen.

Speaking at a fundraising dinner, then Governor Reagan stated that a tax increase enacted in 1967 saved the state from going 1.5 million dollars into debt. That tax increase went a long way to restoring the state's fiscal responsibility. Reagan touted his pushing of that 950 million dollar tax increase was indeed necessary. He charged that the Democratic Party was culpable "for eight years of irresponsible profligacy." He obviously did not like Edmond G. Brown, Senior. The dinner itself benefited James A. Hayes, Republican of Long Beach.

## 35.   January 14, 1970

In 1969, Senator George Moscone, Democrat, San Francisco promoted a school lunch bill. The price tag for that bill was 5 million. Then Governor Reagan vetoed all but 500,000 of it and said it was technically flawed. He promised a new bill in the next session.

Well, that time apparently came, and it was 20 million: five million from the State, six million from the federal government, 5 million from the Department of Agriculture. The remainder had already been allocated to the program. The bill had the support from the entire state legislature. Reagan was not against education or welfare, but he had his own peculiar notions of how it should work.

The statistics that were bandied about were that 500,000 children were malnourished, and as many as 1,250 were in danger of that condition. A bill was being tossed about on a 6 million dollar increase in benefits for children and their families.

The then Governor Reagan stated that the funds would be taken out of the unused state surplus funds. Governor Jerry Brown would later criticize this action as contributing to the state's fiscal woes.

Reagan started to change his tune on taxes as he saw the climate change. "... Some taxes will have to be increased to offset reductions, particularly and almost solely in the property tax. You remember when my feet were in concrete I said I would be guided by the people. If the people changed what I believed to be their sentiment, I wouldn't stand in their way. I'll go no further than that." As I viewed Reagan on his impressive record as governor, he was an orator and a charismatic, and he knew how to change with the wind.

Senator Milton Marks, Republican, San Francisco had proposed a constitutional amendment to the gas tax. That amendment would allow the gas tax to be used for other than freeway construction and maintenance. The funds would be freed to be used for related projects like smog abatement. The current state of the gas tax use was compared to the horse and buggy. Assemblyman George Milias wrote a bill that would allow counties with populations of 400,000 or more to split their grand juries into civil and criminal. Assemblyman Paul Priolo proposed a bill requiring counties and school districts that shift duties to the state to reduce property taxes by that amount. The ballot measure was supported by the teachers' association. Local agency control would save money, according to him.

## 36. THE MORATORIUM
### January 29, 1971

The Santa Barbara oil disaster colored California's politics with a black ooze. In 1969 the damage extended all down the California coastline killing birds and fish. Standard Oil was the one responsible, and they paid heavy fines.

Now it was 1971, and California was in a funding crisis. State Controller Huston I. Flournoy, who was Chairman of the State Lands Commission, and an 8 month old bid by Standard Oil finally met the state's new standards, case by case policy. There was a manmade island two miles off the coast of Seal Beach. It was the best case for resumption of drilling on the California continental shelf. The rigs that were already in production and inspected were not affected. We had just stopped drilling due to political considerations.

Flournoy stated, "This particular well meets the criteria of the policy of this commission with regards to safety." State Comptroller Flournoy continued, "And we will continue to review each application on an individual basis. We will continue to insist on safety features, and each well will have to stand on its own set of circumstances. There will be no deviation from that policy."

It was in 1969, off the coast of Santa Barbara where Union Oil Company had a rig three miles off the coast. That rig started leaking and blackened hundreds of miles of California beaches and impacted wildlife. That well was not in control or jurisdiction because it was in international waters. The result was a moratorium on drilling on the continental shelf of California. It was, however, under the jurisdiction of the Department of the Interior. The SLC was the body that imposed that moratorium on new drilling. The oil industry had been in bed with the regulators, and as a result of this disaster on the California coast, was told to develop safety features for its rigs.

Martin Levine, who was Deputy County Council for Santa Barbara was on record as opposing the Standard Oil Lease. He called it a "first step toward a change of position by the commission that would permit further offshore drilling within state tidelands. When the inevitable accidents do occur, the oil industry is unable to adequately cope with them.

"In substance, our point is that more drilling offers greater exposure to possible incidents and should not be permitted until the inevitable pollution coped with, and that such ability should be demonstrated by the oil companies beyond all reasonable doubt. We are fearful that the granting of this application could somehow be deemed to be a determination by this commission that it is now satisfied that the oil companies have adequate containment and recovery devices. We don't feel that such devised have been developed, and we don't believe the commission thinks that is the case."

A real reason for the granting of the Standard Oil lease could have its roots in the continual recurring fiscal crisis.

Prior to the Santa Barbara incident, 150,000 acres off the counties of Orange, Los Angeles, Ventura, and Santa Barbara were at the potential exploitation of oil companies. The State of California at this time got revenues of 25,000,000 on a yearly basis. These funds were used to support recreational, educational and water resources, according to the *L.A. Times*.

Today huge rigs the size of small islands dot the landscape, and it is sort of funny, but we still have a fiscal shortfall.

## 37. THE FISCAL CRISIS
### February 3, 1971

Governor Ronald Wilson Reagan, one of our most enigmatic figures, was dealing with a cash flow problem in the State of California. The seemingly hope and prayer attitude was embodied in the 1971-1972 proposed budget. The figure for that budget was 6.7 billion. The state had not been in this position since the Great Depression. It is ironic that some years later Governors Davis and Schwarzenegger would find themselves in similar positions. The spending programs alone amounted to $6,738,700,000. The budget was up 4%, or 258 million over the 1970-71 budget of 6.48 billion.

## 38. BEFORE THE AXE
### December 11, 2009

It was just before election time and the wheels of state funding by the federal government through the Congress were delivering their Christmas list. Here is the story as it relates to California, which as of 2012, seems squarely in the Obama camp.

During the course of the year there have been 7,577 pieces of pork barrel legislation spread across the country. The current pork legislation comes at a cost of 3.9 billion according to Tax Payers for Common Sense. A budget analyst for the Conservative Heritage Foundation, Brian M. Reidi, stated, "Clearly the earmark culture has not been swept away." This legislation spent 447 billion nationally. It was strictly a Democratic bill with no Republican support. As stated earlier, there were 7,577 bills classified as pork, costing 6 billion.

Among the items funded by the democrats, 1) 330 million to subsidize nationally the jailing of illegal immigrants convicted of crimes. The monies were to be managed by state and local governments. That figure was put at 70 million the previous year. California received 18 million to subsidize its prison costs. 2) 2.5 billion was slated for the high speed bullet train, but only upon its implementation. 3) 50 million nationally for an improved braking system for trains. In all fairness, this was a reaction to the Chatsworth incident. 4) Funding a bus lane on Wilshire Boulevard in Los Angeles, to the tune of 13.5 million. Add to that $500,000 to the funding of a ditch intended for a high speed train to alleviate traffic through the San Gabriel Valley.

Among those not necessary, but beneficial projects was $200,000 provided for the Aquatic Adventures Science Education Foundation in San Diego. The justification for this program was, according to Representative Susan A. Davis, to"... inspire children to pursue education in the sciences, while encouraging students from disadvantaged backgrounds to go to college." You would have to be a Scrooge to criticize such a program. Let me assure you that Scrooge exists. The criticism for this proposed funding came from Arizona Republican Representative Jeff Flake. That poor guy must have been ribbed something awful for his name. That's a Flake off the old block.

The funding for California went on: $600,000 for a streetscape project in Echo Park, $180,000 for training future weather forecasters in the next generation at San Jose State University, and $250,000 for textile research at U C Davis.
The Republicans who were the critics for whom they played Santa Claus in 2005, causing them to lose their majority in 2006, wanted to regain their footing and direction in what has of late become an adverse political climate for their perceived direction. By criticizing these pieces of pork legislation they were trying to overcome good old-fashioned Chicago politics.

## 39. CALPERS
### January 15, 2010

Calpers is the corporation in charge of the California State pension funds. Assets in the fund are valued at $205,000,000,000. They paid 125 million to intermediaries. William E. Crist, a long-time member who was their president lobbied on behalf of the investment firm for a share of the assets. This was according to the *L.A. Times*. Criticism of how Calpers operates seems to be a continuing refrain.

## 40. GIFTS

Among those having to pay fines were Mike Eng, Democrat, Monterey Park, and Anna Caballero, Democratic Representative from Salinas. The Democratic Assemblyman from Southgate has not decided whether or not he is going to pay the fine, and has hired an attorney. He stated, "It was surprising when I found out who paid for it." He added, "It's incumbent on anyone who hosts one of these things to let people know." Lawmakers, according to critics, have a responsibility to know who's paying for their gifts.

It is an old game blamed on administrative and bookkeeping errors. Only a fraction of those engaging in this practice are actually apprehended, and the influence-peddling game goes on.

## 41. CALIFORNIA SECLUSION RADICAL THOUGHT
### February 26, 2010

Tucked away in our mountain ridge communities are many fringe groups that seek isolation to perpetrate what some would call abuse. I was reading the article in the *L.A. Times*, "Paradise: A Bit of Hell, "and the author, Jaime O'Neil spoke of a child crying for mercy while the parent evokes the wrath of God. Prosecutions have happened. The charges of torture and cruelty have been raised in these towns that seemingly touch God. Families have been prosecuted and brought to justice. The crimes only rise to a misdemeanor in places like Butte County. This I think breeds intolerance when the kids grow up.

Not all people stay in these isolated cubby holes, but move into a larger society that they see as outwardly evil, and even if they find someone that moderates them, that fundamentalism acts like a cancer in diluted form. That leads to branding people as atheist, or name some relative paramount to God instead of accepting what has been popularly called the God-Head. The funny thing in a quizzing kind of way has come to define dysfunction in western society, and has even become the grounds for justified murder.

## 42. STATE SELLS SURPLUS BUILDINGS

Normally the state would hold onto vacant properties for future use, but with the down economy, the General Services Director, Ron Deidrich stated, "Most businesses aren't in the business of investing in real estate portfolios, and I don't think the state should be, either. By doing this we are freeing up hundreds of millions of dollars to help the citizens of California by retiring billions in debt. That is a good thing for California now, and in the foreseeable future."

According to the *L.A. Times*, the state bonds were sold to raise money to build office buildings. Paying off the bonds, it would avoid future interest payments. The cost of retiring the bonds would be about 1.35 billion, leaving about 600 million to add to the state's general fund if the properties sell for the projected two billion.

The sale of large commercial properties has not happened very often of late, when you consider the credit crunch factor. (2008) To get a buyer with enough fluid cash in these times has proven difficult. The result of this underwater market is that people attempt to hold on to properties for a more reasonable profit, as opposed to a loss. State properties were going for two dollars a square foot.

Buyers are looking for the equivalent of a fire sale. When they don't find it, they know that the market is nearing the bottom end of the cycle. Banks are showing signs as of 2010 of being reluctant to take back foreclosures. There is no liquidity in the market. The profits in the banks' eyes are not there. They have the cash, they want what they consider a decent return.

### 43.  February 26, 2010

On a statewide basis there were 11 sites in major California cities that are offered for sale. The properties, once sold would be leased back to the state. The established rent would be 12.2 million on an annual basis. The cities involved would be Los Angeles (the Reagan State Building), Sacramento, Oakland, San Francisco, and Santa Rosa.

As stated earlier, the sale of these state properties come at a time when commercial property, which is always devastated when properties are under water. Private homes are not doing much better at this time. Mansions, like those once owned by famous people that have passed, or those that have gotten into trouble, are a bargain. The butler and the maid come with them, along with the groundskeeper (just kidding).

### 44.  THE INSURANCE INDUSTRY

You know all those high costs for medical care, well, the insurance companies were gouging, and they were caught. Companies like Blue Cross, Aetna Health, Blue Shield of California, Cigna, Health Net, and Kaiser Permanente, not to mention Pacific Care. The State Assembly Rules Committee authorized a subpoena of financial records concerning the reimbursements of doctors and hospitals. Anthem was the first to be targeted.

### 45.  COSTAL CONFLICT

Have you ever had that sucking experience as if you were being drawn into Never Land? A man by the name of John Vincent was sucked in with the fishes and lobsters into an area the size of Lake Arrowhead. The fish and the diver were returned to the sea. In reality, some fish do die. This system has provided energy cheaply, but the state wants the water to be drawn from the surface, as opposed to the floor of the continental shelf. This is not a cheap process, and the power company doesn't want to do it. The changes are probably why we have seen an increase in electric rates. May I suggest solar or wind? On second thought, you might then get chopped seagull.

## 46. LET THE RACE BEGIN
## May 1, 2010

California's insurance commissioner Steve Poizner was a networker, not a bull in the china shop. In 2009 he set up his campaign and, like Brown, was frugal in his spending. He did the circuit, and he was a decent speaker. He had the reputation of an accommodator. He helped Schwarzenegger compromise with the Democratic legislature in an effort to solve some of California's problems. Budget priorities and social issues would be an example, with an eye on the state's indebtedness. These you would think would be good qualities, especially with his business background at GPS, but he was jot Jerry, and did not have the name recognition. This is the story of this man as he pitted himself against Meg Whitman for the prize of being the Republican nominee.

Meg Whitman was something special. I, to this point had never seen another candidate quite like her. Aside from the heavy use of negative campaign ads against Insurance Commissioner Steve Poizner, as I said, was running a low key campaign, as did Jerry Brown in the general election. Her tactics were effective with her Republican audience. Her tactics centered on a tightly-controlled campaign and high-profile national media interviews. She avoided debates with Poizner, instead relying on sound bites. The *L.A. Times* described her style as no holds barred. They were being gracious.

The big criticism was her lack of transparency. She in effect refused to accept the ritual of media public inspection. There were times in the campaign, in my Republican opinion, she was as clear as mud. She did throw a lot of that. She was ignored by the affiliated Democratic campaign committees. She did have one television before the primary. There were no interviews of substance before the primary. It was as though God was running for the position of Governor. The Jerry Brown campaign had one comment: Does Meg Whitman gave a glass jaw?

Now to Jerry Brown, who was our Attorney General at this time? His bid for the governorship was, in a way historic, for two reasons, having served as governor at the age of 36, and his attempt at the age of 71 would make him a three-term governor, something his father failed to do, and having served as the youngest and oldest governor in the State of California. He wanted Senator Feinstein to run, but she decided not to do what he regarded as his obligation to the state. The figure of Jerry Brown, though maligned in history, was still very much respected. It was said he had the tools to fix the machinery of government.

In defense of Governor Schwarzenegger, he was told by the Democratic legislature that he did not have the clout to make the changes needed. The bully pulpit did not work, pleading to the people did not work, and the accommodating became a liability. So it was that the race for the Governor's Mansion began in the year 2010.

## 47. EVEN IN VERNON
### March 4, 2010

The city of Vernon is a largely industrialized city with a population of fifty thousand. Most salaries for elected and appointed officials are above average. The financial cushion in that city is there to maintain stability, and not to fatten the pockets of those in the city. The economy even in Vernon had gone flat (no growth). Revenues were coming in, but the economy was going stagnant.

I will give the salaries as of 2010. The City Administrator has a salary of $600,000. They have $100,000,000 in reserves. It is the philosophy of the city to cut services. What they did was, they eliminated not the coverage to the primary city employee, but they did cut out the coverage to the spouse and children. They also stopped putting matching funds into the pension fund. Donald O. Callaghan, the City Administrator, did call those affected to a meeting and explained that they did have their cushion, but were just exercising sound fiscal policy. He stated, "The bottom line is that Vernon is in sound financial shape because we take tough actions like today. Fiscal responsibility means that you manage your costs. If you see something escalating above your revenue, then you take action to correct it." He commented that all on the board were facing salary cuts. It was said afterward by those attending the meeting the shock wasn't so much in what was said, but the manner in which he said it.

## 48. IT REQUIRES A LICENSE
### May 8, 2010

A tour bus company in Van Nuys operating under the name of Tierra Santa, Inc. owned by Caytano Martinez was running passengers from Central Mexico to Los Angeles. They had been doing so since before 2009. Their license only allowed them to transport within the State of California. There had been maintenance problems, and on occasion their buses were declared out of order by various interstate agencies when examined on the open road. U.S. District Court Judge George King signed the consent decree after information on the Arizona accident was made public.

It happened in this way: The bus was carrying 22 passengers from Mexico to Los Angeles early Friday. It hit a pickup truck in the rear in Arizona and rolled down an embankment. Its windows shattered, and the roof of the bus concaved. The accident happened on Interstate 10, 20 miles south of Phoenix. The bus had just crossed a border checkpoint. Two men and four women passed, and the other 16 were injured.

After he was forced out of business he reopened under another name and was promptly shut down. He was operating on that creative capitalist oops program.

## 49. TAX FREE BONDS
### March 9, 2010

State Treasurer Bill Lockier, in an effort to raise 2 billion dollars, was promoting a campaign to lure investors to Generalized Obligation Bonds left for institutional investors as an example of mutual funds. If the big investors competed, that would mean that California would get a lower interest rate. As we all know at this time, state finances had gone south.

The individual investor market here in the Golden State has been municipal bonds, and local government bonds. The state finances have at this time deteriorated to the point that investors have shifted to out-of-state bonds and securities.

This is similar to the Chinese and their ceasing to buy American debt in favor of other countries with a better rate of return.

The point of this bond sale is to prop up the procedures and institutions that go into putting on an election. The 20 billion deficits will still exist after the sale. How does a bond sale happen, and what are the procedures? Securities will be offered to individuals on Tuesday and Wednesday. Institutional investors will put their orders in when the final yield of the bond is set. (This, according to the *L.A. Times*). States sell their debt through institutions like AIG, Morgan Stanley, i.e., brokerage houses. They make their money on the margin. Win or lose, they win. When they sell bad product, as to say the outside looks good, but the inside is rotten, they have committed fraud and the economy suffers.

The state of tax free municipal bonds and their yields have declined in the last couple of months. The reason is the individual appetite of investors remained healthy and no new bonds were offered at a rate to sustain the market. It was the hope of the State of California that despite the declining economy, investors would find tax free yields on this particular series too much of a good deal to pass up. The rate at this time was 3.6%. These are the thoughts of Wall Street dealers at this time. Here's the clincher: if the tax cut initiated by George had been allowed to expire, the bonds would have been more attractive.

## 50. WHITMAN'S PORTFOLIO
### March 11, 2010

Whitman's asset portfolio is based on risk. She basically invests in distressed companies either to cannibalize, and in some cases build that company if it is a new startup. Startups seem to be her specialty. She has trouble with established companies. She holds the title of the 326$^{th}$ richest American. At a bulk level her assets in 2010 were $1.9 billion. As of this date there were 214 active investments on her plate.

The following is a list of her investments: Perry Partners, a New York hedge fund invested $100,000 to $1,000,000: Chrysler Financial, GMAC and Ford Motor

Credit, specializes in distressed properties: NCH Agribusiness Partners, and according to analysts, her investments could be confused with a pension fund.

Pompel stated, "The fact is Meg has been a successful business person and a manager her entire career. She has diligently paid her taxes in full, and has happily disclosed her assets to the voters of California. She's a passive investor who has managed to put top grade professionals just like any University endowment, pension fund, or any height net worth individual." For more details on Whitman's economic activity, see the *L.A. Times* article entitled, "Whitman's Portfolio Detailed." It is interesting.

## 51. STEVE POIZNER

Poizner and family had their investments in the tech industry: $1,000,000 in Dot UDU Ventures, which invests in computer related firms. $1 million was invested in De Novo Ventures which has as its investments medical devices and bio technology. He was also into information technology.

Poizner was less the scavenger and more the investment growth opportunity person. He would be better at an established firm. That, in my mind's eye makes him the better candidate. Unfortunately, the people saw Whitman as more charismatic, and Poizner had trouble with name identification.

## 52. THE TORTOISE AND THE HARE
### March 11, 2010

I have given you their business models, so to speak. Now I will delve into their character. Whitman was the equivalent of an attack dog. She went as far as a negative campaign in order to define Steve before he defined himself. It was plain that she was avoiding direct combat in the primary. She used his record against him. Poizner, as I said, helped the governor mediate with the legislature on the budget. That requires compromise. The compromises were portrayed as a betrayal of Republican ethics. What worked for Brown in the general election defeated Poizner in the primary.

Poizner's own strategist put it this way: "In essence, she has been running unopposed. Very few people know who Steve Poizner is. The test of his campaign is going to be what happens when people get to know Steve Poizner." Dan Schnur, the director of the Jesse M. Unruh Institute of Politics at USC stated, "If you're a legislator or a donor, or a grass roots activist, and you see your candidate slipping further behind in the polls, you May know that there is a strategy, but it still makes you nervous."

Part of the Poizner dilemma had its roots in the fact that Poizner had spent 3.7 million and Whitman had spent 19 million. These ads were untrue or distorted. She gave you part of a fact and distorted to the other end. It was as if she wanted to avoid the primary process and go directly to the playoffs. She went as far as to send the Poizner campaign an email threatening a 40 million dollar negative campaign if Steve did not drop out of the race. Whitman commented," It looks like Steve is in this for a while. My point of view is that the Republicans have a big challenge in Jerry Brown so my view is that it would be the right thing to pool all our resources... But you know what? I'm happy to compete." She launched a website, www.canttruststeve.com. She attacked him on taxes, abortion, and betraying the party by reaching out to the Democrats to solve the state's problems. That was portrayed as treason.

Back in the Poizner camp, Murphy, one of his strategists stated, "It would be foolish of us to walk into this kind of late attack strategy. If Steve is committed to this kind of kamikaze thinking, and he has the money to do it, we have the resources to engage in a debate about Steve's record, which is very problematical." Poizner had, in this campaign, stuck to the right of issues and tried to brand Whitman as a liberal. He was trying for the loyalist Republican votes in the state. He obviously did not get them.

The tactic that counts on your opponent to do an oops, especially with three months in the campaign was the basic hope of Poizner. It would be Brown in the general election that exposed Whitman's record far more effectively, and he didn't have to become a pit bull to do it.

Off the subject, but nonetheless important, is the Innocence Project. A man by the name of McKinney had petitioned for a new trial on the basis of evidence collected. The students doing the investigating were led by Professor Protess of the Medill Innocence Project. A charge of impropriety was made by the prosecution. The rebuttal was it was just journalistic effort, and nothing improper was done. The judge had not ruled out a prosecutor's subpoena.

## 53. THE DOO DAH PARADE
### March 11, 2010

To lighten things up a bit, the anti-establishment parade based on spontaneity was losing its punch. The idea for the parade itself had its origin in the now-defunct Chromos Bar. The first parade took place January 1, 1978. The Rose Parade would have dominated, except for its Never On Sunday policy. Corkey Peterson stated, "It was a collective consciousness kind of thing. We worked this whole thing from the bar pay phone. People called up wondering what was going on. The parade was like a way to let out steam."

Old Town, where the parade had been held had changed, and the organizers felt that the parade did not match the businesses like Abercrombie and Fitch and the Cheese Cake Factory, so they moved it. The Light Bringer Project was born. The organizers stated, "By moving it, we're peeling a few layers away so it becomes less of an entertainment vehicle and more of a public art event." They chose Lamanda Park, which is an eclectic neighborhood. You have boutiques and auto body shops in the same neighborhood. To the owner of the Antique Gallery in front of her East Pasadena business, it did not enter into the picture whether they would be customers or not. The owner felt it was an opportunity for the people to get to know them. They as merchants hoped that the parade would put Lamanda Park on the map. Those involved stated, "It's a really nice area, and has a unique personality. It's sort of what it probably felt like back in the 1920's, 30's and 40's, except the cars are just newer." Parade organizer Dale Brown stated, "We're not a shirt and tie kind of place." The side streets are independent restaurants and shop keepers. A lot of them are artistically oriented. So goes change.

## 54. MORE ON WHITMAN
March 24, 2010

The former startup CEO of EBay, Meg Whitman, had a campaign strategy for winning her party's nomination. Spend $14,935 an hour or $358,439 a day. Between the starting date of January 1 and March 17, she managed, with no prior public office experience, to establish what was called a soaring lead over Poizner and a small lead over Jerry Brown. Her campaign ads ran in two phases. 21 million in airtime was purchased, showing a bleak California and a vibrant Whitman. The second campaign was a down and dirty effort to show why you could not trust Poizner. Her ads were actually twisted truths and blatant lies, but the object was to win.

## 55. AB 32

There has been a highly flawed analysis. The Varshney/Tootalian Report stated that this bill would cost small businesses $50,000 a year. Add to that each household, referring to a new house or an established house, $3,857 yearly. This would apply as soon as the new regulations kicked in. California State Sacramento Business School Dean and marketing professor said of the Varshney/Tootalian Report, "Their estimates are highly biased, and based on poor logic and unsound economic analysis. The costs they predict are far too high."

This bill did become a law, and it requires industries to curb emissions or buy allowances to bring California's carbon footprint down to 15% by the year 2020. This law is being challenged on the basis that it will be bad for the state's economy. It is argued that it should be tabled for better economic times when the unemployment rate declines to 5.5%. This study, I stated, was used as evidence against the law, and had the study been accurate, they would have been perfectly correct.

It was the Small Business Round Table that called for this study to be made. Remember, statistics can give you man's TRUTH (it excludes the value of all energy savings). Its primary source of logic implies that any savings achieved would be too speculative to count. It is assumed that AB 32 would require new houses to produce as much energy as they consumed. This is not a fact. As a matter of fact, it's a lie. It would add $50,000 to the construction of a new home by their calculations. It was figured in their analysis that net zero energy price tag. They applied this to all housing in the state. The stiffer standards required under the bill would come to $5,000. The majority of those costs would be realized in lower energy bills. These costs apply only to new construction, not existing housing. Anonymous is wrong again.

They arrived at the issue of cars, and the impact on those that drive them. They do agree that new fuel-efficient cars can and will save $36-0 yearly. They also contend not everyone is going to go out and buy one of these vehicles, and those are the people that will be stuck with the tab. They generalized the dollar amount increase to virtually all vehicles in the state, sitting or running. The cost of petrol is usually absorbed by the dealer in the interest of competition, and you would not want to inconvenience a trucker who would be impacted if their analysis is correct. That would be a matter for the courts, and you know there would be a remedy.

Technology is the driving force in our state, as in the other states of the Union. They make the presumption that businesses would not invest in solar, but just go out of business. They would not seek the new products on the market (fair cost benefit analysis). This they left out of their equation. It is assumed that businesses and people will become oblivious to the forces of the market. Being sarcastic, we would be healthier if we walked more, anyway.

There is a converse argument to this. If improvements were made and those who live in California get the jobs to make those improvements, that would lower our unemployment rate. Granted, my argument has its limits, too. You have to be qualified to do the things this new economy would require. What this issue needs, aside from the litigating, is informed debate.

## 56. HEMET

Hemet has a problem. The Los Angeles gangs were and are moving out there. The police are stuck trying to tell the difference between those escaping the violence and those that wish to transplant it. The police describe the majority of those in the area as wannabes. There is an element that is actually targeting the police for assassination. They have attempted to blow up the station house with natural gas redirected by a pipe into the building: bombs have been placed under police cars, and a variety of booby trap devices. The police force does get federal help, along with other police agencies, but the force went from 99 to 58 as an economy measure, and this complicates matters.

What to do? This, to some, would be comical and unrealistic. Grow a head of hair so you don't look like a skinhead. Don't dress cool or wear your trousers to your butt. Let those who are causing the trouble and insist on their identity pay the price. Thinking inversely, if they don't look like the gang type, you have a problem, for that's how the Asian gangs operate. If those of you who live in Hemet, be you cool or not, remove yourself from the fight by changing your image, and Maybe those responsible can be dealt with. To the police, if someone has a history but has straightened up, let him!

## 57. WHITMAN ON HEALTHCARE
### March 31, 2010

Whitman's stand was against President Obama's healthcare bill. She was asked, if she were governor, would she direct the state's Attorney General to file suit to block its implementation in California. First she said she would do just that, and then added she didn't have the authority to do it. She believed the healthcare bill, as it stands would be a burden to the state in a time of fiscal crisis. She noted that Brown was not voicing any objections to the legislation. She added the only persons bringing suit were Republicans.

She stated the high cost of medical coverage was due to the limitation on the number of insurance companies allowed to operate in the state. This was incorrect. If you, as an insurance company meet the California standards, you can sell insurance in California. The limitation comes from, and she knew this, if your insurance company is registered in a state with minimal requirements, you cannot do business as an out-of-state insurance company in this state. That is a protection against fraud.

What she liked about the national health plan was the clause that you could not deny insurance on the basis of a pre-existing condition nor the cancelling of a policy when the person reaches the limit of the policy. She felt there was a question on whether it was constitutional for mandatory coverage paid by the individual if he or she could afford it.

On tax breaks for businesses to lure them into the state, she favored that, but not across the board tax reduction. That she pinned on her opponent. The Supreme Court validated Obama's national health plan under the right of the Federal Government to tax (June 28, 2012).

## 58. NURSING HOME ABUSE
### March 31, 2012

With a down economy, you have inadequate policing of such institutions. The location is Calabasas, and a nursing home that caters to those on the edge. Adelina Campos was doing a bed check when she saw Cesar Alloa in a midair-jump, landing on a dementia patient, a 76 year old female. He then hit another patient with the arm of a chair, also a dementia patient who was cheering him on. He was brought into the justice system, and among the charges were torture. If this is the state of healthcare, why are we encouraging people to live to a great age?

## 59. ACORN
### April 2, 2010

The Association of Community Organizations for Reform Now is now out of business, the victim of sting operations and poor organization. It engaged in what was called highly inappropriate behavior. The sting gone wrong was a man and woman posing as a pimp and prostitute seeking advice on how to avoid the law.

The investigation of ACORN was requested by Governor Arnold Schwarzenegger by his Attorney General, Jerry Brown. The investigation was in response to a video purportedly showing the couple getting advice on how to avoid the law. The ACORN representative skirted around the issue and broke no law. The organization said it regarded the incident as a joke.

Attorney General Jerry Brown stated, "ACORN in California was disorganized and very poorly managed. It failed to recruit, train, and monitor its employees to insure compliance with California law."

It was stated, according to Brown, that two film makers, James O'Keefe and Hanna Giles had approached ACORN employees about making a political film. They posed as pimp and prostitute across the country from July 24 to August 14, 2009. The most offensive remarks to the couple happened outside the state of California. One of the ACORN staff in San Diego went so far as to call the police about the couple. It was the San Bernardino office that treated it as a joke.

Brown continued: "The evidence illustrates that things are not always as partisan zealots portray them through highly selective editing of reality. Sometimes the fuller truth is found on the cutting room floor." The film makers gave the complete film in exchange for immunity.

It was argued that the ACORN organization could be sued civilly for violations of the privacy act outside of California. The reason, shredding thousands of pages of confidential information about employees, members and other individuals, according to the *L.A. Times*, as well as failing to file a 2007 tax return and engaging in four instances of possible voter registration fraud, courtesy of Motor Voter in San Diego.

The ACORN organization could not document how charitable funds for relief benefitting the victims of the California wild fires were dispersed. The probe came to the conclusion, determining that ACORN spent more than it likely raised for fire victims, and therefore further action on this issue was not wise use of the state's resources. You can't get blood out of a turnip.

Meanwhile, Meg Whitman was on the Campaign Trail, bashing Poizner.

## 60. STATISTICS, STATISTICS, STATISTICS
### April 5, 2010

The war of statistics as to who's ahead in this election was most telling. Whitman exceeded Poizner by 40%. In the Senate race, on the Republican side,

Florina was in a close contest with Campbell. Florina had 30% and Campbell had 28%. Jerry Brown had it over Steve Poizner, 53% to 22%. The Whitman-Brown numbers were too close to call, and their contest was being referred to as a brawl.

The battle for the independent vote was split up between Brown and Whitman. Costal California went to Brown by the narrowest of margins. What is called the slippage vote went 3 of 10 Democrats for Whitman and 2 of 10 Republicans for Brown. Barbara Boxer had a rating of 40%. This would be bad news, but her victories run usually 10% over her opponent. She has good relations with labor, women and minorities.

Governor Schwarzenegger, who is not in the race, holds pretty much as previous governors at the end of their terms. He went from 33% approval to 25%, a drop of 8 points. The legislature was much worse. It only had an 18% approval rating.

According to a survey by Quinlan, Greenberg, Rosner, a Democratic firm, 6 in 10 identified with Whitman largely because she jumped from unknown status as former EBay CEO to front runner over Poizner with his more traditional approach. The mix of feel good ads, mixed with negative anti-Poizner ads were having their effect. It's a numbers game.

## 61. LEGALIZE MARIJUANA?
April 8, 2010

What was made illegal in the 1930's out of fear that it would spread from the black musician community has become a culture outside the law in places like Humboldt County. The monetary contribution of the illegal pot industry in that county is $500,000,000 to $700,000,000 in an economy of 3.6 billion. The growers are largely family operations, and the fear is that legalization would bring in larger-production corporate farm-type structures affecting the current culture. The downside in this family-friendly structure is, the kids can't share what their parents do for a living.

Part of the reason for the growth of the pot industry is the decline in traditional industries of the area. The salmon population has declined as the logging and timber industry is but a memory to some, if not most of the population. Their low-tech economy bubble has burst. This new scientific agribusiness that has emerged has siphoned talented people who would normally go to college instead of farming in the hills and siphoning water from streams.

The other part of the argument lies in what price would the crop command if it were legalized. The price could drop to a hundred dollars a pound as opposed to a thousand where it currently stands. It is argued that the insistence on keeping marijuana illegal is the best price support the industry could ever have. There is a joke: The best way to boost the price of wheat is to make it illegal. According to the *L.A. Times*, somewhere between 800 and 2,000 homes are used partially or completely for this crop. That is exactly what it is, a crop.

I have another side for you. To be legal, it would have to be regulated. Accurate books would have to be kept, as in the medical marijuana growers and dispensers. It would be a different world from this free-booting underground society that is so totally visible. Laws would have to be stricter and consistently enforced and the tax man taken care of. What KMUD FM so broadly touts as the way would be in the public eye and scrupulously watched. In a way, marijuana would fall victim to the Dutch effect, and the price would be permanently lowered and have its own economic bubble. Who knows?

## 62. NATURAL GAS
### April 9, 2010

Remember when the American companies wanted to join the tech revolution in 1993? Something like that was happening as of the date of this article. Commissioner Dian Grueneich wanted to install smart meters. These units would cost $200 each. There would be an increase in the utility bills of seventy cents, spread over 25 years. There would be a 1% improvement in the actual gas used. Because of the lack of volatility in the market, it was argued that the expense was not needed. Like the preparation for the future and that urge to move ahead, the Public Utilities Commission voted 3 to 2 in favor of spending 1.5 billion on these smart meters to improve our lives. Fresno is the most northern placement, and right down to the Mexican border. The plan was to install them by mid-2012. We still have our old meters, but we're waiting for the new ones.

## 63. RED LIGHT CAMERAS
### April 23, 2010

It is Big Brother at the intersection. It is that little unimposing camera that watches all. The City of Los Angeles reported that during the month of May the city collected 3.8 million dollars from 32 mounted cameras. That sounds like a lot of revenue, but the bottom line is what the program costs. To top that, a good number of citations are ignored or argued successfully to the defendant's benefit. The city had to kick in 1.6 million to keep the program going. Cost-wise, the system is a wash. The company itself has gone out of business.

Numerically, what is the record for accident reduction using red light cameras? Red light violations were responsible for 40% of an estimated 2,395 accidents in the city of Anaheim at its intersections in 2007 and 2009. According to Sergeant Rick Martinez, in total there were 12,858 traffic accidents in that time frame.

It was hoped that the implementation of this automatic photo system would free up officers for other duties and created revenue for the cities while improving public safety. You realize that's a circular argument. The cameras have a fixed cost, and if people obey the law even marginally, the program ceases to be cost effective.

Garden Grove saw a 40% decline in traffic collisions at traffic monitored intersections. They expanded the program to eight intersections. The city council stated they were pleased that the system did what it was said it would do.

A quote from Pringle, a resident, called the system a ruse. "I believe there is enough evidence now to demonstrate that red light cameras do not necessarily cause safer intersections. I believe many red light cameras are placed around the county and around the state for the purpose of local governments' revenue collection as opposed to traffic safety."

In the effort to avoid having your picture taken in your car you could do one of many amazing things. Sergeant Greg Scott of Costa Mesa reported a 13% increase in accidents at red light camera-controlled intersections. This occurred between the years 2003 and 2009. He added that there was a 20% increase in rear-end collisions. Just guess why that happened. There was a good side to all of this: There was a reduction in broadside collisions by 30%. Injury from the crash scene went down 15%. As you can see, there are two sides to this argument, and maybe a little humor.

## 64. STATE PROPERTY continued
### April 28, 2010

The legislature became more upset with Governor Schwarzenegger over his planned sale of state properties. A non-partisan legislative analyst's office stated that selling structures including the Ronald Reagan State Building in downtown Los Angeles to help close the budget shortfall would eventually cost the state money—about 200 million a year. The report called it poor fiscal policy.

The governor had hoped to sell 24 state properties. He said it would raise 598 million of the state's 20 billion dollar deficit. The governor had his critics removed from the State Building Commission. Schwarzenegger stated, "I can guarantee you that I will never sell state property if it doesn't make any sense from an investment point of view." He added that the properties could bring in 1.4 billion instead of 598 million. I think he wanted to make a solid step before the next governor took over.

## 65. CALPERS FRAUD
### May 6, 2010

Alfred Villalobos was a lobbyist that had tremendous influence over CALPERS, the independent agency that manages and invests the California State pension funds. For leverage against failure in his efforts he gave box seats, luxury trips, and what was described as other gifts to Frederico Buenrostro. In the years from 2002 to 2008, the Chief Executive was the recipient of what was described as tens of thousands of dollars. The thing was that Villalobos was a former vice Mayor of Los Angeles and should have known better. After his time as a public servant he went to work for ARVCO Capital Research. He secured 47 million in undisclosed and unlawful commissions for making the sale of 4.8 billion in securities to CALPERS.

The Los Angeles County Superior Court stated, "Buenrostro played a key role in assisting Villalobos and ARVCO in their fraudulent activities."

The suit itself states that Villalobos compromised Buenrostro along with other CALPERS officials with gifts that put the integrity of CALPERS at risk, and in the process violated the California State Corporate Code. CALPERS officials got trips around the world. Other perks included private jet flights to attend a benefit for Leon Black in New York (Apollo Global Management). The lawsuit stated that Apollo was Villalobos's biggest client at CALPERS. The pension fund decided not to publicly comment on the case. That was the reality as of this date.

## 66. May 7, 2010

Attorney General Jerry Brown made a broad, sweeping statement concerning the suit filed against the two figures charged, and said more indictments would be coming. "This is not the end of this case or the end of the investigation. Other things could follow." To expand on what Brown said, any investigations from his office, or independently could result in further litigation. The prospect was raised for a criminal indictment coming from the local district attorney. Other possible agencies included the Fair Political Practices Commission or other law enforcement agencies.

It is charged that Villalobos's allegedly assisted private equity fund managers, bringing to a close deals to invest billions of dollars of government workers' retirement money by wooing CALPERS officials who in turn influenced the board to authorize those investments.

If I fast-forward you to 2012, Governor Brown is still dealing with the mess that has caused the state's budget deficit.

## 67. WHO'S RUNNING THEIR RECORDS

As we all know, Jerry Brown won the election, but it is good to know, as a brief rundown, what his current stands are. First, I will tackle the economy. Brown swore not to raise taxes unless the voters approved them. He favored a limited reform of the tax system. On this one he had his eye on revising Proposition 13, which he always, in his heart, really opposed. On immigration he is a mixed bag. He has called the Arizona law "legally problematic." He is opposed to sanctuary cities like Los Angeles. He is in favor of the path of citizenship for undocumented immigrants. Concerning healthcare, he favors a single-pay healthcare system. According to the *L.A. Times*, he is "somewhat ambivalent toward the Democratic healthcare law." In a way he is more Republican than the Republican candidates. On the environment, he shares Schwarzenegger's vies on AB 32. His signature went on an agreement in his position as Attorney General that would lead to adoption on a national scale of the state's tailpipe emission standards. On the issue of abortion, he personally opposes it. On the other hand, he has been consistent in his stand that a woman has a right to choose. On education, he supports quadratic education, and contends there is a moral dimension, and his appointments would reflect that attitude. On same-sex marriage he flip-flopped, violating his duty to defend state measures in the courts. Initially he said he would defend the measure, but in the end called it a violation of civil rights. On the marijuana initiative, he would not support it, but was considering how to write the initiative for the ballot.

Concerning Meg Whitman, the winner of the primary in June, where she stood was as follows: She has promised to rein in spending, push for job-creating tax cuts, and reduce regulations to promote job growth. On healthcare, if the economy is not sound, she does not regard it as an absolute right. It would be limited. She supports the repeal of the federal healthcare bill. She has called for a suspension of AB 32. She wants the bill analyzed. On abortion, she supports limited access for women. She favors an absolute ban on late-term abortions, except when the mother's health is at risk. She favors an overturning of the state's decision to fund abortions. On education, she favors a test score system. That sounds like No Child Left Behind, and it did not work. She favors the charter school system. On same-sex marriage, she favors civil unions and says marriage is between a man and a woman. Number one, all marriages are civil unions. Marriage is only a term applied to church-blessed unions. On the M J issue, she vociferously opposes the legalization of marijuana. I can see how she became the Republican nominee, and I also see why she lost.

On Steve Poizner, the state's Insurance Commissioner stated he would seek a moratorium on bond sales which had slipped in the bond market from triple A status to double A status. This would create an inertia in the bond market and cause further loss due to a lack of liquidity. Putting a freeze on state hiring would make it difficult for the state to do its job. He wanted to set up a 10 billion dollar reserve fund similar to what Jerry Brown did in his first two terms. He also favored across-the-board tax cuts. On immigration, he proposed to cut illegal's' benefits. Now, Governor Pete Wilson tried to do just that and passed a law saying so. The State Supreme Court knocked it down. While he at first opposed Arizona's SB 1070, he later changed his position when his concerns over profiling were satisfied. On healthcare, he opposed the federal plan because of tremendous cost overruns that would affect the state's economy. He did favor use of electronic health records as a method of cutting costs and improving service. He was in favor of a moratorium on AB 32 until the unemployment levels dropped. He is in favor of those earthen dams that we used to store our excess water before we drained them to build houses. His argument was that it helped to save the endangered smelt from going into the water pumps in the Delta. He is in support of limited abortion rights and is in favor of adoption programs. Under education, he favors local control and charter schools. He, as a means of control, would deny tenure from the five worst schools and the rights to collective bargaining in teachers' unions. That is one powerful lobby, and he could never accomplish that. There is also that element of federal funding and its strings that would prevent it. He supported Proposition 8, and opposes same-sex marriage. He considers the tax benefits of the legalization of marijuana to be short-sighted.

## 68. THE CALIFORNIA SENATE CANDIDATES

Senator Barbara Boxer is a three-term Senator who was first elected in 1992, and this time faces a challenge from Republican Tom Campbell. Where she stood in the election is as follows: On the economy she supported President Obama's stimulus package and opposed the Bush tax cuts. She initiated a proposal that would tax Wall Street executives at firms that were the recipients of federal bailout money. On the immigration issue, she stands opposed to SB 1070 and stated it was polarizing and hurtful. I wonder what she would think of Machiavelli, because she is also in favor of stricter border control. She also favors guest worker programs and a path to citizenship for those here illegally. On healthcare, she voted for and is an advocate of President Obama's affordable health reform law. She is the author of the cap and trade bill that taxes industries on the basis of their carbon emissions. She is flat-out in favor of abortion rights. She supported Bush's No Child Left Behind Act, but her stand as of the date of this *L.A. Times* article was that it was underfunded. She is a supporter of early education and after school programs. She also supports Pell Grants. Her position on Proposition 8 is plain: she opposed it. She was in opposition to the measure on the California State Ballot to legalize and tax Mary Jane.

Tom Campbell was a senior Representative who was defeated. He had set his sights on the governorship of California, but decided to go for the Senate seat instead when he looked at the numbers. He had extensive government experience in multiple federal and state administrations. In his run for Boxer's seat you would think he would have been formidable. His stand on the economy was a matter of record. He had a top ranking from the Tax Payers Union, and his record in the Congress on fiscal matters, according to the *L.A. Times*. He supported an increase in taxation cuts in the state's education system. He compromised with the Democrats: that was not a good thing to do. On immigration, he stood solidly with Arizona's SB 1070. He was in opposition to illegal immigrants getting citizenship, and supported fines for employers who hire undocumented workers. Analytically, that was probably one of the biggest reasons his candidacy did not take hold. He would have been too effective, and, also, he compromised with the other side. His position on the affordable healthcare reform law, as presented by the Obama Administration was plain: He stated that it was unconstitutional. He was right, and he was wrong. According to the interstate commerce clause, it was unconstitutional, but according to the federal government's right to tax for services, it met the test. On the Cap and trade issue, he opposed the bill, but would look at a modified form. On abortion, he was pro choice. On education, he opposed No Child Left Behind on the basis of testing. On this issue, he proved to be statistically right. He favored the charter school system, and was in favor of smaller class sizes. He also favored controlling administrative costs. He had a liberal side, for he supported same-sex marriage. On the marijuana issue, he supported its use for medical reasons, but opposed legalization as proposed in California. Considering the candidate the Republicans ended up with, I wish he would have stuck to the governor's race.

Chuck Devore was a Republican State Assemblyman, what I would call a Tea Party conservative. He proudly signed a no new tax pledge. When the crunch came and the legislature voted for a tax increase to balance the budget, he resigned his leadership position in protest. His stand on the immigration issue is, to say the least, harsh. 1) Supports SB 1070: 2) Supports tighter border security: 3) Opposes a path to citizenship for illegal immigrants: 4) Wants to put a halt to in-state tuition for illegal immigrants. On healthcare, he stated he would vote to remove the affordable healthcare reform law. You might say he would be a company man, for he opposes cap and trade legislation, and is pro oil. He supports offshore drilling with less invasive types of drilling technology. Remember what is happening at this point in history off the coast of Louisiana and her neighboring states. He is for the right to life, no exceptions. On education, he believes it is a state and local issue with no role for the federal government. He opposes same-sex marriage and is on record as voting against expanded partnership rights. He opposes the initiative to legalize marijuana (he doesn't inhale). He did not survive the primary.

Carly Florina is a hard-nosed businesswoman-former CEO of Hewlett-Packard. She has an extensive business background though some have argued it was checkered. As a candidate, she signed the now tax hike pledge. She has stated she would cut taxes to stimulate the economy. She has stated that she believes that the stimulus package is wasted taxpayer money. (To a large part she is wrong, for the corporate paid back the money with interest, and TARP was a success, statistically. Only with the smaller banks seem to be having a bit of trouble meeting the regulations.) She has also criticized the Wall Street brokerage bailouts which have repaid their funds but not corrected their ways. On immigration, she is a balancing act, for on one hand, she supports SB 1070, and on the other she pushes for a guest worker program. On healthcare, she has pledged if elected to repeal the Obama healthcare plan. She has also pledged to suspend or repeal AB 32. She was thinking high when she stated that she was against a woman's right to an abortion, but would not let that be a litmus test for a judicial nominee. On education, she does not favor increasing the amount spent, but getting more choice and value for that which is being spent. On same-sex marriage, she is a split card. She voted for Proposition 8, and as CEO of HP she voted for expanded rights within the company. You guessed it, she opposes the legalization of marijuana in California.

On battle tactics, Whitman, who one year ago was an unknown, has become a rock star by outspending Poizner, who only possessed 19.1 million for his campaign, which he deliberately did in softer tones, as did Jerry Brown. Meg Whitman was attempting to buy the governorship with air time.

This part of the book is a review of the political history of the United States and its international implications from the late 1960's through the 1980's, and all the principals involved and their contribution to history. If you think carefully, you can see why we are where we are today in 2012.

### 69. November 4, 1970

This is the time before disaster struck and Watergate happened. President Nixon is turning command of the bases over to our Vietnamese counterparts. This includes the military machinery to fight the war. There is a lull in the fighting. We were pushing the North Vietnamese forces out of certain areas. At home, the national races have been sorted out. Governor Nelson Rockefeller defeats a Democratic candidate by the name of Goldberg. Ronald Reagan wins a second term as governor of California. An obscure challenger from Riverside, John V. Tunney, defeats an older Brock for the Senate seat of California. Nationally, the Democratic Party captured 12 governorships that were formerly Republican, with two more hanging in the undecided column. President Nixon's popularity was being tested as well as the length of his coattails. Both parties were preparing for the battle of the Presidency in 1972. Note the Nixon Administration was living up to its commitment on Vietnam, and had in place wage and price controls that were the product of a wartime economy and corporate greed. The people did not like the measures that were being employed. At any rate, the 1972 election came and so did the incident at the Watergate Hotel. Thus began the meltdown.

### 70. FUND RAISING

In the beginning, fundraising and lobbying interests were one in the same. There were no limits an individual or corporation could give. The concept of public financing of elections at the congressional level were being discussed. Nobody wanted to give up the perks. Some Senators and Representatives had a novel way of handling things. They would invite lobbyists from both sides to the same function to get a balanced account. They also made sure it was a charitable organization the funds were going to. It is noted that Senators got more than Representatives because they are 100, compared to 435, and thus wield more power. Note there was no talk of undue influence, but only what was right proportionately.

### 71. PENSIONS AND THE LEGISLATURE

Though opposed by Governor Jerry Brown and Assembly Speaker Leo T. MacCarthy, plans for it going to committee that Monday with approval for passage seemed all but assured. A special session was favored to place the motion on the floor. California State Senate President Pro Tem James Mitchell favored the special session. The bill itself would allow, representatives, in their 30's and 40's who have served in the legislature to collect a pension of several thousand dollars after their time in public service. This would be for life. Nothing came of this, fortunately.

Under what if systems, back on October 25th, 1975, an article appeared in the *L.A. Times* suggesting we follow the Constitution in electing the position of President. No parties would be involved. The applicants would submit their qualifications to the Electoral Board, and the President and Vice President would be chosen from among the applicants. No general election and the Electoral Board would be the controlling body that would be removable. This would be very similar to the Parliamentary system. The people would elect the Electors, and the power would flow from the states to the federal government. Only those powers granted by the states to the federal government would stand.

What happened, well, aside from George Washington and John Adams, things operated very differently? The twelfth amendment to the Constitution in the 1800's required separate ballots for President and Vice President. When you get to the 19th century, nearly all state legislatures had turned over the selection of electors pledged to specific candidates to a popular vote. They passed their responsibility to others. This proved that the original concept did not work.

Today political experience passes for real qualifications, and sometimes not the brightest gets the job, based on popular will. This is something they don't teach in the school textbooks.

## 72. POLITICAL CHANGE: THE EARLY YEARS

It is December, 1968 and President Johnson is about to leave office. Stephen J. Pollak is the man in charge of enforcing the 1968 Civil Rights Act. It is argued that old policies continue. The difference is they cannot continue openly, for the loopholes are big enough to drive an 18 wheeler through. Here is a quote from Pollak: "School desegregation bogs down if Negroes can't live where they want to live, and these rights are defeated if Negroes are denied jobs on account of race." Not policy without attitude adjustments can and does happen.

It is argued that since the death of Kennedy, both NATO and SEATO are our bond to the world. At present the United States has it all over China. I remind you I am talking in the sense of 1968, at least in the nuclear field. Europe is Gaullist, and Britain has recovered from the loss of her Empire. Rumania is starting to assert herself. It is most dangerous living in the shadow of the Soviet Union. We seem to be sitting on our hands.

The US Commissioner on Education in the Johnson Administration in 1966, citing the Civil Rights Act of 1964, declared it illegal for institutions accepting federal money to discriminate against minorities. This is that big hole I was talking about that gave way to the 1968 Civil Rights Act. The first across-the-board school aid bill, passed in 1965, helped to push desegregation on both faculty and campuses nationally. It was argued the progress was satisfactory, according to the *L.A. Times*. The tools were educational parks, busing between sections of the city to integrate children educationally. It was put this way: "Every racial geographic and economic center of the city, supplementary centers for special enrichment of education which bring together young people from different sides of the tracks." This was the idealized language of the time used in describing the struggle for equality.

## 73. THE OPEN PRIMARY

The California Primary of 1976 was interesting. You have President Gerald R. Ford lagging behind, then-Governor Reagan in fundraising, but not by much. In the state it is unusual for delegates to be split in who gets what, on both the Democratic and Republican sides. Twenty candidates were running for president. They ranged from Libertarians to Communists.

California is split into 43 Congressional districts that select 210 convention delegates. The residual delegates, 70, are proportionally chosen. This experiment was later modified.

Look at the talent pool of candidates, Republican and Democrat, which at this point numbered 109. The Republicans have basically Reagan and Ford. The Democrats have Birch Bayh, Henry M. Jackson, Lloyd Bentsen, Fred R. Harris, Morris Udall, George Wallace, Milton Shapp and Jimmy Carter. This was the talent pool of candidates for the year that was 1969.

Here we are: it's 1969. The cease-fire by the Vietcong was broken by the North, but there seems to be a lull in the fighting.

Back in the US, the Mossbacks, represented by Senator Strom Thurmond, Republican, North Carolina, are mulling over changing the environment in the Senate. Senator Everett Dirksen, tried through his positions on the Judiciary and Finance Committees to influence the delicate balance between liberal and conservative. These committees control Social Security and confirmation of federal judgeship appointments. These committees also handle the civil rights legislation of the time. The antiwar bias was growing, and with that modification of the social structure of the House and Senate.

Representative Adam Clayton Powell, a Democrat from New York wanted return of his seniority and lost pay for when the House refused to seat him. He took his case to the Supreme Court and won. He stated, "The lack of pay was not important. The main thing which we have established is that the principle of the three branches of government has been reaffirmed. It affects not only me but 220 million people. You can't have a government in the United States that believes in law and order if the Congress does not believe in law and order." So it was that a grateful Powell took his seat in the House after censure. It must be noted the Court did not decide on the $25,000 fine.

Now President Nixon threatened veto of the Social Security legislation on the grounds of the need to balance the dollar content of the legislation. The goal is to have the revenue gained by tax reforms brought into balance with revenue lost in the proposed tax reductions and added outlays. I gather from this he wanted revenue to match benefits, not a fixed amount. In this legislation was a rider 5% surtax that would be extended for another year. This applied to telephone service and new car sales. There was also a 7% tax credit to businesses that bought new machinery.

On one of my favorite subjects, cigarette commercials and advertising, the National Air Board ruled that despite possible evidence that television stations were not regulating the contents of their advertisements, the cigarette companies would be given six more years of self-regulation to set their house in order. The argument was that, "There was a substantial appeal for youth." The evidence showed they had stopped reviewing contents of commercials in 1968. Today, with all the links established, especially second-hand smoke, the rulings are quite different.

Mrs. Nixon was touring the ghetto areas promoting the arts and literature when she ran across a little black magic. "Mrs. Nixon, millions die, but you don't cry. This hex on you will come true." This was held up on a huge banner. Similar occurrences happened throughout her visit. Black culture coloring books were distributed and said to be a source of pride. As you can see, Society was in flux.

John L. Luis, head of the AFL-CIO died on June 18th, 1969, and was laid to rest6 in Oak Ridge Cemetery in Springfield, Illinois. This was a powerful man who controlled people's lives.

Now to the battle cry of Social Security in Nixon's years. On December 20, 1969, Nixon vetoed the Social Security bill. Senator Ralph W. Yarborough raised the battle cry: "This is the issue. We are the party of the people." Senator Fred R. Harris: "I'll say let him do it. That's the issue that can be easily joined." Now remember, we are trying to disengage from the Vietnam conflict. We have related inflation issues, and the Democrats want to engage in social welfare.

Now to a young man, who happened to be black, at the end of the Korean conflict who refused repatriation, and instead went to China and attended a university there. He returned July 5th, 1966. He declared, for all its faults, America is still a far better form of government. He made the statement that young black men should return home and push for our removal from Vietnam. He stated he still opposed the war, but felt dialogue was necessary. He felt the Chinese system was working for the Chinese, and Mao Tse Tung was very much in charge. He did not view himself as a turncoat, for he did not dessert.

## 74. CONFLICT OF INTEREST

Senator Edward V. Long accepted fees from Hoffa's lawyers for his legal services, not before the committee. He said there was no conflict of interest. The reason for interest in Senator Long was that it came at the time when Congress was investigating Representatives Adam Clayton Powell, Thomas J. Dodd, and Bobby Baker. This situation brought the need for a disclosure law that had not been in existence as yet.

## 75. CALIFORNIA 1968

The voting public of California in 1968 held law and order next to the Throne of God. Republicans were favored over Democrats as advocates of strict law enforcement, over what the Democrats called the need to fix the social network as a means of lowering crime. Support for Proposition 3, which was a bond issue for the State University/College system had support in northern California of 54%, and in the south of 59% of the popular vote. Propositions 1a and 9 were property tax relief measures, and those who opposed the measures were 32% in the north and 31% in the south. Stricter law enforcement was at 18.4%. Programs for housing with family unity emphasis ranked 15.2%. Stricter law enforcement with stiffer punishment was 11.2%. Change in the court system and revision in the legal structure had 8.4% supports. You can see the off-with-his-head mentality. Johnson was our president and Nixon was a rising star.

Michigan Governor George Romney, a Mormon, was launching his campaign for the presidency, along with several figures from the Eisenhower Administration. It was Richard Nixon's second try for the presidency. The machines seemed to be lining up behind Romney. This was Romney's second attempt at the presidency, also.

Thomas H. Kuchel, the current Republican Senator was being rejected by his own party. He was not alone in this club. Frank J. Lauche of Ohio, at the age of 72 lost his office. Edward V. Long of Missouri was defeated at the age of 60. Ernest Gurening, Senator from Alaska, was defeated at the age of 81. He had served a long time.

Nixon and Humphrey were running pretty much evenly in the South, even with Wallace and his Southern advantage. Humphrey seeded to be the better organizer, or at least his poll numbers showed it that way.

Los Angeles politics can and do get dirty. When Sam Yorty ran against Paulson, the incident in Griffith Park effectively put Sam in the position of Mayor. When he ran against Tom Bradley, he used a series of scurrilous tricks and used the proposed construction of the World Trade Center, which was never built, as a weapon against Bradley. This did not work.

What is interesting is who gets the job when the winner claims the prize. On December 15th, 1968, Nixon had his cabinet put together: David Kennedy, Secretary of the Treasury: Melvin Laird, Secretary of Defense: John Volpe, Transportation: Robert Mayo, Budget Director: Robert Finch, Secretary of Health, Education and Welfare: William Rodgers, Secretary of State: Winston Blunt, Postmaster General: Maurice Stans, Secretary of Commerce: George Romney, Secretary of Housing and Urban Development: Clifford Harden, Secretary of Agriculture: George Schultz, Secretary of Labor: Walter Hickel, Secretary of the Interior, and Vice President-Elect Spiro T. Agnew. His cabinet was a mix of people, and Henry Kissinger had not even joined the team yet.

On how the election was won, no pun intended, the Republicans outspent the Democrats 3 to 1. The final figures state the GOP, according to receipts, $22,942,489.30, with expenditures of $7,490,702.82. George Wallace reported contributions of $665,475.74, and his expenditures were $6,497,806.85. We all remember what happened to candidate George Wallace, who ended up running his campaign from a wheelchair.

Now back to the race for Mayor of Los Angeles. The position of the party was to be neutral. Some did not read the manual. Representative Alphonso Bell, a Republican from Los Angeles endorsed and campaigned for Tom Bradley, a Democrat. Not to be outdone, 10 Republican Assemblymen in Sacramento supported and campaigned for Sam Yorty. Other council positions were also up for grabs. There was a major power play in force. The names of these men were, Henry Arklin, Mission Hills, Robert E. Badham, Newport Beach, E. Richard Barns, San Diego, John V. Briggs, Fullerton, Robert H. Burke, Huntington Beach, William Campbell, Hacienda Heights, John E. Collier, South Pasadena, Charles J. Conrad, Sherman Oaks, Newton R. Russell, Burbank, and Floyd L. Wakefield, Downey. Most, if not all of these men represent Southern California communities.

The race card was used in the Los Angeles elections. The challenger, Tom, was a former police officer, and a councilman for six years, running up against a trickster and a three-term Mayor, Sam Yorty, often referred to as Honest Sam. Other council positions were also up for grabs. There was a major power play in force, so you can see the interest of the national parties. In the end, as of May 27th, 1969 Tom Bradley was leading in the polls.

We do not exist in a vacuum. On March 29th, 1969, a eulogy was given by former President Lyndon B. Johnson for a close friend, Dwight David Eisenhower, also now passed. Former President Johnson stated, "A giant of our age is gone. Dwight David Eisenhower began his service to his people as a soldier of war. He ended as a crusader for peace. For both he will be remembered by a scared and hopeful world. A world that loved him well. The sturdy virtues of honor, integrity, courage, and decency all found eloquent expression in his life of his life of this good man and noble leader." These words from one of the most eloquent speakers of our time, though he was indeed the most hated. Just one note: where are the words of eulogy from Richard M. Nixon, who at this time was President of the United States?

Now to Democratic Senator Alan Cranston (California), and the oil seepage that was polluting the coast of Santa Barbara. He questioned in a letter to the interior minister Walter J. Hickel, "Since an increasing oil seepage from the fissures in the channel floors suggest a possible change in the pressure balance, I believe the public should know whether water injected for any purpose is part of operating procedure under platform A and elsewhere in the channel." The long made short, should we drill off our coast or just convert to other fuels and use diesel from Alaska? These questions I ask in 2009.

## 76. CALIFORNIA POLITICAL SOCIAL INFLUENCE

Local ordinances can enforce social taboos. In the year of 1976 the sex business, be it movies or product fell under the nuisance laws, which supersedes other city ordinances. Whittier, being the liberal town that it is (just kidding: they dipped into a 1915 law so they could close down these establishments). This was all to close down the Pussycat Theater. That's my home town.

## 77. ELECTIONS

Here is a tale of two parties formed in 1968: Peace and Freedom Party, and the American Independent Party. As of 1976, their numbers had dwindled to 19,248 registered members. At its start, the AIP numbered 64,248 registered members. The original name of the party was the PAF, Political Action Front. At this point the organization was well-organized. George Wallace was its candidate in 1968, and was running as a Democrat in 1976. The membership in 1976 was 27,927. In 1974 the Peace and Freedom Party was at 12,851, and the AIP was at 21,758. This is the inherent problem of third parties, and they compete with the two major parties, at least here in California.

## 78. EMINENT DOMAIN

On the subject of Eminent Domain, the arguments of fixed income and a balanced public good were being weighed by the city council. The packed chambers reflected the interest of the uptown, whether it was the suits or the citizens. Uneven development at the expense of the poor, those living in apartments or older homes on fixed pensions would have no place to go. What did they do? They built Lutheran Towers for the elderly who could still basically take care of themselves. Those families, mine being among them, were forced into apartments. The issue is also between business and residential. It was there in 2009, and those businesses are not easily targeted.

California in 1976 on about July was the battleground of uncertainties from the Brown camp that gave tacit support to Carter and John. V. Tunney, senatorial candidate running against S. I. Hyakawa from San Francisco. Questions of Ronald Reagan against Gerald R. Ford is a worry in the Carter camp. Carter's ability to capture California remained a question mark. Again, this is just a snapshot in time.

Now to Senator Hyakawa and his stand on the Panama Canal treaties supported by President Carter. After initially opposing the treaty, he has dismissed his comments about stealing it fair and square, to the realizing we are relinquishing control gradually, and are not losing anything in the bargain, so he is supporting it.

Governor Brown, on July 3, 1876, proposed a 12.8 billion dollar budget. There was an 8% increase in education funding. Brown cut 51.1 million from the budget.

17.5 million was cut from nursing homes program. 14 million was cut from various school programs. Representative Ken Mead joined Republicans in blocking 100 million dollars from the budget till Brown gave a more generous allotment to the schools.

## 79. THE NATIONAL SCENE

On the national scene, Representative Wayne L. Hays had a secretary that was not. You might say it was a bedroom affair at the expense of the public. When members of the chamber returned home there was no reaction, and some howled as if it were the end of the world. It was largely a fight among Democrats over Elizabeth Ray on the Hays staff, and the public trust. They wanted him removed from the House Democratic committee. No one knew how to handle this affair.

Now to Tom Hayden, a leader of the antiwar movement. He launched a respectable effort to unseat his rival in the Democratic Party, John V. Tunney. He conducted a foot campaign to reach the common people. Hayden ended up in the high thirties, and John. V. Tunney got in excess of 50%. That is the way of politics.

## 80. TRANSPORTATION

On the Santa Monica Freeway and the Diamond Lane experiment: Initially, Caltrans started this experiment as a way to get people to share rides or take busses. During peak hours, the two center lanes were used. It was a mixed blessing with little alteration in statistics. The debate was whether to keep or drop the program. As you can see, the plan was expanded and is still around in 2010.

## 81. TACTICS

In the Tunney versus Hayakawa race for power, it seemed a race going under two different rules. The Republicans seemed lost. Tunney very much connected at the organizational level. Hayakawa, born in Canada, and a naturalized US citizen stated that the concentration camps in California probably saved lives, for they were not shot at. He is a philosopher, as opposed to a political animal that keeps in touch with the structure. He missed a meeting with President Ford because his aides failed to inform him of it. Hayakawa viewed himself as a teacher, not a balancer.

## 82. MAGIC

On the lure of America, three Chinese citizens made it to Hong Kong. They were not influential people, just people in search of a dream in the United States. Concern was raised over the smuggling issue, over the amount of money they had paid.

## 83. STYLE

The time is October 23, 1976. President Ford is running against his Democratic contender, Governor Jimmy Carter. Carter and his vice presidential candidate, Walter Mondale, have hit the floor running in direct contrast, as has Senator Dole, who is quite the humorist. At one stop, a sign implied Senator Bob Dole was Ford's Agnew. He walked over to the demonstrators, adjusted it and said, "That's better." Another time he was speaking when a military chopper flew overhead. He remarked, "I guess they did not want you to hear for national security reasons." Mondale was more hard-hitting and Fritz was far more serious. It all boiled down to style.

When it came to debates, Ford was the better debater, and Carter tended to get his facts mixed up, whether for political ploy or other reason. Unemployment statistics Carter stated, that during the 1950's there was low unemployment, and the current rate of unemployment was the Nixon/Ford fault. Ford countered after pointing out he had is wars wrong, that during the Korean War unemployment was low because of 3,500,000 troops committed to that war, compared to the military under his administration stood at 1,400,000 in peace time. He pointed out that war has a habit of creating jobs.

There was also a semblance of difference. Carter was trying to connect the dots of Ford to Nixon. Ford was trying to show we were at peace, and no American soldiers were dying anyplace on the planet. He, Ford, extolled the Spirit of 76 and thanked the American people for the privilege of serving as President though he did not seek office, and hoped they, the American people would affirm his policies in November. Let it be known, Ford was an honorable man.

When Governor Carter did get organized, he was eloquent, and did spell out the social agenda. He argued for helping the cities, and how it could take as much as 18 months to set a piece of legislation to the target of public need. He put quite a stress on healthcare and responsible military spending. Let it be known more than either Nixon or Ford, he promoted revenue sharing, especially in the areas of education and healthcare.

When Ford spoke he spoke in detail. He spoke on the revenue-sharing programs. He pointed out he fought for general revenue shari9ng, and pointed out how the congress finally went along with him. Of the funds for that purpose, one third of the states got 6 billion, 300 million dollars to be spent in whatever category was most helpful to the state and locality. Ford continued on, touting his good housing program aimed at cutting payments by fifty percent. He talked of expanding the Homestead Housing Program. This was to hit the community level to help solve housing shortages. He pointed out that Secretary Hill had a 75 page report, with specific recommendations to help local communities.

When questioned on civil rights and the complaints by the NAACP, Ford responded that the Air Force had its first black general and the Navy was under consideration for a new three-star admiral. This was a first in US Naval history. He talked of tackling the redlining issue that affected all persons of color no matter what race or economic condition.

Governor Carter countered that Ford was initially against the Civil Rights Act. He also pointed out that the world has changed since Kennedy and Johnson in 1969. Black entrepreneurs get started in business and are forced into bankruptcy. He felt Ford's description of his administration was a contradiction in its own terms. He spoke in almost Marxist terms of the progress of the South as a liberation of both blacks and whites.

This is just a side note in all of this, but no one talked of the American Native population and their needs in all of this period of time.

Other aspects of the Carter attack centered on the 1,300 indictments in the HUD Department concerning the loss of 600 million dollars in the last part of 1975, and 800 convictions. This was just in home loans. He charged that the Federal Government had become a slumlord.

Without totally exasperating you, this is the flavor of the debate. Today, in 2010. With our massive outreach in federal economic aid going down to extensions on unemployment, we find ourselves in government ownership, with at least partially controlling interests. Mortgage default continues at an alarming rate, though the numbers are dropping. Some have argued we have hit the bottom. I still have to ask what happened to the people that have become invisible, and indeed have a subsistence economy. Is social Darwinism back? You see, things have not changed that much.

## 84. CALIFORNIA SCENE, 1976

The differences were stark, from liberalizing child labor laws to the Humphrey Hawkins 15 billion dollar tax cut supported by Tunney. Tunney argued that Senator Hayakawa simply did not understand American society, and that it would lead to conflict between the old and the young for jobs. Again, look at corporate outsourcing and continued layoffs. Hayakawa argued that adults are not interested in minimum-wage jobs, and would rather go on welfare. Tunney argued the tax cut was necessary to avoid the coming recession. Even back then corporate needed a guaranteed paycheck. It was argued that was part of the Nixon/Ford economic policies. Both agreed the busing of children was needed for the balance of society. They agreed that the B1 Bomber should be built. At that time, 7.5 million people were unemployed. Today 15 million are unemployed, courtesy of corporate consolidation and greed. At the time, in 1976, help would come in the form of welfare. Again, as in this time, growth depended on middle-level corporations, not the fat, bloated larger corporations. We are in corporate decline even here. This continues to be true in 2012.

Barry Goldwater, Jr. had been consistently reelected from his San Fernando base, and was now being challenged by a congressman's wife, Patti Corman, who took potshots at her husband and Goldwater. She was underfunded by her party and was not taken seriously. In 1976 she was a novelty in the mix of novelties of politics.

Howard Jarvis launched a campaign to fix the tax structure, and the angry taxpayers who have seen their taxes doubled, especially in troubled times, are taking aim at the government and big business, which, in this early time could not see their own shoes. There were 28 organizations dedicated to fighting the tax structure, Governor Jerry Brown, and anyone else in their path.

What went wrong? Philip Watson, Assessor, blamed the rising property values. Everyone loves to see their investment go up in value, but they don't want to pay the price. At the other end, too much was attached to the property tax. He said he anticipated an uproar. Remember, wages did not go up, even though the property values did. If your stocks go up and you don't get dividends, how do you pay your taxes? We were trying to artificially build government on the backs of property owners, who were not getting their share of economic wealth being hoarded by corporations. That is why the tax revolt. Are you listening, Big Brother?

It was a tight race. Hayakawa 48% to Tunney's 49%, and the battle tried both men's nerves. In the end, Tunney won by a squeak victory over his Republican opponent. California remains, even to this day, a divided society. This is just a reminder we must respect each other's views and not exceed our own grasp.

## 85. THE 9/11 EFFECT

On September 10, 2001 the political/economic world of the United States was in turmoil. There was a Democratic Representative of some legend, having served 27 years from the 9th district of South Boston by the name of John Joseph Moakley. He had passed from leukemia in the spring of 200, and for twelve weeks a special election was being held to fill his seat. There were two Republicans seeking the position he held. There were also seven Democrats seeking that same position. This account of that election and the general political drama that was consuming this country prior to an event that altered all our lives is telling.

In the 70 years prior to this September date there were only three Representatives that had served in this district. Democrats outnumbered Republicans 4 to 1. It was said that the two Republicans seeking Moakley's seat were just whistling in the wind. What was not stated was that Moakley was a conservative Democrat and had values of another age.

The Democratic contenders for the Congressman's seat were John E. Taylor, Bill Ferguson, Bill Sinott, Cheryl A. Jacques, Stephen F. Lynch, Brian A. Joyce, and Marc H. Pacheco, who was a State Senator in the Massachusetts legislature.

Jacques was the closest rival, with 18% of the vote, according to the state polls. Lynch, who was also a State Senator, had 39% of the vote according to those same polls. Jacques was painting Lynch as a member of the far right, and one opposed to abortion. What he failed to state was that Moakley himself held the same views. Joyce had sent out literature painting an unflattering picture of Jacques's live-in partner. The Republican Candidate, Jo Ann Sprague, was a Korean War veteran and also a State Senator. She was actually expected to have victory on October 16, which was when the special election was to be held. The Sprague record supported the National Rifle and Pistol Association, death penalty advocate, pro gay marriage, and against abortion. He stated, "I am willing to take on anyone who comes out of that primary. People don't vote the Party anymore, they vote the record."

A political analyst, Lou DiNatali described Boston politics as a blood sport. Max Kennedy, who is the son of the Late Robert Francis Kennedy, put his hat into the ring, but quickly dropped out. DiNatali was putting his money on the Democrat who survived the primary.

## 86. THE NATIONAL SCENE

The Democratic Representative from Los Angeles, Henry A. Waxman, called into question in an 8 page memorandum on NBC and its calling of George W. Bush the winner prematurely in the 2000 campaign for President. He stated that there was unfair leverage that influenced other cable and network channels.

Jack Welch, who had retired from General Electric and owned NBC was accused of unduly influencing the decision that George Bush took Florida. Kassie Canter, spokeswoman for NBC, concerning Waxman's statement said that that he sided with Bush was nothing new. She also stated, "and in no way shape or form the result of Jack Welch's influence."

NBC President Andrew Lack told Waxman at the committee hearing that if any tapes existed, he was "certainly welcome" to internal tapes made of Welch on election night. Apparently there were none, and none were delivered. His 8 page memorandum was in response of not being able to get the video tapes which he said he got from eyewitness accounts he did not identify.

Kassie Canter indicated, "In an eight page tome, Congressman Waxman comes up with shocking revelations that Jack Welch was interested in the results of what was perhaps the most fascinating night in the history of presidential elections, and he supported George Bush, not exactly a news flash." She added, "In no way shape or form, the result of Jack Welch's influence."

Waxman's account of what his source said went as follows: 1) Welch and other visitors distracted NBC News Director Sheldon B. Gawiser with repeated questions about his projection decisions, how they were made. 2) Welch had access to raw election data that weren't available to new anchors, writers, producers, or other news anchors. 3) After instruction about reading the data, Welch later concluded that Bush won Florida, and shared his analysis with Gawiser. At almost the same time, John Ellis, George Bush's cousin and Fox News senior desk official called both the Florida and National election for George W. Bush. Welch, reportedly standing behind Gawiser, was asking why NBC was not also calling the election for Bush. Shortly after this, Gawiser did call for Bush, and all major stations did the same. This was the nature of the charge, and his implication of a grand conspiracy. These statements appeared on September 11th in the *L.A. Times*, the same day our country was attacked. This will give you a rough idea of the political state of the nation when our house of cards was attacked.

## 87. A HOME INVASION

To understand how we came to be so vulnerable, we have to go back to a House Judiciary Committee hearing on May 25, 200. The hearing concerned, of all things, crime. The Assistant General Controller, Robert Hast testified on how our airport screening devices at the time, and our security measures were woefully inadequate. GAO agents were able to penetrate key security areas of our airports without an escort and with fraudulent identification.

Hast related the story of Victoria Cummock, whose husband died when Flight 103 went down in the town of Lockerbie, Scotland in 1988. A plea was made at that time to improve aviation safety. She was on a commission headed by then-Vice President Al Gore. We have, nationwide, 450 international airports, and only 54 high-tech explosion detection devices.

What weapons were used by the team of hijackers was not known for certain. No guns were mentioned, based on cell phone conversations. Box cutters and knives were mentioned. The knives used, it was suspected, were the flatware distributed by the airline itself. It was added that if a box cutter were "held to your neck, wouldn't you do what you were told?"

Some experts, like the retired head of the FBI office in New York, Luis Schiliro, related their investigational experiences, among them the explosion aboard Flight 800 and the 1993 bombing of the World Trade Center. He stated, "This is something I can't begin to comprehend. They put this together very, very, neatly. We're just amazed at the level of coordination this would have taken." On the basis of their experience, previous terrorist acts were highly disorganized.

The executive director of the Washington Office of the Monterey Institute of International Studies stated, "It shows that our emphasis on nuclear, chemical, biological and radiological weapons of mass destruction caused us to overlook the more readily available opportunity: airplanes. They had no bombs, and they proved to be incredible weapons."

How did the teams of hijackers get to the pilots and send them back with the passengers, which is what happened. The doors were not secured, and once they had control of the aircraft, it was fairly easy to guide the planes to their targets. "Almost anybody who had knowledge of flying could guide the airplane, "according to Robert Rueth, aeronautical sciences professor. "But they did a good job with the accuracy. It's not a matter of strength: it's a matter of having a bit of knowledge of how this particular airplane works."

Huntington Beach Republican Representative Dana Rohrabacher was critical of our intelligence efforts when he called it, "A catastrophic failure of our American intelligence."

The Rand Corporation's terrorism specialist, Bruce Hoffman thought this was a new breed of terrorist: highly skilled, carefully trained, utterly devoted. He stated, 'They hit two embassies in Africa a few years ago. That really drew our attention. To hijack four commercial aircraft, at the same time. You're really talking about tremendous professionalism and diligence. You're not recruiting someone who is going to panic. Short of having an agent in all four cells, how do you prevent that?"(We found out of course that Al Quaeda was behind all the attacks mentioned, including the September 11, 2001 attacks on the World Trade Center, The Pentagon, and the plane that was brought down by the passengers themselves in Pennsylvania.

Here are the flights and the losses on those flights. 1) American Flight 11 was a Boeing 767 out of Boston, heading to L. A. The flight had 9 flight attendants, two pilots, and 81 passengers. This plane hit the first tower. 2) United Flight 175 was a Boeing 767, Boston to L. A. Seven flight attendants, two pilots and 56 passengers. This plane hit the second tower. (The death toll in the World Trade Center Towers was 2,746.) 3) American Flight 77 was a Boeing 757 out of Washington, headed for Los Angeles. There were 4 flight attendants, two pilots, 58 passengers. This plane struck the Pentagon. 4) United Flight 93 was a Boeing 757, Newark to San Francisco, 5 flight attendants, two pilots and 38 passengers. This was the flight of heroes where the passengers overpowered the hijackers and was brought down in a field in Pennsylvania. The target of this plane was believed to be the White House itself. There is today, on that site, a monument to those fallen heroes.

The day of the attack on the World Trade Center/Pentagon, the nation shut down. Air traffic from coast to coast, and all American territories was shut down. Only military aircraft flew. The New York Stock Exchange shut down. Banks did the same. In California, people were buying up emergency supplies. Schools and public buildings were offering counseling and having shortened days. The entire economy of California and the nation was brought to a halt. The reasoning behind the attacks was to affect the US economy. In this they were successful. Banks pulled their liquidity from the economy. No one could do business. Insurance companies refused to grant licenses and permits. Our economy had ground to a halt as Osama Bin Laden was having tea and toasting his victory.

President Bush stepped into the spotlight and encouraged us to continue life as normal. Unfortunately, the banks had stopped lending, employers were ridding themselves of inventory and downsizing. In layman's language, laying people off. The airline industry and support industries were especially hard hit. This condition lasted for the good part of 2001 into 2002, and only started to recover by 2003. It was at this time that G W and Greenspan came up with subprime mortgages to give lower income people a chance to become homeowners. The problem was twofold: 1) employers were still not hiring, and house flippers inflated the housing market, causing it to collapse, and 2) the job market, which was not supporting the housing market caused the phenomenon we call foreclosure. George made some mistakes, but it was our institutions that were the real enemy.

If you add the tax cut pushed through just prior to the September 11th, the tax which suppressed our economic development, which George regarded as a campaign promise despite the declining economy, and the seven times the prime rate was lowered to stimulate the economy, you could repeat what Clinton said: It's the economy, stupid.

## 88. THE WEST COAST

It is September 12, 2001 and the nation is just absorbing the impact on New York's financial district. At this time Grey Davis is governor, and we are going through a crisis of our own, though it is not full-blown as yet. The people do not know whether we are in a state of war or not. The superintendant of the Capistrano Unified School District stated, "I'm shaken. We are concerned to how children react to this." It was a child that raised the question. Karen Loveless, a west side mother, heard the question from her fifth grade son."Are we going to war? I'll go if I have to." Thank god children don't have to fight, but he probably is in the military today (2012). Field trips were canceled, along with extracurricular activities, and in many cases, shortened days. Superintendent Roy Romer stated, "Young children who view hours of terrorist attacks, fires and human suffering are highly at risk of psychological trauma."

I have an abstract for you. The current situation in Syria, and all the blood a and death that has been displayed on the screen has seemingly had little impact in this country. Either because it is happening to somebody else it doesn't seem to bother us that much, or we have been so desensitized by the Afghanistan and Iraq conflicts that all this blood and guts and crying is like some old horror flick.

Here are a few things that did happen on the west coast, California in particular. Governor Grey Davis shifted operations to the California Highway Patrol campus outside Sacramento. Disneyland closed. Madonna canceled her concert. City blocks resembled concrete deserts. Only the squirrels were out. Downtown L.A. rush hour resembled a grade B sci-fi flick with traffic streaming out of town, destination Cucamonga.

## 89. AN EYEWITNESS

Having said what I just said, here is an eyewitness account by John Kelly: "Then there was this burst of stuff coming out of the building. There was no fire and no explosion. I wondered why the plane was making so much noise and was so low. You could tell it was a passenger plane, that it was in trouble or trying to get close for a view. You'd never think a plane would go dead center into a building. It was like a missile." Here is where Anonymous got the idea what hit the towers was a missile.

They merely took part of a statement out of context and created a story, which they sold the country and broadcast over the internet. Kelly continues, "I thought it was an accident, except he took a sudden left. He went right for it. It was so creepy, I thought OH MY GOD. I just saw 300 people die. My wife says oh my God, they hit the second building. I looked, the plane went through the building and there was a blast out of two sides in all directions." Back to the anonymous report. The reason there was no plane found in the building was that it passed through it. "I saw people jumping, bodies flying through the air. I saw people waving white flags. It was horrible.

"Police and ambulances were everywhere, and within seconds there was no one. You saw everyone running, running. You saw shoes, sunglasses on the street. People dropped their stuff and ran. It was like a nuclear explosion."

Among the dead was a CNN commentator, Barbara Olson, the wife of Solicitor General Theodore B. Olson, who had two conversations with her husband by cell phone from the hijacked airliner before it crashed, according to the cable network report. Her statements were the pilots, crew and passengers were forced into the back of the plane. The only weapons apparently were knives and box cutters. There was no mention in her report of nationality or motive of the hijackers. He aid her words were, "What do I tell the pilot to do?" Theodore added, "That was somewhat typical of Barbara, a take-charge kind of person. But there was nothing they could do. They were all kept in the back of the plane."

## 90. THE FLIGHT OF HEROES 93

The reason we know so much of this flight is because of cell phones. The pilot had locked himself in the bathroom and called on his cell, stating, "We are being hijacked." At the same time, Cee Cee Liles called her husband, a policeman, telling them that their flight had been taken over by hijackers. The time was 9:58, and the plane's rout had been altered south from its San Francisco destination and was over West Moorland County, Pennsylvania. It was stated, "We lost them, "and two or three minutes later, "We lost them." They fought back, and the plane crashed in a field in Pennsylvania.

## 91. A PEOPLE'S CALL TO WAR

We had been attacked, and as it turned out later, we had a list of all those hijackers that were involved. We were even tracking them and their activities. We just failed to connect the dots.

James A. Baker III, a former secretary of state was quoted as saying, "In effect, we unilaterally disarmed our intelligence capabilities. We need human intelligence to penetrate these groups." Either baker was out of the loop or he was not being completely honest.

Richard Holbrooke, who was formerly our ambassador to the United Nations, made the argument that any action should be in conjunction with other nations. He included Russia in this mix. He also included the nations of the Middle East. He did make the plea to bring those who did this act to justice. I have a question. Does that mean invading a country or countries? Russia would not join us because of commercial contracts with Iraq, and had in their recent history suffered a defeat in Afghanistan. Ironically, they have the same reasons for not acting against Syria. Times or nations and their motives have not changed. Holbrooke stated, "Any nation seen to harbor or aid and abet these people must be treated as co-equally responsible."

Former State Department counter-terrorism official Larry Johnson was an advocate to wage war on those who attacked our sovereignty. Failure to respond would seem to mean that the U.S. was unable to fight. "This is a declaration of war. You don't go in for a tie here. If these guys want to cross the line this way, so be it. But so will we. We can't go back now. If we don't act, the U.S. will be seen as unable to fight." The trouble is that the group Al Qaeda was not affiliated with any one nation, though Afghanistan and Pakistan did have them operating within their borders, and these countries felt they had control of them. Why did we not go after Pakistan as well as Afghanistan, instead of invading Iraq, which at this time was not related to the issue?

The answer to Pakistan was simple. They, like George Washington, had the ax. It was simpler to make them an ally, though an unreliable one. Afghanistan was nothing more than a group of warlord fiefdoms with extremists holding influence over the country. Iraq was an out-of-control former ally that was killing its people, but it was not related to the equation.

A former internal Chief of Security at the Justice Department, John L. Martin argued, "Any kind of retaliation must be very restrained, methodical, and deliberate and accurate." You can't make things up and generalize because it's convenient. He added, "Or else you're going to worsen the situation." I can only say we generalized, and it did.

Here is one for the conspiracy theory buffs among us. There was a 47-story annex adjacent to the Twin Towers World Trade Center, and it had caught fire. It was argued that the fire had been intentionally set. Reality check would be the fire in Tower Two caused the fire in the annex. All the occupants had been successfully evacuated. It was the fire from the 110-story tower that caused the fire that started on the roof, combined with the intense heat of the adjoining structure that caused that building to collapse. It was not a case of government arson as Anonymous stated.

## 92. VILLAIN UNVEILED

It turned out to be an attack from a far-off land: Afghanistan, courtesy of a guest in that country that was counted as a fugitive and head of an organization that we would come to know as Al Qaeda, and its leader, Osama Bin Laden. There's an old saying, if you associate with a thief (terrorist) you are branded as one. His organization operated independently of each cell, yet it was tied and funded from a central source. Orin Hatch, Senator from Utah referred to Bin Laden as the mastermind behind the September 11th attack. He was put on the wanted list for the attack on the embassies in Kenya and Tanzania.

How Afghanistan enters the picture is through the Taliban, an extremist Mohammadan sect. They expressed shock at the attack, but stated Al Qaeda and its leader were not behind it. No one took this denial seriously. The editor of Abdel Bari Atwan of the *Alquds al Arabi* newspaper reported that Islamic Fundamentalists close to Bin Laden were planning a major operation, but he did not take the threat seriously. The paper was quoted as saying, "They said it would be a huge and unprecedented attack, but they did not specify."

President Bush had given orders to place U.S. forces the world over on high alert. Bush flew from Florida to a secure location in Louisiana. Vice President Cheney and his family were also placed in secure locations. Congressional and cabinet leaders were also put in secure sites.

Admiral Robert J. Natter, Commander of the U.S. Atlantic Fleet: "We've been attacked like we haven't been since Pearl Harbor." Senator Charles Hagel, Republican from Nebraska added, "This is the second Pearl Harbor."

Just how did Bin Laden and his organization come to hate us so? This goes back to the 1991 war against Iraq that had the support of the U N. Al Qaeda offered its forces in combating Saddam Hussein. The Saudis declined their help in favor of a U.S. effort. The next question would be who is Al Qaeda? The answer to that one is related to Afghanistan and the Moujadine. It morphed into what we call Al Qaeda. Had Bin Laden not been harbored in Afghanistan, the Moujadine would not have morphed. Now we're dealing in circles.

## 93. THE AIR DOWNTOWN

When you travel into L A today it's pretty clear, but back in the seventies and eighties the air had a brown tinge to it, and on a bad day you could taste it in the air. In Downtown Manhattan there was only limited visibility, and it was not smog. Imagine burnt jet fuel, vaporized plastics and metals, not to mention the 2,746 humans that were vaporized, all floating in the atmosphere. Firefighters, policemen, and, by this time, National Guard units were maintaining order and taking it all in. Greenwich Village was having a half-off sale, and they weren't getting any takers.

Those who initially went in for the rescue of others wrote their names on their arms or on the walls of the building they were entering. What I describe here is that sense of prophetic doom mixed with that sense of duty, and the candles still burned and the cards kept coming and the fence stood still.

## 94. WHY WERE THE TOWERS STRUCK?

It could truly be said that these two towers were a concentration of business international. The best way I can state the loss of companies and people would be to list those companies.

100's: Chen, Lin and Jiang–investments: Atlantic Bank of New York–financial institution: Sandra, O'Neil, and Partners–investments: AON Corporation–insurance.

90's: Regus Business Centers–employment agency (this company was on five floors): Gibbs and Hill–engineers: Raytheon Company–manufacturing: Fiduciary Trust Company, Int'l–financial institution (this company was on three floors).

80's: Corporation Service Company - not available: Gibbs and Hill–engineers: New York Department of Taxation and Finance–government (this was on two floors): Harris, Beach and Wilcox–attorneys: Keefe, Bruyetti and Woods–investments (this group had three locations).

70's: Fuji Bank–financial institution: First Commercial Bank–financial institution

50's: Dow Jones and Company–printers/publisher (two locations)

40's: Seabury and Smith–insurance: Fireman's Fund–insurance: Morgan Stanley–investments.

For the complete detailed list, see the *L.A. Times* September 13, 2001.

The long made short was that the world did its business here, and for those wishing to bring down the western world and the influence that goes with it was, in a way, better than Washington, DC. They struck there, too.

I have not said enough about those who fought the fires, maintained order and died doing it. Among the firefighters, many were off-shift, but came down to help. Some doubled as plumbers in the middle of the night. Their families knew each other and played together. They tipped a beer or two. There are shrines even today in police and fire stations. Comrades honoring their own.

## 95. THE SUSPECTS

Fifty names surfaced and suicide notes were found addressed to their mothers. As of this date, four cells were apparently involved, according to the investigators. A good number of them had taken flight training. One case, oddly was not concerned about landing. That should have been a clue. Forty suspects had been accounted for, and were dead. Ten suspects were still at large.

At the White House things had changed. Security had been beefed up. Even now you can't drive by the White House, and there are security barriers around it. Our attackers wanted to change the world, and I believe they did. There rose an anti-Islamic sentiment in this country, and the government even to this day, in 2012 is still fighting it.

After the attack, a throng of Palestinians rejoiced in the streets, stating God is great. The infidels, in their minds, had been dealt with. America had been pressuring for peace and a homeland for the Palestinians. We were even pressuring Israel on the establishment of that Palestinian state. With the attitude in the street making itself known despite the official denouncing of the acts, the U.S. took pressure off Israel and the Israelis were more aggressively dealing with the intifada that was going on at the time.

Israel's Prime Minister at this time, Ariel Sharon, had implied that Arafat might be involved, which he was not. He stated, "The line has been drawn. The world is changed. It is a different ball game. You can't be a little terrorist anymore. You have to make a choice. You're on one side or the other. It's a historic strategic choice of evil and darkness on one side or the civilized world on the other side." There were incursions into Jenin and the city of Jericho. Washington did not raise an official complaint, as they had in the past. Sharon continued, "We are not under any pressure. What we are doing in Jenin hasn't come up at all. Something has changed in the world. Now they understand."

Foreign Minister Shimon Perez stated, "The Palestinians have today a chance to disengage themselves from any sort of terror and enter the responsible world trying to stop the dangers." He spoke of Arafat's dilemma and opportunity to renounce the "world of terrorism or face the rage of the entire world."

Since 1991, Islam has been radicalizing. Indonesia's President, Megawati Sukarnoputri, who was elected after President Suharto was driven from power in 1998, faced at this time a vacuum in effective law enforcement based on democratic values as opposed to autocratic rule.

It was said that Bin Laden's Al Qaeda was establishing itself in Indonesia, according to U.S. Intelligence. "We have known for quite some time that the Bin Laden group had established itself in Indonesia. I think they see real opportunities in the world's biggest Muslim country, and one in which there are no effective controls."

The President of Indonesia was slated to meet with President Bush over the lingering effects of the Asian economic flu that had at this time gripped Asia. That trip was suspended due to domestic trouble.

## 96. AMERICA ASKS FOR SUPPORT

I have given you a taste of what the attitude is in places like Indonesia compared to that of Israel. The Middle East region was and is full of degrees of support and denial at this time.

In Lebanon, its President Hariri, who would later himself be killed in a terrorist attack along with other members of his cabinet, stated, "We have 100% sympathy with the Americans. We understand that terrorism is against humanity and against our religion and principles and against everything we stand for. On the other hand, we want to see all the problems of the region solved."

Jordan, regarded as a key ally in the Middle East, was caught on the horns of its own dilemma. The U.S. had supported Israel's side in the intifada that had been going on since 2000, resulting in 740 men, women and children dead. The majority of the dead were Palestinian. Their spokesman said, "Officially, we told them that Jordan is beside the United States to confront this monster, and we have to finish off terrorists everywhere." Remember, Jordan's population is in excess of 50% Palestinian.

I am reminded of Joseph Stalin's pledge to fight for democratic principles. Our stand on terrorism in other people's eyes is a contradiction in its own terms.

Here's a funny one. Even Iraq's Saddam Hussein condemned the acts of terrorism on September 11, 2001. We all know what happened shortly after that. I have another good one for you. Even Moammar Kadafi offered his condolences for the attack.

President Bashar Assad of Syria offered his full support to the United States in fighting terrorism, but again, looks at their definition of a terrorist organization and ours. At any rate, the President stated, "Arabs have always been fiercely opposed to terrorism in all its forms." There was a qualifying remark to the position: "legitimate resistance against occupation." We do know what he meant by that. The other counterpoint is, Syria today is involved in ethnic cleansing teetering on total civil war.

The Saudis offered their full condolence. Remember that a good number of the hijackers were Saudi citizens. Money for the act did come from that nation.

## 97. BUSH ACTION/ECONOMIC REALITY

In 1991, at the time of the first Gulf War, George H. W. Bush: "This act will not stand." He formed an international coalition under the United Nations Charter and liberated Kuwait. But we did not occupy Iraq, but did set up a no-fly zone that held up, ironically, until round two.

When President George W. Bush stood in the shadow of what was the World Trade Center, he stated that this act of aggression against America would not stand. "Victory against terrorism will not take place in a single battle, but a series of decisive action against terrorist organizations and those who harbor and support them." Bush, as he stood with the volunteers, evoked his concern for the families of the victims, and referred to the hijackers as Barbarians. He vowed to track them down.

At a later press briefing he expanded the meaning of his words as Bin Laden was brought into the picture. "There is no question he is what we would call a prime suspect, and if he thinks he can hide and run from the United States and our allies, he will be sorely mistaken." President Bush continued, "They will try to hide. They will try to avoid the United States and its allies, but we're not going to let 'em. He repeated his father's words, "This act will not stand."

At another junction, Bush's press secretary stated, to a question, "The President will only act when the time is right." He added there is no question America is rallied and ready.

Now with all the flag-waving there was something else going on. The airline industry was shedding jobs. Continental Airlines stated that they were ending 12,000 positions. These were all support staff. Northwest Airlines was cutting flight schedules by twenty percent. People taking to the air dropped dramatically. There was talk of a thirteen billion dollar bailout for the airline industry. Now think what was happening here. That bailout money would have been wasted. The American people and the industry were reacting out of fear. The economy had not suffered a dollar loss, we were just having the consequences of a bloody nose. If banks, insurance companies and corporations would have acted responsibly, we could have been on our feet fairly quickly. Small business would have taken up the slack, and we would have created jobs.

## 98. BIOLOGICAL CHEMICAL WARFARE

By 1998 the fear of unconventional warfare had been on the rise. Here is a note of comfort and concern. While extensive efforts were made to accumulate vaccines to accommodate a massive biological attack, the quality of those items has been thrown into the equation. According to the GAO, the stockpile included expired drugs. Cyanide, while not critically considered a threat, the vaccine for it was wholly outdated as of this article in 2001.

Some more good news/bad news situations: An anthrax attack would kill 80% of those affected if not treated. We did have such an attack aimed at the Senate and the Washington Post Office, and a suspect was found, but no convictions happened from it. We and the Soviets had massive biological weapons, but have been eradicating them as a result of a treaty between us.

The current thrust of the national defense as staged at this time (2001), was aimed at anthrax and smallpox. The supply had been tripled since the year 1998. Courtesy of the 9/11 attack, a 40 billion dollar emergency funding bill had been passed by the congress. It was urged that 1 billion be set aside for potential biological mass attack. Representative Christopher Shay echoed our paranoia at the time when he stated, "I am absolutely convinced we'll have a chemical, biological or nuclear attack. The question is not if but when, where, and what will be the magnitude." In a way he was right. Sort of. A gentleman from Pakistan tried to smuggle a nuclear device through Canada into the U.S., and was caught. The case of the Times Square Bomber was caught by a local policeman, and the bomb that was in the fan was fortunately not put together properly. Among the then projections going back to 1993 stated that an anthrax attack on Washington could kill up to 3 million people. The actual attack as it did occur affected some 40 individuals, and there were ten deaths, much less than the projected loss. In the case of the anthrax attack, it was a disgruntled scientist that was investigated, and he died before anything could be done. Our new coordinating agency, Homeland Security, and our initial color based warning systems did have some effect.

Calmer heads did speak up and kept guarded, but not crazy. Jason Pate, a terrorism specialist employed by the California Monterey Institute of International Studies stated, "There's a threat here, but it's a long-term problem. We need to be worried about the security of the cockpit doors in airplanes, not buying gas masks at this point." We did reinforce those doors and stop the carrying of any sharp objects, including scissors. Also note the change in menus to basic snacks, as opposed to meals. This is because the knives used in first class for meals served were turned into weapons.

As far as any other countries having weapons of mass destruction in the post-9/11 period proved to be mostly an illusion and faulty data. At the close of the Persian Gulf War and the liberation of Kuwait, which occurred of the matter of a debt, the allies had targeted Saddam's stockpile of chemical weapons and degraded his capabilities after the war. He did get rid of all of those weapons. The unfortunate thing is, he also destroyed the paperwork and could not prove that he did it. If you add the killing of 10,000 Shiites to this, and the few mobile scud missiles he possessed to harass allied aircraft, you have some of the reasons for what followed.

Tripping on over to Al Qaeda, in the 1990's an inquiry was made by Bin Laden's organization for aluminum tubes thought to be the type used in the making of a nuclear device, and the fission materials from an African source, but the connection was never proven. The report was discounted, but the rumors had a life of their own.

Under actual attacks other than ours, there was the attack on the Tokyo subway system by the Aum Shinrikyo, a Japanese terrorist group that used Saran gas to kill thirteen people. This one attack by this nationalist group started extreme overreaction in the United States.

The result of all that I have spoken of did have a positive effect, for we created a network to deal with disaster through the Department of Justice and the Federal Emergency Management Agency, and as of this point in the year 2001, 273,000 police, firefighters and health workers have been trained as to when where and how to respond to disaster. These ramped-up efforts that have been put together, we are told, are far from complete.

On the nuclear question: According to the Nuclear Regulatory Commission, our 103 commercial nuclear power plants were not built to withstand an attack from a 757 or767 airliner being used as a weapon of mass destruction. Knock on wood, with the measures taken since 2001, as had been planned, our nuclear plants are now more secure, for we have tightened the environment around them. Now all we need is a tsunami to hit San Onofre, our nuclear power plant in San Diego, and we would have another ballgame.

## 99. FORCES THAT UNIFY
### September 22, 2001

The 15 nations known as the European Union through these structures at this time merged into one voice and Osama Bin Laden had indeed triggered a change in world structures. Now no extradition order would be necessary to prosecute members of what became known as Al Qaeda. As it turned out, the only ones to be truly upset were Pakistan and its constant charges that we violated their sovereignty, and do so to this day (2012).

The nations of Britain, France and Germany were at this time committing themselves militarily to get the nation backing Bin Laden and his Al Qaeda organization. We were having trouble with the Russians and Chinese who felt the concepts of preemptive war were wrong. It must be explained that what became two countries attacked one under false pretenses was regarded to their polemic concepts of when and when not to get involved.
France's president at this time, Jacques Chirac, who was having domestic problems of his own welcomed the distraction and the committing of his nation to a noble cause, though not all French held the same view. Germany's economy was slowing and as cynical as that sounds, would be a way to employ its people. Jack Straw, Britain's Foreign Minister stated, "Given the scale of the death and destruction, the proportion is likely to be significant. What happened on September 11 was abhorrent and despicable, and it requires an international coalition to respond." (Minus Russia and China, of course.)

Standing on more neutral ground, Javier Solana, who was at this time the European Union's most senior foreign policy official, stated, "The center of gravity of the fight against terrorism is not the military. An American reciprocity is legitimate. Each according to their means, the member nations of the Union are ready to engage in such actions. The actions must be targeted. The actions can be directed equally against states that aid, support or shelter terrorists.

## 100. HOLLYWOOD ADJUSTS

It was as if you were back in the 1950's and they were checking for Communists, stopping every car entering any of Hollywood's major studios. There was a vague FBI warning that the studios could face a terrorist attack, and overnight all became the usual suspects, just like in the movie Casablanca. One would have expected the head of Algeria's secret police to be raiding Rick's night club. One would even expect to find Bogart in character.

Police chief Bernard Parks had ordered its 18 divisions to beef up patrols, especially concerning the studios. I remember my profession at the time being affected out her in Ontario, being stopped to be asked why I was taking pictures. The world had truly changed, and to the police we all became suspects. Back to Hollywood and the reports of gridlock. Concrete barriers were brought in to control traffic and limit access. Bill Ryan, a casual observer noted that the precautions exceeded the first Gulf War.

On his own accord, Michael Eisner, Manager of Walt Disney Studios, drove around the outskirts of Disney Studios to make sure that nobody was illegally parked. Disney President, Robert Eiger walked the lot to make sure that the security steps were being enforced.

The Sony Studios spokesman said those having business in its studios were still allowed access, but friends and relatives were no longer to have access to their back lot.

Promotions were put on hold. Fox Studios canceled the planned New York premier of the film Don't Say a Word. Michael Douglas was demoted to conducting two days of interviews by satellite.

The sad reality was that this was overreaction at its worst for no apparent reason than to do it in a padded room.

## 101. HISTORIC FIGURES

Ronald Reagan is possibly the biggest popular contradiction, with lingering favorable memories of his presidency. This is my account of this rising star.

Having basically left the active movie industry, this lifelong Democrat turned Republican, who became President of the Screen Actors Guild challenged a two-term governor, Edmund G. Brown. With 26,717 precincts out of 28,573 reporting, the vote broke down to 3,460,475 to 2,573,123 votes in favor of Reagan. Rumor of his wanting the presidency surfaced, which he denied. "I will do my best to solve the state's problems. I think I will have made my position clear. There is no need for further questions."

As of March, 1967, he had a 53% overall approval rating. The state was in a wait and see mode. Mrs. Reagan was and is the non-political type, dealing with the social and family issues. Ironically, due to Reagan's future condition, she would become a spokesperson for stem cell research.

When asked about his first steps, he came up with a three-point program. Through the use of 150 management specialists, a think tank approach on improvements on potential immediate savings. Second on the list: in-depth studies of specific areas, and the impact of specific reorganized programs. The third revolved around the long-term effect of specific reorganized programs, as they relate to the executive and legislative branch. What Reagan was proposing was the scientific method.

The state at this time had a 200 million dollar deficit. Reagan proposed through his administration a raise in corporate taxation, doubling the state income tax, and a 31/2 cent raise on cigarettes. The Legislature objected to an increase on cigar and pipe tobacco. He believed in sin taxes. Cigarettes at the time had a ten cent tax on them. The Reagan tax plan was authorized by Senator Dukemajian who would later run for the office himself. The 1.5 billion dollar tax bill sponsored by John G. Veneman on payroll withholding was defeated. He was seeking monies and expansion of revenue sources to beat this deficit.

Assemblyman Jesse Unruh would later push for a change in the makeup of the Board of Regents to exclude elected administrative and legislative members. Members of the Board of Regents are elected to a sixteen-year term by the Governor - it would be more accurate to say appointed - and are accountable to the public. Reagan argued the people need a voice, and elected officials are the best way to do that. Unruh argued that the governor was exercising undue influence. According to the governor, "You just have to add some hard, cold mathematics, and look at their present age and add 16 years to it, and you don't make an appointment."

Regan, on related matters, proposed a 365 million dollar budget for the school system in California. Max Rafferty was the one that proposed the measure.

The name of Howard Koupell, an auto dealer, led a recall petition that failed. They came 400,000 short of success. Of the 484,700 total signatures, 236,787 were held valid. He asked for an extension for 20 days to get those signatures. You can see the divisiveness in Sacramento politics, and the people's will. Just look at the conflict over legislative or administrative initiatives in 2009 that have gone down to defeat, and the passions that fueled those arguments.

Among the people that disagreed with Reagan were the *L.A. Times'* Joseph Conrad, who was always bagging on Reagan. My view was and is this late, great cartoonist commentator was one of a kind and they both added spice to life that is sadly lacking today.

Welcome to the era of the Vietnam War, very similar to our Afghan/Iraq conflict in substance. We had Angela Davis, a card-carrying member of the Communist Party, and the Students for a Democratic Society. On the other side we had Ronald Reagan and his view of campus order. Carefully reading the views of Reagan, he was not opposed to demonstrations, just that they should not be held on public campuses.

His proposal for campuses in California went along the lines that campus life was for students, not those who were expelled. A teacher's job was to educate. The only time a loudspeaker system should be allowed on campus is during a sanctioned event. As shallow as that May seem that is what his view was. Social outcry was reserved for the streets, not the campuses.

Using his position as Governor he developed a four point program to restore order to the situation. 1) It would be criminal trespass for a non-student to be on campus for anything other than official business. 2) The term of one year should be imposed on any student in terms of suspension. He or she would not be allowed access any college or university campus during that time. He or she was convicted of a criminal offense. 3) Any teacher or staff member convicted of an offense related to a school disturbance would be dismissed, and only be reinstated through a review board of that institution. 5) This is the telling one, considering it was the fifth of the four points and it concerned any person using a loudspeaker system or even possessing it without the permission of the State College or University administration. Reagan stated, "It is imperative that an educational atmosphere be maintained if orderly educational process was to go forward. It is equally important that the lives and safety of students and faculty and the property of our educational institutions, paid for and maintained by taxpayer dollars. These campuses must be free of violence, threats and intimidations."

If the world were simple, and governments told the truth then Governor Reagan would have been the shining star for truth, but things break down and civil disobedience does occur. Yes, organizations like the SDS and even the educators themselves might be part of that element we call change. This was the reason for the great outcry from the public. Today people are being politically correct, and everybody is putting everybody in a box, but boxes break down and truth does escape.

Robert Taylor was one of Ronald Reagan's friends and colleagues. He passed after 35 years of acting, 24 of them with Metro Goldwin Mayer, was praised by his fellow actor, then-Governor Reagan, who touted his films and his personal life as exhibited by those that honored him and recounted his heartaches, joys and love interests.

On the drug war - that's right the same war we fight today, only with bullets and blood down in Mexico and on our borders—between the period of 1968 and '69 there was a fifty percent increase in drug use despite, or Maybe because of a massive education campaign. The young and Haight-Ashbury 24 were cited as an example. The solution: a massive campaign on drug abuse. The early use of marijuana was cited. I believe this was the time the 1930's film Reefer Madness resurfaced. Ed Reineke, the Attorney General at the time headed up the fight. The term "near-epidemic proportions" was used. Well, California is still vibrant, and the cartels are still doing their thing, only now you can argue something is very wrong.

Teachers' salaries and administrative costs were the propriety above the needs of the students. The accusation was confirmed by one example at the Sacramento college system. President Johns was forced to resign, and it was found out that 50% of expenditures were not being scrutinized. The budget was to face a 20% reduction in the educational system. The system was upside down. Chancellor Glen S. Dunke stated, "All we're talking about is finding ways to reduce the cost of operations so we can get more students educated, and still find a way to provide the citizens' tax relief." In a way this is an oxymoron, considering the initial extension of the tax structure that Reagan put into effect at the start of his administration.

The University of Southern California entered the argument. Chancellor Charles E. Young, and philosophy professor Donald Kalish and the hiring of assistant professor Angela Davis to teach Black History. Her personal view on the matter was, "The factor that I am a member of the Communist Party says something about the kind of mind I have. I can't and I won't keep my political opinions out of the class-room. I think they belong there." Her point was that the students themselves should be free to discuss academic freedom. One must remember the Marxist view is that negotiation and the peace process itself is an instrument of war. This is just part of the dialogical argument.

You can point to the McCarthy mentality that at this point was imbedded in the American psyche. Just read Trotsky and you see the schism in the arguments in the theories on both sides. Remember what happened to Trotsky, and who did it to him, and more importantly, why.

On Reagan's part he thought it was a plot by Young and Kalish to attack the governor's arguments. These arguments are, of course, denied. On this point you have to make up your own mind.

Governor Reagan went to the students and Chancellor Young. The following is a direct word for word list of questions and needs expressed by the students in the California system.

1. Line item on budget requests on individual campuses.
2. Expenditures for individual campuses for 1968-69.
3. Programmed space utilization at each campus.
4. Number of faculty-student contact hours at each school.
5. Actual space utilization at each campus.
6. Augmentation items in priority listing drawn by administrator.
7. Amount of faculty time in non-campus duties.
8. Total amount of money allotted for State Colleges and Universities.
9. Listing of persons on each campus making student cutback decisions.

The above was the meat of the issue that was discussed.

It is good to know that Reagan opposed using the California National Guard as a spy agency. As of November 19th, 1969 his political plans did not include the Presidency. The deadline to file would have been March 20th. He called the tax initiative sponsored by the California Association of County Supervisors, ASSN, a fraud that would actually raise taxes by one billion dollars. According to the *L.A. Times*, he agreed with Spiro T. Agnew that the press had a bias.

Rodger C. Chandler of Yuba City was coordinator of his 1966 campaign for Governor in Northern California. He was his appointee to the CYE Board. He found there was no conflict of interest because the agency itself had no direct involvement. That is good to know. He bought the houses for $5,500 that were valued at $10,000 each. The profit could be $200,000. His salary was $25,000 yearly. Now you can scratch your heads.

To show, where Governor Reagan authorized Connecticut's extradition: The reason, the murder and kidnapping of Alexander Rackly. The one being extradited,

Bobby Seale of the Black Panthers. At this time he was in jail in San Francisco. His lawyer, Charles Garey tried and failed to prevent that extradition. That's one way to rid yourself of a problem.

In the year 19712, cuts were made in the medical program by the administration and the legislature. Cuts, according to the *L.A. Times*, amounted to $140,000,000 deficit that was anticipated. Assemblyman John Burton called Reagan a liar, and that the cuts, according to the language, May be made, not must be made. Amounts paid to doctors were lowered by 10%. Governor Reagan, in his State of the State address: "I would find it more pleasing to me if someone would mention along the line that these horrifying cuts that I had made in Medical so far were mandated on my by the legislature and not something I dreamed up in my mind."

In March of 1970 Assembly Speaker Jesse Unruh charged that Reagan had broken his campaign promise to fix the university system. Reagan's response was, "Now Mr. Unruh May occasionally stumble over the truth, but he usually gets up as if nothing has happened. I never made any promises of being able to solve this." Reagan criticized the leaders of the system itself: "For they have been unwilling to meet this head on and grapple with it." This is the art of campaigning.

This is historic: the Air Resources Board, in the interest of better air standards has required a new gadget, the catalytic converter. Republican Assemblyman, from Riverside, W. Craig Biddle. Governor Reagan signed the legislation into law.

On April 17, 1974 the Nixon question was front and center: whether Vice President Ford, or Governor Reagan, the issue of the issue of the candidates in the Republican Party. Reagan said, "I don't think anyone can endorse Watergate and related incidents. It was an illegal act, but now it's before the courts. I think that's where it should be settled. In the meantime, every one of us should assume that those involved are innocent until proven guilty beyond a shadow of a doubt." Concerning impeachment, "I don't think you have a blanket statement about every candidate. The proper answer is to weigh the evidence and then reach a decision."

Vice President Ford said, "If I were a candidate today, I would not defend Watergate." He urged candidates to count them-selves fortunate that the political sky had not fallen on them. He criticized the 1972 campaign of Nixon and urged the concentration on his foreign policy record and his domestic agenda of accomplishments.

In 1975 a Reagan supporter stated, "We had a hero in Ronald Reagan. We worked hard for him and he made a great governor, but now we have an incumbent Republican president. We have a party duty to support him. Now she is supporting President Ford in 1976."

Now it is time to consider the other side of the White House that panicked. They stampede when the president gets on the phone and twists arms to get people to support him. What's wrong is that it implies some kind of White House favors if you agree. I thought we were through with that sort of thing. That was the reaction of Reagan supporters who were now supporting Ford.

## 102. THE FAVORITE SON CAMPAIGN

Former governor Reagan was bitten by the Presidential Bug. He was sending out feelers on the New Hampshire Primary, and based on mathematics, planned a total of thirty presidential primaries. Though he had not announced yet, he was behaving like a candidate. Sears, who was his early campaign manager sated, "I was very encouraged by the workability of the political situation so far as the primary is concerned in New Hampshire."

Reagan came to Oregon and urged a campaign of civility. He urged for a better America: "Everybody can have a slice of the pie if Government will get out of the way and let the free enterprise bake a bigger pie." He added, "I personally will do nothing to be divisive in the coming campaign. I'm sure the President feels the same way."

The time is March 23, 1976. Reagan and Wallace are competing for the same but different supporters, of who would be the main candidates, Ford or Carter. Wallace had become gun shy, making predictions that did not pan out. Despite being considered the underdog, Reagan felt he could make a decent showing. North Carolina was on the line.

Going back to New Hampshire, the Silmar Tunnel explosion came to light. He defended his actions: "The first time was when I read and terribly disappointed. I would never have condoned it." Reagan continued: "Then I saw to it that there was a complete investigation, that it went to trial." The main gist of the criticism was the cuts made in the industrial safety division. Reagan's response was, "We kept the bureaucracy from growing."

On the issue of $100,000 that was diverted in 1970 by Thomas C. Reed, then Reagan's reelection campaign chairman who was now President Ford's Secretary of the Air Force stated Reagan knew of the diversion, which Reagan denied.

Reagan beat Ford in that state, but since it was not a winner-take-all state both candidates received delegates. The same applied to the Democratic side with Carter and Wallace: divisions going to the other candidates. Ford now had 206 delegates to Reagan's 81. Carter had 166 delegates to 85 for Wallace.

Reagan, in a debate on, of all dates, April 1, 1976, gave insight into his views on world dominance. "I believe the peace of which Mr. Ford speaks as much as any man, but peace does not come from weakness or from retreat. It comes from restoration of American [military] superiority. Ask the people in Latvia, Estonia, Lithuania, Czechoslovakia, Poland, Hungary and all the others: East Germany, Bulgaria, Romania. Ask them what it is like to live in a world where the Soviet Union is number one. I don't want to live in that kind of a world. I don't think they do, either."

Reagan used Henry Kissinger's words against him when he stated, "The Soviets have been inept in Eastern Europe. They have not been able to bring the attractions that past imperial powers have brought to their conquests. They have not brought the ideological, legal, cultural, architectural, organizational and other values and skills that characterize the British, German and French Imperial adventures.

This inorganic, unnatural relationship is a far greater danger to world peace than the conflict between East and West. It must be our policy to strive for an evolution that makes the relationship between Eastern Europeans and the Soviet Union an organic one. We seek to influence the emergence of Soviet imperial power by making the base more natural and organic so it will not be founded on sheer force alone." Now I think on Bush's promise to Asia, and his assessment of China as a rising power and all that it implies. These are my words in 2009. I also think, though rocky with the election of Carter, we avoided falling into the Grand Canyon. Reagan did eventually become president, though he had a failed economic policy, not even his own fault. The Soviet Union did fall, and Eastern Europe was set free. This would not have happened under Kissinger's pattern of thinking.

Admiral Zumwalt was the source of Reagan's quote of Kissinger on the U.S. position relating to our position in the world. As for the general, he said it as a side note, not a direct quote. Meanwhile, Reagan experienced a stoppage in matching funds and gave up the campaign jet, and was going to use commercial airlines. This was widely reported.

As the California Primary neared and Reagan's Texas Primary win, his organization began to implode, and Reagan supporters went to Ford. The win in California was considered the balancing point of the nation.

The issue of normalizing relations with Panama, and the issue of the Panama Canal was a sticking point. Manuel Noriega was a narco president. We had to work with the machine in that nation, and things did work out. Mr. Noriega spent time in a U.S. prison. Note the power of the U.S. at this time.

Reagan charged that the Ford Administration was dealing in secret diplomacy. Governments do that.

The labor union, AF of L–CIO and George Meany, head of the union at the time are leaning to Jimmy Carter over Ford or Reagan. The Unions regard both men as shades of black.

Kansas City was to be the site of the Republican National Convention. The Democrats are slated for New York. The Reagan people got less than parity compared to the Ford people. An official complaint was lodged.

Reagan ironically raised more money than Ford, as of July 10, $13.1 million, having spent $13.9 million against Ford's $11.1 million, spending $11.3 million. This is just a small amount of money spent.

When Carter chose Democratic Senator Walter Mondale from Minnesota, Reagan charged Carter was showing his other side, counter to his anti-Washington stand. According to Reagan, he was not what he pretended to be. He challenged Mondale's childcare bill handing childcare to the federal government.

The delegate count goes like this: 1,103 for Ford, 1,020 for Reagan, with uncommitted delegates at the convention. Vice President Nelson Rockefeller is releasing his delegates little by little. Reagan contended why not leave the issue to a floor fight. President Ford was trying to sew up the convention.

We all know Ford got the nomination of the party. The real story lies in how Reagan lost. With Ford, winning New Hampshire by a fluke. You see, Ford had 20 delegates and Reagan had 24, but the rule is, if you have over 21 delegates, your entire slate is thrown out. Reagan also underestimated the power of the machine that worked against him. This is how you win the battles and lose the war.

By October, 1976, Reagan has returned to writing and made a comment on our policy in Africa and how it was being used as a tool against us. Rhodesia and the Smith Government, and the one man, one vote principle was being cited. What wasn't mentioned were the two tribal factions waiting to kill each other once that buffer between them was removed. At the heart of the issue was raw material: industrial diamonds, uranium, manganese and cobalt used in jet engines, useful to the Soviets. An issue is not always what it seems.

By November 1976, Reagan and the members of his team were on the Ford team, pushing for victory in November. His statements of opposition he stuck by, but in the search for victory you set things when you share common ground. He regretted Ford's faux pas on Eastern Europe and Soviet influence. That aside, he saw Ford as the best choice.

Vice presidential candidate Bob Dole, who now shared Ford's ticket was introduced to his Texas audience of supporters and had to prepare for the Vice Presidential debate. Reagan, who was now balancing his efforts because he had to concentrate on making a living, helped pack the house with people like John B. Connelly. Laxalt and other power hitters were pushing the edge of the envelope.

By August 1977 the Panama Canal Treaty was being negotiated, and the Soviets were looking to secure financial interests in the area. Growing Soviet influence and that of Castro's Cuba were a legitimate concern. Now go to Candidate Reagan's concern over the Kissinger analysis and you see the point, especially at this time in history.

Concern over the direction of the Carter Administration in Social Security, on the raising of fees on both sides does not solve the problem. Insurance experts should be brought in. On the Middle East, including the Russians in negotiations was a source. Gas and oil and when industry should be allowed to expand.

## 103. NORTH ATLANTIC TREATY ORGANIZATION

Our report on NATO starts on January 25, 1977. The Cold War has wound down, but the west became lax. The organization that serves as our defense umbrella has some problems presenting herself in a fight. The Soviets, with their expanded nuclear arsenal could obliterate a consolidating reforming force, modern tanks, troop carriers and self-propelled artillery. NATO has fewer vehicles, and they are considered outmoded.

While NATO has superior air power, the Soviets have been upgrading their offensive capabilities.

The southern flank of the Mediterranean has at this time largely been ceded to the Soviet's naval presence.

SALT 2 is forming, but there is concern over the ability of Europe's hands being tied on the cruise missile development.

With the rise of missile defense systems comes what some consider an antitank weapon. That weapon was the neutron bomb. This weapon leaves buildings and tanks intact and kills people similar to an atom bomb. There was a lot of argument on deployment of this weapon. In the end it was banned. Defense Secretary Harold Brown, who was the chief U.S. negotiator, assured us that the moratorium on basing cruise missiles on land or sea for three years would have minimal effect, for the system would not be ready till after that time had passed. The other concern was the 360 mile limitation. 1,000 miles is considered intermediate. This means the missiles would only go to Eastern Europe!

In Europe, the armed forces have unions. The Dutch have the VVDM. They meet with officers on such things as housing and food, but not on matters of military planning. In Denmark the union is in 2% of the force. Co. J. Juel Peterson states, "Our union is entirely nonpolitical and intends to stay that way. The right to strike, we've never even considered it, but we assume government servants do have the right to strike." In Denmark's armed forces in 1977 there were 13,500 conscripts and 14,500 regular enlisted troops. A young man is paid six thousand dollars a month for a forty-hour work week. In Norway the Officers Association dates back to the 19th century. 24,000 of the 25,000 troops in 1977 were conscripts and they serve an ombudsman role on living conditions and related matters. In Germany almost half of the Bundeswehr pay union dues. Britain and France do not permit unions in their military.

Turkey closed down the poppy fields after WW2 at the insistence of the U.S.. In 1974 they sought to open up production again for the purpose of morphine and codeine. They went to the U N and explained how it could be done so no heroin was produced from the gum excretion. The project started out with 100,000 licensed farmers on 50,000 acres. It was expanded to 200,000 farmers on 125,000 acres. A complete army of vehicles and airplanes supervised this crop. They refer to it as the straw method. Most heroin comes from Mexico these days. The solution is there for them to adopt, and it would take away the tar heroin aspect of this war.

With the Soviets massing troops on the border along with their naval fleet, the State of Norway and its Storting (Parliament) put forth an idea of stockpiling weaponry on Norwegian territory to head off any conflict between NATO and the Soviet Bloc. The British train in Scotland, and conduct exercises in Norway, and Canadians have done naval exercises, but no quick response time. The U.S. Marines did not impress the Norwegians. Too much, Vietnam-style fighting.

A thought occurred to me: our tactics, at least as conducted in 2009 in Iraq and Afghanistan are probably all wrong for engagement in the European Theater.

## 104. ON SOCIALISM

Morgan Glistrop was the creator of the Danish party that favors the abolition of the income tax. In 1973 his party won 28 seats and effectively halted the welfare state. A similar thing happened in Britain and Sweden, the reason 40% accelerated to 60% of the GNP. The common thread of this development and what is happening today in the United States is that they want to retain their social revolution of government pensions, medical care and welfare provisions. What the people on both continents wanted and still want are the avoidance of superficial treatment costs, better hospital planning, more moderate doctors, and the introduction of pharmaceutical and bookkeeping. The stability of pension funds still remains the question mark. This applies to an up-and-down economy.

## 105. ON GEOGRAPHY

On geography, the great Baltic Sea lane was the lifeblood of the Soviet Bloc and served 14,000 Communist flag ships. It was also where the Soviets built and repaired their ships. Modern Russia does the same thing today. This is their Panama Canal!

On the Mediterranean, in Italy there were 45 ships from the Soviet fleet competing with 45 allied and sixth fleet ships. Italy has the largest Communist Party outside the Communist Bloc, and the concern in 1976 was, and is in 2010 the hub of the southern defense. There was concern of a Communist victory in June of that year (1976). There were 13,000 U.S. troops contingent in Italy, reinforcing military links to NATO. Even with a Communist government, a way would be found to maintain a U.S. presence.

## 106. RELATIVE MILITARY STRENGTH

The NATO review of strategic strengths showed an alarming decline in NATO capability, even as the Soviets improved theirs. Without going into severe detail, here's the breakdown: 22,000 Soviet tanks to 6,000 NATO tanks. Your average Soviet Bloc soldier has an 18 month tour of duty with six month rotation. The NATO forces are a month-long stint with no rotation. NATO Nations are essentially an all-volunteer force. The Warsaw Pact has 3,700 increasingly upgraded aircraft, to NATO's 1,800 fighters. The Warsaw Pact, in 1972 could airlift 25,000 troops, and by 1975 had an enhanced capability, defensive and offensive to 100,000 in 14 days. Admiral Sir Peter stated, "My view is that these developments indicate the importance which the Soviets attach to cutting the lifeline between North America and Europe." By the way, they (Russia) still do that today, through trade and alliances. He continued, "... and the oil producing area. This is taking place at a time when the trend is for some countries to reduce their maritime commitment to NATO."

# 107. EUROPEAN POLITICS

Now I am going to take you back in time for some possible explanation for all of this. Among them, Charles DeGaulle blocking Britain's entry into the common market twice. The last time it occurred was in 1967. This continued in the 1960's, stalling in 1974, remaining stagnant in 1977.

By the time of the Luxembourg Conference, French President Valarie Giscard D'Staing saw West Germany pull ahead economically, leaving formerly robust France in the dust. Britain was now a member, and all nine nations had their set of problems. Britain's Wilson was ceding the position of Prime Minister to Foreign Secretary James Callaghan. Aldo Moro, who defeated the communist candidate was on the last days of his administration. President D'Staing was plunging at the polls. In West Germany, Schmidt was looking at state elections in Baden Wurttemberg. Everybody had to put his own house in order. They failed to reach agreement.

It was in the year 1874 Alexander M. Haig, Jr. was about to assume command of NATO. The chief reason for this was it was the responsibility of the United States to look after the nuclear arsenal. It was also the time Gerald R. Ford became President.

Now step back to December 9, 1969. President Nixon was pushing through Patric Moinahan's environmental issues. Even the Soviet Union had a representative at the press conference. Basically, it was stated that if the air pollution problem was not dealt with, by the year 2000 the sea level would have risen ten feet, which is an increase of 25%. Whether the seas did rise to that level, I don't know. As of 2010 I see no evidence of it. It was argued that NATO had to address the issue of total numbers of cars on the road.

The nuclear issue was a hot-button issue and Canada was threatening to withdraw its forces. British Defense Minister Dennis Healey and Melvin R. Laird, our Secretary of Defense put their heads together. The result of this meeting was this statement by Healey: "If the Canadians go along with their planned troop reductions, and even more, if this leads to a chain reaction among other countries, the nuclear threshold will fall, and the point at which nuclear weapons would be used would arise very much earlier." Remember the nation of Czechoslovakia was invaded when they attempted to establish a democracy. This event became a catalyst for a lot of things.

Now back to 1977 and the Carter Administration. There is an interest in cruise missiles which the Soviets see as a way to fatten the defense industry profits. These missiles are capable of being fired from submarines and mobile launchers. The French have expressed an interest in developing such a weapon. They do not benefit from our satellites, and wish to develop systems of their own.

## 108. SHAPE

Before there was NATO there was this thing called SHAPE. In 1951 General Eisenhower was at the heart of Paris, near Versailles. The big question buzzing at the time was, is Eisenhower a Republican. A name out of history, James A. Farley, thought Ike would make an ideal Democratic candidate. In January, he made the declaration that he was indeed a Republican. Matthew B. Ridgeway succeeded Eisenhower as head of SHAPE. Ridgeway came from Korea and brought with him his staff. He had no patience for the niceties that was Europe at this time. There was no fraternization between levels. General Günter took command in 1953. He was gregarious, good-humored, and razor sharp, according to the *L.A. Times*. In 1956 he was succeeded by General Ladris Norstad. He talked with the likes of Adenauer of Germany, Belgium's Paul Henry Spaak, NATO General Secretary Dirk U. Stryker, and members of the permanent council. He had the support of President Eisenhower and John Foster Dulles, the author of brinksmanship. He handled his open style very well. He had trouble with the Kennedy Administration and Robert S. McNamara. It was the Cuban Missile Crisis that kept him on the job as long as he was. General Lyman L. Limnizer took over in 1963 and held the organization together during the French withdrawal from NATO. He was direct and dignified, and the oldest serving member of the military, at the age of sixty-seven.

## 109. THE NEW NATO AND CYPRUS

As of December, 1977 the Cyprus issue had come up, and the country known as Turkey was directly involved. The cruise missile question was very much on the minds of the European powers, along with the talks with the Soviet Union on SALT 2. Howard Vance assured that those interests were being protected.

During this time there was a giant spy case, where three people were indicted, including Guenther Guillaume, an East German agent who was personal assistant to Chancellor Willy Brandt. He got a thirteen year jail term. This incident forced Willy Brandt to resign as Chancellor. He was succeeded by Helmut Schmitt, also a member of the Christian Democratic Party, in coalition with the Social Democratic Party. The Bundstag defense committee announced that the Defense Minister, Georg Leber had been asked to appear Wednesday to explain how three accused spies had been able to penetrate the ministry system and steal documents vital to Germany's defense and the Atlantic Alliance, according to the *L.A. Times*.

The need of an early warning system was led by the potential acquisition of the E-3's and the British Nimrods Aerial Recognizance aircraft, at a cost of two billion dollars per unit.

# 110. THE COMMUNIST QUESTION

We all know that European Communists can be and are loyal to their respective countries. In 1977 the Carter Administration stated its opposition to Communists in Western governments. This caused an uproar in Europe. In America, not such a fuss, for we are basically ignorant as to the movement in Europe. The Europeans generally excuse the rhetoric, but not this time. The State Department, as of January 12, 1978, stated, "Administration leaders have repeatedly expressed our views on the issue of Communist participation in Western governments. Our position is clear: We do not favor such participation, and would like to see Communist influence in any Western country reduced, as we have said in the past. We believe the best way to achieve these goals rests with the efforts of the democratic parties: to meet the aspirations of effective, just, compassionate government. The United States and Italy share profound democratic values and interests, and we do not believe that the Communists share those interests."

Further statements from the Carter Administration viewed Western European Communism, and specifically Italian Communists as more of a trouble to the Communist bloc than they are to other European countries themselves.

The Spanish Party effectively can't get involved with another faction. Having said that, a high government official stated, "It is always hazardous to make predictions about Communists." As it has been pointed out, even though the parties act independently, their words have an impact on each other.

Again, according to the *L.A. Times*: the Italian Communist Party, agreed to continue the support of the Minor Christian Democratic government. The French Party would prefer to block involvement in a coalition based on principle. The campaign strategy of the French Communist Party in connection with the national elections scheduled for 1978, that tactic of coalition, seems to betray the Euro-Communist commitment to democratic government. The Spanish Party rose from 60,000 to 300,000: such numbers are hard to control. In Italy, it's 12,000 local sections. These sections serve enterprises like Fiat. As of 2009, guess who owns General Motors? One in five Communists is a woman, and there has been a decline in youth membership, but that goes across all parties.

Euro Communism believes that the Communist Party can be party to the pluralistic system and not act as a monopolistic unit. For this reason the Kremlin was suspicious of it. Spain's Carrillo is a proponent of such a shared system. He hoped that his ideas would gain a foothold in the Eastern bloc. There is some evidence of that: look at Czechoslovakia before the Russian tanks rolled in. It sort of changes the definition of things when looked at in this light.

Seven nations share the Baltic. It breaks down like this: two NATO, three neutral, and three Communist. The area is so small that the boundaries lie in the middle. Norway challenges the Soviet Union by placing submarines armed with nuclear missiles in its port. There is oil in this region. Commerce passes through this region, and it is constantly used as a chess board.

Norway was worried about future naval commitment in light of U.S. and Canadian commitments during this period of time. Their concern was future Russian pressure. You can look at the region even today with its escalating and de-escalating tensions. It is troublesome to look at emerging Mother Russia as a new reborn super power. You can see the concerns of the newly freed nations and those that were neutral. In a way, nothing has changed.

### 111. U.S. PRESENCE

President Carter assured the allies of the U.S. commitment to the alliance. Turkey's Prime Minister, Bulent Ecevit, expressed concern over the continuing embargo against that country. Prime Minister Schmidt was also assured of continued U.S. support. The embargo goes to Turkey's invasion of Cypress and all the human rights violations that occurred. Other aspects revolved around a fifteen year plan to build armament and forces to build up the non-nuclear end. This was in line with the SALT 2 negotiations. What was important was that all equipment had to be standardized. Schmidt and Brezhnev talked at length and came to a trade deal for 10 years, with a possible extension to 25 years. There was an agreement to draw back troop levels at the border and ease the Berlin situation. Brezhnev was in ill health with a pacemaker and emphysema. Gromyko was second in command and would take Brezhnev's position as president.

All the eggs were in one basket. The NATO fleet was in Naples. The new and old with enhanced weaponry were on display. Parity in the naval field was close. NATO, has two military exercises a year under the watchful eye of the Soviet fleet.

The Soviets have always been big on chemicals, whether it is killing your opponent or disabling soldiers on the battlefield. It is like white bread. NATO, on the other hand, moved to ban those substances. The only reason to store them was so we wouldn't get annihilated if they should decide to use them. NATO forces have little or none of these weapons. It is a first strike weapon.

Back to the cruise missile issue: The Pentagon stated that within 10 years, at a cost of 30 to 50 billion dollars, the Soviets would be able to blunt a cruise missile attack. It is then they would send their ICBM's. The flip side is greater accuracy within ten years. Europe thinks the Carter Administration is making the world more dangerous. The Carter Administration thinks the Soviets will never be superior to us in national strength. We are by far the stronger nation economically. Our productive capacity is superior, and I think always will be. In the case of nuclear weapons, we have equivalency with them, and they recognize that, and vice-versa. Carter projected a 3% growth in military terms, and this will do the job.

Other weapons have a numbers problem. Among these problems is the cheap kill. It could be electronic interference, like what happened in 2008 when that government was disabled by its internet going down and Russian troops just moved in. The fear of the Backfire Bomber led to it being included in SALT 2. The other issue of the SS20 which is an intermediate-range missile was another. The PRV's were being raised as a possibility in 1978. There were 150 models of those. Again, electronic jamming.

## 112. THE IRANIAN REVOLUTION

On November 4, 1980, the U.S. Embassy in Iran was overrun, and hostages were taken. They were put on public display and slated to be tried as war criminals. Mohammed Reza Pahlavi was overthrown. He escaped the country. The Ayatollah Ruhalloh Khum-maini established an Islamic republic, and we became the great Satan. The Carter Administration took our cause to the United Nations. The resolution was drafted, but nothing came of it.

Now, back in 1979 the expansion of the military budget resulted in us being perceived as weak. A TRIAD system was developed: submarine and land-based and long-range bombers, $37.8 billion for operations and maintenance, 882 million dollars, or 7% of the 1979 levels for research and development obligations, and the development of the ICBM system. The X Trident nuclear powered submarines and space defenses,
Reagan's Strategic Defense Initiative, the Pershing II advanced attack helicopter, and MX tank and gun with better intelligence and communications were Reagan's proposals when he came to power.

## 113. RONALD W. REAGAN

Reagan comes to power in 1980 and the Iran Hostage Crisis is resolved largely because Reagan was a wild card. By 1982 things have clearly changed. The Iran-Iraq War happens and we support Iraq. I would like you to tell me why? We enter this period of hostility that exists even today in 2010. The Secretary of State, Alexander M. Haig negotiates with Andrai A. Gromyko. Brezhnev is still top dog, but obviously slipping. Items on the table, the Iran-Iraq War and it's on the Persian Gulf Sheikdoms. You see, it's all about oil. Weapons reduction, in cruise missiles deployed in Europe. You notice how the issue did not go away. They were tackling the Soviet Euro missiles. This was under the START framework.

NATO and its role would soon change. Though they did not get involved in the Falkland Islands conflict, its members were involved in indirect support. It became known as the U.S. Rapid Deployment Force. Argentina, of course, lost the conflict.

66 Missiles had been placed on European soil b y May 8, 1984. They are in Britain, Italy and Germany. Nations in the alliance are balking at the missiles on their soil. The Dutch Netherlands had a popular opposition to their placement. This is according to the *L.A. Times*. The decision to deploy 572 single warhead missiles

slated for placement was in danger of being halted.

Now the Craxi Government of Italy is in favor of a moratorium on missiles being placed on its territory. Reagan's Secretary of State Casper W. Weinberger and his message were not exactly welcomed.

Note the inevitable happened: The Soviet Union collapsed. The reason, they spent 70% of their GDP on military-related items. Look upon it as a chess game for all intents and purposes, for the economic survival of the Soviet dictatorship or for European Capitalism. Remember the discussion on the European Communist Parties. Now you could say, "Aha! I get it." Remember Brezhnev is going downhill. A NATO representative stated, "People are already walking on eggs, waiting for the Dutch decision, and the Craxi idea was not needed now. It could split the NATO alliance." One Whitehouse official stated, "Going public with all of this now will make it harder for those in the Netherlands who want to go ahead with deployment. No one around here is happy about it."

Another reason for the SS20 missiles in East Germany and Czechoslovakia was to pressure the countries to change their will on the matter.

The Soviets were invited to the NATO Alliance military exercises, and invitations were sent to other Bloc nations. The invitations were declined.

Congress was considering withdrawing 30,000 U.S. troops from Europe. The Supreme Allied Command argued that such a withdrawal would lead to capitulation or premature use of nuclear weapons. (General Bernard W. Rodgers)

## 114. GOVERNOR JERRY BROWN

In 1975 the projected 1976-1977 budget was within spending limits. A spokesman for the Brown Administration stated, "This is a chance to build a budget from the beginning. It will reflect, with dollars and cents, the philosophy of the Administration. The basic fiscal policy of the Administration is to redirect efforts without escalating costs. Every budget to be submitted to the Department of Finance must reflect this policy." According to the governor, all programs must meet certain standards of growth in terms of job performance. According to Governor Brown, "I intend to take every step possible to avoid a tax increase in financial year 1976-77." Accordingly, new programs which cost money require corresponding reductions in other programs. Believe it or not, Brown signed into law an 11.47 billion dollar budget.

When Brown was running for governor in 1974, the public employees union was threatening to strike. He suggested a collective bargaining law (forced arbitration). Hustan Flornoy, his Republican opponent did not believe in arbitration, let alone the right of public employees to strike. This was one of many differences between the candidates.

The following is the record of bills passed and vetoed under the Reagan Administration in the closing year 1974-75: Signed 1,546 bills. 102 became law without his signature, and 148 others were vetoed. Governor Brown, in his first year signed 1,183 bills into law, 102 became law without his signature, and he vetoed 146.

Here are the bills signed by Governor Brown (at least some of them). 1) Mandatory prison terms for the use of a gun in a robbery, murder or attempted criminal act. 2) Mandatory prison terms for heroin sellers upon conviction. 3) Collective bargaining rights for public school teachers. 4) Plug income tax loophole that helped Governor Reagan in 1970. 5) Permits girls under the age of 18 to get birth control without parents' consent. 6) Unemployment benefits $90 to $104 per week. Contributions paid by employers increased $600,000,000 yearly. 7) Spanking in schools stopped without parent approval. 8) Medical malpractice reform to avoid doctors' strikes. 9) Employees rights to see file held by employer at convenient time. 10) Allows pharmacists to substitute generic drugs for name brands as a cost-saving measure. 11) Ban the sale of flip top beverages after 1979. 12) Repeal of fair trade laws excepting alcoholic beverages. 13) Prohibit denial of credit on the basis of sex or marital status. 14) Requires honoring martin Luther King Jr. on his birthday in the school system. 15) Board of Governors public access to meeting and expand members to five non-lawyers. 16) Opens PUC to public when they meet. 17) Protects citizens from inaccurate credit reports and agencies. 18) Creates the State Public Defenders office ($42,500 salary). 19) Repeals law that distinguishes between legitimate and illegitimate.

Under vetoed legislation, he vetoed a bill that would increase the alcohol sales tax by thirty-four million dollars. This is his record. There is more but it would be voluminous.

Reacting to the Little Hoover commission on its criticism of nursing home management problems, Jerry Brown essentially said with mobility of society and the expanded expectation of the state oversight, there was to be an increase of taxes. This follows Galbraith's theory of a consuming society. Police and regulatory forces cost money and therefore more taxes, according to Governor Brown. He further stated, "If not, expect imperfections and mishandling of the system."

In 1976, Jerry Brown made his bid for the Democratic nomination. He placed fourth, behind Jimmy Carter, Senator Humphrey and George Wallace. Though he had no national campaign, he had national recognition. His premise for running: no candidate will win the election during the primaries. He predicted a brokered convention. He thought potential victors could be Senator Humphrey or Senator Edward M. Kennedy of Massachusetts. He thinks he will be chosen after several ballots. At 37, he thinks his running is a fresh direction.

Bill 17 sets up a change in the rules of the game. Doctors and dentists will be allowed to advertise and independent oversight boards to give the public a say so in the purchase of health services. Ralph Nader is on board on this one.

Mervin Dymally, Lieutenant Governor would be acting governor when Jerry Brown was out of state. He would have a substantial role in the campaign. Again Brown seemed extremely popular.

In 1975, after one year in office, Jerry Brown had the following programs in place: Farm workers get jobless benefits (unemployment insurance), the services of a public defender were now available for higher cases of appeal.

The following is an example of the Brown Administration attitude to the legislature. October 23, 1975, Senate bill 852, known as the Information Practices Act was vetoed at the last moment by the governor. It was referred to as the Moscone-Carpenter Privacy Bill. It was designed after the federal statute from the Ford Administration two minutes before the deadline. Brown vetoed it. His reasoning, "I will support a bill in the next session to accomplish this purpose of this measure without the attendant problems that the administration believes are unworkable." Moscone theorized that Brown was opposed to that segment of the bill that set up a committee in the process. Attempts to explain the bill to the governor were met with the argument of lack of time and a phone call was suggested.

In figuring out the Brown psyche you must look to his words. October 20, 1974: "You know what is this thing you know, giving a smile to every person you meet? Is that a relationship that's honest? You create a face just to put everyone off. But these politicians you think you know so well. You don't know them at all. I think you just see a face, a mask, and what's that? That tells you nothing." Brown held the belief that his troubles with the legislature stem from his strict enforcement of election laws, dating to his time as Secretary of State.

He claimed a relationship with three legislators, Leo T. McCarthy, Democrat, San Francisco, Howard L. Berman, Democrat, Los Angeles, and David A. Roberti, Democrat, Los Angeles. He did admit, "I change. I admit sometimes I'm up and sometimes I'm down."

He added, "I don't believe in the politics of personality, I think that was the fundamental mistake of the 1960's: the cult of personality. I think we have to deal with ideas and think of the parties as having an agenda and responsibility." His view of reporters digging into personalities of those in government is irrelevant. I think I can see why he was called the Guru Governor.

In March of 1978 Brown proposed at Union Plaza in Los Angeles a subsidized housing benefit for low and middle income groups. His vision was to build a 157 acre downtown LA renovation of existing structures and the construction of new housing. He had the funding of 300,000,000 dollars. It encompassed 45 specific action programs. It must be remembered this is the time he was running for president.

The CDC endorsed Brown by 82%. The gay community decided not to oppose Brown, but did not support him, because he did not stand more strongly behind their cause. Mervin Dymally, his Lieutenant Governor, got 87.2%. The stats were given by Gray Davis, his campaign manager.

Brown's overall rating as governor was 29%, similar to Governor Reagan's rating of 28% at the end of their respective terms.

To summarize all of this, Jerry Brown became our first Guru Governor. He employed such people as Gray Davis as his top aide. As you well know, Gray Davis became governor of the state when he defeated Wilson, one of our more hated governors. Pete basically did just get a bad rap. He also made a few unfortunate decisions, but that is a later story. As a result of a recall petition, Mr. Davis was removed from office and Arnold Schwarzenegger succeeded him. This seems like small potatoes now. Going back to Brown, Gray Davis suggested he use a small Middle American car as a symbol of frugality in government. This idea was later used by Jimmy Carter. The Sacramento Zen Center was his source of spiritual enlightenment. The diamond lanes came into existence in the Brown Administration. Initially they were a fiasco. Jerry had trouble with the bussing issue, and was viewed as anti-bussing.

The Zen Center was in the rundown black section, and shared the neighborhood with the Simbianese Liberation Army. This is where Jerry tried to get in touch with the needs of the minorities and the poor. He was always on the lookout for new ideas. Governor Brown monopolized people's lives, and many quit after one year. Pat Brown, his father and former governor - who was succeeded by the actor-politician, Ronald Reagan, who in turn became president - was a powerful ally.

To give you an idea, where his head was at: Health and Welfare Secretary, was Mario Obledo, son of immigrants. As a lawyer, he championed the Chicanos and the poor.

Decision making had its reflections in the Zen Center, for, in an aide's words, it was as follows: "Jerry likes the Zen Center because it's a place where people can go and meet and discuss things like the 19$^{th}$ century in a coffee house setting. He obviously was fascinated with Eastern forms of thinking." He continued, "And what does Brown discuss? Neighborhood foundation, parks, the Pink Palace, the tenant association, crime, and basically interests of the governor."

Former Governor Pat Brown went into the oil business, as did a lot of people. When Brown, the son wanted to import oil into California, he was accused of collusion in the family business. His defense was that if anything, it was more difficult for his family, and he wished the business did not exist. Brown Senior called the attacks on his son some of the most vicious he has ever seen. An April 26, 1978 Jerry Brown turned forty.

Since this was the second time Jerry had run for the office, light was shone on his 1976 attempt, and a figure of 104 thousand dollars. Brown came back that most of the debt had been settled to the dollar.

The hyperbole had been applied to Brown for roughly three and one half years. The Brown camp made a decision to use the airwaves to counteract the art of negative politics. It was hoped by this strategy the heat would be put on the Republicans.

Pat Brown, a two-term governor who tried to run a third time when he lost to Ronald Reagan, pointed out that the longer you are in politics, the more enemies you get, and the other side of the equation, the more friends you disappoint. Some could question the validity of his assessment.

Governor Jerry Brown celebrated the fiftieth birthday of the State Park System sitting with Pat Brown, and pledged to expand the 240 sites that encompass

855,000 acres, and to expand and make them more and make them more easily accessed by the public. I wish again to point out this is at a time when he is running for president.

On May 22, 1978 he started a media blitz. As I said, he was looking to silence those who opposed him for the position of governor in the primary. They were Attorney General Evell Younger, Fresno Assemblyman Ken Maddy and retired Police Chief Edward M. Davis.

Brown's position on Proposition 8 is favorable, for it gives those whose property was not assessed a 40% reduction. Those who get a 50% would net out even. Senior citizens who earn $8,000 a year would do much better under 8 as opposed to 13. Renters would get $275 under 8, and nothing under 13. He called Jarvis and 13 a fraud.

When July came, there was a reversal. Evell Younger had a medical problem with his kidneys and had to go to Hawaii for treatment. In his absence, Jerry Brown made hay and supported Proposition 13. No one knew the Younger position, let alone Younger. Critics argued he could alienate his liberal base. Looking to the 1980 presidential election, if Brown won re-election, which he did, he could be a threat to Carter. By June the numbers favored Brown 50% to Carter's 41% with 9% undecided. In terms of executive-legislative public approval, Brown had a 45% favorable rating, to 29% unfavorable.

With the passage of Proposition 13 and the voluntary rent rollback, till January 1, landlords were raising rent in violation of Proposition 13. If voluntary compliance does not happen, legislation would make it happen.

Allen E. Rothenberg, then the vice president of Bank of America in San Francisco, associated with the Zen Center took a position I n Brown's cabinet, only to quit 15 days later. He stated, "I like Jerry Brown, but I have a three year old daughter and a wife I like better."

Gray Davis and Jacques Barzagi were the two most influential men in the Brown Administration. According to sources, Barzagi was not the Rasputin the press has made him out to be.

The state legislature, after ten years decided to increase salaries in 1977. Brown promised a veto even if his salary increase were deleted. Here are the figures that were involved: $49,100 to $65,000 for the Governor: Superintendent of Public Instruction, $35,000 to $50,000: Attorney General, $42,500 to $62,935. This figure was similar to the salary of an associate member of the State Supreme Court. You can see the conflict of interest in the state at this time.

The Unitary Tax became an issue. Japanese businessmen did not like the structure and considered it unfair. Brown proposed changes in the system to reflect the complaints and encourage foreign business to come here. In 1978 Jerry was due for re-election. Naturally this concept was opposed by the Republicans.

Brown saw the urban spread to the rural areas was a bad idea. He tried to redirect State resources. He talked of sharing property and sales tax revenues within a single metropolitan region by limiting freeway construction. He hoped to centralize populations. This obviously did not work.

The estimate of a 2 billion dollar surplus by 1978 shows how well he understood economic growth in the state for at least this period in our history. In this package, home owners get relief through 1975. This would have been during Reagan's time as governor.

Wall Street and utility companies were pushing for a LNG plant, to be paid for by a tariff to avert shortages in the state by 1985. Brown opposed the use of public capital for the construction of the plant. He said it would blur the lines between private and public. The reality was there was no shortage of natural gas in 1985, even without the construction of the plant.

Brown had a strong disagreement over his conservative management style. He wanted in place a 1 billion dollar hedge against the need for new taxes and potential economic downturn. These were not to be touched. The AFL-CIO contended this was too conservative an approach, but agreed on the need for a natural gas terminal to prevent job loss.

Brown was slated to meet with President Carter over his energy plan to use coal, of which there were substantial deposits in both the east and Midwest, and to draw down on the use of coal and natural gas projects. He even talked about trade with Asia, and the Panama Canal.

## 115. PRESIDENT JIMMY CARTER 1977

President Carter, at his 100 day mark made initial efforts to know the world leaders and establish his brand of diplomacy on the world stage, but at home achieved marginal results. At the 100 day mark he had a 41% approval rating. 57% rated him fair to poor.

The long-promised urban policy had its hang-ups. The philosophy of not spending money, but through manage assets was hitting a dead end. His critics stated he failed to grasp the needs of people living in the urban environment. For Carter, the presidency was a learning process. On the international stage, his brand seemed slow to catch on.

President Jimmy Carter had an approach to Eastern Europe that was split, should it be through the Soviet Union, or a country by country basis. This goes back to the 1968 Soviet invasion of Czechoslovakia that was referred to as socialism with a human face. Poland and Hungary had a special niche, for their relationship had developed between these two countries and us. Carter's view of Hungary ran like this: "The Administration views the action of the Hungarian Government in the field of family reunification as progressive." According to Cyrus Vance, "Obviously the action taken in this area is positive in relationship between our two countries, and I think helps to facilitate the atmosphere in which we discuss the whole range of problems, and the issues that our two nations will be dealing with." Church-State relations were cited as an example as it relates to the 60% Catholic population and smaller Protestant group (Lutheran). There was an 80 to 100,000 Jewish population at the time. In 1944 the United States held the symbol of Hungarian Royalty, because of the Soviet invasion. It had been stated at the time that the road to better relations with East Germany, Czechoslovakia and Bulgaria have a long way to go. Human rights violations are a key reason for this long path.

It is not that Carter did not put forth an effort, for in his own words, "I came to Washington the first time just about a year ago. I had to do hundreds of hours of study about history and present circumstances concerning the Middle East, Africa, Latin America, Panama, SALT, comprehensive test ban treaties, test ban responsibilities ahead of those responsibilities to the Democratic committee. I don't think I have the support that I needed from the White House."

We have to remember the election of President Carter to his position was, in a way, a knee jerk reaction to the Nixon years. For this reason, he can't be faulted for the learning process.

Statements of public record did draw some concern. "I would like to go out of office at the end of four years with the same cabinet I have now." Think of it this way: he could not have meant he did not intend to seek a second term. He seemed to behave more like a manager-balancer than a leader.

This harkens back to the Nixon proposal of wage and price controls to control the inflation that was rampant at this time, and during the Nixon years. Carter favored voluntary controls, with wages and prices limiting their expansion. Control your greed. This was coupled with lower expectations and conservation.

The president proposed a 400 million dollar incentive to promote minority employment in urban job programs, but at this point in time did not have the specifics.

One consistent theme in all administrations seems to be an anti-protectionist stand, and at the same time, not a free trade policy, but a fair trade policy.

On income tax, the Carter plan for 1979 was a 23 billion dollar income tax cut, 17 billion going to individuals and 6 billion going to business. "The key to success in our international economic policy can promote the economic health of the world with fair and balanced agreements, lowering barriers of trade.

Tracing problems back to the oil embargo of 1973, referring to the congressional deadlock of his first 100 days and the conflicts of interest over energy policy and legislation, and recognizing the limits of the congressional process that unfortunately ended in a deadlock and a failure to produce an energy program after five years, Carter stated, "We have failed the American people."

In all of this Carter maintained that having restored moral standards to our domestic economic scene, we have in this last year restored our moral foreign policy.

In defense of his position on the Panama Canal treaty he stated, "Open always and the United States retains the right to defend the canal with our military forces if necessary, to guarantee its openness and neutrality. The treaties are to the clear advantage of ourselves, the Panamanians, and other users of the canal."

## 1978

President Carter had a farm subsidy policy that he contended was in the interest of protecting the farm system in this country. Some equated it with welfare and unjustified expense. Now remember back to Eisenhower and his refusal to follow the think tank on eliminating the farm subsidy. The family farm is subsidized in all countries. Carter continued, "What's best for the farmers in the long run is best for the consumers." I might add to that statement, the security of the nation.

During the State of the Union message to Congress, he pointed to the declining inflation rate, the creation of jobs, and a two trillion dollar economy. Under points he covered on energy policy, despite the 1973 oil embargo and non-use of our natural resources, I just ask the question, why did we not look to coal, our biggest asset at that time? Under this topic he stated the economy must expand to create new jobs. Private enterprise, not government must be the engine of job growth. (This is sounding amazingly Republican.) We must lower the rate of inflation and keep it down, and lastly, we must contribute to the strength of the whole world's economy. Seventeen billion dollars will go to individuals, which breaks down to $250 per family. On corporate taxes, there will be a $2,000,000,000 decrease in the excise tax. On employment, through the public works service program with a doubled budget, more minorities will be given an opportunity for a better job and get off welfare. His main emphasis still lay in private business. Pointing out the increasing portion of the budget of the GDP, this budget has only a small increase. High unemployment does not stop inflation. The solution is managed by government policy seeing to it that companies don't raise prices on an anticipated demand. Wage increases against future costs, based on no sound principle should be discouraged. According to Carter, that is how you fight inflation. He made no mention on the size and nature of business. (Holding, companies.)

Under undue influence on government via 500 lobbying boards, the Carter Administration is bound to reduce the influence of such bureaucracies on the process in Washington. He is referring to all those back-loaded interests that put riders on the bills passed in the people's business. President Carter had an interest in putting the U.S. as a strong supporter of human rights. In his mind's eye, other nations were beginning to move the way of the United States.

President Carter looked to the idea of the peaceful use of the atom, and control, if not elimination of nuclear weapons from the earth. This proved to be unduly optimistic.

The following speech given by President Jimmy Carter was given at the first State of the Union address, and sounded remarkably similar to Barry Goldwater's speech where he was booed. "We must seek fresh answers unhindered by stale prescriptions of the past. Government cannot solve all our problems, set all our goals or define our vision. Government cannot eliminate poverty, provide a bountiful economy, reduce inflation, save our cities, cure illiteracy, provide energy or mandate goodness. A true partnership between government and the people can reach these goals." This was the logic of 1978.

Like Truman and Nixon before him, President Carter used the Taft-Hartley Act with the United Mine Workers Union after they rejected an arbitration agreement which the head of the Union endorsed. President Arnold Miller, then head of the union stated, "I've tried everything to keep this from happening, but the divisive people in the union got out and distorted this contract so that our members did not understand it. Any action on the part of the government will cause some violence in the coal field."

The reason Carter thought action was necessary was the shortages of coal that were being experienced throughout the country. Potomac Edison and Monongahela Power Company in West Virginia had a 25% cutback in services. It was feared that reduced coal delivery could trigger layoffs.

One of the top union leaders, Floyd Lamb stated, "When Taft-Hartley was applied before, our men didn't go back to work. You can't shovel coal with a piece of paper. You cannot shovel coal with a bayonet. That doesn't have seemed to have changed at all."

Under other opinions, Dennis Scarford, who served as Secretary Treasurer stated, "Once they go back I wouldn't promise there would be much production, but they'll get back on the job. It comes down to if they're willing to take a chance on going to jail, and I don't think they'll take that chance."

Note it did not work for Truman or Nixon, and it did not work for Carter, either. Reagan used it some years later on the Air Traffic Controllers with similar negative effects on the industry and transportation safety, not to mention a reduction in manpower due to people leaving the industry.

One of President Carter's first natural disasters was along the coast of Los Angeles County, where homes were about to lose their foundations and there was flooding. Jerry Brown, who happened to be Governor of California at the time called for federal aid to help the residents of Malibu as the high surf ate away the California beaches. The breakers ran from four to six to ten feet high. Many homes did meet the surf. The swift San Gabriel River claimed one life with its ferocity.

President Carter had empathy for the poor. He chastened the legal profession for catering to the well-off, less to the poor. "We have over layered and under represented. When a poor family is cheated by a merchant, unfairly threatened with eviction, falsely accused of a crime, it can rarely take advantage of skilled legal talent at reasonable rates. Adequate legal help is often beyond the reach of most middle class as well." The president left the stage with a polite ovation.

Comments by members of the profession in the audience, "We are surprised when he accuses us of resisting innovation. This is particularly astonishing when in view of the fact that we are due to meet next Wednesday at the White House on establishing the Center for Defense Services to help the poor accused of crime." It appears Carter was jumping the gun.

I have a time warp for you. The postal rate stood at 15 cents to mail a letter. The average salary was fifteen thousand a year. Postal workers do not have the right to strike. Your average worker at this point in history was getting five dollars and fifty-one cents an hour. Postal workers made eight dollars an hour. Robert Straus was the councilor on inflation. The postal workers' contract was due to expire on July 20, 1978. The President proposed a 5.5% increase in prices. We still had the concept of an economic ceiling on the rise in prices. We still had the concept of an economic ceiling as under Nixon in a peacetime economy.

Under upcoming labor disputes is the Railroad Workers Union, 450,000 workers who had a pay rate of $7.75 an hour. This rate was 20% above the wages of railroad workers a decade ago. Meat prices had gone up forty-one percent in the first quarter. The AF of L had signed an agreement lowering labor costs in 11 southern states. The effect of the agreement was to standardize overtime rates.

On the issue of the TWA and the Clinch breeder-reactor, the president opposed potential weapon use. Use of solar power to power whole cities was mentioned, but considered impractical. We are just today, in 2009 implementing solar panels.

Carter's Middle East foreign policy was put in jeopardy by the proposed arms sale, the sale of F15's and F16's to Saudi Arabia, Israel and Egypt. A non-sale would put those countries in jeopardy.

Senator George C. McGovern had these observations of the Carter Administration: "He hadn't lived up to the promises he has made. He is the most conservative Democratic president since Grover Cleveland."

## 117. September 12

Jack Anderson and his poison pen tried to pin an apparent non-extradition of Robert Vesco on the Carter Administration and how it pressured Costa Rica to expel him instead. Where he settled would be hopefully extraditable. Anderson had charged it was a ten million dollar bribe. A little background on the Vesco case: He fled to Latin America and stated he could get favorable terms on the Panama Canal Treaty that was under negotiation. He had contracted Hamilton Jordan and Charles Kirbo, along with Cyrus Vance. On review of documents, overtures were rejected and his extradition had not been set aside.

When President Carter used the Taft-Hartley Act against the Railroad Union Workers, the Union filed with the courts a document stopping the railroads from doing reprisals against the workers involved in the threatened action actual strike activity. On Tuesday the unions struck Southern Pacific, Union Pacific, Amtrak and other lines in California. The strike could be ended with emergency board procedures. Picketing was extended to eight more railroads and affected 52 lines.

Carter vetoed a water works bill, saying, "It is important that I and the Congress set an example for the rest of the nation in controlling inflation, and this public works bill is exactly the wrong example." The result was the 10.1 billion dollar water construction bill was vetoed.

Wage-price controls were initiated on salaries, restricting increases to 7% yearly. Persons making four dollars an hour were exempt.

McGary was a member of the Federal Election Commission, and was replaced by Staebler. The former refused to leave, and went to the courts to block the president's action. Staebler could sit in the room but not vote. He had not completed the 1976 election report. Remember, this was 1978.

By November 2nd, the president was in Chicago to shore up his alliances with the machine. He visited with Mayor Michael A. Bilandic and other ward officials such as Senator Richard M Daly, who used to control the machine but had risen like the cream of the crop. They were all part of the strategy.

President Jimmy Carter, addressing the world and domestic concerns of world leaders concerning the continuing slide of the dollar, that at this time had lost 27% of its value, acted to enact mandatory price controls, largely because his voluntary approach had not been working. The U.S. dollar lost: West German mark, 27%, Japanese yen, 38%, and the world thought we were not serious about cutting back on oil consumption. The administration had argued we were helping the international economy by buying energy commodities and other goods. (Apparently not.) Now think to Obama's strategy on balanced trade with a declining economy. Now think about the business interests of Carter's time that were thumbing their collective noses at Carter's voluntary efforts, and again do the math.

Though it was understood candidate Carter conducted unofficial research into his support in New Hampshire delegates on how they felt, his most serious opponent was Senator Kennedy of Massachusetts, who was pushing for a comprehensive health care program. Hamilton Jordon urged support for the President and his policies.

Other candidates included Jerry Brown of California, who had not formally declared. Others were Senator Henry M. Jackson of Washington, and Representatives Morris K. Udall of Arizona, both of whom were candidates in 1976, and still harbored some ambitions.

Vice President Mondale stated, "It is not just the domestic programs that will be annualized, so will the defense budget. Don't worry about the passion of this President. President Carter wants to succeed. He wants a compassionate human nation."

Concerning the economies of this administration, as opposed to the liberal plank, Hamilton Jordon stated, "I understand your concerns, but you have to have some trust and confidence in the President. Don't tie your hands with this resolution, "when the delegation asked if their vote would affect the congress. They continued to support the administration budget-cutting efforts.

Responding to the reaction on the economic resolution of the Carter Administration, an aide said, "A catch-all for those delegates who were teed off about anything else, people who didn't get a chance to speak, or who didn't like our policies. It gave them a chance to stick it to us." The platform of the President was adopted with resistance.

Senator Proxmire, member of the housing, banking and urban affairs committee stated that no matter how lean the military budget the president submits, it will be cut. The military budget has a ten point eight percent increase overall for 1980. (Billion.)

Senator Joseph A. Califano was pushing a Carter-backed universal health plan. This is as of March 29, 1979. It would have had 60 to 90 days. It would have been universal health care, starting date 1982. Coverage would have basically been for the elderly and the poor. Note he did not say the children. In the early stages, there would be catastrophic coverage for all citizens. (10 to 15 billion dollars a year would have been the initial cost. Private employers would have been hit with the 2–3 billion dollar cost annually.)

Remember the old Soviet Union and its battle for Afghanistan? Well, Cyrus Vance negotiated with then foreign minister Andre A. Gromyko over the issue of withdrawal from Afghanistan. He also covered the importance of a neutralist government. The reason for the visit was the pending death of Tito. What was then the common market was very concerned about the issue.

On November 4, 1980, with the fall of the Shah of Iran, Mohammed Reza Pahlavi, the rise of the Ayatollah Ruhallah Khomeini led to the seizing of the U. S. Embassy and the Marines that were inside as war criminals. They were paraded through the street and were threatened to be put on trial. The issue was brought before the United Nations to resolve the issue and the release of our hostages. The issue was being debated by the U. N. (November 16, 1980.)

President Carter reached the decision to sell to Egypt and Saudi Arabia, and not compromise our support for Israel. Carter made a reference to the iron triangle of bureaucracies: "Congressional committees, well-organized special interest groups who can mobilize a strong opposition to the reforms we need, President Carter: Too many agencies doing too many things, overlapping too often, coordinating too rarely, wasting too much money and doing too little to solve real problems."

Curbing spending was the main attack of the Carter Administration. He wanted to hold federal spending to 40 billion dollars, as opposed to sixty billion dollars. Federal Reserve Chairman William G. Miller linked the size of the budget deficit to the interest rates. Miller wanted the deficit reduced to or below fifty billion dollars until a balanced budget could be attained in 1982. "If inflation continues at seven per cent there is not much any of us can do to bring down interest rates."

Let's jump to 2009 with the low interest rates and still-declining economy with continued job loss, and compare tactics used in our current economic disaster. This will follow later.

One of Carter's interests was water projects, including dredging the Los Angeles River, and Long Beach Harbor to a depth of 45 feet, courtesy of the Army Corps of Engineers, a flood channel for Gollita Valley and Santa Barbara County. There was an irrigation and water construction project in San Diego County. Note the state that took these projects. Now reflect on Carter's statement on special interest groups.

Back to the postal service and the use of federal troops to deliver the mail, as did President Truman. This was a bargaining chip to hold a multitude of things in mind. Other industries involved in negotiation this given year included paper, cement, retail/food, airlines and construction, all pressure points in 1978.

On arms control and the nuclear question, President Carter negotiated with the Soviet Union military ground forces parity concerning the nations of Eastern Europe. The Soviets, with 950,000 troops would have to draw down troop levels to 700,000. This was the first time the Soviets accepted the concept in principle. On the nuclear question, India accepted the principle of the peaceful use of the atom, since it exploded in 1974. Desai, India's Prime Minister conferred on this matter with President Carter.

Midterm elections have resulted in the loss of power at the Congressional end. The losses are evenly divided. The numbers are roughly like this:

| Year | President | Losses | Seats |
| --- | --- | --- | --- |
| 1946 | Truman | 32 losses, | 54 seats |
| 1950 | Truman | 43 losses, | 29 seats |
| 1954 | Eisenhower | 65 losses, | 18 seats |
| 1958 | Eisenhower | 56 losses, | 47 seats |
| 1962 | Kennedy | 67 losses, | 04 seats |
| 1966 | Johnson | 48 losses, | 48 seats |
| 1970 | Nixon | 56 losses, | 12 seats |
| 1974 | Nixon | 31 losses, | 44 seats |

President Carter complained of loss of Presidential power. The Supreme Court stripped the administrative appointees of absolute immunity and the ability to enforce law was limited to congressional oversight. Carter lamented the loss of the ability to do his job.

Carter relied heavily on Zbigniew Brzezinski over Cyrus Vance, who was the Secretary of State. This caused friction between the head of the National Security Staff and the State Department. This kind of contradiction defined the Carter years.

The main reason Carter had trouble with his staff was second-level appointments who felt no loyalty to the President. He did not want to give the perception of President Nixon's phobia that led to his downfall. Carter got a lot of people with their 60's mentality among his appointees.

Carter believed in deregulation, at least as far as new natural gas was concerned. There was to be a gradual rise in the cost till 1985, when it would be deregulated.

The Jones Bill was a 16.2 billion dollar tax bill that benefitted homeowners and 2 billion dollars in the reduction in the capital gains tax. It applied a maximum rate of 35% on the sale of stocks and other investments, according to the *L.A. Times*. The Jones Bill brackets $15,000 - $40,000 in contrast to Carter's bill that gave breaks to those $20,000 and under. 10.5 billion For individual income tax cuts. The Republicans wanted a $90 billion three year tax program. The personal exemption would go to $1,000 from $750. There would be a $2,300 personal exemption for singles and $3,400 for married couples. This was the bill Carter was going to veto.

## 118. 2013 (Part two)

The following section resembles a daily log of thought on any number of subjects related to state and national interests. Again, it is like having a conversation with a friend on national dialogue. It is also organized in the light of the day in which it was written.

Our taxation credits $116 billion in new tax credits, $400 per individual with an increase for 2009, double that for married couples. Under the alternative minimum tax, 70 billion dollars for 24 million taxpayers would, in 2009, save $2,300. There would be an expanded college tax credit for tuition for 2009 through 2010. There would be $20 billion all for alternative renewable energy incentives for ten years, covering all alternative sources from solar energy, including insulation and hybrids.

On mortgage failures, homes, August 30 must be held by the bank for three years. $6.6 billion, or $8,000 per household.

## 119. THE FIRE SEASON DOWN UNDER

Melbourne and Victoria are in a severe drought, and as a result experienced severe fires resulting in over 180 deaths. People living in the towns are trained to fight such fires. The fires were suspiciously arson-related. Controlled brush fires had wiped out towns and villages.

## 120. ON POLITICS
January 22, 2009

Under the ends of dynasties, Caroline Kennedy has removed herself from contention for Hillary Clinton's Senate seat. Governor David A. Patterson stated she was never in contention, and he nominated a senior member of the lower house, also a woman. There is no blame, there is just the process.

## 121. THE MIDDLE EAST

Israel is doing damage control. In the end, Israel is looking for agreements to prevent weaponry from reaching HAMAS. It is interesting that IRA representatives have been training HAMAS fighters. It is in the evolving nature of these groups like Schinn Fein in Ireland that lead eventually to peace accords in Oslo. Still, we must remember the dead and injured. There were 13,000 dead in Gaza. The most recent incident casualties total 420 children and 104 women. I don't know what the future brings, but what have we wrought?

## 122. ON THE PRESIDENT

When now-President Barak Obama spoke to the American people it was televised all around the world. The Chinese even saw it, translated, of course. They edited his speech. Any derogatory comments on the social struggle of Communism were censored. There was a point in the speech where the analyst was forced to make things up, and she was hard pressed to do so.

## 123. BACK TO THE MIDDLE EAST

In Kurdistan in the northern section of Iraq, assassinations have taken a toll on elected officials in cities like Mossel. The Mayor has lost five members of his family. He leaves office with mixed resolve, looking at himself as a buffer. He leaves for a safe zone in Kurdistan.

## 124. ON APPOINTMENTS

Barak has Hillary Clinton as his Secretary of State. Her vote was delayed a day as a courtesy to the Republican minority. Obama has put restrictions on those that were lobbyists who join the administration for the duration of his presidency. If this holds, it would be as step in the right direction.

Bush Administration in its last days deleted powers from the EPA and forest service. Now President Obama reversed that direction.

## 125. OBAMA ON EXECUTIVE COMPENSATION

The Obama Administration took issue with this corporate practice as counter-productive to our recovery. I have pointed out that these corporations, regardless of their excuse, have no social conscience. Their mentality is the bottom line. This is especially true when corporations are losing money and laying off people. Sorry, Obama, this is the nature of a corporation that has outgrown its responsible stage. Some have gone as far as ordering private jets for their companies: this while asking for a public bailout. Obama is pissed.

## 126. BLAGOJEVICH

The Senate and the House of the State of Illinois has finally axed the rogue governor. By this joint action of impeachment, so ends the great circus and its showman. The lieutenant governor will take the oath of office.

### 127. CORPORATE LAYOFFS

More corporations are proceeding with layoffs and plant closings. Wall Street continues to laugh. Obama is pushing for regulations. This new struggle for Corporate America and Government is intertwined. Caterpillar is the latest: 20,000 jobs lost in the first quarter.

### 128. JUST HOW COLD IS IT
January 29-30, 2009

Back East and, ironically, in the South, due to the cold, power outages have reached emergency proportions. We are talking 6 degrees or lower. When power outages occur they have community shelters. You lack the basic amenities that make up life. There is no privacy, but you May get warmer.

### 129. IRAQ AND POTENTIAL ELECTIONS

In Iraq regional elections are scheduled for today. There are 14,000 candidates and a multiplicity of Parties. This time around the Sunnis are involved for a piece of the pie. This time around there are names and faces connected with parties. The platform of the parties centers on basic services and job growth. The educated and uneducated are fighting their way from the bottom. The difference is their doing it through the ballot box this time.

### 130. THE STIMULUS PACKAGE

The oil companies had a profit of $45.2 Billion dollars in profit. I hope they don't show up on Washington's doorstep. The goal is to help middle level families who work for the corporations and they are losing their jobs. Do you see the problem? Another focus is at middle level business you need the method of controlled cash rebates.. You need mid-level tax incentives, in the energy and service field, even small manufacturing but not to be used for the benefit of major corporations. They will receive the residual from this growth. The price tag is a big $819 Billion Dollars. Senators have added Pork to this bill.

### 131. THE EMPLOYMENT ISSUE
February 2, 2009

The EDD is facing massive filing of appeals for extensions of benefits. The current backlog is 40%. Seventy-eight Million is the annual budget funded largely by the federal government. The chief administrator has been fired. Only a small percentage of the cases have been resolved. The government of California, Governor Arnold Schwarzenegger has proposed a blanket amnesty in what is generally a gnarly mess. Remember they urge you to quit, because it looks better on your job application. Remember we live in a corporate minded economy.

### 132. THE MORTGAGE ISSUE

The mortgage melt-down has hit Beverly Hills. Property values have hit a 30% decline. Even the nuveau rich are starting to be hit where it counts. The stock market continues to systematically slide.

### 133. BACK TO THE MIDDLE EAST
February 4, 2009

Remember the truce in the Gaza, well HAMAS has been firing rockets across the border killing three Israelis. They were obviously bad shots. Well Israel attacked HAMAS much more affectively and the Egyptians are forced to step in diplomatically.

### 134. CRITICISM
February 4, 2009

Former Vice President Dick Cheney has warned that the actions of the administration will lead to a post 9/11 attack, greater than in 2001. He criticized the closing of Guantanamo and basically said time will prove the Bush administration was correct. History often has it's parting shots.

### 135. DEFAULT

Senator Tom Daschle has withdrawn from consideration for the post of Secretary of Commerce. He did not want to cause a rift in the developing Barak H Obama Administration.

### 136. MORE ON JOB LOSS

500,000 jobs have been lost so far this year as the politicians argue over what does and what does not do the trick. CEOs have corporations that have asked for aid due to losses, will be restricted as to raises not in excess of 500,000. They are still conducting a fire sale.
One interesting note change in the way we get our energy, but we are not making the product. G E is the only American company so far in this industry. There is

room for competition. Grants and loans should be made to a market for wind and solar within American companies.

### 137. OBITUARIES

James Whitmore has passed. He immortalized Harry Truman and Will Rodgers. He joins the likes of Spencer Tracy who immortalized Hemingway's Old Man and the Sea. I speak of giants and it is sad to say there are few of those giants today.

### 138. THE MIDDLE EAST

Vigdor Lieberman a marginal far right politician is becoming centrist. With the shrinking Jewish population, the drive to keep the secular nature of Israel itself. His words are being heeded.

### 139. JOB LOSS UPDATE

The revised figure of job losses for the first quarter stand at 598,000. The argument on Capitol Hill over 85 billion in pork. By Pork I mean good things that don't stimulate the economy. This is what plagued the Reagan Administration. Money for the banks is still there. The corporations still have their hands out. There is a stimulus for middle business including green business. But it does not go far enough.

### 140. THE REPUBLICANS

Senator John McCain has inherited the banner of the Republican Party and the opposition to the Obama Stimulus package on the grounds that it is excessive. And does not accomplish the needed results.

### 141. ON THE HEALTH ISSUE

More on the peanut butter issue, and the FDA response. The company lies to the government on checking for contamination. What was the name of the company (Peanut Company of America). They followed the tradition of Monsanto to the tee. Their doors are now closed. Contamination spread to dog biscuits snacks and related products in 43 states.

### 142. SRI LANKA

The dilemma of Sri Lanka is militarily they have shrunk the area controlled by the Tamil to 100 miles from 2000 miles. The problem is they failed to integrate the Tamil people into society. They remain second class citizens. After this group is defeated another resistance group could easily take its place. This is the group responsible for the assassination of Indira Gandhi.

## 143. ON THE LIGHTER SIDE

On a lighter note NFL is trying to tap into China. They keep on being blocked but they keep on trying.

## 144. FOREIGN POLICY

President Obama extended the olive branch. The Iranian Parliament extended a branch of thistles. The demand is our admission of our mistake in Iraq and our position on Israel, our apology for and acceptance of Iran as a nuclear power with its usage for peaceful purposes.

## 145. THE TALE OF ANGEL ISLAND

The tale of Angel Island located off the coast of San Francisco. In the 1930s this was the entry and the prison for many Asian immigrants as well as many other nationalities. Poetry and political slogans have been painted over and filled in. The efforts to uncover these written ideas of history are in some cases unrecoverable. Imagine the Chinese culture and the thoughts of those migrants, seeking a new life and refuge from civil conflict. Some had to lie and say their parents were dead. There were: Japanese, Russians, Koreans, that passed through and were denied entry at these gates.

In the 1970s the restoration began. It was like working on a archeological site, with tooth brushes and small rotating tools. The thoughts and the poetry were uncovered along with words of hate and frustration.

The numbers are like this: 120,000 Chinese, 60,000 Japanese, 12,000 Russians, 7,000 South Asians, 1,000 Koreans, with the remaining being 75 different nationalities, all trapped and locked in buildings and chicken wire pleading for resolution.

Why did some lie? Husbands could not bring wives unless you were diplomats. Children could not come with parents. For them to want to be here imagine what home was like.

In 2005 the restoration was in full swing and today people can tour the barracks and with a little soul, feel the souls that passed Through here.

## 146. THE INTERNATIONAL DRUG TRADE
### February 13, 2009

Western Africa has been battling the bulging drug trade without resources. It is only recently that Europe and Britain along with the United States have helped with funds and training from the DEA. African nations as a whole have said, it is not that they lack resolve but the lack of resources to fight the cartels that come from Columbia and Venezuela.

## 147. PAKISTAN

Remember the Drone attacks of the Al Qaeda stronghold. They were stationed in Pakistan attacking the tribal areas. Senator Feinstein blew the whistle on the CIA. And its operation that obviously had the support of the Pakistani government, even after Mushariff. This is despite the complaints on our activities.

It is now official the group that attacked Mumbai came from Karachi Pakistan. The Indian Government is pressuring for extradition of those arrested. Lashkar El Y Taiba is the name of the organization, and it has been outlawed in both India and Pakistan. It has cultural and social extensions that make it difficult to eradicate. To some these are the good guys.

## 148. A SEASON FOR GIVING

Christmas is a major event in this country. It has a economic base that requires people to buy. This source is cultural and even necessary. In Dubai they have a retail holiday where visitors from all around the globe go on a buying spree. It is necessary for the survival of the economy and tax structure. People need a buying giving season. The winter solstice is just that and falls along the lines of Hanukkah and other faiths that have similar holidays. The bottom line is that we have culture tied to economic survival.

## 149. THE WEIRD EXPERIMENT

We are trying to bring Dolphins to the arctic. They have to be put in warm water to revive periodically. These dolphins come from the Atlantic Coast and are primarily warm water. The Humane Society is upset. We are doing strange things.

On flight patterns, tiny song birds are being studied for the great distances they travel and their routes. One of the findings is that these birds fly up to six times faster north as they do going south. (400,660 from the Amazon, to a basin in Pennsylvania). Geo-locaters are placed on the birds. These devices don't seem to interfere, with the birds functions. It is just interesting.

The Autism vaccine and rulings against it were defeated. No links between the Vaccine and the condition were found. Sometimes I think back to Monsanto and I hope this is not the case.

## 150. THE WORLD ECONOMIC CONDITION

The United States security has been linked to the world economic condition.

Failure of that network unleashes those emerging terrorist organizations that wish to alter the current world situation according to the *L.A. Times* Toney Blair stated: "Most likely potential fallout for U.S. interest will involve allies and friends not being able to meet their defense and humanitarian obligations."This leaves the Non-aligned movement with its allies and bank roll. (The new Powers)

## 151. SIDE EFFECTS
### February 14, 2009

    Yesterday the Stimulus package reached its final evolution and California looks to the Feds for assistance. The total package comes to $789,000,000,000. States will receive on the basis of need and growth. $53.6 Billion goes to State stabilization, $12 Billion goes to special education, $13 billion for the nation's neediest children, $106 Billion for general education, and funding national support was $60 Billion. Critics have argued that this belongs to the states. Ever heard of displaced, value deficits. This abstract argument goes like this: India had a famine and the world came to its aid. The food and other aid were distributed in the cities. This caused farmers to leave their land and the farming industry collapsed. The other argument is artificial. Education spending does little in the field of job creation. The real issue here is the denial of funds, solely because of the cancelation of programs. That is what set the states Oregon and California in particular into its current set of troubles. California also had CALPERS related funding problems. The loss to California was $8 Billion. How much and how the states spend the money becomes the issue.

    The State of Washington is set to receive $4.6 Billion due to Federal regulations it has a $6 Billion Dollar shortfall (Deficit).That is how the states of the Union in complying with federal regulations got into the red. This example applies to the state of Idaho. People don't want a new prison built and defeated a bond measure to prove it. Now the stimulus funding builds the prison. I guess they have to leave the prison empty. What fool would do that? The ACLU was becoming involved. The authority to do things is based on a sea of mud.

    Some state Governors were opposed to receiving Stimulus money so it was written into the bill that the legislatures could override the Governor so the interest of the state could be served.

    Oregon needs realignment of a internet exchange so they can turn a landfill into a business center stimulating jobs. There are regions like rural Marian County and the Pee Dee region that were former manufacturing hubs that went south with the economy. Do you rebuild what is lost or save what is? The same argument applies to Detroit.

    The reaction in California, on the negative side: (Remember the India Famine argument.) "Spur permanent growth in government programs and spending that will hamstring future budgets, and plunge our nation into further debt every year. Remember government mandated programs? This quote is from Jerry Luis, Republican of Redlands."What is good depends on where you live."

## 152. THE BREAKDOWN

Here is the money breakdown nationwide: Under spending $67 Billion Dollars extended unemployment benefits. Increase in Food Stamps was $20 Billion Dollars a year. Job training $4 Billion with $3 Billion for temporary welfare payments, $85.7 Billion for infrastructure as in bridges and interstate projects. $24.7 Billion for Amtrak related projects, $8.4 Billion for mass transit, $7.2 Billion for broadband internet service, $4.6 Billion for the Army Corp of Engineers, and $4.2 Billion for repair of Defense facilities, $141.3 Billion for health care. $86.6 Billion for Medicaid related expenses under the Cobra program, $19 Billion to modernize health information technology, (Here is the pork 10 billion dollars for the construction blue print related think tanks. Don't forget the anti-smoking program 1 billion dollars. $8.8 Billion, in block grants to states. $41.2 billion for energy, $11 Billion for a smart energy grid, clean up nuclear production sites. Energy efficiency and clean energy grants 6.3 Billion, $5 Billion to weatherize modest income homes, To improve the efficiency of federal buildings $4.5 Billion, Electric vehicle battery grants $2 Billion (This one why not have a conversion tax exemption.) $87.3 Billion for education: $44.5 Billion for prevention in cuts to school district, 25.2 Billion for No Child Left Behind (This one wouldn't that be covered under the regular budget, 2 Billion for Head Start again the same argument, 9.5 Million for housing, $4 Million for public housing repair, $2 Million for shortfalls in public housing accounts, $1.5 million for Homeless shelters, and note the level of importance paid to this issue. Now think about the people that have fallen between the cracks.

## 153. February 21, 2009

On the nature of man and gold, we ignore the intrinsic value of things and sell our past to be melted down for potential foreign interests. Our major export is scrap metals and plastics just like a mercantile system we are the colony.

## 154. MEDICAL FRONT

Cord blood saved from an infant at birth was used to save the child's life several years later. The enriched antibodies that are a mix of mother and child stimulated the child's immune system.

## 155. THE JUDICIARY

On languages and the court system: currently over 100 language interpreters are employed by and through the court system. There are over 5,000 languages we classify as living. Taking Spanish as an example silence is taken as understanding or mental illness. People come up her to escape the drug war in Latin America. There are Indian languages in Latin America. This is one of those human tragedies that affect history.

### 156. IN THE OOPS COLUMN

One thing the Obama Administration discarded the idea of charging people on the basis of miles traveled. All new vehicles would have been equipped with this device. People would start buying used cars from private parties and that would really hurt auto sales and if they made it mandatory on all vehicles: I can just imagine check points for that purpose. Two states have such a system and they are depressed.

### 157. ON HEALTH CARE

The health care fix will be financed nationally through higher taxes. Remember compulsory health insurance, well it's possible the target is automated records to avoid duplicate procedures. The congress projected the idea for public health insurance competing with private health insurance. At present Obama is not weighing in on the issue. That could be a mistake.

### 158. THE DRUG WAR

South of the border there is a war being wages. The sad thing is the market they supply is us. Families see their members kidnapped especially the landed elite and some of those cases have relatives in the United States and they send their money to their families. Police forces have been compromised. Military has been asked to move in. People have been forced to resign from police positions in order to save lives.

In the United States arrests have been made in connection with this war. So far over 500 individuals are in custody (Sinnaloa Drug Cartel is the main organization presently.

 The bottom line is whether President Chavez of Venezuela support of Columbian Rebels continues to operate in his country. The emptying Mexican villages and other Latin country's that come to the United States and bring with them inadvertently problems of their home land to our home land this will cause a change in the whole continent.

### 159. THE ECONOMY
### February 1, 1996

The Federal Reserve board for the second time in two months lowered interest rates as a preventive measure. The prime rate was lowered one quarter of a percent.

The intended ripple effect was to stimulate, sales from cars to homes. Chairman Alan Greenspan by this action sent signals that further reduction would happen in the coming months. The Dow Jones Industrial Average gained 13.73 points jump the day before.

Sun Won Sohn chief economist at N W Corporation headquartered in Minneapolis stated: "The Fed is concerned about a slowdown. It is not becoming a recession yet, but clearly the risks are on the down side. It was said that the lowering of the rate was largely a symbolic gesture.

### 160. THE Y2K AND NEW ZEALAND

This island nation became the testing ground for the sum of all fears on how computer systems would react to the year 2000. We all know everything went fine, but this island about the size of California had the eyes of the world upon it. They promoted tourism up the rear and put on a show to reflect the thousand year history from the birth of Christ to the modern era.

There was a selfish note here. It was also to get rid of the old jokes about the resettlement of the sheep. They wanted to encourage investment and tourism in this island nation. Ships had to have proper navigational systems before they were allowed into port.. There was an alert out for cyber terrorism, and companies were in touch with their component companies in this island down under. In the end we all survived.

### 161. ROLLING BLACKOUTS
### September 13, 2000

Here in California, especially Southern California we experienced two days of rolling blackouts. Pomona, Claremont, and Montclair were affected from 9:20 to 2:10 PM. 47,000 customers and forty communities were affected.

### 162. THE BLAIR WITCH PROJECT
### March 20, 2001

Hype and the things that make it a success are constantly, changing mode. A thirty-four year old computer whiz was offered $10,000 a week for creating a fake web site concerning the film Blair Witch Project. They threw out all conventional rules and the site exploded along with ticket sales. The movie itself took 1 million dollars to make and grossed 128 million in the first five weeks. The filming techniques were horrible. It was jiggly, but it captured the minds of the movie going audience. The work that was considered extracurricular made him $150,000. He wrote fake articles and used pictures he got from magazines. None of it was true. The movie wasn't even true. So much, for truth.

## 163. THE E BUSINESS
### April 2, 2001

It all started with Y2K and the great fear that the tech world would gobble up the concept of standard industrial production. Companies over-spent by 50% in technology innovated changes. Y2k came and went and with it the tech bubble soon collapsed. Companies still wanted cheap toys but they wanted them cheap.

The reason the Feds lowered the Prime rate, because they feared a slowdown and they wanted to head off a recession. Markets adjust, so do tech companies. On March 8 Intel Corporation announced layoffs of 6% or 5,000 jobs that would simply go away. It also expected a fall of 25% in their profits for the first quarter. Cisco Systems said it would eliminate 3,000 to 5,000 fulltime positions along with 2,500 to 3,000 part time positions and temporary jobs.

All these people that trained and geared their skills to the tech world found themselves in the position of gardeners and minimum wage workers. When asked in 2001 why this was happening, now Edward Yardeni chief investment strategist of Deutche Bank stated: "We simply over invested in technology, over the past decade. Alex Brown in New York stated: "During that time spending on computers and communications equipment grew 50% per year. That's really quite extra ordinary. "He continued to put forth the theory that too much capacity was created. In the real world there was no need for it, so companies had to rethink the bottom line. In part the fault lies with venture capital and investment bankers. Daniel Murphy of Frontegra Growth Fund for North American Capital Management: "There was an enormous amount of capital that was poured into all these companies that were coming. The Y2K bug caused companies to deplete revenues in the tech sector. Now they were lost and people in that field were no-longer needed. People thought that something had fundamentally changed in the economy. The expectations fell as dozens of companies became history. The other affect was that traditional industries felt under siege from the tech companies and finding qualified people an illusory yet defined environment. The good thing is they have time to figure out the environment. The good thing is they have time to figure out where they are going. Add the 9/11 effect and you get more uncertainty.

The E Boom was not understood by those traditional industries. They confused it with E Commerce. E Business is an automated system: that balances ordering inventory, business to business and business to customer relations. It's an enhancement of productivity. E Business in the Health Care Industry helps to streamline things between the doctor, hospital, staff and of course the patient. Up to 10% has been reduced through E Business models. On the retail/ industrial side the supply chain between the manufacturer, transportation, and inventory control right down to the retail.. Think of it as an electronic check and balance.

The information technology worker is still needed. The problem lies in what the companies call: appropriate background. The industry still lobbies for importation of foreign workers because of the shortage of qualified help. In a poll conducted at the time of this article (April 2, 2001) 1,400 chief information officers projected a 21% growth in the market. Eugene Paceell who works with bank brokerages and insurance companies stated: "I have been on the beach for two months and expect to be there for one more month. I've been out of work for more than one month before this."Those that are working are doing agency work.. They state big recruiting efforts have been largely put on pause.

Robert Montgomery Chief Executive Officer of Head-hunters net. Stated: that they are recruiting passive employees." Although many are secure in their current positions, 48% are still looking for a better opportunity and 78% would consider switching jobs today. "Today work or the lack of it is considered commiserate.

## 164. FANTASY GAMES
### April 2, 2001

It seems that one of those side affects we refer to as war relates to sports. Call it an escape. You can put together a football team with the top players of your choice. There is still a bottom line here called profit and usage has reached specific proportions depending on tour interest in the game. Some areas are 54%, and others are 84% as in sports news. To fantasy sports, 13%. You can buy equipment of your favorite team. It is a major industry even in times of high unemployment and a post 9/11 World.

## 165. THE ENERGY CRISIS

California and its projected rolling blackouts have Governor Grey Davis pleading with Washington for help. The argument on capping bills is rejected by the industry, for they say it creates long lines as it did in the gas crisis of 1970. It would create a shortage of supply from the industry end.

In Los Vegas, Nevada where the rate for casinos is 25% attendants are converting to energy saving fluorescent bulbs and time switches, temperature control of rooms that are not being used.

California Edison Company is heading for bankruptcy at this time. Governor Davis is talking about buying the Edison transportation department. This would settle California for years to come. The administration and the utility have worked out several draft agreements. Lake Edison has been under consideration in the courts.

## 166. LINUX/MICROSOFT

Linux services 27% of the industry and Microsoft has 41% of the server and products market. The 24% growth rate on the part of Linux at this time is greater than Microsoft's 20%. What happened next is telling: Computer corporations like IBM, Dell, Compaq, Oracle's 1,SAP R/3 gives Linux a chance for a bigger market share as of 2001. Larry Augustin head of Linux stated: "I think it is fair to say virtually everyone in the Fortune 500 and Fortune 1,000 is experiencing with Linux and are open source software in some way. They were much more willing to go with the younger technology. Larger corporations are going to be much more cautious in where they go. It takes time for technology to move its way in there.

What makes Linux so desirable when you compare it to Microsoft? The explanation goes like this: Linux is what would be called an open system. It is available to anyone who wants it. It should be noted that companies are paying little or nothing to install it. The critics of the system have played the part of doubting Thomas as to this being a selling point. Dick Sullivan from IBM stated: "It is not that the operating system itself is inexpensive, but the real estate it requires from the server standpoint is also smaller than other operating systems that are available.

Now Microsoft has won the desk top war, but it is the laptop that is the wave of the future. In 2001 Microsoft had 41% of the market compared to 27% for Linux and Unux with 15%. Nova net Ware less than 20% was projected to grow to 24% which is greater than which Microsoft Windows. The collective minds of the industry according to the *L.A. Times*: "They understood before anyone else the reflection point that has happened in terms of those who make decisions to purchase technology. Eight years ago it was bought by a technical person, on the basis of technical merit. Today it is a business person on business merit. Since the server market is where it's at Microsoft is going there.

## 167. THE CONSORTIUM CONCEPT
### April 2, 2001

In this time of history health care has a cost of $1,000,000,000 in the United States. $250,000,000 goes to administrative costs. To build a network from scratch is too expensive and not practical. NEHEN uses an incremental approach blending existing and new technology.

Simply throwing technology at the problem does not solve the problem. 12 Boston area firms tried building a system that would cover all inclusive problems. The long made short they failed.

The Health Portability and Accountability Act of 1996 were passed. It protected employees who wished to keep their health insurance, even with pre-existing conditions The idea was conceived of a system simpler in nature that targeted certain aspects of a program. That resulted in NEHEN in the year 1997. Each member sends other member requests for information over the internet using web browsers. Answers are sent back to those that asked.

How does it work? Banks have different systems but they share a network of automated tellers. Be it a clinic doctors office, or insurance company, they employ a data translator they refer to as Lingua Franca. They went to the decentralized data base. It is described as Peer to peer with everyone competing directly among themselves. (This according to the *L.A. Times*.) The cost reduction was reduced to ten cents per transaction. If I might state the obvious they are networking.

The matching information and the person involved say with your insurance company. You use Sophie instead of Sophia as listed on the policy. The claim is rejected and it could take weeks, months to straighten out.

Success has its own negative impact. If a program is successful as NEHEN is, you have a reduction in staff. People lose their jobs. Here's a quote with reverse inference: "The social good we should aim for is redeploying people to activities that really make an impact on health care. The more premiums we can put to medical care and less truly administrative activities, we think we're serving our members better."

## 168. STOCK MARKET

People that buy stocks live for dividends. Companies cut costs and see a rise in profit which is on occasion taken by share holders as dividends which makes them think they should buy more stock. This is what I called a false positive. Job consolidation means less wages paid and depending on the market share expanding or shrinking could be signs of real growth or cannibalization. Sometimes companies put themselves in debt to avoid hostile takeovers. Some do mergers with companies that have debt to protect themselves from hostile takeover. Some press for protectionist legislation under the monopoly laws. Then again some share holders want to be bought out. In a way I am making it simple and in a way I am not. Don't forget about marginal buyouts.

Just think you as the employee file applications to work for these companies. Depending on the motive of management you could end up doing multiple jobs or be caught up in a consolidation. Movement. More on this later.

## 169. EMPLOYEE EVALUATIONS
### April 8, 2001

It is argued that the process of evolution gets in the way of itself. It is also argued that the whole procedure has gone the way of the mammoth. The procedure can actually impact company performance of the various departments. Firms in the consolidation mode use it to press older employees out of the company in favor of less costly younger workers. Remember the importance that has been placed on the bottom line.

Coen's and Jenkins a research team on the subject of employee evaluations stated: "For too long we have been redesigning appraisals because of their dismal track records and to little avail. Appraisals try to serve several different functions, which is part of the problem. We would suggest rebuilding the functions organizational movement: feedback, coaching, development, compensation decision making and legal documentation. You would assign individuals to each classification to handle personnel. All the while the company has to know where it's going and what its stated goals are. Add to that the wishes of management and shareholders. If you're going to analyze your employees and their direction you have to know what you as an employer – manager are doing as an officer of the company. Add to that the market conditions. Integrate with a spoon (That was a joke) you'll understand where you are and why.

One expressly sad note: the tech industry at this time in history is imploding. Intel Corporation and Cisco Systems in the first quarter of 2001 laid-off 38,000 employees. It is argued that the tech industry in general is on a slide barring the development of a new product that I'd say would need new hires to make that product. (Temporary agencies)

## 170. QUALITY TIME

It is possible that management has become so disconnected from the people they are managing that they don't know the problems that are brewing in their company. You want to do better at work but at times your opinion does not seem to matter. You even fear losing your job that now feeds your family, that house you have a mortgage on, health conditions you have acquired as of late. The point is you want to do better at work and improve things for everybody. To the employee, middle/ lower management you feel powerless against perceived outside forces. It would be nice if middle and upper management had a better idea and input from those they are supposed to be close to.

The following is a suggested guide for those on both the management side and the staff side of a review. Call it a survival guide.

1: Before a performance review compile examples of work received from colleagues, include documentation of personal and professional attributes, personality strengths and communication skills.

2: Create a list of things to improve. Prioritize your weaknesses and select three to work on immediately.

3: During the interview tell yourself. I need to listen to this. It will help me grow personally.

4: Stay tuned to what you are hearing.

5: Be as objective and unemotional as possible.

6: Do not interrupt.

7: Ask yourself is the feedback specific and action oriented. If not ask for specifics, so you can understand the critique.

8: Summarize and restate what you hear to ensure you heard it correctly.

9: Create an action plan for attaining your goals.


It is argued by taking these steps you might even become a critique. One thing I used to think management while I was labor and found I often was shooting myself in the foot, with my own gun. But I do agree self examination is necessary.

## 171. THE LANDLORD CONCEPT
May 5, 2001

The value of labor and the land mass it occupies puts pressure on wages if they do not go up in proportion to housing. Most people rent these days and the landlord class has succeeded in bumping up rent to the value of property while wages have remained stagnant.

In the South Land / Los Angeles County and the surrounding area rents have gone up 9% from the year 2000 to 2001. This is a time-capsule study on where the rents went up and why. Sustained job growth pushes up rents double the rate of inflation. Renters paid an average of $1,187 in the January period of 2001. There was a 13% jump in the price of the priciest apartments, In the area. This according to the first quarterly report by Real Facts Novato based research firm. Rents rose an average of 10% to $1,175 in Orange County. There was an increase of 9% in the remaining counties to $1,106 in Ventura Counties. Riverside was $797 and San Bernardino was $788.

Remember this is just after 9/11 happened and many lost jobs and had to move to apartments in congested areas. Could it be the landed class in these corporate-owned properties were gouging the economy when it was on the decline.

## 172. DEREGULATION
May 6, 2001

The energy crisis was upon us. Once proud Edison workers were seeing their company face bankruptcy and the villain was deregulation and corporate mingling in deals they never should have been making. Mathematical logic no-longer served the corporate purpose. People who had given their lives and built traditions found that it didn't matter anymore.

The *L.A. Times* told a tale of a soft spoken Mr. Rodgers type by the name of John Balance. He was in charge of the Edison transmit ion and distribution grid for

32 years. In the 1960s he entered the field strait out of Berkley. At the age of 53 he still feels alive when he thinks about those early hot summers when he would install temporary grids when outages occurred. He took pride in what he did. You know, maybe that's the secret to the whole thing. Now the corporate structure as of that year could not lick a postage stamp. The skill level was washed away with reorganization plans and unrealistic contracts. To think this issue would eventually topple a Governor.

I think back to a list of questions an employee goes through in that critical examination on how well he does his job and I feel compelled to have management question their own behavior.

What went wrong as the new economy emerged? Edison cut its staff through a series of layoffs and voluntary retirements in the 1990s. In 1998 in order to comply with deregulation it sold 12 gas powered plants and bought the electricity back through state supervised market prices that fluctuated daily. Other retailers were invited to jump in but real competition never materialized. It was an iron clad rule that prices do not drop, they soar. By December 2000 it was clear that the market was dysfunctional. Under the deregulation law Edison could not raise rates. The utility was now out of cash and that led to cutting power to consumers. Chances are the employees were told to keep their mouths shut, for management and state government knew what they were doing. That is my problem with the acceptance of supplier's authority when they could be wrong.

## 173. THE EDISON COMPLEX

Something happens when you artificially adjust the price of something. Under deregulation the price of a Kilowatt rose from 3 cents to 30 cents. The rates did not go up. The result was every time you or I watch television, turn a light on or off Edison lost money. Note it was not leaving lights on or the act of running your air conditioner that was the primary cause. It was the initial cost of the unit of power itself. This was because they had to buy power from others who were trying to make a buck. They no-longer controlled their sources of energy production. It was part of deregulation and the concept of outsourcing. Those who made the decision to sell their power grid, probably for some share-holder dividend did not account for the greed and sacrificed profits in the long term.

It is argued that when you go to work for a utility you are looking for a nice steady place to work not Mr. Toad's Wild Ride. This ride caused 2,000 employees to get pink slips. It caused retirees to consider whether they could afford to retire. They were seeing their salaries and bonuses, go out the window, or was that down the rabbit hole?

Governor grey Davis was at this time looking into a rescue plan for Edison that avoided raising rates. The legislature was grilling its executives and accountants on how they arrived here, not knowing they were at least partly the cause.

Charles Basham runs the Edison internal website at this time. He stated: "I've seen this time and time again over the 21 years I've worked here. We work best in crisis." Alan J. Fohrer stated: "We have an opportunity, but we have to move quickly. The problem gets bigger every day."

## 174. EDISON TIME LINE

It all started in 1886 when small independent power companies brought lighting to southern California. In December 1897 West Side Lighting Company and los Angeles Electric company merged to form Edison Electric of Los Angeles.(EELA) As of February 1899 the Santa Anna River goes on line carrying 33,000 volts a distance of 83 miles. It had the highest transmission in the country. In 1901 Edison buys small high risk electric companies. It has been argued that certain businesses work better as monopolies for they provide more efficient service. The acquisitions were to make a more stable regional system. By July1909 the entity became officially Southern California Edison. By 1911 a public utilities commission is formed to regulate and monitor the corporate financing. Consolidation and franchising of this and other utilities. In 1917 Pacific light and Power Corporations is acquired. This is where Edison gets its huge Hydro Electric plant at Big Creek in the Sierra Nevada. This doubles Edison's assets. By 1922 the local Los Angeles government pressured Southern California Edison to sell its los Angeles distribution system. In the periods from 1933 to 1938 they cut the salaries of management and lowered the work week from 6 to 5 days. In 1941 due to the war the coastal regions are blacked out. In 1947 through 1980 the utility doubles its output and builds 10 new power plants due to the increasing demand of 1,000 people per week. In 1957 peaceful use of the atom comes on line with the Santa Susanna Experimental Station. In January 1968 the San Onofre Nuclear Generating station comes into being with the joint effort of Edison with 80%. The partner, Sandi ego Gas and Electric Company. In the 1970s conservation becomes Edison's byword. In 1982 Edison ventures into the Solar field with Solar One the nation's first Solar plant. Here is where the trouble starts. In 1994 the Public Utilities Commission sees retail competition as the best direction for the electric utility. I think the politicians of this period had their hand in things. This is when Edison Stock tumbles. By January 1996 the California Assembly Bill 1890 poses a framework for deregulation and becomes law. By 1997 Southern California Edison sells 12 plants. By 1998 the deregulation bill takes effect and the Mad hatter tea Party begins.

## 175. May 12, 2001

Now we all know if you don't maintain your car you have trouble in the long run. Think of the selling of those 12 plants and the need for profit at the same time skimping on maintenance. Remember we have started to gear up for the perceived Y2K threat. What happens? The cost goes up because down time is viewed as lost revenue. The Mega Watt hour, the sold for $30 went up to $1,500. Off line time went up 350%. Governor Grey Davis and the legislature thought the utility was with-holding power. They traced the problem to 1998. This of course led to the Recall election when Arnold Schwarzenegger replaced Governor Grey Davis.

## 176. THE URBAN RETAIL REACH

The cities with their great densities bring great diversity it all becomes a matter of traffic flow and foot traffic. When the trades appear flat with no sales of consequence an idea comes into the heads of the major mass marketing chains. The inner city, South Central Los Angeles, which lacked services, but had people in a largely untapped economy. Be it low income or the underground economy combined with foot and slash freeway local traffic. Major retailers have flocked to develop services and provide jobs for the inner city. It is viewed as a reliable market. They aren't going anywhere.

Phil Angelidas who had a major hand in the CALPERS policy stated: "I think it is important that these programs are set up now. "Among the obstacles: small lots, environmental damage, security is often a potential concern. A little down-town capital could be eye-catching. This is especially true in the downtown tight money market.. He stated: "As the economy slows, capital tightens up. Then it searches for solid opportunities, where there's a reliable market."

The other draw is that mystery wrapped in intrigue is the underground cash economy that has not been examined. I seriously doubt you would get willing participants in a study of an income class cloaked in the dark.

The location was Wilshire Blvd, and Union Ave. It was eight and a half acres. On it was rising one of the largest developments in remembered history. Home Depot, Food for Less, and Rite Aid. The complex was built to serve some of the poorest immigrants. Though incomes are low it is one of the densest, population's west of the Mississippi according to the *L.A. Times*. In each household you have multiple wage earners. It was the artery that upper and middle income traffic flows through. There was a quote in the *L.A. Times* that stated: "The retailer asks you: what are the demographics? What's the traffic count? What's the household income? If you can give them the numbers they want to hear they're willing to open a store."

The changed perception of South los Angeles has caused the financial world to put on the table developments that would have been unthinkable in the 90s. Grubb and Ellis broker Armando Aguirre have signaled that the message had traveled to retailers and developers up the financial food chain, if you would to lenders who started to seriously look at projects. In other areas of los Angeles in Chesterfield Square another Home Depot and Food for less, Are under construction.

There were even back-up tenants willing to move into spaces that would normally remain vacant. The Latin American population was more than willing to part with earned income to satisfy their needs. It is ironic that the former areas of affluence have turned at this time to effluence unless it's a fire sale.

The Federal Committee Reinvestment Act was the major funding to spur development in the inner city, but as of the date of this article May 12, 2001, major financial institutions were considering building. Now here's the rub September 11, 2001 things turned negative and in the end Bush got the blame for the economy.

## 177. THE CENCUS EFFECT

All of these positive things I have spoken of, do have one common ground, that army of men and women who talked to all of us and mailed us forms to fill out. It did not matter if you were legal or undocumented. It was to find out who's here and what the needs were. In the period starting, the 21st Century.

On the business end of things it was the tool used to target their markets. This would apply to banks as well as investor and potential retail outlets. This was my obvious reference to development in urban areas.

The data gotten from the Cenci's borough is aggregate and contains no personal financial information with the advertizing commercial agencies."We do not receive credit header data, personal names or information from Equifax."The quote added: "We do not receive credit header data to target those areas of geography, in fact the aggregate data forged with entities like Ford Motor Company and Proctor and Gamble, Sobxho Marriott Services Inc, Mendelshon Media Research, and Data Base America. These agencies from the private sector help to determine the needs of the people. Recently private agencies have had other ways of determining the peoples marketing needs through purchases that are made.

## 178. THE ENERGY ISSUE
May 15, 2001

The Public Utility Commission based in San Francisco was grappling with the Southern California Edison energy crisis. The appeal for a rate hike an it's affect on customers was being debated. Governor, Grey Davis was in the fight of his life and was pressuring the PUC to reform the system and put the recommended rate hikes for electricity and gas into affect. Loretta Lynch the President of the PUC commission stated: "The proposal was for a 9 to 60% adjustment. Pacific Gas and Electric would experience a 7 to 40% increase. Out of fear of dampening the business environment and in the same breath encourage conservation there would be an increase in residential consumer rates. There was a 130% baseline created. According to the PUC this is how it would work. The fear is that the commission is caving in and taking (the increase off big business) customers and putting it on residential users above the 130% baseline. The issue this point was still under debate.

The price of natural gas had spiked in California and a charge was levied that the PUC conspired by stocking supplies to drive up the price of natural gas towards California. Bill Shirman Head of El Paso Merchant Energy stated: "We obviously disagree with that." He pointed out that the prices in California had spiked and that combined with logistical problems of moving of moving 1.2 Billion cubic feet of natural gas a day to the California contract combined with the affect of unusual weather. He noted that California did have high gas prices. Norma Dunn added: "We did nothing wrong. We need to look at this in context with all shippers were trying to move as much gas as they could into the state." It was pointed out that a company that controls the large part of any market enhances its ability to dictate prices. And other conditions. (Note the argument for deregulation and competition is in this case totally false.) It was argued that the El Paso firm and its prices were 20% of the market. And in line, and should not raise the concern of what they called the anti-competitive edge.

It was argued that because California had no north, south piping system within the state that the true are of distribution was restricted to southern California. Judge Curtis L Wagner Jr. stated: "The question of the geographic market makes a tremendous difference in how El Paso merchants market share will be measured and the results. If the market is Southern California and not the entire state the figures tend to demonstrate a rather high level of concentration. In El Paso Merchant."

Sandra Rovetti of the PUC in her opinion had not considered the price impact of unusual weather and price outages in her charge that the company had wielded monopolistic powers.

### 179. May 23, 2001

The Federal Energy Regulatory Commission was holding hearings. The fact that the price of gas in California, was five times the national average, of the rest of the country. In the 1990s as has been stated the Congress moved toward deregulation of natural gas. The California experience is one of shock and awe. California Senator Feinstein moved to re-establish a cap on natural gas. Los Angeles Representative Henry Waxman was requesting the same of the commission.

It is important to note we are talking about 1% of the daily volume used by California. The ramifications were more political than real. That aside the BTU nationally sold for $13.54. The logical extension of remarks was and is that the power generating plants were powered by gas. The argument goes that this exponential feed of natural gas caused the electric bill to rise in California. FERC has the function of a National utility Commission. The Chairman at the time Curt Herbert was opposed to re-establishing curbs on natural gas.

President George W. Bush was about to appoint two new members to that commission. The president told the commission it had to aggressively investigate the cause of high natural gas prices In California. With the same stroke of the pen so to speak he nominated Patrick Wood and Nora Brownell to the five party board.

The commission said it would reopen the debate on the price cap for natural gas in response complaint's from California's committee quote: "We don't know if this is the actual cause of high prices, but even if it is not the direct cause, people have been pointing to it. This is the response we have been hearing from the people on Capitol Hill. Now think back to the forced sale of those 12 generating plants and the built in need for profit from a competitor and you might have part of the answer. Not the snide comment that was given by the committee.

What the commission controls is not the wellhead price but the transportation but the transportation of the natural gas pipelines that do transport the gas. This according to FERC is only a small portion of the cost of the gas. The gas can be resold and shipped to a new buyer. The cost is one dollar to ship one million BTUs from producing bases in Texas to California. The mark-up. The mark-up at the state border was nine dollars. The trouble comes in the language of the contract was all inclusively delivered of the gas.

It could be interpreted that the Davis Administration made one hell of a mistake. For a State Attorney General which he was to make such an error speaks volumes.

### 180. May 25, 2001

Here's where the other shoe drops. Now remember George W. is an oil man. We had a crisis here in California and George supported putting a cap on natural gas delivery and sale. Now we have the interior Secretary Gale A Norton who succeeded James Watt, had proposed opening up select spots along the California coast for natural gas drilling. Since the 1980s there had been a ban on drilling on the continental shelf. This ban had been upheld by every president including George H. W. Bush. George W was seeking to overturn that ban.

The following was a letter sent to George W. Bush from 50 members of the House of Representatives: Many of us represent areas whose economies rely on vibrant coastal communities. Tourism is a major industry for these areas and a staple for their economies. Off shore oil drilling directly threatens the economic engine and the people of the communities know it. This went on to weigh the nation's supply of fossil fuels against the demand. The document itself concluded those three miles out could be called the outer continental shelf. "Should be viewed, as a significant source of increased supply of natural gas to meet the national demand for the long term.

### 181. THE JOB SCENE

It may seem like the good old days when you read this section. Thousands of workers were added to the payrolls in the first few months of 2001. The figures in April were not out yet, but it seems California was following the national trend when a 4.3 Unemployment rate rose to 4.7. President Obama would love that rate that was under the newly elected George W. Bush.

## 182. ENERGY THE SOLUTION
June 19, 2001

Two potential deals were brokered by the Davis Administration and one by the Sempra Group. Both plans involved the sale of 170 high voltage lines that went from Orange County to the Mexican border. Both would require legislative approval.

The president of the Senate Pro-tem John Burten, Democrat, San Francisco stated that the Sempra agreement looked to be the better deal. "It looks in some ways that Sempra is giving more than Edison. This agreement was the conclusion of four months of negotiation. Would not require the state, to take over the power lines.
It would eliminate the $750,000,000 debt owed by Edison was in a fundamentally more stable situation for it had no appreciable debt to generators. Edison's debt stood at 3.5 billion. The difference between the capped retail rates and the high wholesale cost would be placed on a balance sheet. The San Diego rate payers were essentially on the hook for the $750,000,000 balloon payment. Residential tax payers would be charged as much as $400 and small business would pay up to $1,400. Larger commercial users would pay up to $12,000. This would be subject to the California Public Utilities Commission. Under the deal outlined by the Davis Administration along with his legal advisor Berry Goode Sempra would have to make a consecutive number of accounting changes in addition to settling the various claims to the satisfaction of the PUC to bring the 270 million amounts to zero. The San Diego utility would write off 219 million of the 245 million that was overcharged to customers. The quid pro quo would be SDG and E would agree to sell power from San Onofre Nuclear Power Plant at relatively low price.

Here's the kicker. Sempra would agree to postpone any rate increases for the following year and agree to make an investment of $3 billion over six years to upgrade systems of delivering electricity to 3 million customers. That amount would increase to 3.5 billion if the State of California did not take over the San Diego Transmission system.

The reason the state plan to purchase the transmission lines remained controversial was that they were going to pay double what they were worth. This was according to Robert Mitchell Vice President of Trans-Electric a Washington based firm. He offered $1.8 billion for the grid. His argument was that there was little chance that the legislature would approve the Davis Plan. Mitchell at this time approached Sempra and offered 700 million for its lines.

The states position is that the lines are worth 2.3 times their book value. Mitchell believed that the lines were worth 1.2 to 1.4 times, their book value. Mitchell stated: "At one billion dollars this is considerably overvalued but if Sempra can get that type of money for its transmission lines congratulations. I don't think it will happen."

The reason for the price offered by Sempra according to the CEO was related to the amount needed by Edison and PG and E to be credit worthy not the actual value.

It was also noted that SDG and E were not the same situation. On the States end it felt that it could make up the extra revenue through long term bonds and collect fees from the transmission grid operator.

It should be noted that despite the thoughts of projected growth, the economy, job loss, companies leaving the state set in motion a recall of Governor Davis.

## 183. FIBER OPTICS

Formed in 1998 level three, that worked in conjunction Nortel Equipment have lost their share of the markets. As a matter of fact many of the start-up companies that were buying Nortel level 3 products had gone out of business. Nortel Networks corporation stated it had lost19.2 Billion dollars, in the second quarter. It was explained that most of this was a paper loss. Level 3 was one of Nortel's customers. They built data communications systems. Both firms were hit by a rapid drop in spending.

Level three as a result of these revenue losses projected lower sales of 153 billion in 2001. It added to that expected lower sales of 162 to 172 billion in the next two years. As a result of these expectations they made adjustments in their work force by laying-off 27% (1400) positions. It also lowered sales projections to approximately 2 billion for 2002.

Paul Sagawa a telecommunications equipment analyst with Sanford C Bernstein and company stated: "Companies in this sector have a very hard road ahead. These companies have borrowed too much that some will never be able to pay back the money." Sagaway estimated a thirty percent drop in demand for the years 2001 through 2002. The long range plan of Level 3 was leaning to its budget of 2.3 billion between 2001 and 2003. They also planned to sell noncore businesses. And real estate. They said they would continue to (Court) business from the baby bells.

You can see these people in this time of emerging technology and how heavy borrowing affected their bottom line. In 2011 there was a solar company backed by the Obama Stimulus programs that declared bankruptcy. They pleaded the fifth before the Senate Subcommittee. They probably had a similar story.

## 184. THE MEDIA

One of the great foreshadowers of disaster is the decline of advertizing. Our top media companies were at this time experiencing shell shock. The severe drop in advertizing! Several media executives went to wall street and explained that though they would make their year it would not be without pain. Cost cutting draconian style seemed to be the order of the day.

Peter Kahn the Dow Jones and company chief executive analyst that the financial publisher which publishes the Wall Street Journal saw no let-up in the year long advertizing retreat. He added that the cost cuts should help them meet their second quarter forecasts. Advertizing has not picked up at all, nor do we see it picking up at all during the balance of the year. According to nine analysts 50 cents a share with the top of 77 cents a share were projected. There was a profit of 93.7 million or 1.06 for the year 2000.

The Washington Post stated that a soft advertizing market had cut ad based revenues by 8.4 % at its flagship newspaper and 5.9% at its Post, Newsweek Stations television units. "There are no surprises people can't figure out where we are going. Most companies are just hoping things don't get worse."

Night Rider, Inc. the publisher of the Miami Herald and the San Jose Mercury News stated new add revenues fell 8.6% for the month and 5.1% for the year to date. The publisher had to eliminate 1,700 jobs. That amounted to 10% of the work force. The *New York Times* Company reported that revenues fell 17.1% In May of the previous year. The Flag ship *New York Times* dropped 19.5% in May. People just don't want to buy in this time frame apparently according to the *L.A. Times*.

## 185. IT'S A PLASTIC WORLD

Gerber is doing away with glass jars that have saved many craft makers in the class room. The new containers are square and tamper proof. The conversion came after much marketing research and as a result saw a 20% increase in sales. Save those jars they will be collector's items.

## 186. GROSS DOMESTIC PRODUCT
### July 28, 2001

A funny thing is happening in corporate land, while the people had not pulled back in buying therefore holding off a recession. The corporate structure is consolidating and laying off people Robert V Diclmente U.S. Economist at Smith Barney Salomon in New York stated: "The investment slide is really in full force. We know it's coming from the company announcements but when you see the number it looks pretty big. JDS Uniphase Corporation and Compaq Corporation were announcing a new round of losses and layoffs. The economy in 2001 was showing an inverted pattern. He added: "Consumers are the only ones saving this from turning into an actual recession.

## 187. NOW THE REAL DAMAGE
### September 26, 2001

The erratic flow of stock exchanges around the world as a result of the attack on September 11, 2001 set into action an economic downturn world, wide that economists were afraid to call a recession for all that was implying. Our GDP dropped a good 2%. There was no reason for this drop it just happened. I do have another suspicion that we were causing this affect ourselves. It would now be an excuse for consolidation. Maybe Corporate industrial, Tech, sectors viewed this as a means of recapitalization at the expense of the workers.

William Kline a chief economist for the Washington Think Tank stated: "I'd prefer to call it a global stagnation, because recession implies a more extreme downturn. (He continued) but extremely sluggish global growth is what you're talking about through at least the second quarter of the year."

In the year 2000 the U.S. GDP was 4% and it had just dramatically dropped 2% in 2001 leaving us with a 2.8% GDP.

William Kline continued his comments concerning the growth of India and China and their economic engines. He stated they were basically a domestic consuming culture at this time and we could not trade our way out of this situation by dealing with them.. It will be noted that we did try to our peril. He stated: "You're not going to have a global boom premised on exporting to China Mexico is in a recession and Canada and Europe are next to zero in world trade. Remember the year about which I am talking about (2001) People don't send salesmen or bankers to visit countries if they think they're all going to be at risk. You don't send your personnel or build factories in places where they're going to be blown up or attacked."Here might have been the reason for our invasion of Afghanistan And later Iraq. Our perception, that if we did not act, we would be inviting our own destruction, if not by war, the fear of doing business with us. That May have been the reason for President George W. Bush when he promised to keep the Asian economy open when he was at that global summit.

It would be those who evaluate risk that determine our future as they did in 2001. Insurance Companies, that arrange international contracts. Contracts in the Caribbean to Singapore had seen a drop in Hotel travel. In the U.S. there was expected to be a 25% drop in lodging reservations for the rest of the year. Our best east coast insurance company put Thailand on hold. The Japanese insurance firm delayed bidding, on a major contract. Several multinational clients according to the *L.A. Times*. Said: (That these representatives would be putting off nonessential travel.

This Twilight Zone marathon was apparently unexpected. There had been a reduction in exports on the part of Europe, Japan, and the United States which account for over half of the trade of the developing countries in Latin America and Asia. This was before the events of 9/11 . The dollar value according to the *L.A. Times* had dropped 2% after rising 22% in trading value in the year 2000. Remember all that consolidating I was talking about and the profits from that activity. Could this somehow be related?

### 188. THE LIABILITY OF 9/11
September 22, 2001

Pan Am Airlines was exploded over Lockerbie Scotland. It was judged to be a terrorist attack. In 1988 Pan American Air Lines was blown up over Scotland and was sued in that year. It took till 1996 for the settlement of flight 103, which amounted to $500,000,000 split between 270 claimants.

The three aircraft that were involved in the 9/11 attack were owned by American and Continental. They were judged to face Bankruptcy due to the loss of life on the three aircraft. They were absolved of the deaths in the 9/11 attack on the ground. The American Trial Lawyers Association put a moratorium on suits for three months so the aid could catch up to the people. That needed it, and would not be competing with the lawsuits.

If you step back in time to England during World War 2 the German bombing of London you would find the houses that were bombed and lives lost were compensated by a national insurance policy.

American Airlines and Continental were given War Insurance on flights over 180 days coverage was restricted to foreign flights originating in the United States.

Tom Campbell a former Congressman from Silicon Valley stated: "Did the airlines suffer from anything of their own doing or did they suffer because they were American targets? It seems overwhelmingly the later. It is more just and fair that the financial loss be spread over all Americans."

Lee S Kreindler the New York attorney who sued on behalf of 225 Lockerbie victims' families stated: "It is a whole new world since Lockerbie. We now have Federal statutes that limit suits against terrorist countries who are on the State Department list. "Frozen assets in this country that are awarded to plaintiffs could be taken from those funds. As cumbersome as the solution would have been the states where the hijackers came from and their root organization could have been perused In the courts instead of invading their country.

### 189. THE AIR-MARSHAL PROGRAM
September 28, 2001

This program was created in the 1970s to deal with hijackers to and from Cuba. It was in 1985 that then President Reagan expanded the force as a result of the flight (TWA) 847 in which a navy Diver was killed. Interest in the program had waned. According to the transportation department Air Marshal Deployments dropped 48% from 1992 to 1996. They stated that the program had administrative deficiencies and with that excessive back staffing. There were charges of them having excessive weapons.

Your average Air Marshal works in the cabin or pretends to be one of the passengers. Whether the Air Marshal concept was viable today with the organized team of terrorists became a relevant topic. Just how affective would one Air Marshal be? It was thought a better use of funds would be electronic scanning devices. Coupled, with trained security.

The bottom line was that 15,000 applied for these jobs. Black water at this time was doing the training for this kind of a position and they depend on the funding of the government.

## 190. NEW JERSEY

Three years before 9/11 hit there was a competition to get firms to move to New Jersey. They offered the New York Stock Exchange all sorts of rebates and tax exclusions if they would move. They did not. It was initially feared that New York would resemble Detroit.

When the World Trade Center was turned to ashes, New York firms either went to the Southern part of long Island or they crossed into jersey. USB Warberg proved that New Jersey was viable. In 1998 it moved its trading floor and three thousand employees from Parkv Avenue to suburban Stanford. As of the date of 2001, 4,000 employees are in Jersey and three thousand are in New York.

Michael Carey President of ESDC stated: "The economic future of lower Manhattan is on the line.."Lehman Bros. occupied the 38th and 40th floors of the World Trade Center's North Tower. It also had a marked presence of the near and by now uninhabitable building. The day of the attack all but one of the 600 employees made it out of the building. It is stated that they moved into the Sheraton Manhattan Hotel."We locked up the Mini-bars and moved out the beds. The hotel had been a good short term solution. We need something more stable."They signed a lease for a 150,000 square foot office structure in New Jersey."It doesn't matter really where you work you're a computer terminal and phone line away from Wall Street.

The initial offer made to business was to move your company to this 250,000 community, New Jersey promises: pay no city income tax, no corporate tax, no commercial rent tax. The state offered up to a 80% rebate of their state income taxes for attracting 25 to 75 new employees here.

New York itself had a direct response: Rudolph W Giuliani took a series of steps by granting millions of dollars in tax breaks to law firms, brokerages and businesses. The point was to keep them in Manhattan. That thing called pride and tradition prompted the traditional businesses to stay. The American Express spokesman stated: "We are committed to having our headquarters in New York City. Referring to the specifics of things, Molly Haust basically stated that it was too early to tell how things were going to work. 4,000 employees were temporarily in Jersey with a few employees on Wall Street.

## 191. THE CHRISTMAS DILEMMA
### October 22, 2001

The Mall retailers were putting their fingers to the wind Richard Giss a retail analyst stated: "Companies are defiantly being cautious, but I think they will ultimately hire the people they need. This is the retailer's time of year, that if they're going to make a profit they're going to do it now."

Being specific the Target Store at Foothill and Haven in rancho Cucamonga, It's manager David Parker stated they would hire 80 to 100 temporary employees each year: "We will be hiring at least that many this year (2001) There are several reasons for that. We're undergoing remodeling right now and with the economy slow stores like Target which attract price conscious consumers May not be affected as the upscale stores."He inferred that even before September 11 it was projected to be a soft Christmas. He continued."We pride ourselves on quality service. We don't want anyone to wait in long lines."

The General Manager of Ontario Mills Jim Mance, stated that he was expecting a solid season."We will not see an increase in hiring or layoffs. We're still showing sales growth here. We're up 3% in August and just last week we had a 8.26 increase in traffic from the same week last year."He stated that the higher priced items that the higher priced items were being discounted, because they might not sell well this season."He continued: "I don't think you're going to see people buy a lot of things that aren't necessary this year. They'll buy what they need and can still feel good about. Every-ones interest right now is just reinstating people's confidence in the economy."

Federal Express and United Parcel Service find that their business peaks in December. FedEx spokesman Steve Barber stated: "We don't hire seasonal help as such. What we do at our hub operations, when the crunch comes is to use what we call permanent part time employees. And increase their hours as we need them. At this point it is hard to predict what this holiday season will be like. There is lots of uncertainty out there and it will be a while before we know what we're going to need."

UPS and it's managers essentially was a photocopy of Federal Express and stated they were hiring 90,000 seasonal employees nationwide. That was last year's figure. They expected to match or exceed it.

## 192. FEDS CUT RATES
### October 22, 2001

The Bench Mark rate for the ninth time has been cut. The is the rate the banks pay to the Fed for money use. The rate was lowered by half a point to 2.5. The last time the rate was this low was 1962. The President and the Congress wanted to take action while Allan Greenspan was urging caution.

Paul A McCulley Chief Economist with Pacific Investment Management Company a New Port Beach Mutual Fund.: "They show we're in a recession period. It's not a risk, not a probability, it is a fact. When you in a Recession you're supposed to get aggressive and antirecessionary policy. As stated the rate has been cut for the ninth time in 2001. The terrorist attacks have significantly heightened uncertainty in the economy. That was already weak. Business and household, spending. As a consequence are being further dampened. The technical affect of the Fed Action was affective to a point. People did buy, borrow, and invest. J P Morgan Chase and Company,

Bank of America Corporation, and Bank One Corporation lowered their interest rate from 6% to 5.5%. Other banks were expected to follow the pattern. The Stock Exchange dipped then rose 1.3%. The tech savvy industries rose 0.8%. As a result of the Fed action there was a miniboom in mortgage refinancing The fixed rate fell to 6.72%. Analysts predicted that refinancing would reach $875,000,000,000 in 2001. This would top the 1998 number of 780 billion. The Feds had hoped for more of a lift Out of this action. Fed Chairman Paul A. Volker stated that we're indeed in a recession.

If you look back at the beginning of the arguments presented you see how the slide actually started in the late 1990s and for all intensive purposes the corporate structure valued their bottom line over the employment and prosperity of the country. I will give you that we're switching from the old economy to the new economy but the new economy is yet to be defined. The planes that struck the twin towers, pentagon, and brought down in that field could not possibly have hurt us as much as we have hurt ourselves.

### 193. PAKISTAN

On Pakistan the former Premier Narwaz Sharif head of the Islamist Party has been banned from holding office in the Coalition government. The current government seems incapable of managing the country. The economy is being sustained through the World Bank. And other foreign countries. This is a nuclear power. The Zardaris government seems to be using the judiciary to stay in power. It is trying to fight the Pushkin problem, Taliban, Al Qaeda, but losing the hearts of the people.

### 194. TOO BIG TO FAIL
March 13,2009

Bail out madness continues as AIG for the fourth time is at the trough, for 30 billion more dollars went their way. This company operates internationally. It is argued that it is too big to fail. The consequences of failure are a worsening global situation. My argument is that they are so big they can't avoid failure. For those who put their duckets into this brokerage firm, they are potentially out of luck. They don't produce anything. They are just a brokerage house. (Enough said)

What gave George Bush such power to over-ride our civil rights. The concept of Memo is akin to administrative law as opposed to legislative law. The January 15,2001 memorandum for the files (Steven G. Bradly Assistant Attorney General) many of the office of legal counsel opinions issued between 2001 and 2003 no longer reflects the views of the justice department. They should not be treated as authoritative for any purpose."Has the light come on in your head?

### 195. AMERICAN ISLAM

Okay hear I go remember the concept of Islam exceeding the boundary of the nation state. It would be like a Catholic holding the views of the Pope above this nation. Think of the concept of cohesion and culture. Now think of the complaint by the American Muslim community that they feel excluded from our culture. This fact occurs despite the fact that they are better educated and have a tendency to be self motivated and exceed in professional fields. Now think of the person that thinks he's right and your wrong and you have the reason for the general situation.

### 196. JUSTICE

The innocence project is being opposed by those in justice related cases and the DNA testing involved. It is argued by the system that there is no constitution al right to the DNA defense to prove innocence. There are 232 cases currently contesting the verdicts arrived at. What is the legal system afraid of?

### 197. PERSUASION

The short messages on a computer, used by politicians and citizens alike. It is called Twittering. John McCain once a critic of the practice has pointed out its widespread use. He also argues against rules, that could bring about political correctness.

### 198. THE NASTY EGG HUNT

There is a red hot treasure hunt going on. A small amount of Isotoph formerly used in the industrial process are now in some corner some-place have become of some concern in terms of making a dirty bomb. The result of this, concern on the part of homeland security. On the positive side concerned workers were glad to get rid of the materials.

On the Election for Mayor in Los Angeles and other officers Villaraigosa the current Mayor is being challenged by two others and there is a council seat open in the fifth district. As of Friday the District attorney's race, six candidates are running for that seat. Early ballot count 84,281 is the current count. The last election count was, 95,087.

You have a migrant who is undocumented. Add to this being caught and sent back to Mexico. He or she is caught for violating their agreement. He is supposed to get 20 years. This is federal time. The federal government is not taking action on some cases. California has been sentencing them for parole violations. The amount of time is four to eight months at a cost of 10 million dollars a year which the state can no-longer afford. 12,000 undocumented migrants have been housed by the state of California. Schwarzenegger had reduced the amount put into the prison system. By400 million dollars. The situation is under review.

Political correctness is taking its toll on Political officials. My comments in this book have not been politically correct. The incidents about watermelon and chicken have been raised. I suppose the next thing is serving goat at these functions Oh I forgot that's politically incorrect.

On the subject of proper, when is the use of the tazer by the police on a 12 year old autistic child. He was hitting the officer but there are times when reason should exceed force. Think adult before you act.

Down in Sanpedro there is a town called. There is a town called Wilmington One is the tourist trap and the other is known for its recycling centers and junk yards. That's all changing. A Tea Shop has opened. The Green movement has come to town with green jobs. Maybe the Bible is correct the high will be made low and the low will be made high.

California is better than 84% of its rainfall and the DWP is using old data to justify new projects. They wanted to sell 10 billion in water bonds and were turned down. So you now have a drought. It is not 100% but it is not the worst it has ever been.

Nancy Anne Departe is now the head of Health and human Services. A former member of the Clinton Administration appointed. She was an advocate for the pour and women's rights. Her origins are in Kansas and she is frustrated by a republican dominated state.

## 199. THE WINDS OF CHANGE

President Obama is about to reverse a last minute Bush decision on streamlining the paper work on drilling, lumber, minerals, and mining on National Park land. This is a good thing.

President Raul Castro is stream-lining his government. Rogue a Fidel appointee was removed and not put anyplace. Others that helped shift the economy of Cuba after the collapse of the Soviet Union was shifted to a position in science, the military and a consolidation of positions. Raul is open to dialogue with President Obama but all our President wants to do is relax the useless embargo that has caused a steady flow of business from Europe to Latin America.

In Europe Sarcozi nationalized the French Auto Industry by gaining majority stock. It worked and France is moving ahead. George Brown of Britain has 70% of the Bank of Scotland but the bank refuses to lend and stimulate the market and England's economic meltdown that occurred on Browns watch.

The Middle East has shown promise, consternation, and hope. On Iraq the courts have sentenced Chemical Ali to death by hanging. The court acquitted Aziz at least temporarily. He could get death if he signed certain papers that sent people to their death. The court proved it was balanced. On Iran Ahmadinajad is viewed as a moderate. Concerning Iraq and is on a state visit there. Clinton talks are expected to yield little fruit. She continues the Bush strategy of isolation. Palestinians are being urged to compromise. In exchange for aid and Israel is being pressured to ease its restrictions. This is just a summary but we will see.

Cludad, Mexico is on the U.S./Mexico border. 1,600 people have died in this border town alone. The total troop level is expected to be 7,000. 1,000 Federal troops have arrived to reinforce the 500 already there. The war goes on.

Guinea Bissau a nation in the grip of narco terrorism has lost its President Joao Bernardo, Vieira was the lone assassin associated with a Narco Revolutionary group. This was not a coup. General Batista Tagme na Wate of the American Union condemned the assassination and those involved will be brought to justice. This is a nation struggling for its identity.

On the Stock Market and AIG with its inability to generate jobs. It only generates the maintenance of the structure, Which does not generate income. There was a 300 point drop in the market. The small investors are asking their Brokers: (Is it time to leave the stock market with what's left before the system goes bust.) Remember marginal buying and the municipal bond market is geared to generate revenue and not necessarily performance.

## 200. SOCIETY ADJUSTS
March 7, 2009

Proposition 8 was declared Constitutional but since 18,000 Same Sex Marriages were allowed to stand. The movement is designing another ballot measure to undo Prop 8 in 2012. The argument on the part of the justices is that it takes time to educate people. Note they did not use the argument on legislative procedure and disallow the measure or deny any marriages legal existence. Remember I said the movement vowed to move against judges that helped the issue stay constitutional.

President Barak Obama to the relief of both parties at least the centrist parts of those parties has applauded the reversal of the Bush policy on Stem Cell Research. The Department of Health and Human Services in charge of the National Institute of Health, spinal cord injuries, Alzheimer's and heart related therapies. California is in the game courtesy of Proposition 71 in a building designed for that purpose that was funded to the tune of 3 billion dollars. Prior to the reversal mice were used that were genetically altered, but they netted narrow results. We have opened the genetic box and we don't know what we will find.

## 201. THE MONTAGE
March 18, 2009

Here is the argument that is hitting close to home, a study on medical treatment and heroic measures are tied to a belief in God. If you don't make an effort to preserve your life you are some-how letting God down. It was always pointed out that these measures tend to lead to lesser quality of life especially in cancer patients. These same people also seem to have not enough protection of their estates.

On the Postal Service they are consolidating and making it necessary for you to go to the Post Office. You know those collection boxes you put your mail in well they're starting to take them out. 3,700 Mail Boxes in Los Angeles have been removed. People have been petitioning for them to be put back. It seems that services convenient to the public are being eliminated.

Will the trouble of the Catholic Church ever end? Rodger M Mahoney of Los Angeles has been called to testify in Fresno California, where he was stationed about some rogue priests that were not removed due to child molestation charges when he was in charge. Some of these cases have been resurrected in 2009.

Remember Sarah Jane Olson of the Charles Manson group. She moved to Minnesota and became a soccer mom. She had two children seven years ago in 2002, was apprehended and sentenced. She has served her time and wanted to be paroled to be with her husband and children. The California Governor Schwarzenegger approved it so she gets to be with her family. This is just another episode in the Twilight Zone.

There has been a spike in the housing market. Maybe are now low enough in some areas and those two person households are seeing the advantage to buying in the six county region chiefly in San Bernardino County with 583,000 homes sold in February. Home sales stayed stagnant in the areas of Beverly Hills, Santa Monica, Lacanada, Flintridge, Ranchos Palos Verdes, and Long Beach. Apparently there are a number of people who are possibly a foreign buyer looking for a good deal. I know the employment picture has not picked up.

President Obama is winging through California. The Orange County Fair Grounds were the first stop, followed by Pomona. In all cases the passes to see the president admission was not guaranteed. This May be an accident but it occurs while this AIG mess is in the headlines, Nixon went to China, Obama goes to Pomona. That was a joke.

On water the State of Colorado, forbids the capture of water in containers of any size. A fellow built a water tank and was told to tear it down. You have to let it go to the earth and flow to the river. It was proven that 99% of falling rain never reaches the rivers. Legislation is in the works to make it legal to harvest water.

You know all those commercials you see on depression: Astra Zeneca and Seroquil have buried studies critical to the whole class of anti depressant drugs for they all have the same side effects: weight gain, Hypoglycemia, and Diabetes. These affects occurred courtesy of fifteen studies and their law suits. I have a suggestion for the depressed. I get depressed. Look inside yourself and find something positive for we all are God centered.

On Anti-Semitism: a American Rabi went to Siberia to help re-establish Jewish Cultural traditions that he found were all but forgotten. After six months he was expelled as a undesirable. He set a cultural fire in the country. The problem in the country is that there are not enough Rabbi's. So they rely on foreign Rabbi's, which the state deports if they are successful. Such is the state of Russia.

On the Drug War: Senators like Feinstein are putting both the U.S. and Mexico in the same boat in the drug war. Guns flow into Mexico as the drugs flow north. Hit squads operate in the U.S. and Mexico. Greater cooperation and intelligence is needed along with material support to prevent the collapse of our southern neighbor. The Bush Administration called for the meridian initiative to be reactivated.

## 202. March 23, 2009

The Governor's race is starting in California. The San Francisco Mayor Gavin Newsom is running as a centrist candidate. Edmond Brown Jr. challenges his validity as a centrist candidate. Edwin Ramos was arrested and released prior to his triple homicide. He was an illegal immigrant. The charge of being soft on crime Newsom's draw is: "Look I'm the guy who comes from the private sector. I've created thousands of jobs. He was referring to his 14 different businesses.

Newsom cited that as Mayor of Oakland for two terms: "At the end of Browns two terms in 2006 Oakland was the murder capital of California. "He continues: "with a homicide rate three times that of San Francisco. It was also designated as the fourth most dangerous city in America based on FBI statistics." It just gets heavier from here.

The Mass transit Authority in Los Angeles was due to replace its aging rail cars. They want to double the amount of cars in service. A spokesman for Vilaraigosa Mayor of los Angeles: "The Mayor believes that we need to explore every possible avenue to make sure we measure sales tax investment yields maximum benefit. The L A Mayor at this time is running for Governor.

On California and infrastructure, reconstruction of the Freeway System. It is a mix of public and private ownership, This I don't like and avoid the use of those routes when-ever possible. The other is the gas tax increase to pay for road construction. It is estimated between 18 and 20,000 jobs would be created.

In this age we are seeing the collapse of the physical newspaper in the interest of a electronic one.. We also see the rebirth of the local paper. It is just local news, obituaries and local sports. The carbon Valley Journal died but in the vacuum of its death gave birth to a voluntary community newspaper with a circulation of 2,000 and the written word will always be with us.

On Space and the Space Station, the Shuttle Discovery used it's jets to alter the orbit to avoid space junk. An earlier event forced the astronauts into the Soyuz Space Craft. Soon the shuttle system will be retired and a new age will begin.

Remember the Red River Valley? That old song has new meaning in a flood stage alert. The National Guard and local prison and even the high school football team were pressed into service. In North Dakota in Fargo and the sister city across the way were affected. Flood stage expected 40 feet.

## 203. March 7, 2009

There is a changing strategy in business instead of trying to save jobs companies are automatically laying people off and downsizing if not going out of business. I have described how businesses finance themselves and look to demand. It is almost as if we are imploding in certain sectors of the economy. The unemployment rate has reached 8.1 nationwide. A friend of mine is giving up his house and moving to Colorado for a job and for the sake of his family. In all fairness he did engage in land speculation and lost. It has to be said in this economy we have all taken chances and lost with leveraged funds. Businesses used lines of credit to finance business and payrolls. This led to artificial expansion. This led to perceived loss and our current dilemma. This current generation coming up is going to have to live with this jobless slowed economy. This courtesy of the new definition of progress, and corporate thinking.

Medical Marijuana is giving confusing signals as it grows. Prosecution of cases were temporarily suspended and then started up again. There is a case of a now convicted marijuana operator. Charles Linch of Moro Bay was about to sentenced. Those that support medical marijuana are rallying to his defense.

Location California the tax refunds are off hold and in a couple of weeks would be going out. All those disadvantaged were thanked for their patience. Unfortunately many were displaced by landlords that did not get their money. Many lost their jobs because the private sector did not have the same level of understanding. The State did have to borrow but it would be short term and paid back by the end of that year. There would only be one monthly day off.

## 204. CONVICTED

Raymond Lee Oiler was convicted on five counts of first degree murder in 2006 for the Esperonza Fire. Those that died were: Captain Mark Louzenhiser, Jess McClean, Daniel Hoover, Najera, Jason McKay and Pueblo Cerda. 48,000 acres were lost and lives were changed.

The Jis Jam Iyyat Ul Islam is being targeted, along with the LAX recruiting center and Israeli Counsilet, its master mind Kevin James age 32 got 18 years for conspiracy charges. The letter he wrote saved him from life in prison. The organization was effectively eliminated.

The legislature has introduced a bill making it a misdemeanor carrying jail time for hitting a dog or cat or farm animal without reporting it to the police on site. The bill was applauded by the Humane Society as a necessary step.

## 205. ENERGY

Fossil Falls Lake has a conflict in the interest of Geo-thermal energy and the amount of water it takes to run the plant that provides electricity for Inyokern County. The local gun club opposes the measure because it would permanently damage the estuary. I have an idea start using solar panels to power the city. That way you save the estuary.

## 206. ASTRONOMY

On astronomy the Kepler Satellite is to be launched to find a earth based planet. The telescope is wider in range than the Hubble Telescope which is narrow in its range. This is a joint JPL NASA venture. Scientists have selected 150,000 suns and systems. The hope is to gradually isolate targeted planets and systems.

## 207. EARTH MATTERS

The Obama Administration is upholding the Bush Administration's decision on removing the grey wolf from the endangered species list. Similar things happened with the American bald eagle.

## 208. March 22, 2009

AIG continues to mystify the nation with its antics along with the total ignorance of Government courtesy of the Federal Reserve. After four times at the public trough they gave bonuses to the tune of 165 million dollars as a means of retaining talent that caused the mess in the first place. It was learned that the Federal Reserve knew about the pre-default bonuses but argued they were contractually bound. It was later learned they could have invalidated those expenses. Similar situations occurred with General Motors labor contracts and their renegotiated requirements to get the bail out.

## 209. THE VOTING RIGHTS ACT

The voting rights act is coming under attack as being out of date. The margin of voting patterns in previously segregated societies, Gregory S. Coleman stated: "The question is now at what point do we wipe the slate clean and accept that we are all equals, with equal rights (Quota System) equal treatment and equal expectations, and special treatment shouldn't be provided to anyone."The Supreme Court justice Anthony M. Kennedy acted on limiting the scope of the 1965 Civil Rights Act. The laws goal is: "To hasten the waning of racism in American politics, not to entrench racial differences."The case in and around North Carolina case and the balance of race to voting population in districts. The exception is in those districts where black and Latin populations are dominant. You can't break up the district to dilute a vote in a given population. In the south before a state can redistrict they must get permission from the Justice Department. (According to the *L.A. Times.*) This is considered a badge of dishonor. Among the challenges slated for the Missouri and Arizona will be looking at rolling back Civil Rights laws. The leading affirmative action activist Ward Conerly stated: "We will say, how do you account for the election of Barak Obama? I have an explanation George Bush and the curse that was placed on McCain by the present administration, by the American public.

## 210. THE TIMES THEY ARE A CHANGING

It is the sign of the times that I hate to see come for I like holding the physical paper word. Senator Pelosi is arguing for the justice Department to consider a electronic media factor when considering proposed mergers that created corporations that are too large to function effectively. The Mergers themselves could cause the extinction of the written press.

## 211. ON THE WORLD

The Cartels moved into the human Cargo business. Drugs can only be used once but people can be used again and again. The authorities have not addressed this issue that has changed the drug war. This problem exists in New Mexico, Arizona, Texas and California. It looks as though we have entered a new era.

Location Pakistan the Chief Justice removed by Mushariff and not reinstated by his successor, was reinstated by the power of public demonstration. Peace has been restored and the perceived will of the people honored.

The Monarch has once again returned to Mexico to breed and grace us with a show. This is a altered landscape that moves within the reserve. It is a young old thing that is protected by the people. The poaching of the woods continues.

Operation Russia and precisely the Olympic Games in 2014.Several candidates are after the job. A former NKGB agent turned industrialist, a spy killer wanted as a international criminal, a liberal novelist slash social crusader, looking after the peoples interests and you have Putin as the power broker.

Location Tibet: Thousands of Tibetans surrounded a police station. It was over the suicide of a monk who had a Tibetan flag in his room with literature. He threw himself into a river and drowned. Last year at this time there were demonstrations across the region.

Location Italy, a small island, on the trade route to Africa. The instability of the continent has caused massive migration. They have the same problem we have with Mexico. The Government is concerned about migration. Interior Minister Alberto Maroni is cracking down on migration. He is concerned about immigration, but the country needs the migrants. Boats designed for ten are carrying fifty. Old fishing boats are being used. Side note Pope Benedict is in Africa. He talks of the slavery of the poor and the continued bloodshed of the continent. Angola's independence in 1975 and the resulting war that ended in 2002 were blamed in part on tribalism.

## 212. U.S. POLITICAL STRATEGY
### March 28, 2009

The Obama Administration has stepped into the arena of the Afghanistan War. General Halbrooks and Petraeus are left to integrate the civilian efforts on improving the lives of the people and to fight the Al Qaeda influence/ Taliban. The war effort will have 4,000 more troops in Afghanistan and an increase of 1.5 Billion dollars in the war effort.

Tom Anderson a former Main Law Maker: "We want to be able to support the President and his efforts to protect the American People from the threat of Al Qaeda but the policy announced today will fail to do so, and instead make a significant step towards a perilous quagmire."

On the other side a former Congressional analyst for the CIA said: "We should be thankful the maximalists have won the debate. The American people will be safer because of it.."We are hearing the old familiar term bench marks. Remember the Obama reaction to the Bush policy? The Obama Administration stats to echo the Bush Administration according to the Administration: "We can leave as the Afghans can deal with their security problems."The Afghan forces number 90,000 but the goal on the part of the administration is 134,000.

The flip side of all of this lies in Pakistan and the deteriorating condition of the country. The Kybar Tribal region 200 people were trapped in a Masque as a suicide bomber exploded him-self killing fifty people. They were digging the survivors out by hand. The old ass hole joke still prevails.

## 213. HOME FRONT

On the domestic front Fargo and the neighboring towns in Minnesota they were stacking sandbags like frozen turtles. The Red River was expected to crest at 43 feet. Entire communities were on alert.

The small investor was considering getting back into the market. The larger investors were in a buy and hold approach, in hopes of a continued rebound that started March 9th and it was at this time up 19 points. Remember the small investors were wiped out at the initial collapse because of their margin buying. That was a trick to get more money in the market. They call these Common Stocks purchased through Mutual Funds. At any rate they are being tempted to get back into the market. They just don't know.

Location Oakland California four police officers were laid to rest. The heart of all law enforcement showed it's colors and the ceremonies were matched by the eulogies. The sad fact is that Oakland is one of the most violent cities in America. I believe what we watch on TV has contributed to the insensitivity to such incidents. I refer to the live police shows that are presently shown. Ordinary people don't act on fantasy but the criminal mind does.

We are moving closer to train service between Los Angeles and Long Beach. Several bids have been put in but oddly the Italian firm is in the running. Where are the American companies?

On the California budget crisis, tax hikes are inevitable. There will be 1.8 billion dollars in deficit spending and one billion in reduction of state benefits. For the higher wage earners there will be a increase of 0.50% or 9.3% to 9.53% approximately. Those teaching in the state could lose jobs along with other social services.. Note in 2010 they did lose jobs in the teaching sector. Class size was projected to increase. These are the signs of the times.

The Free Choice Act has lost key support in the Senate. Senator Feinstein stated: "This is an extraordinarily difficult economy and feelings are very strong on both sides of the issue." Critics say: "this proposal is unacceptable. This Bill was written by CEOs. Basically it is argued that it takes the privacy out of choosing Union Membership, though this is in dispute.

A national Health Plan has hit a major change element, the taxing of health benefits. It is argued that the public is aware of the built in cost factors. There are an estimated 46 million uninsured in this country, and the price for establishing a system could force a rethinking of how to handle health care.

Under a curious note tea served very hot has the potential of causing cancer of the esophagus 124 degrees to 154 degrees it is not confirmed but suspected.

Jack Dreyfus the founder of Dreyfus funds has passed. It is the oldest of the Mutual Funds if not the most stable.

## 214. CHANGE AND WORLD ELEMENTS

The Sintu Gin Tang Damn in Indonesia burst after heavy rains killing approximately 100. The earthen damn could not take that amount of water caused by heavy rain. It wiped out the village in its path.

In Iraq according to its constitution a referendum was to be held in 2007 on the autonomy issue. This lack of action is causing a rift in relations with the Kurdish region with its oil and the Shiite dominated government in Baghdad. It felt that external sources are complicating a solution that could be handled by the people in the region.

## 215. CHINA
### March 31, 2009

There are two, china's in Kashgar. One is Muslim and it's people are largely European. They coexist, with the dominant Chinese Culture. When Mao declared that all China would be in one time zone the Uyghur's who follow the Sun, now compose 40% of the population. The Buddhist's also have resisted, and it is argued a cosmological significance. The Uyghur's are tolerated in Xinjiang province. They practice a country within a country.

## 216. ECONOMIC ISSUES

Ron Paul coined the phrase Economic Fascism and I believe it to be a correct one. President Obama in his effort to reign in General Motors and Chrysler who have accepted Federal Bail Out monies were forced to let go of their CEO Richard Wagner. This is what happens when companies get to big for their own britches, deliberately kill competition historically speaking. They deliberately killed alternative technologies simply because they did not want to go there. Chrysler vehicles along with G M would have their warranties covered by the federal government if they went into Bankruptcy. Under incentives you can deduct the sales tax from the price of the new car from your income tax.

On the attitude towards change the argument is once a horse has been let out of the barn you just can't stop half way. You have to complete the change. They have brought back the incentive to buy American.

## 217. FOREIGN LANDS

Location Israel Benjamin Netanyahu the hawk is Prime Minister Designate of Israel. He has become a pragmatist, willing to work with leftist parties in his country diluting the influence of the right. You see politics is the art of compromise. His judgment has been tempered with the rise of HAMAS on the Gaza strip and it's extreme counterpart Hezbollah. It is argued that limiting Iran's influence especially in the nuclear area peace can be achieved.

His party favors expansion of settlements on the West bank. This one fact alone provides a interesting twist to the plot.

Location Dubai, Sulim Yarnadayev a Chechen resistance Leader was gunned down in Dubai. The Chechen president who adamantly denies any involvement in his death (Ramzan Kadyrov) He calls him a hero and demands his assassins be brought to justice. The Kremlin is suspected.

## 218. NATIONAL DEBATE

On immigration Napolitano the new head of Home land security is shifting course. The Clinton Administration used a carrot and a stick approach with balanced results. The Bush Administration while saying the target was the employer rarely followed through but instead concentrated on labor through ICE. The new affect on those who knowingly hire the illegal immigrant will be targeted. We will see if this approach works.

The EPA is exercising some muscle under the United Nations Charter, limiting emissions believed to cause cancer, asthma and emphysema. The ports of Los Angeles, Long Beach and the East Coast are impacted.. 95% of all vessels are foreign owned and not under the jurisdiction of the United States. By operating under the U N Charter you would impact the world. Lisa Jackson is the driving force directing the current effort. Emissions of nitrogen oxide are scheduled to be cut by 20% in vessels built after 1990. By the year 2016 an 80% decrease is expected. 360 Ports are affected globally from the great Lakes to the Gulf of Mexico the impact will be felt.

The Red River in North Dakota flood waters is receding, but now sand bagging of homes and in-climate snow storms remain the reality. Several residents have chosen to fight with sump pumps and other measures.

## 219. INTRIGUE AND CHANGE

On Cartel violence 2,000 deaths have occurred in Juarez Mexico, in 16 months the army has been called in and A K 47s have been used in the Tijuana Battle. These weapons came from major North American cities in the southland and up north. Senator Kerry favors re-establishing the ban on assault rifles. It all goes to the traffic flow and checking cargoes going south into Mexico. If we put a check on our own house we would solve their problem.

Iraq's Interior Ministry gives us some insight into what's happening in the government. The corruption and infiltration has largely been eliminated and those feared death squads are history. How the opposition is handled, as long as it is peaceful and an element of Democratic change it will be welcome. If this is true it will be good news.

In England the cheap labor that was the Common Wealth became that of Eastern European Poland Sin particular. Polls were offered incentives to live and work in England. It was cheap labor for high tech industries, pubs and such. With the recession and global melt down the Polls are returning home to their native land that is outperforming Britain. This is the nature of migration, and Mexican families are returning south of the border as jobs disappear on our landscape. It amounts to the same thing.

The Taliban in Pakistan caused the deaths of 20 police cadets. At this gathering a hundred were injured. They are fighting the government for dominance of the nation. It is very likely this group had perfect knowledge of the targets and knew the operational environment well. They had a familiarity with law enforcement operations and their cadets and studied them very carefully over a period of time.

On the Arab Summit we have a case of the jitters. In 2008 there was a 6.4 rate of growth. So far in 2009 it is 0.4% rate of growth. The cushion of oil sales will carry the countries for a while. Now think of an abstract strategy and our Iraq involvement. Now think about our connection to Kirkuk and you have the reason for economic woes in the region. Rivalries on who gets what treatment and who's somebody else's puppet are affecting the summit. Policy wise they are speaking with one voice. Qatar is a place of intrigue these days.

## 220. OBITUARIES

Maurice Jarre composer of epic films like Laurence of Arabia,170 films and television scores are to his credit (Grand Prix, The Man Who Would Be King, Zhivago) He collaborated with David Leon and produced our legacies over five decades. He was 84 years of age (1924-2009)

Monte Hale a star among the singing cowboys like Gene Autry, Dean, Rex Allen, Tex Ridder. He died at the age of 89. He was one of the main collaborators of the Gene Autry Museum. He has his own massive list of films.

## 221. A WORLD APART

Aquila Italy was the center for a 6.4 earth quake that toppled history to it's roots. In 1915 some 33,000 people lost their lives and though the toll May not be that high in modern times. The loss May be potentially in the hundreds. Entire mid-evil villages were flattened. In the last six months seismic activity had been noted and people say we have not taken precautions (Berisconie)"This is not the time to argue. It is the time to act"

Location South Africa, the African National Congress between Moketedi and Zuma has been won by the later. Charges of corruption have been dropped in the interest of justice. It was argued to be actually political pressure. The anti-corruption Scorpion agency was accused of abusive tactics by the Zuma camp who were being blamed for repeated filings? The world bank and especially Leonard McCarthy (Vice president) $450,000 was paid to Zuma between 1995 and 2005. Involved are bribes received by Zuma in multi-billion dollar arms purchasing agreements with the French. According to MPSHE, for purposes outside and extraneous to the prosecution itself.

Thbeki lost in the power struggle with Zuma over the African National congress and so lost his chance for the presidency. According an official release of the ANC: "The inhuman and undignified treatment of Comrade Zuma suffered at the hands of state prosecutors, was not only disgraceful but also brought our criminal justice system into disrepute. Hellen Zille Head of the democratic alliance charged the MPSHE with 16 cases of fraud and racketeering. Charges were altered and apparently forgotten.

Location Baghdad four cars exploded reminiscent of the bad old days. No real political reform has occurred by Iraqi standards, The Sons of Iraq were to blame this time. Al Qaeda,the Bath Party, Alsares Militia all are elements in the struggle. The army is not seen as a plus and people worry about when the American troops withdraw from the city. Will there be renewed conflict? The bottom line, 36 are dead.

## 222. SCIENCE

On Earth-quake predispositions Radon gas has continued to be a element in prediction of the event, but accuracy and timing seem to miss the boat on occasion. You say it will hit in one town, it hits in another. Still with a relative time frame, they were within a week of the L'Aquila quake which was ignored by officials. In the end it goes down to economic value to public safety and unreinforced masonry which is why many people die.

On donating your body to science for the benefit of mankind, one word: Don't. You're dismembered and sold basically parted out. What happens to the soul and the reburial of remains? For all you cut-ups out there have respect for those you are practicing on and their families irrespective of their most recent case.

## 223. A QUESTION OF INTENT

It's a case of Hart who raped a boy who was mentally disabled. He was given life. The trouble was that he was just as mentally deficient. He has already become somebody's toy. Texas attorneys and civil rights groups argue that he does not belong in prison.. He was not capable of understanding the charges against him. He was not capable of understanding what he was agreeing to, let alone the act. He can't be free but he shouldn't be where he is.

## 224. DETAINEES

On Guantanamo two Uyghur detainees who originated in China and are Muslims. They live separate from Chinese society. For seven years they were detained before they were granted a writ of Habeas Corpus only to see it overturned. They were not convicted of anything and had no connection with Al Qaeda. They were to be set free in the United States. Rumsfeld what were you thinking.

## 225. A NEW DIRECTION

President Obama is completing the G 20 Summit and the astonishingly concrete results, on the global recovery agreement that was shoring up European Allies including Turkey who has supplied bases in the war effort. The assurance of U.S. support and the in-person promise that we are working with our Islamic neighbors.

## 226. OBITUARIES

Jerome Waldie who introduced the impeachment bill on President Nixon after he fired Archibald Cox special prosecutor on the Saturday night Massacre. He championed the rights of the poor. He died at 88.

## 227. ECONOMIES OF SCALE
April 7, 2009

Gates is looking into changing the direction of the Pentagon turning spending away from the big ticket items. Like the C17made in long Beach. And the new modern helicopters in favor of nonconventional warfare programs and drone programs. The budget for the military stands at $536,000,000,000. Resistance in the congress is expected. Economies in California will suffer under these programs in California and lead to a downsizing in our military capability. Robert Gates according to an Aid: "He came to fix the war, but in trying to fix the wars, he ran into institutional hurtles. He realized in order to fix the war he had to fix the institution. Missile spending is on the books for discussion."Now think about Czechoslovakia and the missile deal with them, and remember the Russian statement on what they would do to that country if we followed through. They would invade the country with their forces the northern industrial section and we do not have troops in place there. They would then annex the region.

## 228. BACK IN THE USA

Santa Barbara California is back in the game of apposing drilling off their coast line. They are arguing for alternative energy programs, and conservation once more. Just remember old oil is still out there and the people still don't want change no matter what they say. Change only occurs in times of stress not opportunity. Still I think engine conversion companies to alternative fuels supported by tax incentives is the way to go. Not everybody is going to buy a new car, especially in this economy.

On saving species like the leather Back Turtle, It is estimated that there are 150 to 350 turtles left in the oceans. If not protected they could go extinct. Saving measures don't use plastic bags turtles eat them. They also get run over by cars on the beach. There are four other varieties but this one is in trouble. You have to be sensitive to a creature that has been around for 110 million years.

Location Los Angeles: Symptomatic to the situation to contracts with city employee unions Mayor Villaraigosa has proposed a modification in Union contracts. Cuts in hours and benefits, to save the cities ever expanding budget along with divesting assets to raise money for the city. It involves lowering of expectations for dollars rendered. The city police union does not like sharing the load, and considers it a violation of a campaign promise. Remember I was referring to the Latinization of America. Well this is part of it. It goes hand in hand with the loss of a tax base and a declining economy.

## 229. DISCLOSURE
April 17, 2009

The Obama Administration released Bush Administration documents on Guantanamo. What was argued was the selected treatment for certain candidates. The insect in the box trick with Al Qaeda suspects. Apparently they have a thing about bugs. Sleep deprivation and restraints up to 48 hours. As of 2005 a prisoner could be water boarded six times in two hours. In the documents it did not state whether any information was gained by the tactics involved. It was mentioned about the mentality of the time, and the need for retribution, at the time.

On his way to the Latin Summit President Obama stopped in Mexico for a visit with President Calderon. The two areas they had agreement were on the green house effect and the corruption that has gotten so deeply into the Mexican Government. It was argued that the Cuban Embargo was the least affective instrument of change. It was also noted that things hadn't changed in years. That's the old rule: The more things change the more they remain the same. It's more like shifting a deck of cards and sometimes there's a card missing. Machismo seems to be the order of the day. They love the man not the policies of his country. They voiced the need for immigration reform. In this country. At the summit Obama was a rock star, especially in Brazil.

There was an earth quake or should I say two just north of Kandahar. The dead numbered 15 and a hundred injured. The place was flattened.

## 230. CALIFORNIA

The people are protesting the oil leases that were granted under the bush Administration. The California Coast line is 1,500 miles long and drilling on the continental shelf can inspire disaster. Toney Lions is heading up the California effort. Among the elected officials present Representative Barbara Boxer of California, Oregon's Governor Ted Kulongoski, Lt Governor Garamondi, They recalled the 1969 oil rig blow-out in Santa Barbara. I remember that one myself, dead fish and birds. I recall the oil slicked rocks. It was sickening.

## 231. THE BATTLE OF SAN JACINTO

The battle of San Jacinto ended the conflict that ceded Texas, Arizona, New Mexico and California to the United States. The battle was lost by General Antonio Elmontes who were equal to Sam Houston's forces. Which were 1,100 to the strong 1,200 defeated Elmontes forces by ambushing them in gully like conditions. General Santa Anna's forces were captured a short distance away. From that location, ceding the western territories to the United States.

Anger at the loss of life at the Alamo where 350 secessionists were slaughtered fueled the anger of Houston's troops. If no surrender occurred the Mexican troops, 1,200 of them would have been slaughtered. Artifacts found at the sight consisted of pellets and used ammunition clumped together as if it were still in pouches and Bayonets, buttons of uniforms. The surrender was in 1836.

## 232. CHANGE

Robert M Gates is openly moving on openly gay persons serving in the military. He noted that issues have to be resolved and laws adjusted to meet the situation. This was not in the article but it follows logically. Families on base is a unique question. The counterpart that is the civilian would have the right to live on base. Stepping away from the big ticket items in favor of unconventional warfare is another quagmire. Just think about what I'm saying.

## 233. ONWARD

High speed rail is moving a step closer to reality from coast to coast. We are talking about short distance regional systems like Chicago to Michigan areas, Los Angeles to San Francisco and things like that. Travel within Florida not using airports, as major get about systems. It would create essentially more diversity. The amount of money to jump start the proposed system 13 billion dollars.

Concerning John Madden and his retirement, it should be celebrated as a new chapter in a man's life. He has been on CBS, NBC, the NFL as an announcer. He brought light and excitement to the sport world and was and is appreciated by all generations.

## 234. ON CIVIC RESPONSIBILITY

There is another reason AIG and other companies should not have been bailed out. Tim Newman is a Sheriff who went to Iraq to train the police forces in Baghdad and the surrounding areas. He lost his leg to a road side bomb in Baghdad. His claim was denied for an artificial limb.. He stated: "It's like we're disposable soldiers. AIG collected 1.5 billion dollars from U.S. tax payers. They earned 600 million in profit. Right off the bat they rejected 44% of the claims filed, related to the war for compensation. Over 1,000 cases ended up in court. There was a movie with a insurance company called Great Expectations. They were driven out of business in the end. Maybe this should happen to AIG.

Location India: A group called the Nasalizes a Maoist group May be involved in disruption of India's election process. Land-mines have been used and assaults on polling places killing 17 in various fashions. It is designed to intimidate the poor in Eastern India. The military solutions are not the way to go according to the government. At the root of the problem is the government's inability to address the people's needs in a society based on the Mercantile trade system., which was and is part of the Caste System, that locks people culturally in place's they don't want to be, so when the opportunity rises people act.

### 235. THE PROGRESSIVES

Child protective services is not what it's cracked up to be. I know of a case worker with a family and herself had problems. It seems it is a requirement for playing priest in the social service sector. 32 children have died in foster care or families with known deficiencies. The article in the *L.A. Times* details abuses and the need and attempt at reform. We need to do a better job, and not just protect job security.

FDR is becoming the yard-stick for the Obama Administration. His bail-outs are equated with the programs of the great depression. The difference is we are propping up institutions that are behaving badly and are out of touch. They only cooperate for their own benefit. The house of cards will fall. But the rules will change.

### 236. CONSPIRACY
April 26, 2009

What we did as a form of Xenophobia just after 2001 has come home to roost in 2009. The CIA and its related agencies have repeatedly been asked to review their policies. Just after 2003 through 2005 and again in 2006 and recently in 2007. They failed to do so. The government stonewalled the situation playing on public fear. The main reasons given for the practices were the information of the two masterminds who broke under interrogation. What do we have today as a result, well a organized opposition that controls sections of Pakistan and its people. By the way they are getting recruits from these people. Iraq's renewed car bombings preying on fear of the people in Iraq. The Taliban in Afghanistan control sections of the country, despite our efforts. All we did was compromise our own civil liberties. To what end?

### 237. THE CHANGE ELEMENTS

Frank McHugh owns 140 major housing units in Los Angeles. He rents to those who would be considered undesirable in exchange for one simple rule, don't complain about interior conditions: rats, bed bugs, unsafe spaces between buildings. Deaths have resulted. A young child fell to her death. Combined with their deaths there was a law suit. Code enforcement has fined and put McHugh in jail. A number of prosecutions have been attempted and failed, for the fines and incentives don't work. It all comes to McHugh divesting himself of the properties he owns in Los Angeles. You see in the end he still wins the poor lose.

On change elements largely due to security needs we are looking into wind and solar as a means of providing needs of our troops. The vast acreage of government land that acts as a buffer will be used for solar panels similar to Kramer's Junction on Interstate 395 north in California.

On abortion there is a new tactic, the undercover sting. A girl goes in claiming to be a 13 year old and pregnant and impregnated by a 25 year old. She is 20 and not pregnant. She manages to tape and video her disclaiming knowledge stopping the rape charge. This was broadcast over the net. Planned Parenthood has this ladies picture posted at its clinics. She has had photo opts with leading conservative and anti-abortion groups. This war just takes another turn.

Alaska and the oil industry seems integrated into one-another. Palin is seen as pushing off shore drilling in migratory waters. All sectors of the state seem to want a piece of the oil pie. Deals are being made to hopefully assure there will be no ecological disasters. In reality there have been 40 spills in the state. I remind you we are talking about 2009. They choose not to talk about it. It all boils down to jobs.

Bonds are being sold in countries like China, India, and Brazil to aid underdeveloped countries, as opposed to long term loans. The IMF according to its annual spring meeting is making efforts to clean up the banking system and boost world economies. It is proposed that the world economy will stabilize by the end of the year 2010. This is according to the World Bank quite separate from our efforts.

## 238. SPECIAL CERCOMSTANCES

Here's one for the horny class. The use of depositories delays ejaculation and prolongs the sex act by up to three minutes there were 300 men involved in the study. It is not available in the U.S. as of the date of this article. Now that is an upright argument. Oh yes, there is a cream but it takes 45 minutes to work.

Remember those old vinyl records well there back. After the decline in the number of record stores there has been a rebirth of new machines that allow you to play vinyl records that are coming into existence starting at $80. This rebirth will not be a blast from the past and go beyond pocket books. These new machines have adapters that make it possible to upload to a computer. Progress is a circle.

## 239. H1N1

Mexico and the world is seeing a new flu that blends swine, foul and Man. It can spread person to person and has caused 140 deaths in that country. The mass transit system was shut down and all public buildings were affected.

In the United States, 8 deaths have occurred with 40 cases discovered and treated. There is no known serum and antibiotics are useless. The strain in the U.S. became less viral.

## 240. AMERICANS AS TARGETS

In certain ways I feel we are back to the Carter Administration.. Reza Sabira an American Journalist was arrested on espionage charges by the Iranian Government for unauthorized contact and convicted in a one day trial. He is on a hunger strike taking only liquids. The world has protested and this seems to be a test of strength verses weakness on the part of the Obama Administration.

## 241. POLITICS IN THE AMERICAS

Arlin Spector a Republican Senator has crossed the isle many times out of principle. He is now a registered Democrat. He represents the State of Pennsylvania, and was regarded as a Rockefeller Republican. That is how I view myself, but I don't plan on hopping parties any time soon. According to the GOP he has voted with the party 62% of the time this quarter. Some on the Democratic side say he is just trying to survive re-election. At any rate if he sticks with the democrats they will have a 60 seat majority.

## 242. CARTEL WARS

In Tijuana seven police officers have met their deaths at the hands of heavily armed assault team. The attack occurred at a substation. The police have been ambushed as they try to keep order. Their numbers were depleted by half for cooperating with the Cartels. They were waiting for reinforcements of their number.

On the bombing of the London transit system. Three of the five arrested were acquitted or gotten lesser charges. Walheed Ali, Mohammed Srakil, Sadir Slalam, the charges that stuck, conspiring to attend training camps in Pakistan. They were accused of assisting four bombers who boarded the trains on July 5, 2005.

## 243. April 29, 2009

Two things related to Pakistan. The first we were training their army to fight the Taliban slash Al Qaeda forces. There equipment is old and the men are tired of fighting. The second is launching an all out assault against the Taliban bases near the capital. They are fighting in the Buner region.

## 244. SOCIAL PRESSURES AND CURES

On this bout with H1N1 flu, 68 cases in the United States. It has popped up all over the world. There has only been one death and that was a child from Mexico. That has not stopped three private schools from closing in California. 36,000 pass each year from the flu. These are mostly the very young and the very old. Remember there is no vaccine for this flu. When the Spanish Flu hit in 1918 scores of thousands died and it started as a mild flu and no attention was paid to it.

Fourteen children have recently died in the foster care system of abuse. The organization represents the Social Workers is saying they are doing their jobs, but some children slipped through the cracks in the system. I knew a Social Worker once. She now has passed. She has stated they were more interested in their paychecks and breaks and often did not answer their phones. I suppose there is good and bad in all professions, but the bad will get the attention.

Attorney Jerry Brown is targeting the Maywood police department for their practices of tazing hand-cuffed suspects, Riverside has received most of the attention on the subject. (2002-2007) there are reports as late as 2009.

The Supreme Court has stepped into the satellite programming issue. The ruling is they can be fined for anachronisms like FUCK or slang like Shit. Scalia argued that families need a safe haven. Even the skit by George Carlin has been targeted concerning the anachronism FUCK and slang term Shit. If you wondering where the F word came from, it initially goes back to Salem and those charged were largely women who were put in a yoke in the public square with the charge abbreviated for their crime.

## 245. SCIENCE, TECHNOLOGY, AND POLITICAL CHANGE

They have found the link in the DNA of Autistic people that is at variance with the general population. It becomes a matter of linkage between cells which determine how they communicate. Sometimes a link is missed or there is more than one cell. This same discrepancy is not found in the general population deemed normal. 65% 0f participants: "A variation of 10 Cadherin and 10 cadherin in 9 in a region of the Genome that controls cell adhesion molecules in the Brain."

## 246. POLITICS

Bloggers are active in Egypt trying to end Hosni Mubarak's Presidency, Radicals use the internet as a means of war. Mohammed Abdel Aziz has been arrested a number of times in Alexandria but has been released to continue his blogging on his computer on the overthrow of the government. He ironically wanted to establish Sha-ri'a Law which is far more restrictive. The movement is growing and traditional pluralistic government in the area is under fire.

## 247. OBITUARY

Bob Oats died at the age of 93. He was a sports writer for the *L.A. Times*. He covered and wrote 39 Super Bowls. He is in the Hall of Fame. In the literary world he is a giant. And is writing for some sports team in heaven.

## 248. OBAMA'S 100 DAYS

It is now 100 days since Barak H Obama took office. He promised an openness in his administration unparalleled. I would say he delivered on that one. He has started most of his projects he has spoken of. He has met with the leaders of Latin America and Europe and caused some controversy in doing so. The stimulus Package is yet to prove itself but he delivered it. His direction is unproven. It runs counter to Social Darwinism and even Mills. His tactics must be given time to prove themselves.

As to my fears of this propping up what is destined to fall, for those that run those behemoths cannot see their feet. They control too much to be affective leaders and protectors of this economies trust. I have said all I need to say in previous paragraphs, on the subject and the nation has chosen it's direction. I do not wish my country ill and can only hope I'm wrong. Only time will tell.

## 249. WEST COAST SYNDROME

Academic freedom is the freedom to think and yet question what is right. U C Santa Barbara had a study on the Holocaust with pictures of Gaza and Palestine children killed. What is good for the goose is good for the gander. If you are the good guy you can't do bad things. We are not shocked at Iran for their atrocities because we envision them as villains. Yes it is legitimate to compare two struggles.

On California the governor proposed a 10% cut in the states salaries but not in the elected members of the legislature. It is simply a symbolic gesture and there is no more on the way.

June 30 is the day Vietnam fell to the Communists. Those who stayed were unable to leave were put in re-education camps, and many died. I do believe the figure for the deaths was in excess of 100,000 souls lost. Others took to the Sea in boats of all kinds. Today Southern California 159,000 Vietnamese live work and contribute to our culture. They are angered when they see the Communist flag proudly displayed. These are the signs of the times.

Fees are going up at U C Campuses, in California. It was argued that the stimulus money would offset any difficulties to families. The Student Organizations, are urging a revamping of the financial loan programs. Our sins are coming home to roost on us.

Underwater projects and the stimulus package that has been in the end finally seen a possible completion date. Dredging harbors and saving habitats of turns, and other species. Here are some expense breakdowns 27.5 million for the flood control along the Santa Anna River. This is one part of a two billion dollar project that is 90% complete. 1.98 million dollars to look at the condition of the San Pedro breakwater and dredge the L A River.

The jobless population is higher to 12.2%, or an increase of 4.5% from the third quarter in the last part of 2007. From 4.8% to 8.6% as of the first quarter of 2009, from 4.7% eighteen months earlier. To the figure that was 20% foreign born, and two thirds of Los Angeles are foreign. This includes the county area. Janitorial services according to the Union dropped, by 108 to 210. The Union is 25,000 strong, educated immigrants had their unemployment rate go to 6.3%, from 2.6% eighteen months ago.

Foreign degrees do not carry the weight of U.S. Degrees and so the educated immigrants had to take less skilled jobs. It is this factor that led to job loss. To top workers that argues against the need for immigrant worker programs. A consumption oriented people and shop in places like Wal-Mart or K-Mart and don't frequent sidewalk cafes. White in general don't consume as much and really don't stimulate the mass economy. Bear in mind most of these products don't originate in this country and just add to our balance of payment deficit.

Charter schools and their health benefits or retire and retain benefits. As the economy goes down we as a people are going to lose ground and we won't have to worry about private health care.

The Voting Rights Act of 1965 and the challenge of section 5 that penalizes the Southern States and not the northern ones like Ohio. The result was a alteration to a less intrusive form subject to appeal.

## 250. THE DRUG SOCIETY

Powdered Cocaine traditionally a white drug and crack cocaine was far more severe as a penalty. The result was pending legislation that would level the playing field. The big concern was that all those convicted on the Crack charge, would have automatic appeals flooding the judicial system. Congress is walking around the bush in attempting to address the issue. I have an idea automatically adjust the sentences of the crack convictions to the powdered convictions or the other way around so a lot of lawyer's fees don't have to be paid.

## 251. MORE ON THE 100 DAYS

The Administration points to more job loss going hand in hand with corporate re-organization, using stimulus as a tool.

On Health Care the link is made between job growth and medical preventive medicine. How to pay for it is a tax increase? Sweden walked away from that in 1973. His stand is that it will ease the burden on private companies and he's right. They will discontinue coverage to the employees or severely restrict it. One way would be to limit hours to technically part time. When economies of scale are down, the poor be damned. Now we are back to Social Darwinism as it pertains to the private sector. Smith Cline Beckmann is already taking these steps in 2010. The Keiser Plan seems to be followed and that one is bureaucrats unlimited.

On Foreign policy several fronts: Pakistan and its nuclear arsenal which is separated in three spots. He assured the nation that the U.S. Government is on top of the issue. Also the issue of the Taliban and they are standing up to the Taliban. The War in Afghanistan is also taking center stage with the U.S. standing down in Iraq. Korea is on forced quiet mode even with the North Koreans revoking the Armistice agreement.

Support for his policies remains high and the important thing is that the people believe and it is the power of the people that can save the nation. I only wish our corporate structure had just as much commitment.

On Water-boarding and related torture techniques May yield information but as Winston Churchill stated during the bombing of London: "We don't torture."Referring to the 200 German soldiers they had captured. Obama stated: "Churchill understood you start taking short cuts and over time, what's best for the people."The UCLA spokesman (referring to the Obama statement) stated: "Inevitable conclusion that government officials who authorized torture must be held accountable for violating the law." No conflict no matter how noble the cause, you don't lie about what you're going into as far as conflicts go. The Good Prince must maintain a level of integrity in pursuit of luck and good fortune. (Don't be clumsy.)

## 252. H1N1 (continued)

The flu that is sweeping the world that is being called pandemic has affected the sale of beef and pork. Not to mention chicken. Russia has stopped buying U.S. beef and pork: it is affecting the farming industry. Pork products from Mexico are on the banned list. Egypt killed its entire pig farm industry. This is despite the lack of proof of animal to human transmission. The numbers on those to be vaccinated run between 36 and 50 million. The virus is a cross species virus and seems to affect the very young and very old.

## 253. AMERICAN FOREIGN POLICY

As the withdrawal date for U.S. Forces from the cities approaches car bombs have been systematically placed to start sectarian violence. At times the people have been angry at the security forces. Sader City saw 41 die and 81 injured.

Lebanon is due to have elections in June. And a fight is building between Pro and Anti Syrian Forces. The Generals implicated in the Harrari Assassination that killed 22 others. The generals were set free after being imprisoned since 2005 as a release of the presser cap.

Turkey has been fighting the PKK along Iraq's northern border. The IEDs continue to be the weapon of choice. Nine Turkish soldiers have met their deaths courtesy of roadside bombs. The Marxist PKK wants an independent Kurdistan. This is why we invaded Iraq from the South as I stated, in the last book. TRANSITIONS1941.

The Mexican Government of Philipe Calderon has been using the military to fight the Drug Cartels. Unfortunately they have been violating the rights of Mexican Citizens in the process. In the years 2007 through 2008 were where most of the abuses occurred. There have been seventy complaints charged and the military to date has not dealt with its own. Mexico's Human Rights Organization has argued the use of Citizen Courts to meat out justice.. So far the military has resisted. We are talking about crimes like rape, home invasion, and murder.

Notice the strange lack of U.S. presence even in the areas where we are the most involved.. I do believe we have become irrelevant to an extent on the world stage.

### 254. BANKING INDUSTRY

Ken Luis Chairman of America's Board of Directors and the architect of the Meryl Lynch, Country Wide Mortgage Companies did not help the bottom line caused B of As stock to fall got the axe as he should have. His defense was it improved the first quarter earnings.. My comment is at what cost? In the end as a result of this purchase, B of A had to be bailed out. This is what I mean by being too big for your own britches. Again are you listening Obama.

### 255. OBITUARY

Jack Kemp a major promoter of the Lapher Curve that was the trade mark of the Reagan years has passed of cancer at the age of 73. As a debater and a Vice Presidential candidate with Senator Bob Dole in his bid for the Presidency, gave then V P Mondale a run for his money. He was a worthy adversary.

### 256. ECONOMY

On the auto industry and Detroit especially Chrysler which at this time is going through Bankruptcy and is doing what they call going dark. Even those on pensions had their payments electronically disappear from their computers. In time Fiat will control Chrysler and all management will be from that company, but despite all that money that was given the company will go begging.

### 257. PEST CONTROL

There is one industry that is booming. The pool mosquito problem and the Silver Mosquito Fish that looks a lot like our guppies. With all those foreclosures in Nevada, California, and especially Florida the pond scum mosquitos have come to the forefront. Why did not the people just drain their pools? I guess they were just angry.

## 258. SOCIAL AND HEALTH ISSUES

The H1N1 Virus has been mutating. Scientists looking into the deaths of a San Diego boy eventually drew lines that led to a boy in Mexico though no contact had been made. The virus had its origin in Western Pigs and those found in the Orient. It appears to be mild but can kill a person in their middle years. One hundred and fifty have died worldwide. How these two viruses joined is a mystery. Workers back in Mexico are thought to have infected pigs in Canada. (Human to pig infestation and the U.S. The rest is human to human contact. This flu is a social economic disease.

One bright spot in all of this Pandemic situation, is the Catalina experience. Cruise ships are making their regular stop. This boosts revenue for the island that had been devastated by the fire that blackened its terrain and basically killed it's tourism industry.

## 259. THE UNION ISSUE

On the issue of competent teachers and Union membership that protects them. It is hard to rid a school system of non-performing teachers that have seniority, or a tenured teacher. Everyone has a bad day and we expect things far beyond the work day from our teachers. Sometimes they get complacent or just give up. They are just thankful they have a job and rely on the union to protect them. Of Tenured teachers one out of a thousand in the L A Unified School District, Long Beach fires 6 in a thousand, San Diego 2% of its Tenured teachers are fired, The child abuse factor seems to disappear. The source of this is the *L.A. Times.*(May 3, 2009) Here's a quote from the industry: "You're not going to fire someone who's not doing their job, and if you have some-one who's doing something extremely grievous there's only a fifty, fifty chance you can fire them."Is that why all teacher lay-offs with the budget crisis as an excuse.

The Country is divided 47% to 40% in favor of the Obama plan. With Barak changing the direction, and his projection of a grim fight to retain our economic soul. When Senator Arlin Spector crossed party lines, he also said he would not be a rubber stamp. This is after being pressured by the White House voted against the President's plan. Al Frankin though an apparent winner was still fighting for his office which he eventually got. On the Supreme Court and the Sueter retirement to give Obama a chance to make his mark on the court.

## 260. OUR FRIENDS OVERSEAS

In Iran a seventeen year old girl was sentenced to hang. She pleaded with her mother to save her. Her crime was an Islamic one. She killed her father's cousin for raping her. The seventeen year old woman by the name of Dara was hung.

Remember the Chinese Earth Quake in northern China where 70,000 died. Among their dead children in a school that collapsed on them. The survivors to the family having new children even those above the age of 35 years of age. To those people children are a safety net, for there is no Social Security in rural china and the old need the young. The Chinese are a practical people down to the peasant on the farm.

On the Swat valley in Pakistan where the truce was imposed on the people who were placed under Shari'a Law. The Taliban used it as a base to push out into other areas. They were supposed to lay down they're weapons. They did not. Now the Pakistani Army is fighting to push them back into the Swat Valley that used to be a tourist area.

A funny thing happens when two groups want to kill each other and the mediator steps in. The negotiator gets hurt. In Gaza Hamas and Israel are essentially at war. Egypt was trying to broker a peace between the two. Tunnels were built to smuggle arms in support of the Palestinian side. One of their tunnels just got blown up by aircraft killing two men inside.

Amadinajad in his campaign for re-election has been busing students to create the illusion of big crowds. This at the expense of economic reform A bus crashed killing a student in this group. This was reported on by opposition candidate Ahmid Mir Hussein Mousavi on his web site.

Mianmar formerly Burma where in 2008 a cyclone killed 110,000 people leaving 350,000 destitute living in camps. The Marxist government seemed indifferent to their plight, and only grudgingly accepted world help from the non-aligned nations. Their season is approaching and they look at the sky with fear.

# THE ECONOMY 2009

## 261. FAST FOOD
### April 30, 2009

The profit margin tells it all. Society has not slowed down but their pockets have gotten slimmer. The trick seems to be offer a product within the 25% to 30 % range of profit. There are two to three scenarios that fast food operates on, under a dollar, one dollar to a dollar twenty-five is next to impossible. You can get those mini-burgers and they will get you through the day. Quizno's came up with a product (Torpedo Sub-sand-which) which you can get in Turkey, ham, Pepperoni, and Capicoli.

There is a jump in trade improvement when you reach $6.99. Qdoba is a Mexican chain owned by Jack in the Box. It is largely located in San Diego area. They offer a combo meal that boosts their profits. (Any full sized chicken entrée with chips and salsa. It made more profit than their steak combo.)

The food wars are all about convenience and cheapness. You might say something to get you through lunch. It is argued that you can eat out more cheaply than you can fix it yourself. There's an old saying by Walter Crankcase (And that's the way it is.) I just made that up.

## 262. Treasury Bonds

The interest in Government issue Treasury bonds is determined by the Central Bank buying securities. When they don't it causes long range Treasury Bonds to rise in their yield. They were basically playing chicken with bond traders. What they did as traders was dump treasuries causing bond prices to rise. The ten year T note which is a bench mark for mortgage rates rose 3.9% from 3.0%.

The Treasury announced its plan to stimulate sale of 30 year bonds as our borrowing had reached unprecedented levels. The Government sold $26,000,000,000 in seven year notes at a yield of 2.63%. Those that engaged in safe government bonds and won in 2008, lost in 2009. As Treasuries ballooned with yield moving higher the bond market hoped that the fed would pledge to expand its purchase from the 300 Billion dollar target. Chairman Bernanke and his peers did a stare-down with the bond traders. The words were: "Continue to evaluate their timing and over all amounts of all purchases of securities in the light of the evolving economic outlook and conditions in financial markets."The sense of the argument lies in this, long term treasury are up because investors are feeling better about the economy and more willing to buy stocks. Corporate bonds and other riskier assets (This according the *L.A. Times*). The demand for risk free assets is ebbing while the support for risk free government paper is increasing rapidly. Hence higher treasury yields. (Michael Darda) economist MKM partners. 30 year mortgage rates have been treading water for four weeks.

Tony Crecendzo bond market strategist at Miller Tabak and Company stated: "Only if the anchor treasuries lifts so much that it causes the boat mortgage rates and cooperates with other fixed income rates in the private credit markets-to drift will the feds have to expand its program."This was a note that he sent to his clients.

### 263. GROSS DOMESTIC PRODUCT SHRINKAGE

There was a 6.1% decline in the first 3 months of 2009. This was the sharpest drop in 40 years. The Wall Street bunch saw it as a positive thing. The Dow Jones industrial Average jumped 2% to 8,185.73. Investors saw low business inventories as a sign of increased economic activity that would spark economic growth: (People buying goods and services) The good news from the real GDP report was that the most severe phase of the recession was behind us. (Brian Bethune) his global insight. It was that business went into a stall in the first quarter in the production of goods. They cut inventories and their staffs. The amount made was 104 billion.

Sung Won Sohn Economist California State Channel Islands Camarillo stated: "With lean inventories production will be cranked up in order to restock the depleted shelves in coming months.."He referred to consumer spending as the largest piston in the recovery. Too bad he was not referring to employment."The largest piston in the economic engine" kept the economy going in the lag time.

Those with jobs were put on to multi-task and do multiple jobs. This resulted in an increase in pay that was spent on durable goods. There was a growth rate of 2.2%. The rate of take home pay rose 6.2%. This combined with declining energy prices amounted to the equivalency of a 250 billion dollar tax cut. The economy was not as soft as the GDP numbers indicated."

Meny Grauman an economist at CIBC World markets INC. stated: "We can easily blame it on Uncle Sam." He state that government spending dropped unexpectedly by 3.9% thus adding a percentage point to the GDP decline. The exports fell by 30% in the first quarter. The auto industry melt-down added 1.4% to the figure. There was a housing slump and investment decline of 38%. In the last quarter of 2008. The GDP shrank 6.3%. It was also noted that the unemployment figure stood at 8.5%. The economy shrank by 3.3%. The notion that a recession had ended turned out to be false.

### 264. CREDIT CARD BILL

Change has come to the credit card industry. Congress considered and passed legislation changing the way credit card companies do business. In pressing for passage of the bill Treasury Secretary Timothy F Geithner stated: "Deceptive complex card rules hurt responsible borrowers and turn their lives upside down. Jacking interest rates, and unexpected fees. It was estimated that 15 billion dollars in fees were collected annually. Under the new no on raising interest limits on existing balances retroactively. Assessing extra fees for credit card holders who go over their limits and marketing to those under the age of 18 double billing was outlawed.

Edward L Yinling stated that the legislation should strike the right balance between protecting the customer and assuring availability of credit. Well intentioned legislation such as a credit card holders Bill of Rights could have unintended consequences of limiting responsibility.

## 265. REVOLUTIONARY LAW
### May 20, 2009

China threw out Common Law and instituted people's revolutionary law. Lawyers defending the people's interests against the state are often placed under house arrest. Or have their licenses suspended.. A mother daughter and son under house arrest who made it to Thailand had security officers in their bedrooms with the lights on. The girl was watched at school for rear of using a cell phone. This is the potential use of revolutionary law which is remarkably similar to Shari'a Law.

This diverse segment I hope is thought provoking as to our influence in the world at this present time. Remember law and culture, determine the norms of society. It does not matter Communist or Islamic, when you have peoples law you are seeing Plato's vision of the common man and democracy.

## 266. OBITUARIES

Albert Hamilton Gordon born July 1, 1901 passed 2009. He was a Broker/salesman who sidestepped the great Depression. He would outlast the tickertape parades and outlive all of his friends. In the 1980's he ran the Boston Marathon This man was a success story.

Mary French the author of many feminist novels that basically stated that most men are rapists and controllers. She urged women not to see themselves as second best. Her book the woman's room was considered her best work. Her views were based on the life she experienced. Dead at 79.

## 267. INDIA

Location Nepal and the cast struggle between Maoist Soldiers that were promised positions in Nepal's traditional army in exchange for laying down their arms and joining the government. The military does not trust the Maoist forces and is protecting it's elite status. The friction led to the removal of the top military figure in conflict with its prime minister Pushpa Kamal Dahal which in turn promoted his resignation to avoid the violence in this fledgling democracy. So far only street demonstrations and tire burning. The military has so far maintained the peace.

## 268. CALIFORNIA AND THE NATION

The deepening crisis in California with the labor agreement reached that it was said would save the state millions was balked at by republicans in the legislature the labor package was put together in expectation of passage of the proposed new taxes.

On California's economic woes: Van Nuys's Airport had a revenue slide and as a result of increasing fees driven pilots away from that airport. It seems the people that run the airport don't want to adjust to the declining economy. Sometimes you have to lower your fees to increase your revenue.

Victorville 2007 was in a building boom when reality hit and the buildings that were in various stages of construction had become home to squatters. The result of all of this led to the wrecking ball and the sale of potential home building material for pennies on the dollar. Now all that remains is rubble.

## 269. IDENTITY THEFT

On the Supreme Court and its rulings. Identity theft was defined and limited. The analogy of eating a sandwich and knowing there was cheese in it was used. Those illegally here with false social security numbers and knowingly charging things to others will be imprisoned or deported. Corporations that will foul the land have to be held responsible but not pay the entire cost of the clean-up. These were the things cited by the court on this day.

## 270. WASHINGTON

Jeff Sessions a radical mix of conservative and social values is to head the judiciary Committee vacated by Arlin Spector. The Democratic read on the Senator is that he is a purist and not accomodatable. He is fair but insensitive.

President Barak Obama has acted too close to the tax loop hole that allowed corporations to take breaks and simultaneously ship jobs over-seas. In these times job loss and corporate greed it is about time.

## 271. May5, 2009

Pakistan is a useful tool of America. Since it's creation Joe Average Pakistani. America would prefer a dictatorship that acts expediently to the messy democracy where the people (Men) are turning against the Taliban as they interfere with their valued. Our drone attacks no matter how precise don't help the popular opinion of America. The hope that they had for the Obama presidency has faded The people of Pakistan are waiting to see what happens as a result of the Pakistani visit.

Berleskoni is one of the most enigmatic leaders Italy has ever had and the most durable. Having survived repeated scandals, and numerous affairs. He retains a 56% popularity rating. He is right of center, and one of the most vibrant politicians despite his divorce from his wife of 19 years. He is Italian.

China in its reaction to the H1N1 virus is a direct reaction to the SARS Epidemic, that visited China with such devastating results. Mexican citizens were singled out, whether they had been in country or not. Calderon even took a swipe at China, and its policies. The traditional flu kills 10,000 people annually in Mexico. The resulting thinking this was less lethal numerically speaking.

## 272. OBITUARY

Dom Delouise the ultimate funny man with a string of movie credits that hit many categories few can come close to. I could list films but I believe you know them.. In his later days he was primarily on television. He is making God laugh now.

## 273. PRIVATE THOUGHTS

I have come to the conclusion that men should not be teachers for guilty or innocent they are always viewed with suspicion. Also on the whole men are not politically correct. A woman had an affair and married the kid when she got out of prison, but on the whole women are more trusted than men.

## 274. ON THE LIGHTER SIDE

I have a provocative angle on this gay movement and unwanted advances of those of the same gender. I have a joke that explains this: A trapper returns from the mountains with a good load of furs. After getting paid he asked (Got any women) and the grocer said (No but we have Joe over there.) response (Are you sick?) He gets drunk and goes back to the mountains. This happens two years in a row. On the third trip down he asks the same question and gets the same reply (Tell me if I did do it who would know?) Grocer (Well there's you and me and frank and Sam) Trapper (Why would they have to know?) Grocer (because Joes not going along with it either.)

## 275. HEALTH CARE

The issue of health care and the emerging debate. The numbers don't match, all facts show costs would rise. The problem still exists. The debate over the Canadian based system points out the limits of general care. The emphasis on health only works if you are healthy. As the population gets older they get sick.. None of us leaves this world in perfect health. To have the richer elements of society pay for it takes the responsibility from the poorer class who can't afford it to begin with. That's why they die. It goes back to Spencer's Social Darwinism. The Hospitals focus and look upon patients as meat, no matter what the public face is. We will figure something out but costs will impact the public purse.

## 276. ASTRONOMY

Now to the Hubble repair. Hubble was launched in 1990 and initially had to be repaired because it was fuzzy. It has taken some great pictures telling us about the universe. The upcoming repair is fraught with danger but the results will be a telescope 100 times more powerful than it originally was. What is going to add to the Hubble efficiency? Six new Gyroscopes with fully charged batteries with four repaired or replaced cameras. Included in this work-horse, a wide field camera number 2. It is said 100 years from now the Hubble will be remembered. It is scheduled to be replaced in 2014.

## 277. END OF A DYNASTY

On back notes in political history Caroline Kennedy failed to get the senate seat because of her indifference to the grain. This despite the Dynasty prone New York System. At any rate Governor Patterson thought it would be unwise to appoint her.

## 278. RELIGIOUS DIALOGUE

On reconciliation with the Muslim World, Pope Benedict the 16th prayed with the Amoms at a Mosque in Jordon. Most thought it was his contrition had not gone far enough. They were however gracious. The Palestinian issue was raised and the bias of the church towards Israel which he was to visit the following day. A note of concern, the Muslim Clerics seem to be saying (I accept your apology but why don't you agree with me?)

There is a tale of salt and welcome in Israel. With no salt one must be aware especially a dinner guest. This tradition les at the heart of Muslim/ Jewish and Christian Clans. People have lost their heads over it. It all goes back to the land.

## 279. AFRICA RUSSIA

Location South Africa, and the strange mix of institutions that form the coalition that is known as ANC. Now President Elect Zuma, who with the help of the Communist Party and other subgroups defeated the previous President Mbeki for control of the ANC. He promised reform and improvement in the employment situation.

Russia is a hard place to be successful. You have to be persistent or fall apart.

Boris Snordinov was an entrepreneur who made felt packed boots. He fought politicians, gangsters, corruption, He had laid-off workers but he vowed to reinvest and sell his product, when all around you they ask why try.

## 280. THE HEART OF DOGMA

The battle for the heart of Islam goes down to how much freedom your women have in the culture of Islam. It is almost a Marxist Corporate Society. Basic thugs get a sense of Religion and in sufficient numbers can turn society. Pakistan's one size fits all solution was too simple and obviously failed. Corruption and the inability to provide basic services led the people to give tacit support to the Taliban. Though harsh they delivered when the government did not. Military dictatorships seem more effective than democracy. When you're a farmer the government that governs least governs best. As Pakistan is trying to put the genie back in the bottle, with the invisible hand of the United States. You see they hate us. We have to see what happens from here.

## 281. ECONOMIC FORCES

Here is the blending of two or should I say three levels of economic conflicts. College kids are competing with older workers for what is a starting job. The youth are getting discouraged. At the other end of the stick less people are dropping out of school. The rates have been dropping since 2006, where they were in excess of 26% to 24% in 2008. The average is stated at 20%. Now blend this with the overall education level. Consider our agricultural workers. Education matters. The other thing adults should not have to be taking starting jobs. That are minimum wage that just went up to $0.25 an hour as of July.

## 282. May 16, 2009

General Motors who were bought out by Fiat are going through bankruptcy are going to close at least 1,100 dealerships with the possibility of 500 more being added. Chrysler did not make the list public. The dealerships involved had 18 months to unload their inventory. America loves a fire sale and this was going to be a big one. This translates into the loss of 100,000 jobs.

On education the LA Unified school District, Teachers union staged a 24 Hour strike on behalf of the children. Class size was expected to go from 20 to 45. Senior math classes were to be eliminated and English classes trimmed. 39 teachers were arrested in protests in front of the school district headquarters. Somebody made money today, the court system. No reflection on the migration issue but our increased population and decreased revenue has put a strain on the system.

## 283. CULTURAL INFLUENCE

Last year in 2008 70,000 Latino's entered the United States. The population increase has put a stress on services. Los Angeles is experiencing an increase in its population as a result of enforcement of immigration laws. Los Angeles is a sanctuary city at this time. This combined with high foreclosure rates in San Bernardino and Riverside Counties that will not be able to take the strain. There is higher enforcement of immigration laws in these counties. Mexican truckers are going out of their way to avoid these areas. The growth rate of the Latin population goes like this: Los Angeles had a 70,000 increase in population or about 1.5%. The rate of growth has been flat due to increased enforcement in San Bernardino and Riverside Counties. Hispanic ownership of homes has been declining along with increased foreclosures and job losses. The Latin population due to this increased enforcement has been retreating to the cities where there is a fuller slate of services. This is where it all stands presently. Over-all in 125 counties there has been a 10% growth in the Latin population. There is resistance and accommodation but never a reversal.

The other side is the disproportionate use affecting other environments. Among them the battle over water use in the Inyokern Valley. Los Angeles by its policies are putting middle California's agriculture and smaller / middle sized communities at risk. It is draining the economic life out of the rest of the state. Latin's shop at Wallmart while other groups tend to support smaller economic units of activity. Bigger units over time have a tendency to merge and collapse leaving nothing but dust after they have destroyed the smaller competitors.

## 284. THE PROPOSITIONS

Proposition 1F limits in time of deficit the ability of the California legislature to give themselves a raise. It is argued that these highly paid servants of the public have a different level of responsibility with large staffs and work year round. With our ever increasing budget deficit 21,5%. This is part of a package of bills designed to eliminate that deficit.

Proposition 1A is part of the deal which Governor Schwarzenegger worked out with the legislator. That is his job being a balancer. He warned of dire consequences if the package failed. This proposition was to set up a rainy day fund in the good years for the lean years. It was proposed by Governor Brown earlier but never became a reality and this one had a similar fate. Local controls and similar responsibility are all part of this. Believe it or not this is all part of the Lapher Curve. The people I have talked to don't believe it's real.

## 285. WHAT POLICE DO

How do you feel about a kick in the head? Well according to an attorney for the El

Monte Police Department, it's legal. On the other side a Criminologist by the name of Samual Walker, University of Nebraska: "Unprovoked and unnecessary" as reflected on the video. The police position was: "Unfortunately these things never look good on video. Sometimes officers have to use force when dealing with bad guys." This quote was from Dieter Dammier attorney for the police officers association. The officer initially came upon the subject alone. The subject hadn't been searched and was a Parolee and gang member. Now think about the fact that he was on the ground and the officer had the gun. If he moved he could have shot him. The other factor is that it is permissible to use the distractive kick on the subject. Water finds it's own level.

### 286. LEGISLATORS AND THE WAR

Pennetta CIA Director disputed Senator Pelosi on what she knew and when. Pennetta insisted that she was briefed on the interrogation techniques including Water Boarding and did nothing to correct the situation then. Now think about the campaign and how the democrats treated the issue with the Republicans. I say these things only to make people think.

### 287. MILITARY TRIBUNALS

President Obama has revitalized the military tribunals. They say they are trying to say it will be more balanced. The actual record of Tribunals is that they have far more acquittals than convictions.. The two convictions were the Shoe Bomber and the Dirty Bomb Plotter Jose Padilla. He came to the same conclusion that George W. Bush came to. This is despite all the rhetoric of the campaign. We had 250 individuals to deal with and they need good legal counsel.

### 288. SHUTTLE PROGRAM

The Atlantis Astronaut Team replaced the gyroscopes and batteries and upgraded two cameras involved. The space walk lasted eight hours. There was a lot of second guessing on installation. This repair was to last to 2014 when the newer Hubble design is launched. On other objectives President Bush set his sights on return to the moon: President Obama reiterated President Bush's plans. And set the date of 2020.

### 289. ON THE SUPREME COURT

President Obama is looking for a Justice to replace Justice Sueter. His candidate Moro of the California Supreme Court. Katrina Moro was a activist judge with strong pro-abortion Rowe verses Wade leanings. His second choice was Judge Sonamiar nominated by George W. Bush she had a 20 year paper trail.

## 290. OBITUARY

Zao Ziyang a top member of the Central Committee who refused to go along with the Party on Tiananmen Square. He argued that western diplomacy and capitalist markets were necessary to competition abroad. He refused to lead the crack down on Tiananmen Square. He was fired from his position and put under house arrest. He smuggled his story out through a children's book and opera recordings. He passed in 2005 and his book has just been released. You can't squash the truth.

## 291. PEOPLE IN THE NEWS

Pope Benedict the 16th ended his tour of the Middle East with a visit to the Holocaust Memorial and a statement that Palestinians deserve their own state and Israel needs a peace with secure borders.

Poxanna Sabari was released from charges of espionage courtesy of Austria which maintains strong Iranian business contacts. Switzerland was the American connection. You might say the charges were set aside. In the interest, of justice. The reporter wants to think before speaking later.

## 292. BRITISH PORK

Britain is fed up with private pork of both parties in the Parliament. Everything from banditry to security systems was charged. Everything from banditry to security systems were charged to the people's purse. None of this is illegal. The trouble is in times of job loss and belt tightening the parliamentarians just don't get it.

## 293. GUANTANAMO

On Guantanamo repatriation continues with a French citizen of Algerian origin. He was held since 2001. He wants to live with his family in the country (Lakhdar Boumdiene) He was charged with the Sarajevo U.S. Bombing Plot.

## 294. JUSTICE?

The issue of fighting global terrorism was looked at as a intelligence issue not a matter of justice. Geography did and does matter, whether it's Algeria, Afghanistan, or Pakistan or any other hot spot. This was the reasoning behind Guantanamo.. Just recently some techniques have been put into play sleep deprivation among them.

## 295. CORRUPTION

Location Sacramento: President pro-tem of the Senate 2004 through 2008 when he left the position in November to battle with the FBI on corruption charges was absolved after a six year investigation, cleared him and all involved of any wrong doing. Representative Don Perrette of Oakland can now breathe easier.. Now future think and remember that name should Jerry Brown be re-elected to the governorship.. Jerry was Mayor of Oakland. It was argued that none of the activities rose to the level of criminal involvement.

## 296. END TIMES

Peter Falk the actor who worked his way into our hearts now suffers from dementia. His wife Catherine Falk is battling his daughter who was adopted in the first marriage over conservatorship. It all revolves around family seeing family.

## 297. LOS ANGELES POLITICS

The Analdosbreda Contract to bring the modern Bullet Train System to los Angeles with its green jobs is faltering. Mayor Villaraigosa has sharply defended this program as a means of raising revenue despite the 3 million dollar price tag. The deal is basically in danger of collapse. I don't see why we can't get an American Firm, to build this system or one like it. Basically the deal revolves around a 100 car option.

A coalition of forces has banned together to bring suit in the California Supreme Court. The ACLU and other groups are challenging the constitutionality on the voters will on the matter. A number of gay rights groups think this action is premature and destined to fail. Their plan was to launch another initiative or take action in the legislature. There was an anti Saudamy law passed by the initiative that is thought to be an argument against those challenging the Proposition 8 controversy.

The following relates to the Gay rights issue sort of: A man by the name of Drumund was appointed to the Parole Board and was denied for his antigay bias. He had changed that position to a pro-position based on experiences when his views were challenged. After a year of altered behavior Governor Schwarzenegger appointed him to the Parole board, which rejected him because of his proposed bias against alternative gender people. Political realities are very interesting.

On how politics works at the city level: Location Los Angeles. The power to appoint is the power to control. The pension fund is controlled by members appointed by the Mayor. There is a debate on how the monies are being used in the council. At present there is a tug of war.

Metro Link could be due for a change from public to private, because of the Chatsworth incident. People in Moorpark remember that one. It related to cell phone use. The privatization also cuts costs and transfers maintenance responsibilities. These are argued to be lax at present.

## 298. THE SUPREME COURT
### May 28, 2009

Soto Mayor was nominated to replace David H Suiter on the Supreme Court. Her non-stand on abortion and Rowe V Wade has made her a clear target. Otherwise, her legal trail is exemplary. There is no serious opposition but not universal support. One other thing is she is type one diabetic.

## 299. A WORLD APART

Two things North Korea has stated it will no longer honor the Armistice that ended the Korean conflict. It also started reprocessing spent rods to make fission material.. South Korea has joined the non-proliferation effort and gotten the scorn of the north. It closed the Railroad that was functioning between the two nations. It said it would no longer tolerate the south and U.S. ships in its territory. Remember the Pueblo. I hope we don't have another one of those.

## 300. IRAN

On Iran and its upcoming election for president, there are four candidates in the field. It's electoral system is touted as unique for it has clerics as guardians of the democratic process. When a reformist wins there is a schism between secular and non-secular parts of society. Mohammed Katami had a rough go of it because he was a reformist band bucked the clerics. Then came Amaddinajad their choice. The four candidates are: Askar Owladi, Hussein Mousavi, Mehdri Karoubi, Mohzen Rezel, and you have Ahmadinajad, who is the incumbent presiding over a stagnant economy under sanction. Will they keep it honest?

## 301. MEXICO

Mexico is a interesting place now. Colderon is attacking the Mayors of the provinces and he has arrested 17 so far. The Governors are basically untouchable. Three parties contending for the presidency are PRD, PAN, and the PRE, which is favored to win. The election was approximately 40 days away. This is like their Senatorial or regional election that determines the new base.

## 302. ISRAEL

Relations between Israel and Washington hinge on the settlement issue. The provision that is causing the controversy is the concept of natural growth. The Arab position insists that no natural growth occur except for Arab growth.. The Arabs can have as many kids as they want. This is the rub. The other rub is that the settlers don't have a compulsory draft while the rest of Israel does. This creates a two tier society within the Jewish community.

### 303. PAKISTAN

The war in Pakistan for the Swat Valley has taken some strange twists. The only time deaths occur is when there are lapses in security. People are killed with grenades, car bombs, and shiny new guns. The idea is by killing the people you can make government stop fighting you.

### 304. OBITUARIES

Ralph K McPherson the son of Amy McPherson has passed. He leaves a wife and two children. He brought the Four Square Church into the mainstream of America. The concept of healing is prominent in the church. It is part of the American persona.

Jane Randolf the star of the B movies Cat People, and The Curse of the Cat People She died at the age of 92. She was part of the older Hollywood culture.

### 305. THE CORPORATE MENTALITY

The year is 1987. The Grey-Hound Corporation has been to the State of Arizona. There was a hostile bid to take over that company. The legislature was asked to intervene. Around the country similar situations were developing. They developed as a result of a Supreme Court ruling relating to Indiana Statutes. Boeing Company of Massachusetts came to the aid of the Gillett Company. Brace Jovanovich Inc. which is located in the State of North Carolina asked for that States protection to protect itself from Burlington Industries. The State of California had scheduled hearings on the subject for the fall of 1987.

The Arizona case started when a man by the name of Teet's started lobbying by making stops he does not often visit. He visited with the Arizona legislators and then Governor Evan Mecham.

Heavy trading in stocks had been noticed. It was suspected that Irwin Jacobs a Minneapolis based investor or another corporate raider might make a takeover bid to do what is called Green Mailing a company. The practice forces it to pay above market price for an investors stock. John W. Teets basically wanted to meet with the legislature and for it to have a special session to write Greyhound A law. If it did not do so he inferred that this (very Republican) State could not claim to be pro – business. Teet stated: "The question is are State Legislators for business or are they against it. The Grey-Hound bill was introduced on July 21, 1987 and passed 43 to 12 in the House of Representatives. The vote was 25 to 2 in the Senate. The Governor immediately signed the bill. The law's intent was to prevent unfriendly takeovers financed by heavy borrowing. Those that buy the company can-not liquidate it with-in three years of purchase. The author of the bill was a lobbyist by the name of Michael Preston Green. He called it: "The most well balanced in the country....A model to which other states will be looking."As history has proven out that is an awfully optimistic statement.

The interesting thing has proved to be that Jacobs never put together the 5% as charged and the special session was not really necessary. The other thing is that the Securities and Exchange Commission would have had to have registered that sum. He pulled a fast one.

Grey-Hounds earning potential had slowed from 1.5 million shares to 137,000 by July 21st of that year. The other thing came to light that Greyhound had what they referred to as a (raft) of devices to prevent hostile take-over's in place. If a hostile takeover did occur a poison pill in extra stock would be given to stock holders to prevent such action. Golden Parachutes were also in place for the executives just in case there was a hostile takeover. Teets would have gotten 2.8 million if such A takeover was attempted.

The real reason for Greyhound's action was to force action on two other pending bills: a Workers Compensation and Tax distribution bill that were extremely popular at the time. These bills were also considered at that special session. The bills under consideration were contingent on each other.

One of the potential reasons for this pressured law was that at various points in time The Greyhound Corporation had threatened to leave the State of Arizona because of bills in the legislature. I'd say this was a case where the tail was wagging the dog. Greyhound was the only Arizona Fortune 500 company in the State. They said A corporation had gone from employing 2,400 to half that number.

Legislation like that in Arizona has become very popular. It is argued that the Stock holders themselves should take up anti Hostile takeover rules but increasingly the greed factor steps in and the stock holders don't mind the quick extra buck. They as a unit are not behaving responsibly or integrity in the matter of their own investments

The time it took for Teets to lobby the Arizona Legislature was 22 days. Boeing when it was threatened by T Boon Pickins took 11 days. Dayton Hudson only took a week.

Dayton Hudson saved themselves from Burlington took the nature of a crusade from Labor Unions charities and local officials who showed support for the retailer. Most of the time labor and small business don't get involved with anti-takeover legislation for sometimes they want to acquire or be acquired. The idea of the fast buck and Americas love of a fire sale do not work to our benefit.

Other side-effects include unintended consequences. After Dayton Hudson after acquired the retail chain they closed the Detroit store and laid off 1,000 people.

Massachusetts law in cases of a hostile takeover roll-back the stock to a time before the attempted acquisition. This was to prevent the gobbling up of masses of stock for a quick profit. There is also a constitutional question regarding the states' rights to infringe on a corporation with heavy assets in the state, but are headquartered in another state.

Corporations also have a tendency to move from one state to another for no other reason that that state offers more protection. This was the case. Such was the case of the Singer Company. Military uniforms division that moved its firm from Delaware to New Jersey.

In the city of Seattle the Boeing plant went from 105,000 workers to 35,000 workers. This devastated the city and even to the retail end. Paul Sommer's Research director stated: "What it means is Seattle just lost most if not all of its growth opportunities for the next couple of years. David Brewster publisher of the Seattle weekly had a contrasting view: "Seattle's capacity for denial. Its belief in this stuff that it's a hot city will mean this is not much of a blow as you might think. "He cited a Kidder Peabody analysis that ranked Seattle as far as retail activity was concerned at the bottom along with help wanted advertizing. It was also noted that they would not trade places with southern California for anything. The funny thing was that Boeing is still part of its economy as it is today in 2011.

## 306. STOCK MARKET PLUNGE 1987

The world fell this day as its stock market exchanges crashed. It was argued that the national interest over the national concern has told everybody from London to Tokyo and here on the shores of the United States that we are a world village linked economically and was need sensible trade policies. That was 1987 and even today though for totally different reasons our corporations and our national interests have to trump greed.

## 307. CORPORATE POLUTION
### November 25, 1989

The location is Chatsworth in Los Angeles County, Diceon Corporation was dumping toxic waste and two employees Rolland G. Mathews, and Peter S. Jonas were about to start their nightmare.. It has been pointed out that insider trading was rampant in the 1980s and still happens as in Anderson, AIG, and others in recent history. The environmental factor was becoming big and major companies were violating the sovereignty of this land in the late 80's and 90's,

The Government agencies were moving on the corporations through newly developed laws. On October 31, the district attorney filed complaints against Diceon, Mathews, Jonas, and former director of manufacturing Richard Thomas for illegal disposal of hazardous wastes. If convicted the company according to the *L.A. Times* at that time would face huge fines and three years in Jail. Heavy metals and caustics were being dumped into the sewer systems according to the report.

According to the Article the U.S. Department of justice was going through a reformation in terms of hiring personnel, and developing new technologies to catch corporate polluters. They want to catch these criminal in their board rooms At least that was the case in this article..

### 308. CONTINENTAL AIRLINES BANKRUPTCY
#### December 4, 1990

Citing buying to many air-craft and fuel prices, total social cost Continental Air-lines filed for Bankruptcy. Its creditors included Ameritrust of Texas, General Electric Co., Douglas Air-craft Co. and the Boeing Corporation. There was a 2.2 billion dollar debt, that was part of 5.9 billion dollars in liabilities. Continental valued it's assets at 4.8 billion.

Hollis Harris Continentals chairman was over-seeing its restructuring. Continental did fall and pass into history. Now they have made a TV show out of it

### 309.
### 310. THE IDM BANKRUPTCY
#### November 20, 1992

Long beach was home to the IDM Corporation that rode the bubble of the real-estate market. It largely had small investor largely living in California. They faced losses up to 300,000,000 dollars Michael J. Choppin bragged about two decades of success. He built buildings from offices to homes. With the collapse of retail property and later homes in general, he and the people he sold the homes to were now financially flipped. 12,000 investors were affected. Economies of scale must reinforce each other. One can't rise and the other stays the same or decline.

Down-Town los Angeles has a one in four commercial buildings that were at the time vacant. When the market started to go down the corporation borrowed excessively in hopes of a turnaround that never occurred.

### 311. SECURITY PACIFIC
#### November 24, 1992

Bank of America merged with Security Pacific Corporation. One third of the acquired banks were closed mostly in Southern California. Security Pacific was the main competitor of Bank of America. 450 locations were axed. Lowering the number to 990 branch offices. The branches to be closed it was thought to be in the lower income communities. How many employees were to be let go was not disclosed.

## 312. MARTIN MARIETA

General Electric Corporation sold its Aerospace business for 3 billion dollars to Martin Marieta, a firm that deals in defense electronics technology with the Government. This makes them a serious threat to the smaller firms in California. With this merger it surpassed Hughes Aircraft formerly the leading defense contractor in California. Hughes posted a 7.7 billion dollar profit in 1991. Martin Marietta was boost to 12 billion in annual profits. According to the industry guru's this would be the start of a wave of consolidations. Norman R. Augustine Chairman of Martin Marietta at the time stated: "Companies that combine will be the survivors. There is room for strong survivors not weak companies."(Just a note here what is wrong with competition? At some point you get too big to see your own shoelaces and you fall taking your employees with you): "We have proved adept at managing build ups to win wars. Now we have to manage the build downs to win the peace." General Electric was to receive 3.5 Billion. This package included 1 billion in preferred stock. G.E. gains an advantage in Fairfield Connecticut if Martin Marietta boosted its stock. G.E. was also to get two seats on Martin Marietta's board. Companies that faced a rougher road were: TRW, Lockheed and Hughes. This would be because of the leaner defense budgets of the government.

## 313. COMMUNICATIONS TECHNOLOGY
### December 14, 1992

The tech wars were beginning and problems were cropping up. Despite assurances from the industry, there were outages, blocked calls, on 35, 911 emergency systems. This included lines serving airports, nuclear facilities and military sites. This according to the *L.A. Times*.

Speaking of now archaic thing the Federal Communication commission gave the industry until May 1 of the following year to introduce new Technology that would help firms to keep their toll free numbers in the event that they switch long distance carriers.

Here's one for consideration 19,000 credit card users had informed the FCC that they were concerned that major telephone service disruptions would occur if the new Tech. Was tested and installed during the critical holiday period. Companies were pouring capital into new systems at a rate that your average Joe would question. Allen Toffler wrote a book on managed change called Future Shock. What I am speaking of here is one of those consequences.

## 314. RETAIL GIANTS
### January 4, 1994

Due to the rise of discount stores the giants of the board-walks have seen a need to join forces figuring bigger is better. R H Macy and Company and the Cincinati-based company Federated department Stores have seen fit to talk merger to grab a greater, share of the market at the expense of the smaller establishments that surround it and control operating costs.

The Broadway Stores are owned by Carter Hauley and are Los Angeles based were looking at May Department Stores Robinson and May Company for possible economic consolidation.

Isn't it funny that these establishments think consolidation over product and service in their respective communities? True you are talking about three different markets when you compare full service stores to discount houses to small owner operated shops each with its own niche. To think you can expand your base out of your jurisdiction and not hurt your own economy is folly. There is a May Company Store that was shut down in the mid to late 80s and id still vacant today in the Montclair plaza in Montclair California.

### 315. AIRLINE PRICE FIXING
March 18, 1994

There is an organization called the Airline Tariff Publishing Company. Conversations akin to coded messages were being used by six major airlines to fix prices. The justice department found fifty separate instances that date between 1988 and 1992. An example would be foe a flight from Chicago to Dallas the fares across the board were raised $138. During the course of 1993 through 1994 these same airlines have been cooperating with the Justice Department while they were appealing the decision. Asst. Attorney general Anne K Bingaman stated: "Although their methods were novel, Their conduct amounted to price fixing plain and simple. The companies involved were: Alaska Airlines, Continental Airlines, Delta Airlines, Transworld Airlines none have admitted guilt. The nature of a monopoly is that it establishes a bottom line. It is the appearance of choice where there is none.

### NORTHROP GRUMMAN
April 5, 1994

After a seemingly endless battle over the purchase of the Grumman Corp. Northrop won over Martin Marietta paying $2.7 Billion or $62 a share while martin Marietta of Bethesda Md. Stood pat at $55 a share. Northrop needed this purchase to maintain its independence. Grumman is the company that built the B2 Stealth Bomber. What was good was that the headquarters would remain in Los Angeles as opposed to being shipped back East. It also put the company in a position to influence the twenty-first century which it has. Again it is a pity in this world of defense budget cuts that it creates the apparent need to gobble up other companies out of shear survival. The other sad fact according to a company official: "The combination of

Northrop-Grumman is still going to have to get a lot smaller than the companies are separately today." That meant job loss.

### 316. April 6, 1994

The federal Communications Commission had in prior years rolled back cable rates. A T and T had been dismembered. A T And T was attempting to buy Mc Caw Cellular Communications INC. U.S. District Judge Harold H. Greene the judge who presided over the breakup of A T and T ruled that the acquisition of McCaw Cellular was a violation of the landmark consent decree. (That he set up in the first place.) The corporate lawyers were convinced they could make him change his mind.

### 317. THE SOURCE OF THE G M BAIL OUT
### May 12, 1994

Labor Secretary Robert B Reich in the name of the Clinton administration ordered General Motors to reimburse the pension fund to the tune of $10,000,000,000. The reason was that the fund was federally guaranteed and the funds would keep the pension fund solid for the next decade. If it were not reimbursed to was argued that it would lead to a massive tax-payer funded bailout similar to the savings and loan crisis. It is a fact that the Federal government guarantees what was at this time in history 41 million souls that benefit from private pension plans were the responsibility of the tax payers. Now think of the potential reason for Bushes bailout and Obama's Corporate Bailout Plan.

### 318. THE EGG WENT SPLAT

The arguments for increasingly creative instruments have turned bankers into speculators slash insurance firms that deal in the *What if* syndrome. Imagine an egg is a contract and instead of dealing with you one on one after the deal is made I throw it against a wall and it becomes a huge mass. You have to have a fix for each of the problems if the egg hitting the wall. Eventually you run out of options. Here in detail is the why and the how of my statement.

Merrill Lynch and Company with its department Director of Global Derivatives John G Heiman stated: " We're in the early days of all of this. It's still possible to lose money the old fashioned way." He called the developing of innovation a life cycle expanding to meet new needs and situations that need not be feared. Merton Miller a Nobel laureate, economics and a professor of finance at the University of Chicago state Germanys' Deutche Bank sustained a $751,000,000 loss with the collapse of what he called garden variety real-estate He refers to depravities as a novelty item. He inferred that the fact that some of the calculations on economic models had a ominous ring to it. They as a practicing part of corporate life have bonded. There are laws that require firms to use derivatives as a hedge against loss.

The managers of New Jersey's State Pension funds was not permitted to invest $35 million out of $350 million into foreign stocks until they came up with a device to hedge the investment against losses in currency fluctuation. The device known as a currency forward would be used in a country like Britain where they would fear the currency would rise in 6 months. Assembly Option futures were designed to guide projected growth over exacting amounts of time. This could be considered top down economics. This theory does not necessarily reflect the growth of a product. It could even cause job loss due to artificial projections that flat wrong.

The systems required to track and create new directions, would have to be incredibly sophisticated. It was argued in the industry that change could occur instantaneously. This was the pressure that was put on the banks.

Now you would think an economist thought all this up and you would be wrong try a physics major. Splitting particles of matter in this case is similar to splitting financial documents. Again I refer to the concept of an egg hitting a wall and spreading. And you have to define the splitting of the egg from the sum of its parts. Our master mind is a man by the name of Dexter Charles Professor at Massachusetts Institute of Technology. He has degrees in Aerospace engineering and business. It could be said economic models break down in economic turmoil. A quote from Halsey Bullem: "We're not keeping pace with the rate of innovation. The rate of change is so great that you're presented with an instrument that makes you scratch your head, figure out what it's purpose is, and how do you break it down into something understandable?"

Banks would find customers that wanted to turn a floating interest rate into a fixed rate. A banker would find someone that wanted the opposite and they would swap obligations. As of 1994 there were few direct negotiations on loans just abstract arguments. There was and is a bottom line of questioning that comes to light will the action mitigate the action in the portfolio or increase it. This according to the times.

There is a thing called a basket option that that allows users to hedge against similar multiple risks at a lower rate than hedging them separately. Come to think of it I saw a commercial about bundling insurance policies that sounds remarkably like this.

Regulators even in 1994 had this fear that the instruments used by bankers to satisfy a complicated range of transactions were being sold to a unsophisticated customer who did not understand what they were signing. Joseph P. Bauman Chairman of Bank of Americas Swap and Derivative Association stated: "I don't agree with the premise that anything is being done that is so complicated it can't be understood. If a company management can't understand a transaction, they probably shouldn't be entering into it."It was being argued that even the most sophisticated investor felt challenged by esoteric devices. He continued: "It is very difficult for an outside investor, even one as big as us to determine the true costs of some of these transactions."When I was in College and I produced a paper that did not make sense I got a low grade or an F. Should not the same standard apply to business.

### 319. CLASS ACTION LAWSUITS
### January 19, 1993

The world of class action law suits almost never matches its own set of realities. Prudential solicited investor in an energy oil and gas venture. The fees paid by the investor exceedingly favored the company. The deal fell through largely because the facts surrounding the investment were inflated and misleading. Prudential had in fact stopped investing in the oil and gas venture while soliciting funds. Funds solicited from retired investor were 6 billion in the 1980s. The analysis was that they stood little chance of getting a profit. Fraud was proven on Prudential's part and wrong doing on the part of graham Securities(Based in Louisiana The settlement was viewed as far considering the cost of going to trial.. The partnerships were regarded to be worth only a small portion of the original investment. 37 million common pool.25 million for future payments 13 million advance on administrative expenses. 285 million that small investors lost)Investor would be offered shares in the new company. Action criticized because Graham would be in charge of the new company.

### 320. THE ORANGE COUNTY BANKRUPTCY
### December 14, 1994

The County buys bonds and stocks to generate income for the county. If those stocks are bad or the publicly issued bonds upon maturity would have a diminished return. Creditor would be paid from the sale of public land as directed by the court. The schools according to the Secretary of child Development Maurine Dimarco assure the teachers they would be paid.. Richard Marshack the bankruptcy attorney assured all that funds would continue to be deposited in the counties business accounts but that all would share equally in the losses. Sacramento urged hearings on ways to prevent such high stake investments with public money. Wall street looks to potential liquidation of the counties portfolio. Finding buyers is not impossible but investors look for meaningful returns. The long term securities would be replaced with short term investments. There was objection to the selling of the 5.5 million dollars in securities that the county had left. Bennett a city official said: "If we do nothing, the casino stays open and the dice keep rolling. This court needs to help us close the casino and put the dice away and start dealing with the substantial problems."He added: "Do anything to undercut the county's ability to get control of the situation. It's important that what happens here reinforces a positive market perspective.. The Federal bankruptcy hearing was scheduled for Dec. 6, 1994. 4 and half years was the average age of a bond as opposed to 2 and a half years. Exotic bonds were 60.1% and were harder to liquidate. Conventional securities were valued at 95-96 %.The head administrator was criticized an all essential public health services was the only thing that remained. Governor Pete Wilson had no sympathy for the county's financial situation.

The expert that advises California on its bonds was a man from the Citron called Leifer. His fees were high but his reputation exceeded itself and he was replaced when the pressure for competitive bidding rose. He never purchased bonds but gave advice and knew how to get low rates of interest.

## 321. THE FLOW OF COMMERCE

The arguments that flow between protectionism and fair slash free trade are the stuff of wars and alliances. The agricultural subsidies that all nations have so they can preserve their farming industry also set up barriers to the international trade of produce. If a nation is dependent on foreign trade for its basic consumption commodities would be hurt severely in a trade war. The exchange of goods on the international front is contingent elements of an alliance The degree of self-sufficiency also determines how badly your hurt in a trade war. The Smoot Hawley Tariff act of 1930 cast us as the villains of world trade and caused a drop in world trade by two thirds.

Modern estimates are that you could you could stimulate the domestic auto industry by restricting foreign cars coming into this country but the after affects would come back to bite you. GATT was an effort to stabilize trade between nations while protecting sensitive industries. The first effort started in 1990 in Brussels but bogged down when Europe refused to dismantle her agricultural subsidies as requested by the United states. In 1994 in Uruguay round the industrialized world went quite a distance in balancing fair trade among nations emerging and established. The reduction in tariffs went from 40% to 4% in 1994. President Clinton at this time is trying to negotiate a deal with Japan and Europe. He did thankfully reach a balance for we are still here today.

## 322. THE INFLUENCE GAME

Just how do corporations influence legislators? The answer to that would be organized campaigns. Postcards and mass signed grievance petitions are the least affective.

The National Rifle and Pistol Association in fighting the Gun registration and semi-Automatic Weapons Ban used its 900 number in conjunction with its 3million members and 10,000 affiliate clubs to send a drafted letter and automatic patches directly to the law makers and successfully blocked that legislation at that time.

Jack Bonner and Associates a Washington based firm used phone banks and postcard mail to act in the interest of the B2 Bomber, the auto industry and stricter fuel requirements standard,. Stalled the reduction in interest charged by credit cards. As you can probably guess slipped in here some-place in this expanding of the economy.

Representative at this time David R. Obey Democrat Wisconsin made the following statement: "This is a corruption of participatory democracy. It means that those who are well organized with special axes to grind will have an advantage over persons genuinely interested in the issues."He recalls when he first came to congress 24 years earlier the letters he received: "Most of the mail was from the peoples gut. Simple letters they scratched out when something was bugging them. Now the overwhelming majority of mail is ginned up by some Washington interest group trying to keep themselves in business by scaring the Hell out of people frothing them up to write or call their congressman."Some representatives have developed litmus tests to detect hype from reality, so not all is lost.

## 323. WORLD TRADE
### May 20, 1993

Japan and the United States were locked in a little argument. We favored a weaker dollar making our goods more attractive in Japan and Japan favored a stronger dollar so they could get a better price for their goods. We at this time are running record deficits with Japan. Our China deficit is there but not as big as it was to grow. In Europe we have a surplus but it is shrinking. We have a surplus with Russia and Mexico. The old argument is still applied we want more money for our goods and they want less.

## 324. DETROIT
### February 7, 1995

Detroit is on the mend and a man by the name of archer is behind it. He is a consensus builder. Archer stated: If Detroit goes down anymore than it has it hurts all of us."This was said to a largely white crowd of 200 in Oakland County. These were executives."We need to be pulling together in tandem." he delivered this message from Grosspoint to Bloomfield. The sound is Motown and it had a soothing ring instead of that of flight and despair. This man who happened to be a teacher, lawyer and state supreme court justice has established a coalition of integrated hope. He added: "Detroit is the most troubled city in the nation. It can succeed. It gives hope to others. His partners Mike White, and Seattle's Norman Rice are considered to be at this time a new generation of Black leaders running U.S. cities. It is moderate style mixed with Civil Rights goals it was very much middle of the road. You see progress can be made.

## 325. ANTITRUST ISSUES
### February 15, 1995

The Justice Department rejected a set of negotiations with Micro-Soft. U.S. District Judge Stanly Sporkin and Anne K. Bingaman failed to reach agreement on changes in procedures in the way Microsoft licenses its product.. It was alleged that the negotiations left competitors deeply dissatisfied. Sporkin in his 45 page opinion found that Microsoft: "Has a monopoly on the market for personal computer operating systems. The two parties have been unable and unwilling adequately to address certain anti competitive practices, which Microsoft states it will continue to employ in the future.."

## 326. CORPORATE NOMADS
### March 17, 1995

The location is Ontario California. The Marriott Residence Inn. Employees operate out of modular offices and fluid work environments. Flexible schedules work to the benefit of the working parent that still has the impression of a corporate office. Home work with a plug-in at locations like the Marriott redefine community service.

## 327. WESTINGHOUSE ELECTRIC CORP.
### August 2, 1995

CBS has agreed to be purchased by Westinghouse Electric Corp. This creates the largest TV Radio group in the country. The new company was to be called Westinghouse/CBS. The sale amounted to 5.4 Billion in cash. The merger has the approval of both boards. It is estimated that CBS has a viewing audience of 25% of the nation. It is also a sign that the Feds are relaxing the rules on who owns what in the telecommunications field.

## 328. DISNEY TO BUY ABC
### August 1, 1995

Walt Disney Corporation has created the largest media giant for 19 billion affectively wedding New-York and Hollywood. It combines the number one television network with the movie industry. The amazing part of this merger was that there was no overlap or consolidation of business structures. This merger dwarfed the Time Warner merger. It would be the second largest acquisition in U.S. History after the 25 billion dollar acquisition of RJR Nabisco by Kohlberg Kravis Roberts and company in 1989.

"This creates a company with global reach that can meet the ongoing demand for entertainment in the multi-channel environment around the world."This according to

Christopher Dixon an analyst for Pain Webber inc.

### 329. THE BOEING McDONNELL MERGER
### November 17, 1995

     Two giants, one primarily Commercial and the other primarily military. There data strong in their respective sides..Both had interlocking boards reflecting each other's interests. Even before the merger they were in bed with each other. They were already peering down and outsourcing. When the talks go public a lot had already been decided. At issue were reduced defense dollars and an aging population at the plant. Management was downsizing by middle and upper management decisions. People were asked t multitask at increasing levels.

     On the visible corporate side Mc Donnell's President Harry Stonecipher publicly hinted after having a profitable quarter. This was done by squeezing the employees. He was looking for a buyer, and Boeing had been courting the issue Remember Boeing and McDonnell had interlocking directorates. Remember Lockheed and Martin formed a substantial merger for exactly the same reasons

    What really swung the deal was when based on the negotiations McDonnell's stock rose from 4.375 to 90.375 and Boeings stock rose from 1.875 to 75.875. Common sense would say something was a-foot. The resulting transaction amounted to 11 billion dollars. It was argued at the Federal level that the two lines did not compete with each other.. In reality there were plans for outsourcing and or outright deleting the commercial line because it was not as strong. Boeings rankings in the previous year were 4.7 billion in military sales and 16.8 on the Civilian side. McDonnell had 7.8 Billion military side and 3.2 civilian side. Things were paradoxically reversed..The long made short they did merge.

### 330. R. J. RENALDS TOBACCO
### March 20, 2001

     In 1998 the Tobacco Companies reached an agreement to not target youth in their advertizing. Winston, Salem, Camel Doral and other tobacco producers complied to the letter of the law. We are not talking about them. We are talking about R J Renalds and its aggressive advertising campaign to capture market share. Their ads ran in ALLure, Guns and ammo, Hot Rod, In style, People, Rolling Stone, Sports Illustrated, and Vibe. It was argued that these publications play to the youth and therefore violate the agreement signed by the tobacco companies in 1998. R J Renalds is being prosecuted for advertizing in these magazines and targeting youth.

     The State further contends that the number of adults reached by advertizing was consistent with the amount of advertising done It is argued that that many young people could have read these publications and gotten turned on by the advertizing.

Santiago Superior Court Judge Ronald Prager holds the firm in contempt and wants to impose monetary sanctions on the firm which manufactures Camel, Winston, Salem, and Doral.

I could be wrong but I do not believe magazine ads are oogled by the youth let alone the adults. Give the public some credit.

### 331. JAHWA, A CHINESE SUCCESS
### April 2, 2001

Paul Woodward a marketing strategist specialist in Hong Kong wanted to prove that Chinese could compete in the cosmetic market as they had in old time. G.E. was 29. The Revolution had just happened in China. He returned to Shanghai. Finding he could not find work except the most lowly got his basic education and pursued the cosmetics business his family had been in. The Cultural Revolution wipes out his business. When it returns he finds American companies have filled his niche. His family company had been around for a 102 years (Kwong Sang Hong) The history went back to a time when foreign ships brought perfumes and such to China. The foreign goods were a must have item. G.E.'s fathers company created a superior and cheaper alternative that grew with the Nationalistic fervor. The whole thing got knocked down to making cold cream in Mao's China. He returned to the business in the 90's but was not satisfied so he bought two lines that were Jahwa and merged and did marketing. His products are currently in his department stores. Why is it that we have to go to China to find America?

### 332. THE FORTUNE 500
### April 2, 2001

Energy companies were the driving force stating in the year 2000. Exxon Mobil moved ahead of General Motors with 219 billion dollars in revenue. General Motors fell to number 3 with 184.3 billion. Enron rose to number 7 position from number 18. Duke Energy was number 69 and became number 17. Reliant energy made it to the 55 position formerly occupying position 114. Wall mart Stores hit 193.3 billion in the year 2000. Other companies Ford Motor Company, General Electric, Citi group, Enron, IBM, A T and T, Verizon communications.

According to the *L.A. Times* (Energy companies benefited from a surge in revenue brought about by falling supplies, utility deregulation, Soaring natural gas prices, maneuvering to keep oil prices high, by the organization of oil exporting countries.) It is also the shortage of electricity in the west that drove up energy costs This caused an increase in sales in companies such as ENRON and Duke Energy. Now think about the promises of Grey Davis.

## 333. PG&E: THE BONUS ISSUE
### April 8, 2001

At the time P G and E filed for Chapter 11 bankruptcy it had 2.5 billion dollars in cash. What it did with this money cost a governor his office and the people of California their trust? 50 million in annual bonuses were given and what they called a long delayed Merit increase for the same workers. This is according to the *L.A. Times*. Governor Grey Davis and he was right on this one stated Management suffers from two afflictions denial and greed. President pro Tem John Burton stated: "It does not look good. They have a business and a P R problem. The president of the Foundation for Tax Payers and consumer rights. "Talk about manipulating the Corporate finances to benefit management prior to Bankruptcy. It is the kind if arrogant misstate against the public interest."

## 334. SOUTHERN CALIFORNIA EDISON
### May 8, 2001

John E. Bryson president and CEO found himself in the position of a beggar to save the employees and staff due to the pending bankruptcy of Edison. It was perhaps the arrogance of P G and E that caused the agony of Edison.

After a long tussle over perceived irregularities it was argued that Southern California Edison paid out to share holders as dividends funds that were necessary for the operation of SCE. Were the funds essentially stolen from SCE by the international organization?

The other part of the gripe was the demand by the state that it get certain properties in exchange for bonds that were issued by the State of California to cover the shortfall in expenses. What a corporate entity sees as profit a state sees as collateral.. They were discussing some hydro electric dams that had been in the inventory of Edison for years.

## 335. EARTHLINK
### May 11, 2001

Reed E. Slatkin founder and chief financial officer stands accused of taking money and not investing it as per agreement. Federal regulators accused him of creating a Ponzi He invested some but not all and apparently pocketed the rest. This is according to the *L.A. Times*.

## 336. AOL
### June 19, 2001

Microsoft and AOL have been working together for years now and  AOL's

Netscape is not as good as Microsoft's Internet system. With Microsoft panning to go to a web in the year of 2001. AOL provides Micro soft with users to help it sell its products and systems. It was and is as Merrill Lynch stated, both companies need each other despite the posturing.

## 337. FORD MOTOR COMPANY
### June 19, 2001

Chief Executive at the time Jacques Nasser was pressed on the Quality job)no slogan in light of what has been happening with its Firestone tires. J D Power and associates had come out with a list that put Ford in an unfavorable light. Their vehicles listed 162 defects at the bottom of the list. Volkswagen even rated above them at 159 defects. The industry average was 147. The Ford Explorer was being pummeled by the industry. It's truck branch is especially being struck by general motors. 146 is the number of defects in their models which is one point above average to the good. The funny thing though Toyota, Honda, and Nissan exceeded them all.

## 338. TECH MERGERS
### September 5, 2001

Carly Florina who would later run for the Senate under the Republican party had her field not in politics but in the convolutive Tech world. The falling demand for Hughlet Packard products despite a great amassing of capital contributes to the merger syndrome. Companies like Dell, IBM or Cisco systems could pick and choose from the weaker companies. Many so called mergers could be Stock swaps. The State of the Tech sector in 2001

Michael Murphy editor of the Technology Stock Letter stated: "We are going to see a lot of consolidation but unfortunately it will be companies that are looking to be rescued seeking a suitor before they run out of cash."Lucent Technologies and Nortel Network corporations it was argued would be seeking safe harbor in this contracting economy. It seems odd to me that I am speaking of such abstract instruments as ancient fodder.

Glen Robson managing director of Morgan Stanley Dean Witter stated: "A lot of companies are preoccupied by their own internal operations given the current climate. They are reluctant to take on the challenge of integrating another firm in this environment."

Acquisitions don't work. Compaq acquired Digital Equipment Corporation in 1998 for 9 billion dollars but continued to lose ground to Dell according to the *L.A. Times*. H P stock took a dive of 18 points leaving the stock at 4.34. on the New York Stock Exchange. Cisco made 23 acquisitions last year only to suffer a multi Billion dollar loss in 2001.

## 339. CHINA
### September 26, 2001

Here's what can happen in a company town when your letter reaches the right person. In Hebei where the great wall of China extends to the sea. There is a town called Shanhalguan. An American tourist toured the great wall had fun, returned home. He wrote the head of the province thanking him for the wonderful time he had touring the wall and the city. The city manager extolled its citizens go out of their way to be friendly towards Americans. The pattern that followed would be similar to all of us being celebrities in a small town The entire population was to go out of its way to make their visitors feel at home. I'm talking about awards and everything. As I say only in China.

## 340. ENRON: THE TRIAL
### February 1, 2006

The trial of Enron was pivotal in the perception of Corporate Trueth. The Prosecutor John C. Hueston laid out the strategy used by Lay's and Skillings He illustrated the point with a new penny and how even if the stock went up by that Penny it was going forward. Lays and Skilling would silence / lay-off those who figured out their strategy. Cooking the books through derivatives and creative math. I am getting ahead of myself for as of this date the trial had just gotten started and they still had their allies. Remember my description of the Tech industry with all its collapsing variables.

It was argued that Enron's partners maintained the credit line then suddenly stopped it causing the death spiral into Bankruptcy protection. Meanwhile all those investors were being bilked. This was a case of rigged derivatives gone bad. They said they took a simple company and turned it into a tech company. In reality they rigged things to seem like progress when there was none.

## 341. *THE TIMES* OF LONDON
### May 7, 2004

Murdock was a media giant and actually still is today At this time he owned the Guardian and had just bought the *London Times* a paper that was over a hundred years old and one of the bench marks of London. He changed its format and it became more like a tabloid. He contended that people were not interested in say the sports or poetry page so he condensed them. He concentrated instead on the angry celebrity. He cultivated people like Tony Blair and got their stories. In his mind's Eye he was making the paper relevant.. This would change later with startling revelations but I think you can wait for that tid-bit.

## 342. IN KIND OIL CONTRACTS
### September 17, 2009

The way this program read was right out of a movie. Ken Salazar Head of the department of Interior, was trying to figure out how to extend drilling privileges to Federal lands. Products for services was a mechanism. The trouble was when the book keeping broke down, some payments were not made or made in kind. I am referring to sex and special favors. These contracts have been disallowed and when the remaining contracts expired in 2010 the program would come to an end.

Officials stated that: "the program is an effective means of ensuring that the American people receive fair compensation for development of federal resources."The Royalty in kind collected the equivalent of 4.3 billion in Royalties in 2007 The latest period for which data was available as the Interior department spokesman said. He also indicated that the program would run through 2010.

That is all well and good but what of the irregularities in the program and the noncompliance originating with the corporate entities. The program had its run did its job and if you can't fix it it's time to go.

## 343. THE TARP ISSUE
### September 17, 2009

Citi Groups Executive Vicram Pandit sat before officially thanked the American people for bailing out Citi group to the tune of 45 billion dollars. He noted that Citi would need no further assistance. This was echoed by Herbert M. Allison Jr assistant to the treasury that oversees TARP Pandit stated: "This is a different company."Asked about breaking up the company he responded: "We are selling 40% of the company. We are breaking it up."In December 2008 Citi repaid 20 billion dollars. The government also removed 102 billion in guaranties. The remaining 25 billion owed the government was converted to 27 % stake in the company. He stated: "We look forward to helping them make money on that investment. Citi owes a large debt of gratitude to the American tax payers." When asked about the reduced size and limited scope combined with the initial 45 billion dollar bail out disproportionate to the other banks. Allison stated that there is no Corporation to big to fail and with the new regulations in place a failing company would be dismembered. Pandit added: "I don't think banks should be using capital to speculate." He stated that it had substantially cut back on proprietary trading.

When questioned on a banker's impartiality Pant stated: "It is difficult to avoid the impression so for the company to curry favor with the hand that feeds it. This is a tough position for me because if I say what I believe and it happens to be in line with what somebody else believes in the administration, it looks like hey you know because the treasury is 27% shareholder.

Treasury said that the government netted 1.54 billion for the sale of stock warrants that it received from Bank of America as part of the 45 billion dollar bail out. "Pandit continued: "We don't want to be a shareholder in that company" referring to Bank of America said it would sell: "In an orderly manner. The regulators want us to make prudent loans. We are doing that."

### 344. NORTHROP GRUMAN
September 17, 2009

In the 1990's there was a merger due to the shrinking defense budgets. Courtesy of 9/11 they experienced a growth in unmanned warfare. Now with the slowing of defense spending and it's CEO Ronald D. Sugar reaching the age of 61 was due to retire in June. Wesley G. Bush Northrop's President and chief operating officer is due to take his place. Bush is 48 years of age. Sugar stated: "I've had a great run. Like an athlete you don't want to step down too soon. But now it seems the right time to pass the baton." They make unmanned air-craft satellites, and nuclear submarines. They are one of the leading employers in California.

### 345. FINANCIAL RED-LINING

Two subsidiaries of AIG are paying 7.1 million dollars to settle a discrimination law-suit. This class action law-suit had 2,500 African American defendants who were borrowers under the subprime loans which caused the melt down in the housing market. After lawyer's fees 6.1 million will go to the parties in the suit. Thomas E. Perez Assistant Attorney general in charge of the Civil Rights division stated basically that this was the first time a lender has been held responsible for failing to ensure that brokers charge appropriate fees. It had been the Wild West for this had not been done before.

### 346. FILM MAKERS
December 10, 2009

Mohsen Makhalbaf is a quiet man who is the thorn in the side of Iran's radical government. He took with him thousands of Tech say Iranians. They went from Afghanistan to Paris where he pursues his passions. He speaks with fellow firm makers from around the world. Today he is the spokesman for the green movement at least he was in 2009.

### 347. GENERAL MOTORS
December 2, 2009

There is change in the wind at this car company Fritz Henderson a long time head of General Motors is being replaced by Edward Whitacre. At the heart of the matter is direction. Henderson wanted to sell General Motors European division. That was going nowhere. The sale of the Saab line still had several prospects.

Fritz Henderson according t sources: "One of the major criticisms of Henderson is that he is a` G M lifer. Whitacre being an automotive outsider came in and said we need to change the way things are done. Saab though the deal fell through still has buyers. They as a car company want to focus on four marques: Chevrolet, Cadillac, GMC, and Buick. Whitacre stated: "Fritz has done a remarkable job in leading The company through an unprecedented period of change. While momentum has been building over the last several months. All involved agree that changes have to be made.

Several things pointed to this have happened, the Saturn brand that was being offered to Penske fell through. Plans to sell the Saab line to a Swedish sports car maker Koenigsegg fell through. There was a deadline on the SAAB sale that if it were not met there would be an orderly closing of the line. Magna International inc was to buy Opel this was rejected. Add to this the fact that the Federal Government owned 61% of G M Stock his request for resignation had to come from the board. Henderson succeeded Richard Wagner who was ousted by the Obama Administration. Henderson was known as Chainsaw Fritz.. He was not afraid of tackling the hard decisions. In less than a year Fritz steered G M in through and out of Bankruptcy. By November it was stated that G M was in a position to start paying back the U.S. and Canadian governments.

When Whitacre arrived on the scene he argued that G M should not be giving up market share despite a shrinking brand portfolio. Abandon giving large sum cash rebates known as juice sales. Whitacre made his name turning a small Telecommunications company SBC into AT&T. He admitted he knew almost nothing about cars. Whitacre will handle the company till a successor is found.

### 348. COMCAST
#### December 3, 2009

Steven Burke is taking the number two position in Comcast. His family members are all heads of companies in the entertainment field. Before taking on the position at Comcast. He was with Disney. At the age of 51 he decided to help build Comcast. This he has done bring it into alignment with NBC. He in his credentials has been called on to help in the Euro-Disney theme park. It is said he prefers a number two spot that acts very much like an anchor with potentially more influence.

Presslller stated: "Steve is one of those unique entertainment executives who both understands and appreciates the operational side of the business as well as the creative process. His life is very disciplined. He rises early jogs and spends time with family before going to the office at eight o'clock. He is at home with the family in the evening..I bet they talk about entertainment at the table.

## 349. BANK OF AMERICA
### September 15, 2009

Bank of America would have paid 33 million dollars to the Security exchange commission for its payment of 3.6 billion dollars in bonuses to Merrill Lynch and company executives.. They contended that the punishment was too light (SEC) U.S. District Judge Jed Rakoff in New York scolded Federal Regulators that they did not dig deep enough into Bank of America to see if they intentionally set out to deceive the shareholders concerning their plans to pay bonuses to employees of Merrill Lynch the previous year. This was when Bank of America was trying to buy Merrill Lynch. This comes on the heels of the S E C again it failed to detect Bernard Madoff's Ponzy scheme. The casting of the spotlight was in response to the agencies willingness to settle out of court instead of getting at the truth.. All this comes about at the one year mark of the collapse of Lehman Bros.

## 350. THE BANKS
### June 10, 2009

It was argued that a crippled banking system with endless support from the tax payers would be a anchor on the economy. Ten banks that took the TARP bail-out money have started repaying their debt. It is argued that private capital and trade securities are returning along with consumer confidence. It is also been put forth that the auto industry needs to be able to borrow to maintain inventories and do business. This would also apply to other non-banking sectors. The treasury secretary stated: "I think it's fair to say that the force of the global storm is receding a bit.

## 351. THE TANGLED WEB

I just gave you a rosy picture of the banking system and its ability to lend to stimulate business. Now here's the down side. The Saint Regis Monarch Beach the luxury Hotel and grounds that has gone down in the history books as the place where AIG (American International Group) held their massive party after accepting Federal Bail-Out money was scheduled to go on the chopping block the following week.

It seems that they owed $70,000,000 courtesy of CITI GROUP / GLOBAL MARKETS REALTY GROUP. There was negotiation to avoid the public auction that was due for July 7$^{th}$. In the year 2007 the banks had not yet seized up and the business flow was high enough to float a $300,000,000 loan. The Makarchains and their partners had no difficulty at that time.

The Hotel itself was state of the art, the best in the world. It had all the bells and whistles. A quote from management: " If you're going to build a five star luxury resort hotel that will out-do every other deluxe hotel on the planet, you don't scrimp on the sheets."

This monument to excess became the cruel joke of history when AIG held their function with all the bells and whistles just after getting the Federal Bail-out. There is nothing wrong with opulence but they should have declined the honor. There was a 20% drop in business after that. They got a bad rap. The Presidential suite alone went for $3,200 a night. They were talking about splitting the place up into separate establishments.

## 352. THE HEALTH CARE ISSUE

A National Health Care plan was working its way through Washington. At the time the opposition to the Obama proposal was not united and Republicans and Democrats were seeking common ground. You must remember 2012 was a long way from 2009.

The areas of common interest such as retaining your health insurance after you are no longer employed by a given company was an issue. The concern over the cost that was going twice as fast as inflation was a consideration. Strangely the issue of abortion had not come up yet. There was the worry among the middle class that new taxes would be applied. The size of the roll of the Federal government was a hot issue. The cost of the program and who would bear it. ($1,5,000,000,000,000) over the decade was a major obstacle. Sources of raising revenue ranged from higher taxes on the wealthy to taxes levies on sugar based soft drinks.

Those putting forward legislation on the Health care issue Senator Edward M. Kennedy in his version outlines numerous government regulations that would insure that every American got insurance. Representative Henry A. Waxman Democrat of Beverly Hills in cooperation with Max Baucus Democrat Montana: Chairman of the Senate finance committee. Put together a bill hoping for Republican support.. The republicans put forth their version of ideas so they would be included in the mix.

There were three areas of commonality : Improving the quality of health care by encouraging doctors and hospitals to embrace the most effective treatment. Curbing the explosive costs that run twice the rate of inflation. The proposal was to move to computerized medical records. Making health insurance readily available to all citizens. Now I ask the question what about the undocumented? They have been paying taxes some using other names not their own.

Senator Charles E. Grassley Republican (Senate Finance committee, Iowa) stated: " It is just very, very difficult."He was part of a bipartisan group that was seeking a way to solve the health care problem in this country. The battle would rage on.

## 353. HOUSING PRICES FALL

When you buy a home you do so with an eye on the future. You expect steady gradual growth over the years. You expect a little waver that follows will curve but you don't expect to fall off the cliff. Remember the banks still want their money though your property is worth half the value you paid for it. Your income did not go up and you might have fallen into the long range unemployment trap.

The prices of homes for new buyer as of this date had become a bargain at half the value the previous owner paid. The trouble would be that banks don't like to lose money and can just sit on that property as a tax loss. If you were fortunate enough to purchase property you might have to take a short sale. You are essentially absorbing the loss the bank has just incurred. Welcome to the wonderful world of real-estate.

### 354. THE CAT FISH ISSUE

There are two species that look very much alike but have different origins. The American Cat-fish scientific name is Ictaluridae. The Vietnamese species is Pangaslddae. There is a difference in the fin structure, head shape placement and size of the eyes. They are two different species.

With the warming of relations between the U.S. and the Democratic Republic of Vietnam comes trade. Our Cat-fish are corn fed and raised in tanks. The Vietnamese have a much lower standard.. They have been importing and selling to restaurants their product. This has caused the shrinkage of the catfish farms in this country by roughly fifty percent. We lost our shoe industry to Asia years ago. World trade or no you protect your native industries. This could be considered an Obama dilemma. I have not heard anything related to this issue but time will tell.

### 355. A TRIP TO THE MOON
June 27, 2009

Forty years ago man put his impression on the lunar surface. Google in conjunction with NASA has given us a virtual tour of the moon. Apparently it is quite realistic. Buz Aldren described as a place of Magnificent Desolation. They had been working on the project since 2005. Go to Moon in Google Earth.

### 356. FLAT SCREEN TV
June 29, 2009

With the switch to digital from analogue has come the change in taste as in perceived upgrade. Other reasons center on the economy and more people spending time at home. Vacations get put off because gas is too expensive. Change has a relative value some even considered buying a flat screen for $2,700 with all its light Emitting Diode affects.

## 357. GOVERNMENT STIMULOUS RECESIONS END?
### July 17, 2009

It was stated that the worst recession since the Great depression was in 2009 about to come to an end. The experts said that the recession was actually worse than described. Government statistics stated that the economy shrank 1% in the second quarter. It was followed up with the notion that with a cession like this the rebound is generally strong.

The other side to this argument on this seemingly marvelous recovery was the Cash for Clunkers program that rebated, to the buyer of a new car in exchange for the old bas guzzler $3,500 to $4,500. The cost of the program itself was extended, by 2 billion dollars. That would carry it for the next several days. Dealerships were staying open abnormally long hours in response to the public demand. It was touted as one of Obama's major successes. It was actually an artificial stimulant that affected the second quarter. Incidentally sales returned to an abysmal normal after the program ended. That great recovery we were going to experience wasn't even close, though there was some job creation.

## 358. PUBLIC SECTOR JOB LOSS
### July 18, 2009

California had in 2009 a 11.6 unemployment rate. As of June job losses numbered 66,500. The public sector in June shed 6,700 jobs. This was after dropping 14,200 in May. In California that golden state of opportunity our teachers that serve our public schools are getting lay-off notices. How many you ask? The answer 17,500 state wide. Yes. Virginia there is trouble in paradise.

It all stems from that energy crisis that hit us that I have described. For all of the efforts of our Governors Democrat and Republican the crisis remains. Arizona at this time was doing better than us.

## 359. THE NATIONAL HEALTH PLAN
### August 1, 2009

What President Obama saw as a prerequisite for recovery was a National health plan. There are differences between the House and senate versions. Here is a basic breakdown of the program.

Who's covered under this plan 94% of non elderly residents to a peak of 97% in the senate version

What is the cost. In both the house and Senate plans up to 1 trillion dollars over a ten year period. Beginning costs in the senate version 615 billion

How is it paid for? There would be a tax increase to cover $544,000,000,000 over the next decade over the next ten years. This particular tax would apply to single people making over $280,000 a year. The rate for couples would be $350,000 yearly.

How is it subsidized? Families with up to 400% of the poverty level. What is that in the real world $88,000 for a family of four. Small businesses would qualify for tax credits that would help them buy insurance for the employees.

How do you choose insurance? The answer to that lies in the openly competitive market place or there would be a Government option to help create competition.

What exactly would be the benefit package? (Preventive Mental health services along with Oral and vision services.) Out of pocket costs would be capped. Over time this basic package would be the standard for employee employer insurance coverage. There would be no denial for pre-existing conditions.

What about that option the Obama Administration was talking about? To insure the concept of competition in the medical insurance field there would be a government insurance run close to the way Medicare and medical is run today. This was the essence of the plan.

Now review the economic facts as presented and the corporate mindset that has been put forth and ask yourself is providing help to the people in this country a starter in job creation.

### 360. THE FOURTH OF July
June 29, 2009

There is a major dilemma in small town America, with the loss of income comes the loss of discretion. You can no longer go to the movies so you sit home and watch I Love Lucy, that was a joke. Seriously middle America has come to a crossroads, retain employees, help food banks, maintain library services or have a fireworks show. When the question is put that way, it has led cities to either simplify or cancel their celebrations. In many cases good Samaritans have been found to subsidize a shorter show coupled with a community carnival incorporating business interests and bobbing for apple sauce. Still others have raised the revenues to put on a 20 minute display.

Any society must celebrate its birth. That is how we keep loyal citizens. Even in bad times that good feeling is necessary food for the soul. That is why funds will be found, parades will go on and picnics will be in our lives. That is what we call America.

### 361. THE COUNTY FAIR CONCEPT
September 11, 2009

The economy was doing nothing in terms of real growth, but everyone loves a fair and everyone loves a deal. The los Angeles County fair offers that thrill. The venders have a opportunity, especially small firms to sell their goods to 1.3 million people.

Jim Galpin who sells patio furniture: "If I hear someone say, the economy and the recession one more time I'll go crazy."Daily about 12,000 visitors ready to spend and invest in motor homes, technology, food venders, horse racing, he also alluded to the mass over time 1.3 million I spoke of earlier. You would normally get 18 days of sales. In 2008 the fair opened five days earlier. That added 265,000 people to the mix. For a stall 10 by 10 it would run $2,500 to a 2,000 square foot area that would be 40,000 dollars. We food peddlers and carnival ride operators that pay a percentage of their sales during the fair.

The concept of being able to offer discounts up to 45% appeals to the vender and the bargain hunter. Many times the merchandise is last years and the line this merchandise won't last long. Big ticket items like Yamaha wave runners were selling for $15,000. The line would be I May not be here tomorrow.

A vender who sold furniture stated: "I heard it was a great fair to be at. If I sell 40 sets of furniture I'll be happy."Eddy Secard who owns the pool and spa location always sells at the fair. I have been part of that crowd that roams the acreage and it is gorgeous. His latest twist is above ground swimming pools because in this economic environment no-one can afford a $50,000 swimming pool.

The economy is moving and people do get hired on a temporary basis. Our economy is a economy is one that is in transition. The service economy is extremely transitional. The point is that any fair has its economic advantages.

### 362. THE AUTO INDUSTRY
October 2, 2009

Auto sales at this time in history the auto sales plummeted to the lowest in seven months. With the cash for clunkers program now defunct potential car buyers were thinking twice or was that three time. Accumulated sales amounted to 745,,997 cars and light trucks. According to the industry it was a 23% slide for the year from 2008 when the gross figure was 964,000. In plain English the cash for clunkers program generated less business in 2009 than the industry did in 2008.

### 363. U.S. INVESTMENT ABROAD
October 4, 2009

The idea that we design and control the elements of production are over in a economy designed to spread innovative hard goods to other countries. The idea is that if you stimulate foreign markets the benefits come home to roost in yours. Investment in China/ India would create jobs in the united States. The old ways of developing your markets no longer fit the mold. This according to the Harvard Business Review.

It is stated according to the *L.A. Times*. (More of the products of the future need to be designed built and marketed in those local markets with design making power placed in other hands.) This sounds to me like reverse mercantilism.

It is argued that without foreign customers (Power Curbers Incorporated) located in Salisbury North Carolina that makes construction equipment, would have gone bankrupt."We're fortunate that infrastructure development is going on in other countries. Seventy five percent of these corporations' sales were international. This had grown from 25% in 2007.

Because of the rate at which we are growing Corporations like General Electric are relying on the emerging economies to benefit their bottom line. Countries like Kazakhstan have a assembly plant that builds trains and diesel engines. There is a factory in Grove City Pennsylvania that makes the parts for those trains and engines.

General Electric has an Ultra Sound machine that has as its target rural China. The device has a production base near Shanghai. Engineers employed in Waukesha Wisconsin along with other locations around the world benefit from the growing sales.

It is put forth that the weaker dollar will help U.S. exports and as a back handed action encourage American companies to invest here at home.

The sad fact is that we don't matter to the corporate world. They do better abroad than here. In 2004 General Electric had 165,000 employees in the United States. It employed 142,000 outside the United states. As of 2008 it had 152,000 employees in the United States. It had 171,000 outside the United States.

The issue of outsourcing, U.S. Tax and Currency policies are telling them to invest over-seas and not so much in the united states. Again American consumers are urged to buy but the jobs end up somewhere else. Following this logic according to Engler who represents G E: "A decision to build a plant in China doesn't alternatively mean it would have been built here."Over 2,000,000 American jobs have been lost to overseas locations as a result of this recession.

What is happening that companies in order to survive are seeking expansion in foreign markets. Power Curbers a small manufacturing firm was seeking to expand its market in China. It is attending trade fairs and boosting its website. What we manufacture only a quarter goes toward export. The firm Messenger was in 2009 only operating at 60% of capacity., using a reduced work force and part time employment to avoid those related costs. In 2007 they sold 37% or 40 million in sales abroad.

The other major component that was employed in the 90s and 2000 through the start of our great recession was acquisition.(Merger) Kraft Foods Incorporated had express an interest in buying Cadbury an English firm. A significant part of the rational was to gain a foothold in China.

For all the gold in China. Pardon the pun you have one unforeseen difficulty. Chinese bureaucracies coupled with the mad dash of competition that exists in the country. China is not a oral country. It is a practical one. Its leaders can broker a deal allow piracy. In all fairness as of late 2010 through the present they have been cracking down on counterfeit merchandise.

Just a short story I worked for General Electric in the late seventies. Even then they were relocating to Brazil because of their labor policies. You see brazil was anti-union. When the workers tried to organize they hung its leader from a tree. This is a true story.

## 364. MANSIONS
### October 4, 2009

Built in a time just before the bubble burst these huge white elephants that adorn our coast in California have fallen on hard times. The owners of these palaces held out for their price for years but with the recession that actually started as early as 1996, these gorgeous pieces of architecture are going on the chopping block.

Esmael Adibi a Chapman University Economist stated: "Sellers there now have to unload and in order to do so they must reduce their prices. The example of Igarashi who had to cut their losses and move on. Some owners were forced to do so by their lenders. When you have too many palatial mansions in a economy that is contracting some housing is just forced off the cliff. So it is that all those beautiful palaces in Newport Beach, and new port Coast, Laguna Beach, and Manhattan Beach by Irvine to the Palos Verdes Peninsula have lost value at the top of the market.

## 365. THE LOCAL CORNER STORE
### October 12, 2009

The location is South Los Angeles and the issue the density of small grocery stores that serve the people in these areas. Jan Perry who represents the 9th district which is 14 square miles wants to control the density of these stores. There are three major stores in the area. The proposal was put forth that they be one forth mile from one another. There are 58 stores in the district as of 2009. In West Los Angeles there are only 14 such stores. The issue ironically is not one of density as the ordinance implies. It is about obesity and the young population. I do suspect it goes across all age demographics. The people in this area generally walk or take a bus to these stores be they a chain or independently owned.

Janis Perry has the point of view reinforced by a Rand Study that the people in her district are heavier than in other sections of Los Angeles. She stated: "It's a carrot and stick approach."

Roland Sturm who helped put the study together that higher obesity rates and poorer communities together basically stated it is not helpful to regulate the stores. The study stated that 26% of the residents in South Los Angeles were considered obese as opposed to 18% in other Los Angeles Counties. Even he said: "I would hesitate to prohibit the development of these stores."

Margaret Chabris spokes woman for Seven Eleven stated: "Convenience stores whether they are Seven Eleven or other provide needed products and services to communities especially low income and high crime. Sometimes larger super markets won't venture into tougher neighborhoods, but mom and pop stores, locally run convenience stores will. They provide food groceries and paper products, money orders, ATM services and over the counter medicine around the clock. They can also be a safe haven when some-one on the street, or in the neighborhood is in trouble and needs a place to go or make a phone call."The exact number of stores to customers is 58 food stores to 100,000 residents in South Los Angeles. This makes the area unique. Culture is part of economic life.

### 366. THE POP UP STORE
October 17, 2009

In this recession we all know malls with empty stores. It just does not give a good image. What the pop up store does is that in peak times when a manufacturer wishes to push a product or products. They don't have to have a lengthily complicated lease that makes them responsible for taxes, janitorial and in some cases a percentage of the profit.. It creates flow in the holidays. Even store front displays with dot com addresses work to increase the traffic flow in a mall.

The target is the casual shopper who finds something really special that they were not intending on buying. Retail Corporations like Toys R Us or Holiday Express toys take up a shop that would normally be vacant. The location could be the Irvine Spectrum center, Montclair Plaza, anything nationally or in my case the southland. The stores range from Halloween shops to a limited edition of Levi jeans. Also stalls in center walk ways offer opportunities for that miniature tree or piece of art, or have your picture taken in 1800s mode. Small and large businesses are welcomed by landlords who find space hard to fill.

### 367. BANK OF AMERICA

B of A was having financial trouble. Being a commercial giant it was judged too big to fail initially 25 billion was the bailout figure. They looked into buying Merrill Lynch. This was the tip if the financial crisis and Luis its CEO wanted to back out of the deal but Federal Officials according to the times pressured him to follow through adding a 20 billion dollar bail- out so he did it. Now remember B of A had a1 billion dollar loss in the first quarter. The company recorded an 11.7 billion dollar expense to cover future loan losses from a 6.5 billion dollar provision in the third quarter of 2008. B of A fell in stock price 4.6%

Kenth D Luis suggested that the losses might have peaked. (Third Quarter) He warned that losses potential were there in the fourth quarter. The loss spread over shares was 26 cents after paying 1.2 billion in dividends on Preferred Stock.(How can you pay dividends on losses? To continue the analysts expected a loss of 12 cents per share. According to the *L.A. Times* in the last third quarter B of A earned 1.2 billion That averaged out to 15 cents a share. Third quarter preferred stock dividends included 993 million owed to the Federal government on its 45 billion dollar investment. Bank shares shrank 84 cents to $17.26. This was five times their price at $3.14

Goldman Sacks was riding high from resurgence in their securities trading businesses. 3.2 billion in the third quarter. Luis tells B of A that the acquisition of Merrill Lynch was improving the banks financial results. In actuality the brokerage losses had multiplied. He thought of backing out but did not due to pressure and that extra 20 billion. The long made short the acquisition of a dead beat Merrill Lynch put B of A in the red.

## 368. COMMERCIAL TRANSPORTATION
### October 23, 2009

There has always been a fight between commercial and residential use. In the Port of Los Angeles Long Beach is due for an upgrade in the bridge that raises and lowers for the cargo coming in and out of los Angeles harbor. The whole station was at the time due for an upgrade. The residents that live by the station have banded together to fight back

Elva Carrillo and her husband run a small private school that is associated with the Apostolic Faith Church in Wilmington. They live 750 feet from the proposed truck express way. She states: "There are at least 21 to 28 days a year when the air is so bad here that we do not let the children go outside to play. You can feel the trucks rumble day and night. How much should we endure."With the Carrillo's in this complaint, Natural Resources Defense Council and two community groups. They were going to court against CALTRANS and the (Diesel dependent cargo movement industry.) The result of this lawsuit could determine the continuance of our commercial economy.

## 369. HOLLEYWOODS PROPS

Culver Studios was a huge place. It's props and technical equipment earned them a nice living. James Cella was President. He has had to lay-off half of the people who worked for him and others were reduced to a 20 to 40 hour week. The business is just not there. It has moved to places like Michigan that offer a 20% tax credit. The new reality shows do not use props to a great degree.

The founder John Zabrucky secured a location in Vancouver Canada thinking he would head off situations but completion mushroomed and he could not keep up. His firm like others relies on TV production, small scale film makers but with the sharp drop in the economy and the rising costs associated with film production, complicated by the writers' strike, and the year long fight between the studios and the Screen Actors Guild led to the present predicament in 2009. Available jobs in the industry had dropped 13,800 over the previous year. This was according to the Employment Development Department.

The year 1996 seems to be a bench mark for from that date on things started to crumble. By 2008 there had been a 50% reduction in films major and minor shot on the streets of L A. Television production an industry that has kept actors and all that support the production working continue to suffer also. 44 of the 103 Pilots were shot in locations as diverse as: Canada, Illinois, Georgia, New York, Louisiana, and New Mexico.

In all thirty States of the Union have offered tax credits to the movie/ television industry to move out of the state. California finally responded with a tax credit but it is thought to be inadequate to hold the industry in this state.

Jack Kyser chief economist for the Los Angeles Development Corporation: "L A is at risk of losing a good part of its signature industries, just like it did the Aerospace industry in the 1990s. Remember the show Deal or No Deal? Originally it was housed in Culver Studios located in New York. It moved to Connecticut.

As of 2009 it still hosted the Bonnie Hunt Show but its over-all business slid from 85% to 46%. 25/7 Studio Equipment has seen its share in the business shrink dramatically since 2007. Sorenson its owner stated that a major studio can generate seventy five thousand dollars in rental income from a company like his.

One must think of all those affected Hollywood/ New York down turn. People who put their lives into the business now only to find what they did no longer matters.

## 370. THE TIMBER INDUSTRY
October 28, 2009

The California lumber industry has been pummeled as has the housing market. The logging industry. At the heart of California's Red Wood Empire the five operating saw mills have had locks put on their gates. A person who only had a high school education could earn $20 an hour. That has seemingly passed into history. The trucking industry that had geared itself to the transport of those trees were idling their rigs.

The pulp industry, you know the ones that the an entire tree to make a tooth pick.(Just kidding). The pulp mill in Samoa 40 miles south of Orick which had in 2009. When it operated the plant put in excess of $11,000,000 into the local economy. Nate Zink President of the Association of Western Pulp and paper Workers Local 49,: "Now we're being forced into the job market and there aren't a lot of jobs out there."

The affect at the community level is felt also. Take the town of Orick with a population of roughly 300 where out of a stand of trees a herd of elk could appear. They are being forced down to Southern California and the apartment life that really does suck.

Henry Spelter an economist for the U.S. Forest Service stated: "Most of the wood in California stays in California and housing in California is in horrible shape."William Melvin co-owner in Melvin and Turner Chopping stated that he had been unemployed all summer. During the housing boom his saw never saw a dull moment (Another Joke) He paid off his house and now at the age of 50 he is becoming a plumber.

Companies for a variety of reasons: lack of old growth lumber, permits to cut new growth lumber, lawsuits over tree preservation, slump in the housing market have caused the closure or reduced operation of mills and cutting operations up and down the coast of California, having a deep economic impact on the people that live here.

### 371. THE FEDERAL HOUSING ADMINISTRATION
### December 3, 2009

FHA loans have long been the key to home ownership. Without such a loan families like George Ramirez and his wife Leticia could not have purchased their $275,000 home with a 3% down of $8,250. George was the sales manager for Citibank. He stated: "These loans are actually going to help people who are looking for the American dream, and if they start restructuring it's going to hurt them."

FHA related loans in 2009 made up 38.3% of all homes purchased in the southland. The figure was 32.5% in 2008 which was two points higher from the previous year. The Data source was MDA Data-quick. Any changes in the program were not expected to be finalized till January 2010. The main reason for this would be to not hinder the recovery of the housing market.

The Obama Administration was considering raising the minimum from 3% to 3.5%. It was argued given the current housing market, it would prevent some families from accumulating the necessary minimum down payment. Say for argument sake you have a $300,000 house. The minimum payment would be $10,500. If the down payment grew to 5% a buyer would have to put down $15,000. it was argued that it was quite a bit more and harder to save.

The temporary expanded roll of the FHA is only because the market is in such bad shape. A gentleman by the name of Donovan testifying before the service committee stated that he doesn't want to change the direction of the FHA from its historic role as an aid to first time buyers. He did have a concern related to the fact that the FHA is supposed to have a reserve fund equal to 2% and it currently has a reserve of 0.53% in 2009. He argued by raising the rate from 3.5% to 5% would reduce the risk of foreclosures. He May have been correct in a sense but with continued job loss even the well qualified engineer would face foreclosure.

### 372. OLD TECHNOLOGY STATE EFFICENCY
### December 9, 2009

The State of California in2009 had not upgraded its computers used in processing EDD information and extensions as granted by Congress.. Initially in 2002

California received $66,000,000 for the upgrade of its systems. By 2009 they had not done the job and stated it would take $300,000,000 to bring the states computers up to snuff. Ironically the same failure occurred in 2008 affecting approximately 100,000 Californians.

Back to the current dilemma. The regional administrator for California Richard C. Trigg stated: "We note that California is already experiencing difficulty in several performance areas including first payment timeliness non monetary determination timeliness appeals., timeliness appeals aging. Despite corrective action plans performance has continued to decline over the past year.."

To bring this to a personal level Sandra Merchant (46) of the City of Benicia who stated that her life was literally from check to check from the EDD. She had a job in information technology that she lost in July of 2008. She stated: "If I don't have the check I wouldn't make it. That would be the end of me. Basically the only thing I do right now is survive."She makes her rent but must ignore her medical needs. She receives monies amounting to $950 every two weeks and the occasional loan from her parents. She used to make a salary of $12,000 a month. She continued: "There's a really big problem where the EDD is looked at like its lower on the scale than the DMV but it's a critical function. If they don't get those checks out, it will be anarchy. It is bad out here."She was commenting on the log-jam of overloads on the phone system. The unemployment rate at this time in California was 12.5%. In all fairness the Federal Government did send $60,000,000 to remedy the situation to help them bring things up to code. As was pointed out the estimated cost of fixing the system was $300 million. These are hard times.

## 373. ASSIGNMEMENTSS FOR THE BENEFIT OF CREDITORS
January 3, 2011

This is the alternative to Bankruptcy. It is a non-court mandated function. The filing for a ABC is somewhat simple and has been in practice since the 1930s. Instead of going to court you appoint a trustee to liquidate the company. The business owner hires a assignee. A insolvency lawyer or specialist with experience in ABCs often hired. He takes his fee sells the company assets and distributes those assets to the creditors. The Assignee has a fiduciary duty to get the highest price for the assets.

The bowers had a business that used to employ 20 people. Business declined and they put their own money into it. Things did not improve. At the advice of a banker they knew they filed for a ABC and hired Gourmeet Singh as the assignee. The complications of a ABC filing are that the business must be incorporated, It does not close other potential creditor leans. The less under water the business is the better. If personal property is involved such as a mortgage you are still responsible for that.

Gourmeet Singh stated: "We signed the agreement and right away took over everything. We had the locksmith right there and had the locks switched they were out of the business. Then we some people to take inventory of things."This process saved these people a lot of cost and kept their credit clean with no red flags that you would get with a chapter 7 or 11 Bankruptcy. Done right it's clean and simple, wrong it's on going.

### 374. ALL IN THE NAME OF SECURITY
### January 14, 2010

The North Island Naval Air Station maintains and repairs the flotilla that is the U.S. Navy. Civilians work on the island in conjunction with navy personnel. There was a Ferry that helped break the gridlock of traffic for the civilian employees that work on the island. Going to work has been for these commuters like a mini vacation starting at Cabrillo ending at the island. The ferry has also conducted tours of the bay. The ride to the island has always been free subsidized by the State of California. The reason was to relieve the congestion on the high-way that leads up to the base.

Thanks to the shooting at Fort Hood by the naval Chaplin who is just now going to trial in 2011 the powers that be viewed the ferry ride as a facilitator of terrorism. It took just another bit of joy out of our lives. The move probably made them smile. I would compare it the Helicopter ride that lasted 25 minutes that took you over the damn and all over Laughlin Nevada. That was canceled just after 9/11 for the same reasons.

The long made in short in all of this is that the state did save some money because it no longer had to do certain things related to security. The bad thing was it eliminated another draw for the tourist dollar. It also forced people back into their cars.

### 375. FREIGHT BY RAIL
### January 14, 2010

A sign that the economy could be improving is how much freight travels across this country to be carried by trucks to their final destination. The sad fact is that the Rail Road freight haling business has been in decline since before the recession.

Warren Buffett has stepped in and bought Burlington Northern Santa Fe Corporation for $34,000,000,000.He did this Buffett stated: "All in wager on the economic future of the United States."This line services Southern California along with the ports of los Angeles and long-Beach. The other line that follows this route is the Union Pacific Corporation.

Since the most recent record keeping has been in place the industry has suffered a 33% drop in lumber and wood products carried by train. Trains carried across this country 34% fewer motor vehicle parts and 8% less coal. The year of 2009 saw declines most of them very steep (In every major category of Rail Road traffic)

The decline in rail transport from 2008 to the start of 2010 have been dramatic to say the least. The break-down goes as follows: a 48% drop in motor vehicle parts, a 49% drop in metallic ore and metals, plus a 47% drop in lumber and wood products.

By December the world had changed and traffic increased. Grain, chemicals, petroleum, and auto parts had increased and the number of idled cars had decreased. The nations sea ports also saw an increase. That was a sign that consumers were again buying. Wall Street saw the increased traffic as a sign of the water level raising all boats.

### 376. HOME SALES
February 27, 2010

The housing market experienced a slump in sales largely due to foreclosure sales amounting to 38% of the market. According to the National association of realtors sales were the lowest since June but 11.5% higher than in 2009. It was said that the market was critically weak and probably would not recover in 2010. The Congressional action on extending the tax credit had little effect on the market according the *L.A. Times*.

Christopher Thornberg a principle with Beacon Economics in Los Angeles stated: "The Tax credit wore off. Now that the tax credit has been extended it is no longer functional. We will get a push close to the end of it, probably in March."He stated that prices and sales would plunge on April 30th when it expires.

The rather down housing market news came from the Government report that the U.S. Economy in the last quarter of 2009. The GDP rose at a annual rate of 9.5% in the fourth quarter. The U.S. Commerce Department stated that the real growth was up 0.2% over the previous projection. Among the biggest contributors to growth were the Private inventory Investments exports, personal consumption expenditures and non- residential fixed investments. Business inventory restocking accounted for much of the gains. That was expected to dissipate in the coming months.

You see where things were going government stimulus not reinforced by the markets had little long term improvement because it had little effect on the bottom line JOBS.

### 377. FORECLOSURE DILEMMA
February 27, 2010

The glut of houses going into Foreclosure and public sale had become so great that a vacant house was a vandalized house. The result was a form of adverse possession. Even though you stop paying your mortgage, receive a three day or quit notice, no one comes to remove you from that house that you loved and lost.

Gary Kirshner a spokesman for Chase Bank Stated: "If the persons in the property there's less chance of vandalism, and their probably maintaining the house. In the Inland Empire it is estimated that 100,000 home owners are living rent free. I personally know of a case that has been going on for several years and to my knowledge as of 2011 he is still in that house here in Ontario.

The story I will related to you is one talked about in the *L.A. Times*. Rick Sharga and his wife hadn't made a payment in 90 days but the house was not placed in foreclosure. The astounding thing was that the number of foreclosures in 2009 was 2.9 million. Our economists had predicted that the number would be 3.2 million. If you go back to some earlier segments these same guys were saying the recession was near an end. You can now scratch your head. Back to our story. It is now taking a bank 229 days to foreclose on a home as of 2010. It used to be 146 days in 2008.

Mr. Sharga continued: "For some reason banks are being more lenient with home owners who are behind on their loans. Whether it is a strategy to try to slow down the volume of foreclosures or simply a matter of a banks being able to keep up with the volume is something that banks only know for sure."

Some banks like City Bank are doing what they call Partnering. Those that are on the verge of Foreclosure provided they turn the deeds of their homes over to the bank can stay in their homes for 6 months rent free. I have another twist to this. They have lost track of their troubled real-estate and are looking for voluntary compliance. They would later come up with a thing called fast tracking where they are foreclosing on you while they are negotiating with you. In some cases people won but lost their homes in the same breath.

The other trick is the bank can sell your house and not tell you. This is the story of the Harrison's It was stated: "Mortgage lenders are so backlogged that some people are able to slip through the cracks."This according to the institutions. David Harrison stated: "It has been frustrating, a real pain in the buttocks."The Harrison's missed their first payment in 2008. The man lost his job and his health care. She lost her part-time job. They applied for modification with Country Wide which is now part and parcel of B of A. They were told they had to be three months behind before they qualified. They stopped making payment. It was then that they received a notice that their property could be sold. They then were told that their home was now bank owned property. Why did we bail out the banks? If people can fail banks can fail.

### 378. SMALL BUSINESS RISING
March 1, 2010

The small on line businesses are on the rise and have been for some time. It is possibly one of the few bright spots in this economy and why the government now wants to get in on it. The Artisan who lets say makes customized walking sticks and has a website to promote the sale of such sticks. Handmade Jewelry and purses . A percentage of the sale is usually taken by the service.

ETsy.com was one of those sites. Rose Braunstein owns Eagle Rock Jewelers an online company. She stated: "It's a great vehicle but because so many jewelry shops on their it's hard. Right now I have a very small craft empire."She hoped it would grow with her networking system. There is no set up charge to set up a store front. As stated earlier the sites make their money by charging a percentage of the sale. Etsy charges 3.5% and 20 cents to list an item. The amount of money made by the site goes up when items are relisted on a daily basis. According to the Craft and Hobby Association consumers spent 27.3 billion dollars on arts in 2008. This is one of many companies that are part of that new invisible economy that the government does not currently track. So you can say there is economic activity in cyber-space.

## 379. THE PAYDAY LOAN

When you think of these services you think of the person employed who has a bill he wishes to avoid late charges on. Of late the unemployed have been paying 459% annualized fee for an average of 10 transactions a year. It sounds like a lot but to the guy who's trying to avoid that late charge the solution makes sense. This is the economy we are in.

Just how-many out of work people take advantage of this service in a field 2.3 million in the state of California. 1.4 million is the answer. The weekly benefits are between $40 and $250 a week. 26 weeks seems to be the maximum. It is generally a $15 fee for $100 borrowed. When criticized about the rate of interest charged the Community Financial Services Association of America defended their position saying that critics do not understand the reality of scraping by."Who are they to decide. We issue billions of dollars in credit. They issue platitudes and pats on the back. These people need money. They tell them to go to their relatives. These people have bills to pay. These people need to go to job interviews. They need credit."

The default rate on such loans is between 2.5 and 5%. Certain states of the Union do not allow them to operate with-in their borders.. Since their formation in the 1990s they have been accused of preying on the poor. it would be a bit like selling your food-stamps to pay a bill or help accommodate others just to get by. These loan companies are not allowed in: Arkansas, Georgia, and New York. In some locations in California the unemployment check is not considered a valid income. That 's the way it is.

## 380. THE YEAR OF THE PINK SLIP
### March 2, 2010

Teachers are the heart of the educational process. When you lay them off for budget reasons and hire substitutes that you rotate certain curriculum does not get addressed. Certain skills do not get perfected. Add to that the language barrier in the immigrant neighborhoods and you have a recipe for disaster.

What you end up with is gaps in the education system that show up when these children have to take the state examinations. Their base of knowledge is so sketchy and limited that they appear stupid when they are not.

Some teachers that have been laid off have stayed on as substitutes with far less benefits but the inability to establish a consistent curriculum for say a good study of history, the U.S. Constitution to the Civil War into Civil Rights period ETC. Some teachers have bypassed or limited study in certain periods just to keep up. How about the Math and science departments in abridged versions to the slow learner. I think you get the point don't skimp on the kids, their our future.

### 381. AMERICAN DREAM VALUE DILEMMA

This is a story of Nevada with its sprawling real estate boom that that in 2003 inspired Don knight and his wife to buy a ranch property close to the mountains for $180,000. In 2007 he thought about moving to California then the mortgage crisis hit. His home that had increased in value to $350,000 and then plummeted. In 2008 his wife Janet was laid off from the lumber company that went out of business. It was so bad she could not even get a job in a gas station. In 2009 there ranch style home with acreage was worth $177,000 They were about to join the folks in Vegas who were using scuba gear. They got the estimated values of their land to property taxes for 2010. It was $153,000. They went to the arbitration court armed with evidence that a neighbor with a similar house and a pool was valued at $132,000. They contended that their house was worth $125,000. They had received a tax bill of $1,500 This was a hard thing for them to pay considering they were now both unemployed.

The State of Nevada has a law similar to Proposition 13 in California that caps property taxes. The thing is when the price of property rises they complain that the homes are too pricey and when they fall their tax bills did not drop quickly enough. This is according to the *L.A. Times*.

When the Knights stepped forward to press their case stating the comparable home valued at the 132 thousand figure it was pointed out in the debate that it was a bank sales and as such went 25% less than valued. They placed the value of their home at 140,000 dollars.

Here is another case with different connotations. A woman by the name of Moret bought a lavish house for $185,000. Her husband was dying of Cancer. She brightened up the place and he passed. She went to sell it. After four years in 2004 she went to sell it for $875,000. Her sale never became reality and in 2009 it was valued at $439,000. That's what you call the crap shoot. She went before the board hoping to lower the value to $245,000. Property in Nevada is extremely volatile

### 382. THE TECH STARTS UP
March, 5, 2010

In 2008 President Obama initiated his stimulus program. Parts of that program had little or no affect, but the money placed in the Technology slash Green industries bore fruit.

John A Challenger chief Executive of Out placement for Grey and Christmas INC. stated: "After three long years of putting off technology investment companies inevitably want to take advantage of the new technology that's available."(After a fall in spending in 2009 of 8.2% it rebounded 6.6% in 2010.)"Tech will be one of the sectors that will lead the economy out of the recession."

Sharmila Shahani Mulligan Marketing Vice-President of Aster Data systems stated: "We've seen this happen before. There are areas of tech that are big opportunities. Data management is one. Mobile is a big one. With things like this Google device and the phone, people are developing applications and advertizing is growing."

The idea that you can store your data not on your computer but a side mechanism is wetting the imagination of the industry. It is to the point where people are getting jobs in newly started firms that are five years or less. This is where the ball generally gets moving.

For some reason the concept of a public offering and acquisitions if you will are part of the logic for venture capital to be put into play. That is what has happened here. Greene the San Mateo recruiter stated: " Acquisitions are a sign that things are turning. Companies now have money or stock and can afford to go out there and acquire companies. And companies that have funding are hiring and the first place they are hiring is engineering."

Steve Fredrick General Partner Gro-tech Ventures located in Washington D C, stated: "Numbers from the Kauffman Foundation the Entrepreneurship show that two thirds of the jobs created every year in the U.S.. are at companies that are less than five years old. If it weren't for these startups job creation would be negative."

Initially the situation was described by those in the field as this: "Part of the problem is that recruiters and tech companies have such a long laundry list of qualifications it would be hard for anyone to qualify. In leaner times when the unemployment rate is lower the list of "must haves" shrinks."

At the start of all of this the Electronics and telecommunication firms initiated what they called planned job cuts,(174,629) people laid off in the year 2009. John A Challenger of Grey and Christmas stated that the worst of those cuts was in the first quarter. He stated: "Small companies are more nimble and are often responsible for job creation in the U.S.."

Kevin Kimball was one of those laid off from Hitachi Global Storage Technologies Incorporated. It was August 2008 His path to aggressively network on line. He landed a job in 2010 as senior Director of Marketing and communication at Force 10 Networks, in San Jose. He is now a mentor for six other people in their job searches. He stated: "It's only anecdotal but hopefully the trend of my Mentees is a microcosm of something larger."

Red Slice a Seattle marketing and branding company through Maria Ross the owner stated: "Those that are laid off from their marketing teams during the bust now realize that you can't grab new market share and grow the business without effective marketing back in place. Marketing seems to be the first to go when job cuts are made. Until the High Tech companies realize they can't reach their revenue targets with-out it."The venture Capital has started to flow. Let us hope it is for the good.

## 383. TOYOTA'S RECALL
### February 25, 2011

As technology grows there are problems. Design flaws that do not initially revel themselves, but only rise in the day to day habits of drivers.

A sticking accelerator pedal was initially blamed on lead footing that got caught in the carpet and not a manufacturer defect. It was only after a large number of accidents occurred with that single problem in mind that the authorities started looking at the manufacturer.

Toyota ended up recalling six models with recall dates going back to 2003. The Lexus was found to have the same problem. The Highlander and the Lexus RX could be repaired by repairing the carpet trim near the accelerator. The repairs to the Lexus GS models involved replacement of the plastic pads imbedded in the carpet. The 4 runner, Rave four and Lexus LX Toyota is still developing a fix as of the date of this article but will have to modify the gas pedal and replace the all weather mats.

To date there are 10 million Recalls for sudden acceleration since 2009 four months later Toyota determined that sticking pedals could produce sudden acceleration. In 2010 it has paid federal fines totaling $50,000,000

It was determined by the NHTSA that Toyota's original floor mat recall what was wrong and it took 400,000 pages to do it. David Strickland stated: "As a result of the agency review the NHTSA asked Toyota to recall additional vehicles. Now that the company has done so our case is closed."

Bryan Lions spokesman for Toyota stated: " We are confident that we have properly addressed the concerns here." On the consumer end Barbara shepherd of Harbor Springs Michigan stated: "Either Toyota's investigators were incompetent or they just had their heads in the sand."

The exact number of vehicles recalled as a result of the massive complaints 379,000 Highlanders, 272,000 Lexus RX and SUVs.

Beyond the 116 deaths attributed to the defects Toyota faces hundreds of personal injury, death and economic damages law suits in the Federal and State courts.

Steve Berman a Seattle attorney stated: "This sort of revelation calls into question the veracity and credibility of other declarations the company has made. If you ask an average consumer whether a Toyota is worth more or less as a result of these serial recalls the vast majority say less."

These are comments captured in time and the performance of anything should be weighed throughout time and not just one slot of time. If the problem is fixed then it is, but the company should have been more honest and less accusatory.

### 384. THE BORDER'S LIQIDATION
### February 21, 2011

Borders is a place of culture trapped in a down turning economy. It offered a place to sip coffee and read a book along with enlightened discussion. That is not the economy of today. If you do have such a store it must be in a convenient well traveled location.

Jordon Francke 27 a customer at the liquidation stated: "As long as there's a deal I'm going to take advantage of it. It's just the changing landscape of literature these days, it's all electronic. I can only imagine it's a struggle for a place like borders to stay relevant."

Kathleen Oreilly age 52 at the Pasadena store stated: "I spend several days a week here. I actually debated whether I wanted to come, because I was worried I'd be too upset to see the store torn apart."

The critics of the chain argued that they as an organization messed up badly in its move into the digital age. These are those that look to the Wall-Mart models of mass distribution.

The reality of the situation is that 6,000 of the chains 19,000 employees will be laid off but the store representatives state they are not finished but will be back after reorganization.

### 385. THE DOUBLE DIP?
### February 23, 2011

Standard and Poor's / Case Shiller index gave indication that 20 major United States cities dropped an average of 2.4% in December 2010 from the same month a year earlier at 1%. Experts said that the situation could very well get worse. Robert Shiller economics professor at Yale University stated: "My intuition rates the probability of another 15%, 20%, or even 25% real home price decline as substantial. That is not a forecast but it is a substantial risk."

Karl E. Case a Wellesley College economic professor stated: "It looks very much like a rocky bottom with a downward trend. It is so discouraging. It's possible the mood could change very quickly."

This attitude and forecast is somewhat related to the world. It goes from the unrest in Libya and rising gas prices. The Dow Jones index of 30 blue chip stocks lost 178 points or 1.4%. The stock market closed at 12,212.79 amid a global sell-off in equities.

## 386. SMALL BUSINESS AND THE TAX CODE
### February 28, 2011

Small business has delayed putting together its tax bill in California largely because the legislators have dragged their feet.

Here are some of the provisions in the revised tax` code. To state the obvious, the more tax deductions less taxes. 1 Federal tax credits earned last year can be applied against income tax paid in the five previous years using a method called Carry back. That can trigger a tax refund for some firms.

Small businesses can deduct immediately as much as $500,000 of the cost of what's known as real property. This includes machinery equipment and furniture in the year that its bought. The deduction cap is twice as much as it was previously. It can also be applied to some real estate improvements. This includes those made to restaurant and retail properties. The deduction begins to phase out when the cost of purchase exceeds $ 2 million. Previously the phase out was $800,000.

The Federal small business health care tax credit is also for the 2010 tax year. Firms that can meet its strict requirements which include paying average wages of not more than $25,000 to workers who can be full or part time. To get the full tax credit say it could be a boon.

Earle Baer CEO of Price and Item media INC a Malibu on line based publisher of community websites including ...ThisWeekInSocal.com. This firm has five employees.

Due to the budget deficit the state attorneys are looking for ways to raise revenue in the business sector. The state has suspended for two more tax years 2010 and 2011.The rule that lets businesses apply losses from one year against income in the future year. The suspension of the exception has been changed to businesses with expenses under $300,000 from $500,000 previously.

The States Zone enterprise zone program has been sacrificed on the altar of economic necessity. There were 42 such zones.

Credits are still available for the 2010 tax year but May not be around in future years if Jerry Brown and others have their way.

One state credit is still available. It is the little used new jobs tax credit specifically for small businesses. It cuts as much as $3,000 off the tax bill for each qualified employee hired. It applies to companies with 20 or fewer employees. As of 2009. The business must have ended in 2010 with the employees it hired in 2009.

These facts are pretty much verbatim due to the specifics of the data presented and the source is the *L.A. Times.*

## 387. VIRTUAL SHOPPING

The IPAD is about to revolutionize the way we shop this season according to the guru's of retailing. J C Pennies is thinking of doing away with those holiday lines we wait in. One could call it a catalog store inside a department store. The OPAD becomes the register and products don't necessarily have to be on premises. Through the IPAD you can comparison shop from what is in another store.

I see problems with this concept for you still need to buy inventory and there are still different prices for differing volumes of good. How in a cash strapped society where credit has become such a problem do one or more customers decide who will buy a limited number of styles and sizes. How readily do you get them from the supplier. Can you insure you will get the sales price for a dress or your favorite shoes. A retailer has to decide has to decide how much of a thing he gets, so he is not stuck with it when the great return and exchange war starts over all those unwanted gifts.

Yes it would be more interactive, but could the store handle all the variables. Ken Nisch Chairman of JGA seems to think it is the wave of the future.: "Everybody has something in development. This is not going to be a novelty, it is going to be a sea change in how retailers transact and interact with customers.

Other companies have joined in this concept slash experiment. Stores like Nordstrom with their service policy where and how would they be able to maintain it. The store itself has a return policy that says if you don't like it bring it back. This is why Nordstrom's is so incredibly popular despite their prices. The concept of low and stock rotation.

Sandeep Bhanote chief executive of Global Bay Mobile Technologies: "It is taking retail outside the four walls where customers are. You're talking about changing the way you do business. That's what this is all about."

The cool gadget on the counter that helps the customer browse while the sales rep. Helps somebody else a form of multi tasking but how about merchandise control.?"We are developing additional mobile capabilities for our sales floor including testing mobile check out and equipping our sales people with better tools at the point of sale."Is this a greater or lesser degree of service I don't know.

388. TARP
February 28, 2011

When this program was launched it was put in this way like taking all your assets and putting them on 00 on the crap table. Three years after this program was launched to the tune of seven hundred billion dollars the results have been surprisingly good. Those judged too big to fail have paid back the TARP fund. Ted Kaufman a former U.S. Senator from Delaware stated: "It's turning out to cost one heck of a lot less than what we all thought at the beginning."

In mid 2009 the TARP program was projected to lose up to three hundred and forty-one billion dollars. The figure as of 2011 has been reduced to twenty-five billion dollars. The decision was made to pump TARP money into the banks instead of large scale purchase of Securities that were backed by toxic mortgages. It is pretty much a common consensus that the bail outs worked at least at this end's

## 389. ETHANOL
### March 3, 2011

Ethanol produced from corn destined for the gas tank. Plants built expecting t fuel America hit a rough patch in 2008 and plants were moth balled and some were sold. With the new push for renewable fuels these same plants are coming back to life.

In 2010 production hit 13.2 billion gallons Valero Energy corporation who bought some of these plants during the downturn and Marathon Oil Corporation, Sunco incorporated are seeing its closed factories come to life, taking in and processing corn putting the smell of yeast in the air. Pacific Ethanol Corporation which weathered the Bankruptcy is seeing vindication in its investments.

Neil Koehler Chief executive of the Sacramento firm stated: "Ethanol is an important part of this country's energy picture these days. There is a mandated production rate of 36 billion gallons annually by the year 2022 from its original start in 2008.

## 390. PUBLIC EMPLOYEE UNIONS
### March 12, 2011

The place is Wisconsin and the issue collective bargaining rights for health and pension benefits. According to the Union they were willing to pay more out of pocket for what they get but to Governor Scott Walker that was not the issue. He stated: "In the end this bill goes back to what we said last fall.(In his mind he was protecting middle class jobs and that he wanted to make government at all levels better. His goal was to protect the good employees who might have been laid off.) What we're doing here in Wisconsin is leading the way to a better alternative."

It is interesting to note the police and firefighters were excluded from his bill. He tampered with their Union negotiation rights things would be different. That aside such legislation does seem to be taking hold.

## 391. FARM WORKER UNION REFORM
### April 1, 2011

This is April Fool's Day but the issue is serious. In the past when Cesar Chavez initially organized the farm workers employers would intimidate them to not join the organized labor group. These are the same employers who complain they can't get their crops harvested because no-one wants to work the fields.

The State Legislature has just rectified the situation. By a vote of 24 to 14 they authorized Unionizing without the petition that had been required. Governor jerry brown is expected to sign the bill into law.

Senate president Pro Tem Darrel Steinberg Democrat Sacramento who introduced the bill stated: "There are countless cases and countless stories of farm workers who are told that if they join a Union they will be out of a job the next day. They are told they will be reported to immigration."Now think to the argument by the growers that immigration laws interfere with their ability to bring in their crops. Are we talking 1pluss one equals one.

### 392. AMERICAN APPAREL INDUSTRY

The companies name is American Apparel Incorporated. It stated might have to seek Bankruptcy protection because sales have gone down. Among its troubles two sexual harassment law suits that were filed in March. Last year there were $533,000,000 in sales which was a decline of 4.6% decline from 2009. There was a loss of 86.3 million in 2010. The outlook for 2011 was also going to be in negative territory.

The rising cost of cotton combined with ongoing debt issues were included in the 127 page document filed with the Security Exchange commission. It was added that the situation as described were not as dire as expressed according to the founder and chief executive Dov Charney.

### 393. WHAT AFFECT A SHUT DOWN
#### April 2, 2011

The answer to that question is complex but basic. All essential services would be funded. Some services considered somewhat essential would be furloughed. Discretionary services that benefit the public could be closed.

You know that Air Traffic Control staff would be paid as well as security functions. On the House and senate side elevator operators and key staff would remain. As I said federal enforcement would remain as usual. Checks to our military could be delayed. Agencies like the Environmental protection Agency would cease issuing permits. Social Security would not be affected unless the shut down lasted for months. Medicare would be viable for a short period. The National park Service and Smithsonian would cease to be open to the public. The federal housing Administration would not be able to guarantee home loans. I think you get the idea what would happen. Fortunately it did not go this way.

### 394. JOB GROWTH

The job market seems to be returning with the addition of 216,000 new jobs. The unemployment rate at this time was 8.8%. During this time the Obama Administration has been fending off efforts at cutting the budget.

Chris Rupky chief Financial Economist for the bank of Tokyo- Mitsubishi in

New York stated that there was: "Powerful forward momentum."He was referring to the job market.

On the individual level there are signs of improvement. People who had given up were now putting out there resumes. The Obama administration was being compared to the Reagan or Clinton Administrations in terms of job growth.

Austin Goolsbee Chairman of the council of Economic advisors: "Obviously things can go wrong but this continues to be a very solid trend that we've seen over the last year. Yes it was a deep hole but we're growing our way out of that hole."

Here are some cases Mathew Mabry from Bakersfield at 37 a Air Force Veteran on Thursday signed up for job search help from Jewish Vocational services. He stated: "During the summer I was in a funk. I didn't look for jobs."He landed a job at target that has given him confidence to look for a full time position. Nelson Hyde Clark of san Francisco who was laid off in 2008 He started posting on Craig's list and is again looking for work. There are other stories but you get the gist There is some hope in the air now.

## 395. THE ANTI UNION PUSH

With the economy being down as it has and the inherent nature of Union contract restrictions a back lash has developed. Legislatures with fiscal troubles and recently elected Republicans especially in the Governors seat has lead to draconian legislation aimed at restricting the power of Public Service Unions.

It started in Ohio and Wisconsin and now Tennessee is getting into the act. Ron Ramsey Lieutenant Governor of that state has been vocal: "Now it's Tennessee's turn for legislation to prevent Government employee Unions from locking tax payers into long term Union contracts that we can-not afford."According to the National Conference of State legislatures there has been a explosion of State Legislative bills to the tune of 744. These bills exclusively target the Public Union Movement.

John Logan the director of the Labor studies program at San Francisco State University: "In almost every state, I read of at least one more Bill to restrict Union Rights at the state level."The attack on collective bargaining rights in all the states of the Union. In New Hampshire enacted a bill that could be called Wisconsin on Steroids. In a number of states there is a restriction on collecting Union dues from public employees. The State of Florida in its House approved a Bill that not only bans dues taken from pay checks but requires permission be acquired for dues to be used in political activity.

The man who started it all Ohio Governor John Kasich signed legislation tougher than Wisconsin. Do you remember the massive protests. Washington State approved a bill to make it more difficult for Airline and rail-road workers to Unionize.

In my state of California with our liberal Democratic Governor a seven point plan has been introduced to address the problem of pension excesses.

My comment is this: we are going through one of those phases where the public sector due to its nature is judged inferior to the private sector and especially in a economic down turn how dare they consider themselves to be secure at our expense.

## 396. WHAT ABOUT GOLD
### April 5, 2010

All markets have an arc that is to say at the beginning of the arc the price is low as the crisis continues the price rises. With the deepening of the recession the cost of gold and silver goes up until it starts declining again or has a sudden drop.

Kimberly Sterling is a market analyst and her clients ask about investment in gold as a hedge against the bad times. She states the price is high now and there is a potential risk of losing not the gold but the price it was valued at the time of purchase. She stated: "Gold is a bubble now and it's too late to get in. It is like somebody who bought Real-Estate in 2006 at the height of the bubble. You could get hurt really badly."She continued to say that if you had gotten in ten years earlier you would have done very well.. She compared gold to Mutual Funds, Exchange Traded funds, and futures contracts that have risen with the ever rising price wave. She continued: "Gold is one of those things that pops up in times of uncertainty and crisis. But when it pops up it's too late to get in."

Do you know what that means? All those commercials on buying and selling gold are a scam perpetrated on the American public along the way of Gullible's Travels.

## 397. THE GOLDMAN SACHS HEARINGS
### April 30, 2010

What Goldman Sachs did with the bail out some good some bad but the excesses they said came from other funds causes you to wonder.

Senator Carl Levin Democrat, Michigan stated: "There's a fundamental conflict of interest that needs to be addressed."What did Goldman do wrong: make secret bets against the very securities they sold to the investor. His is according to the *L.A. Times*.

Levin and his group plan to press for legislation to outlaw such practices. However the way they are going about it has been called into question Senator Bernie Sanders Independent of Vermont stated: "I think this bill is not tough enough. If this bill becomes watered down so it really is something that Wall Street eventually accepts. I will not vote for it."Sanders has joined with other republicans for stiffer measures.

The thing about corporations like Goldman Sachs that are nothing more than glorified holding companies is that they think they can do anything they want and when congress gets involved more often than not in the end they create a misdemeanor.

## 398. THE BUSH HOUSING TAX CREDIT

You heard me this one sits in the Bush presidency and was expanded under the Obama Presidency to $8,000. California joined in with a $10,000 credit sponsored under the Brown Administration. This stimulus has had an effect and cussed a spike in home sales. Richard Hoffman President of Coldwell Bank Residential brokerage stated: "The stimulus has worked. Buyers are confident that we have seen the bottom of the real estate market and we are on our way back."

This optimistic outlook is not share by those who study the economy. Dean Baker co-director of the center for economic policy research in Washington stated: "We had a serious uptick due to the tax credit but whatever boost that gave us is now at an end. So I think we will see resumed declines. The only real question is how fast."The funny thing is after Congress created the eight thousand dollar figure they waved the repayment requirement. The initial deadline on this program was November of 2009. Baker continued: "The bulk of the money was going to people who were going to buy anyway. It is a short tem fix to the market that is going to be reversed to some degree down the road."

Here is an example one of those lucky recipients: Keith Alverez, and Bunim Murray qualified for a $18,000 credit. They found a fixer upper . They found a home for $300,000. it was going to need work and a lot of it.

What the gentleman said about the reversal process came true and the housing sector stated to slide.

## 399. JOBLESS BENEFITS END

With the uptick in the housing market and the perceived drain on the economy of paying people not to work through EDD payments the group called the 99ers found their benefits ending. The feeling was that they would actually seek employment.

Three point five million people are affected. It is argued that they can go on welfare and get food stamps. That's true especially if they have families but they have to grovel to do it. The hard fact is they will allow you one year then they will remove you from the rolls if you are single and basically in good health.. The bottom line is you must continue to look for work and they will still cut you off if your single.

Donalee King is 51 years of age and part of the 99srs club. They have formed apolitical movement called the May DAY SOS Campaign. She stated: "The have not's are going to be in great multitudes and they will up rise."

Here is a case of a laid off factory worker by the name of Schafer. He had to turn to his mother and her Social security to help with the family a wife and three children. She was a substitute teacher and they don't make much but she was still working. They can't meet their bills. I hope things have gotten better for them.

## 400. PRISONS AND THE ECONOMY
### May 3, 2010

Small towns across America are dying. There is no work. In the state of California in a drought stricken town thirty five miles from Fresno cowboys roam the street looking for work. The businesses are going broke Their only hope seems to be a prison that they hope will bring jobs to the town.

The *L.A. Times* tell the example of a restaurant operated by Wanda Leung. She has no business drawing $1,000 monthly just to keep the doors open. She prays for the opening of the prison.

## 401. THE MIXED RECOVERY
### May 4, 2010

Nationally there was economic growth but no job creation. Again people are spending money but it is coming out of their savings accounts.

In the construction industry the growth rate was 0.2% as of March. The sad thing is this growth came from federal programs not the private sector. Much of the construction was related to temporary stimulus money. That spigot will soon be shut off.

What is encouraging is that at this point in time production in the month of April grew at the fastest rate in six months. The rate of growth according to the Institute for supply management: the manufacturing index rose from 59.6% in March to 60.4% in April.

Companies are rebuilding their inventories as the demand for goods increases New orders are a gage for future production. There has been a jump from 61.5% to 65.7%. The industries that have been growing the fastest are clothing/fashion related and non-metallic goods. The rubber industry also reported a strong growth in this time frame of 2010.

As I stated earlier it is consumer spending that has been the main driving force. There is a missing argument in all of this. That argument is the hiring of employees. Companies are using existing staff having them multi task. Those that invest in technology do so to cut labor costs. To bring this economy up people have to work.

At the height of the great depression heavy machinery was deliberately put on the sidelines so men could be put to work with shovels. We are using technology to displace our workforce and we tell them they have to retrain.

## 402. THE DAY THE DOW DROPPED
### May 7, 2010

In 2008 Lehman Bros collapse caused other firms to seize up. A lot of money was lost that day. The new of the troubles in Europe was causing the DOW to slide a good part of the morning then what came to be argued to be a computer glitch to drop 700 points in fifteen minutes. The panic that followed along with the selling fell to 1,000 points or as close to it as you can get 9,869.62. The board rebounded and finished the day with 347.80 points (3.2%) at 10,520.32. It was as a drama at least as great as when the great stock market hit in 1929.

## 403. SPAIN'S ECONOMIC TROUBLES

The European Union has chosen austerity as means of getting through the Crisis as they call it. The unrest that has happened in Greece and threatened to infect was dealt with a bailing out of the economy but only after severe austerity measures and budget cutting on the part of the government and the civil service sector were put in place. Spain now grapples with potential crisis.

The young in Spain those 20 to 30 years of age have been idled and cannot find work. Those in their 50s hare seeing career changes after long periods of unemployment. The government has cut back the public sector but not had the reaction as occurred in Greece.

Ariadona Perez was laid off from a job she had for three years. For the next twelve months she is go to receive 70% of her salary. That was in 2010 terms $1,300 Euro dollars a month. She stated: "If I had children and a mortgage I'd be screwed. If in a year I don't find a job then I'll do whatever."

As of May 2010 the crisis in Spain had been going on for 18 months many after years in a given profession find themselves changing professions. Here are a few stories from the economic crypt. Mainer at the age of 50 is training to be a blackjack dealer he has stated: "If I have to work at McDonalds or a bar I will. A person can be proud but there's nothing wrong with lowering your level of work."

Spain's President Zapatero has called the shrinking job market Spain's greatest social problem. As I stated at the top of this article the young have been idled through no fault of their own there are just no jobs. There is at this time a 40% unemployment rate among the young. "That's astonishing that nobody wants to hire these people."

Spain has a fairly liberal unemployment package that pays up to two years and there is reduced compensation after that. Collectively the benefits add up to 3.5% of the economy. Greece had to implement austerity measures in exchange for 146 billion Euro dollars to prevent default on the part of that country. Fortunately Europe in general is stagnant moving towards recovery with an average of one to two percent growth. It is argued that speculators are holding back the economy. Now think of this country and the labor practices multi tasking. The use of technology to reduce labor costs and you should see a parallel.

## 404. RETAIL STEADY AND SLOW

There are 28 major retail chains in this country. There performance has been less than stellar. If you averaged their growth in terms of sales there would be a rise of 0.5%. According to Thomas Reuters service sales increased at 10 retailers and fell at 18 other retail outlets.

The economy has something to do with the situation at this time in 2010. Lana Staton a bartender lost her job and stopped shopping except for the grocery store and necessities. Wall-Mart and Target were the places she liked to shop. After getting a new job as a communications operator in January she resumed her favorite past time shopping. She stated: "I'm not back where I was but at least I'm shopping again. It feels really good."

The Easter calendar shift caused a growth of 4.8% Michael Niemira chief economist at the International council of Shopping noted that the momentum of rate of sales was still healthy and that retailers like Target Corporation reported sales on higher ticket items. Costco wholesale Corporation posted an 11% gain. Neiman Marcus had a 10.9% margin. Stores catering to youth fell because of less discretionary income.

Again consumers were buying products but very little hiring was going on and those employed really had to hustle. Companies are squeezing more profit out of their available resources and the economy anemically goes along.

## 405. THE AIRLINES
May 8, 2010

The Airline industry is about to tier. I'm talking about a highroad and a low road and nobody will get to Dublin before you.

They are cramming people into non reclining seats and all things will cost Maybe the restrooms will be free. The reason for all this Spartan luxury a spokesman for the airlines said it best: "The Airlines say they're just giving the passenger what they want low fares. But is that all they want. No they also want a little comfort and a little dignity. If passengers really wanted better service the airlines would offer it."

There are only three legacy carriers left United, Delta, and American Airlines. The major airlines are concentrating on international flights, leaving the lowlands to the smaller carriers.

Glen Tilton United's chief executive officer stated: "This combination will provide a strong platform for sustainable long term value for shareholders, opportunities for employees and more and better scheduled service and destinations for customers."

So fly the friendly sky's to where ever and don't mind the lack of circulation in your legs, you didn't need them anyway. That was a joke.

## 406. THE BUS SYSTEM
### May 11, 2010

    We have a bus system that travels at the extreme. Either there are too few on a given rout at a given time or so many and I have wondered this all eight wheels would go flat. The ridership is a circus of people. You have those like myself 62 and up(That right I ride the bus) the infirmed in wheel chairs, migrant workers, hip-hop types, The homeless, and other questionable people at the back of the bus.

    The bus companies claim a lack of ridership and raise fares on those that do take the bus. The commercials I see are this homogenous blend of middle America riding the bus with smiling faces, not a New York potential brawl mix which I see on a regular basis. The drivers on the whole are cool. There is always that occasional stickler with an attitude. I don't know of a person given the choice that would rather take his car for social reasons. The other reason is that buses cut off at seven on weekends and on week days nine o'clock. Most people has strange working hours and to commute by bus would make them late.

    No the matter is not just ridership or fares though those are a factor. Whether it's the Foot Hill Transit district, Metro Link, L A Commuter Express, or the Big Blue Line in Santa Monica which probably has a homogeneous group of smiling people, It is a matter of culture and independence here on the West Coast. It could possibly work better with longer running bus times that were convenient than those that drive cars might take the bus, who knows.

## 407. MICROSOFT
### May 12, 2010

    Partly out of the reaction general service software offered by Google Microsoft was offering a free version of Word and other programs. These programs won't have as many services as the paid version and would have advertizing, as opposed to the desk top models that would have access to the apps included in the regular office licensing fees. The paid versions account for 29% of company profits along with 51% of its operating income. Google Apps account for only 4% of the market and are web based sites..Generally when you use a program like Word you don't necessarily want to go on line.

    McLeish stated that Microsoft needed a defensive move against on line Apps from Google and other rivals that are pushing this concept known as cloud computing. Microsoft currently has 81% of this market.

## 408. THE BOEING STRIKE

    There are two sides to a coin and your about to hear about them from me. Boeing over the last several years has been laying off workers during times of slow down and expecting other workers to take up the slack when things speeded up. They were outsourcing the Janitorial and security and were moving to down grade the job of tool crib attendants to tool kit handlers. They were thinking of outsourcing that job also. You see outsourced jobs do not carry benefits. I know these thing for I have been told about these practices. I know I have forgotten a few things.

Now here is the companies side. Lay-offs and cuts in production rates were affecting the delivery dates of the C17s (They did not have the manpower to build the planes).The United Auto Workers Union number 148, with a force of 1,700 actively went out on strike hampering Boeings ability to fill its orders.

Ironically this strike is over the smallest of points the decreased contribution by the company to the pension fund and increased co-pays on the health insurance. It is argued by employee that over the years and contracts the company has sought and received concessions from the union because of the economy.

Loren Thomson, defense policy analyst Lexington Institute stated: "For a program that is facing extinction this is not a smart move. As a customer anytime you see a workforce walk out on a program, it makes you think about how reliable and how punctual delivery dates will be."

Now for the employee/ worker who as an individual and a group has poured their good intentions into a contract only to be snubbed the attitude is: "I've been working with this company for 25 years and our Union has given up so many concessions to Boeing in my time here." Ray Luciani stated: "For a lot of us who made the C-17 a cash cow time is winding down. Well we're retiring soon and we just want a fair shake for our work."

To the old timers when McDonald Douglas became Boeing things changed and the cost cutting and job elimination began all in the name of partnership between the Unions and management. I know that's the old, old story.

## 409. THE DEEP HORIZON DISASTER AFTERMATH
### May 18, 2010

On April 30, 2010 Transocean who owned the rig and British Petroleum who leased it had a dispute over maintenance and how to do things. They were drilling the deepest well they had ever drilled in the gulf of Mexico when the rig blew up and sank from sight. The lives lost that day were mourned by those on the shore. Some accepted it as fate while others considered sewing for negligence on the part of the company. These are some of their stories.

Stephen Davis and Mark Davis filed lawsuits against Transocean and British Petroleum also known as Beyond Petroleum in Harris County, Texas. Both men laid claim to injuries they sustained that would make it difficult to provide for their families. At the time of the accident there were lawyers on hand coercing those involved to sign in exchange for unspecified promises. Most did sign and now they are being ignored. Texas Attorney Toney Buzbee who is representing the two men stated: "Most of these guys the overwhelming majority are guys with a high school education. There's probably no other industry they can make this kind of money in."They are each seeking 5.5 million dollars.

Shane Turner who was a co-worker on the Deep Horizon was there in the packed pews. He was lucky, he was on shore when the rig blew. Turner who was 40 retired from the army in 2008 as a sergeant first class talked of the accident. He maintained there's a lot more attention paid to safety off shore than in the service.

People on the east coast have a different way of looking at things. It is an intrusion on the part of the federal government when they interfere with making a living disaster or no. All the time the oil was spreading off their coast and eventually hit their beaches. It was only later that the alarm bells really went off.

### 410. PUTTING THE BRAKES ON RENTAL DECLINE
April 7, 2011

It is argued that the economy in California is improving with competing factors. There is a squeeze on apartment rentals due to the collapse of housing. Increased supply of foreclosed homes pushed down rental properties. Things have stabilized according to market analysts. Foreclosure houses are turning into rental slash leased houses.

According to MPF Research: "Single family homes that are being rented out compete with traditional multifamily product, high-rises or garden apartments. That supply is very hard to calculate. A company or hedge fund that just bought 100 houses they have the ability to offer more affordable rents which lowers the rental market as a whole. The bigger guys are not going to haggle, they just want to get them rented."

It is argued that the housing market is a great spot for buyers who have the cash to enter the market. Some at present prefer to lease but have an eye on purchasing as they feel their confidence building. Again there are many sides to this coin and as you will see many turns. That leads me to another bad joke One good turn deserves another. Two birds talking.

### 411. AMERICAN ENTERPRIZE
April 23, 2010

In the town of Daggett a place I have often wanted to visit. There is a small convenience store next to a sometimes brothel that is located off old route 66. A man by the name of Joe owns the place that has been in business for 130 years. He spends 12 hours a day seven days a week with the goal of moving on. He is now forty five years of age and he hopes for a better life.

## 412. OIL MONEY/ THE SUDAN
May 18, 2010

We all know that oil stocks give the richest returns and our universities invest in a variety of portfolios oil stock included.

Harvard University through the Harvard Corporation invests the alumni funds for the benefit of the school has grown to depend on the oil industry. The government of the Sudan was using the profits from sales of oil to suppress the south. Southern Sudan is Christian and Northern Sudan is Muslim and they hold the cards. All they had to do was pay dividends to Harvard. Harvard after long years of reliance on that stock has divested itself of it.

States, Universities, high-schools had stock in the Sudanese oil venture. There were 95 universities, States like California and cities like Los Angeles. All these organized groups were enacting divestment procedures. Again this is after long years of reliance on that income. They helped to finance our social programs and we helped finance their war.

The Human Rights Watch concluded in 2003: "The CNPC and Petronas operations....have been complicit in Human Rights violations. Their activities are inextricably intertwined the (Sudanese) governments abuses: The abuses are gross: The corporate presence fuels, facilitates or benefits from violations."

Similar complaints were lodged against Petrodar Operating Company. This is according to the European Coalition in a report filed in 2006. The coalition is composed of 80 religious and peace groups. The CNPC owns 41% of Petrodar.

According to the Canadian Government an airstrip at Heglig in the year 2000 operated by the Sudanese greater Nile Petroleum Operating Company was the staging area for military attacks on civilians.

Oil revenue is part and parcel to a majority of Sudan's operating budget and the CNPC was a major purchaser of its oil. Add to this the fact that Sudan was and is getting money from Chinese oil Companies. Remember the Chinese are not moralist. They're pragmatists.

Jed Emerson from Oxford who at that time was an expert in asset management referred to warren Buffett as a kind of guiding light to redefine the roll of business today. He referred to the thought that people think the market as a lot of answers for many problems that exist in this world. He stated: "That will be true only when investors come to the table with enhanced expectations. If they say we won't turn a blind eye, to things like child labor, environmental devastation and Darfur."

Michael Useem Professor of Management at the university of Pennsylvania, Wharton School stated: "Saint Warren has built additional credibility as a wise informed observer of what's good for companies, what's god for governance and where the country should be going.

## 413. BUFFETT

Salomon Incorporated was in trouble in 1991 It was about to collapse because one of its traders broke Security laws. Buffett at that time was a Salomon director. He in essence restored the banks ethical culture. The down side to Buffett was that his ethical concepts did not extend to social or environmental concerns.

The analysis went something like this: Bershire Hathaway had 4.6 billion in eight companies. They were dead last in the ranking of 100 investors in oil and natural gas in the United States. Goldman Sachs at this time determined the ratings on social environmental and governance performance. Bershire deliberately bought into oil companies that lacked a social responsibility. Berkshire stock is transferred to the Gates Foundation. It is the rehabilitation of this stock as measured by Goldman and Sach's along with other foundations efforts to improve its philosophy that "All lives, no matter where they are being led have equal value."

Berkshire Corporation holds 64 million dollars in Pharmaceutical companies with a pricing structure that tended to keep Antiretroviral drugs out of the reach of HIV/AIDS Patients in developing nations. That's funny in a way for they would be one of their most important clients. Among shares owned 28.5 billion in companies with records of Human Rights Abuses and of course 921 million in Wall-mart.

We all know that Wall Mart has been put to the test and forced to pay fines concerning the Child labor law, Union organizing, and adult working conditions. What can I say America loves a fire sale. Add to that General Re Corporation $652,000 in the altria group the U.S. largest cigarette maker.

It should be noted that the Gates foundation screens out tobacco companies out of their investment portfolio. Buffett did not respond to questions concerning environmental, Aids related, or tobacco related companies.

I hope this puts Mr. Buffett in perspective to the corporate view of the world.

## 414. FED FORECAST

The San Francisco based Federal Reserve forecasters have concluded that we have arrived at the turning point in the economy. The basis for their judgment was that consumer spending on key goods was up in a sustained pace. For the first quarter. The sales of software grew at 10% over the 2009 period. The consuming public according to surveys of purchasing managers were buying new cars, clothing, and homes again. A spokesman for the organization Williams stated: "It's kind of like part of the process, you cut back for a couple of years and then you need to replace things eventually."

Not all were in agreement with this concept of recovery citing that 70% of the major retail chains did not meet their expectations. They cited the worry that stock market volatility would affect spending by the wealthy who by the way are leading this come-back because everybody loves a fire sale. Pardon the pun for I did not know there was a U C L A Anderson Forecast. They stated: "You still have a very constrained balance sheet on the part of consumers."It was noted that not even business spending was guaranteed to recover at a strong pace. This thought was from Christopher Thornberg of beacon Economics. In his forecast for the month he called for slow growth during the remainder of 2010 into 2011. His reasoning banks are still stuck to use his term with delinquent loans. He also pointed the sovereign debt crisis that could affect borrowing. What if we lost our triple A credit rating? Would our interest rate be higher or lower depending on the other world economies just one of my little scary thoughts. At any rate Thornberg stated: "The financial market is still volatile, the banks are in a mess, the commercial real-estate market is still a mess. They're ridiculously optimistic.."

### 415. PROPOSED HOSPITAL UNION MEMBERSHIP U.S.C.

Tenet Health Care Corporation its facilities for 275 million dollars to U.S. C. The U.S. C University Hospital Health Sciences near down town los Angeles is what it is known as today. There was an organization that represented the interests of the Hospital workers called the SEIU. It is charged that it has collaborated with management to prevent unionization of the center with all of its components.

The Union movement that is seeking to become the bargaining agent for the workers at this time in 2010. It was charged that two union activists were suspended for soliciting members for their Union. charges that SEIU is in bed with management. The Hospital has gone as far as hiring the Weissman Group a Ohio based consulting organization known for its ability to prevent Unionization of companies. There stated purpose according to them is: "To help managers avoid inadvertently violating any labor laws."They engage according to advertisement: "Union avoidance consulting and strategy."

Adriana Surfas, an SEIU spokeswoman stated: "Management created an extremely hostile environment so that workers who supported Unionization feared what was going to happen."Collaboration based on fear led to charges that the SEIU were in bed with management. 700 workers are affected, professionals from: Surgical Technicians, Physical Therapists, Pharmacists along with other staff that run this beautiful University.

Looking at it from all angles and the dynamic change that would happen in terms of a voice coming from those who make the operation work. Management should not fear input and at the same time the potential new Union affiliated members hold the responsibility of keeping their representatives in check especially this Public service sector.

### 416. RETIREMENT LIVING WITH STYLE

I have written of this troubled economy on its good and bad points, but here is the lighter side for those that did it correctly and kept it all. There is a Village in Northridge worth approximately 90 million dollars. Its residents pay between $4,600 for a studio to $6,800 for a two bedroom plus den unit. There is a full service bar and these people can drink as evidenced by the bartender. The dining room is set like a restaurant. The amenities are that of a hotel and the people that live here live well.

Here are some case studies if you will of those that call this place home. Mr. Dawson is a former skater and at the age of 83 relocated from her home in Rancho Mirage enjoying a drink and hors d'oeuvres. Her late husband was a developer of country clubs. She is not worried about her son: "My son in Porter Ranch found this place."Clair Freidman stated: "The decorator must have made a fortune, but don't write that down."Clair in her profession days was a school guidance counselor that moved to California from Florida.

There are 240 apartments and 35 assisted living units. Management states that occupancy should in the end be about 300. I guess you could call this one of those success stories.

## 417. HOT MONEY
May 27, 2010

Sometimes illicit funds are funneled into banks. It is a way to make the money clean. Developers are often used along with so-called charitable organizations here is such a tale.

Tom Vessey was Chief executive of Redlands Centennial Bank. Real-Estate was its specialty. As home values soared so did the fortunes of the bank. In 2007 at the peak of the housing boom profits were 9.3 million. Its loan portfolio had swollen to 522 million from 191 million just four years before.

E. Wayne Simmons was one of the banks biggest borrowers. He was a Calimesa developer for up-scale housing. His projects included J P Ranch. It faced the Arrowhead Country Club. He found that first Centennial bank was eager to finance the inland Empire housing projects. The bank had positioned itself as a frontrunner in the area competing with Bank of America and Wells Fargo. The bank itself was owned by 400 share holders.

They were involved in community service such as teaching finance at the local high-school. They were on the board of the WMCA. They were even involved in the symphony association. Community representatives stated: "1st Centennial provided us a lot of cash and was highly supportive."

They invested in the Inland Empire as the bubble was growing and such investments paid off as long as the construction was completed. Other banks were brought in to finance larger projects. It also began to offer exceptionally high interest rates to attract borrowers from across the country. Many of these relied on brokers to spot the best deal.

Regulators viewed the high level of brokered "Hot Money" as a red flag on account that these funds cist more and depositors are more likely than local customers, to pull their money out when better deals come.. Bear in mind the bank would have extended hours for last minute business. The volume did not match the scope of the business so one morning the authorities came in and changed the board and the CEO and life went on.

## 418. SMALL FIRMS AND HEALTH INSURANCE

The accelerating costs of health insurance that exceed the cost of inflation by twice its number affectively stop smaller firms from hiring if the concept of health insurance is `included. The cost to a small business is 180% compared to 146% for bigger companies. The only cure for a small business is to go with a simpler plan. If a state has certain requirements they have to think about doing business somewhere else.

Denis Tootelian Director for the Center for Small Business at Cal state Sacramento stated: "If health care costs and other costs go up, it's going to make it more difficult for small business to hire and the lack of employment growth is going to be a drag on the economy. Hiring is one of the most critical factors for getting the economy back on track. If they have the option they will probably think of doing business somewhere else."

Stephanie Cathcart Spokes-Woman for the National Federation of Independent business in Washington stated: "They are concerned that the costs aren't going to go down, they're just going to go up. They're going to be paying new taxes, new fees. It's kind of a double whammy on them."

The California insurance industry in setting rates for small business insists it is not out to gouge the small business man or woman but are merely trying to strike a balance between affordability and a legitimate profit. Blue Shield stated that its rates went up 20% in 2009. Anthem Blue Cross cited a 13% increase from 2009. The Anthem Blue Cross spokesman stated: "We understand that one group that has been most hard hit by the economic downturn of the past few years is the States three million small businesses, who we all rely on to be major contributors to our local economy. We want to be competitive in the market place, but we also want to take care of our members. We work each day to do both."

Scott Hauge who heads Small Business California an advocacy group stated: "They just don't have the profit margins to pay this cost. It goes right to their bottom line. It's a killer." Keiser Permanente has raised its rates 12% from 2009 to 2010.

Here is the incontrovertible fact half of the 6 million Californians working in this state get their insurance from their jobs. The industry needs to meet its needs to stay in business. No-one can take a perceived loss on their books real or imaginary as to the profit base so the costs continue to rise. Just one thing insurance companies own real estate and other business holdings don't they count in the equation?

## 419. HEALTH RISKS AND STAFFING LEVELS

When you cut your staff and you make products the public uses, consumes internally you would think there was a certain standard. McNeil Consumer health care, a Pennsylvania plant that makes Tylenol and dozens of other Pediatric medicines. There was a complaint about an odder on the outside of bottles of, Tylenol. bacterial contamination of raw materials and, shoddy equipment maintenance. There was a failure to investigate 46 consumer complaints sighting: "regarding foreign materials black or dark specks, "in the products. The complaints dated back to before the recall according to the FDA.

Tylenol and over 40 pediatric products were recalled, among them Motrin and Zyrtec along with Benadryl . Seven deaths were recorded and several complaints of adverse reactions.

McNeil along with Johnson and Johnson who make these products were once considered the standard of the industry. But due to cut backs in labor what they called austerity measures contributed to the unsanitary conditions.

A plant in Puerto Rico a FDA warning at the start of the year about (Tardy and inadequate handling of complaints about the odor outside the Tylenol bottles. I wonder what that smell was? Could it have been dissatisfied employees? At any rate it sickened the users of their product.

The Fort Washington plant in suburban Philadelphia experienced cuts in labor and other belt tightening efforts as they put it. These efforts it is argued jeopardized the 62 billion dollar empire of Johnson and Johnson. The plant itself was forced to suspend production. According to a McNeil spokesman. This has been the fourth recall involving adult or children's Tylenol since September. Earlier in the month the FDA extended its warning to include plants in Lancaster, PA, Las Pieras, Puerto Rico. The lack of training of temp. employees was specifically noted.

I think there are some basic lessons learned here. 1 Don't lower your labor force to the point where maintenance of your equipment and product are in trouble. Avoid too much outsourcing for they can be more of a headache than a cure. If you betray your employees it is hard to get their loyalty back.

## 420. GIFT CARDS/SMALL BUSINESS
June 7, 2010

Innovation is the progenitor of invention and small business no matter what category as long as it deals with the public is learning to adapt. As little as two years prior or 2008 plastic gift cards were just 2% of the market. The percentage as of 2010 is between 8 and 10%. In twenty eleven I expect it will be double that..The reason if your company is on line you can give your customer a greater advantage and a larger selection.

Gregory Grove is the President of E Card Systems, a gift card supplier in Brentwood  Tennessee. His target market is small and mid-sized businesses. There is a monthly fee of $500  and  $300 for the machine. He points out that this industry is on the ground floor when it comes to small and midsized business. What I see is small business mimicking big business.

Here is one of those living examples of what I have been talking about. Mark Hennessy  is a second generation owner of the Santa Monica Art and Architecture Book Store (Hennessey and Ingalls) Opened its second store in Hollywood two years ago (2008) it added Plastic gift cards about the same time it dropped paper certificates. He stated: "I could probably go a whole month without selling a gift certificate. But with the stores shiny cards displayed by the register and promoted on line, and able to be used for on line purchases I sell more gift cards."

Even Plastic Surgeons use them. Dr Loyd M. Kreiger in  2008 switched from paper certificates to plastic E Cards. He has a practice on  Rodeo Drive. Many according to the doctor are bought to cover small procedures. Occasionally He sells a gift card that covers more extensive procedures. He also uses the cards as promotional come-on's as he puts it.

This idea of a E gift card is however regulated by the state and federal government as to keep unscrupulous  use of a good retail gimmick.

### 421.  SO YOU WANT TO START A RESTAURANT
June 7, 2010

To start a food service establishment you often have to meet expensive and contradictory requirements.. This is largely because there are contradictory rules that in some cases are designed so the applicant fill fail or go broke trying to succeed.

I will give some examples from personal experience and some as gleamed from the *L.A. Times*. So let's get into that moving ride the restaurant opening experience.

The year is 2009 and the location the Emmons building on Euclid Avenue. You will see a corner space that has been  a photography studio, shoe repair shop and a café / restaurant in the late 1990's. It was owned by a preacher with ties to the city hall. The interesting thing was that according to city hall it was never a café nor were permits issued. There was a memo allowing a grandfather clause connected to the theater but that has been lost.

I give you this background because when we meaning myself and David Perez. We were told it was never a food establishment. The entertainment license that we were using to show old movies that was also grandfathered was also lost.

We had one inspector tell us we had to put a sealer on the floor and to another it was not a requirement. Ventilation would have cost a fortune despite the fact we said we would be using  microwave and cold sandwiches. We spent fund upgrading the molding after another inspector said plastic molding was acceptable. We could not even pop our own popcorn according to the city rules. In the end we made it a clubhouse and did ghost tours. Check on the internet  the Granada Theater slash Emmons building is a genuine haunted establishment verified by the TAPS organization. The building went into foreclosure and we could not put on concerts and the building that housed Hollywood faithful sits vacant today.

Now for a more positive note Los Angeles a good deal west of Ontario of which I spoke earlier has simplified and standardized what a person or organization needs to do to establish a restaurant business in the city and county areas of Los Angeles. They were plagued by the same thing I described to you about Ontario until they made these changes.

The first step in opening a restaurant is you are assigned a case manager. This is according to Raymond Chan who is the Executive Officer of the Los Angeles office of Building and safety. The city has worked a arrangement that ends conflicting rules that county health departments impose those wishing to help get the economy going.

Building a restaurant involves almost all the building trades Mechanical, Architectural, Health, grease control and electrical. Each one of these departments has different inspections. If you have an established business of the same or similar kind it seems the process should be simplified.

There was a restaurant owner who satisfied one inspector with one type of grease trap system only to be confronted with change then the department heads changed and he was told to put another in at the cost of $40,000.

Jeanmarie Dumouchel who has been project manager and designer of four down-town restaurants took in a pilot project under the new system. She stated that the difference was dramatic.

## 422. SMALL BANKS
### June 10, 2010

The stricter rules and paper trail to prevent what happened with the big banks would cause undue stress on small banks. It is stated that small banks would be exempt from much of the overhaul, intended to control the larger banks who were responsible for the Subprime mortgage melt- down

Nancy E Sheppard chief executive of Western Independent Bankers a trade group in San Francisco stated: "Although small banks would be exempt from much of the overhaul, the provisions that would apply would make it harder for community bankers to serve their customers and expand lending. It would create two difficulties for segments of the banking industry, too big to fail and too small to comply."

The Senate version of this legislation would specifically put a limit that new oversight would apply to the thirty or so banks with at least $50,000,000,000 in assets under their control.

In my view as a layman the banks should conduct a KISS Keep it simple stupid. Don't make loans and then hedge those loans as securities in Hedge funds. That's how we got our toxic assets. That's my view.

## 423. BANKS AND SAVINGS
### June 12, 2010

You're not going to believe this, but 48% of households have their cash in banks and credit unions. This is 11.2 million households. What are they earning on this money that they have so thoughtfully put in our financial institutions? The answer is quite surprising. As of May 2010 the accumulated savings of this 48% of households is $5.6 trillion which is an increase of 209 billion since the start of 2010. These deposits are earning less than 1% annual interest.

There have been many investors looking for a better return in the field of Mutual funds. Even bond portfolios which hold 2.4 trillion. Individuals and institutions still sit with 2.8 trillion in Money Market Mutual Funds. What is the average annual fund yield in 2010. The answer is 0.04%. Some of the money fund cash is owned by U.S. companies. That figure is 1.8 trillion in liquid assets. This is according to Federal reserve data.

I guess the bottom line in all of this is if one percent of the population controls all the wealth of this country and we are encouraged to save, we are earning next to nothing for that effort. They still don't hire people.

## 424. ON THE ISSUE OF POT

Marc Emery is considered the king as a progenitor of the various simulative marijuana plants. He published a catalogue with the aim of putting a pot plant in every house putting the drug people out of business reducing the police to busting people who possess these plants.

He has marketed openly: Blue Hawaiian for euphoric high anxiety control, Crown Royal who's flowers are a flat golden brown and high in THC, Hawaiian Sativa with a menthol flavor that tingles the taste buds. He has been arrested and pled guilty for selling seeds across this country. He was arrested in Canada. he stated: "In fact I have done these things so I admit my guilt. We are winning."

## 425. FORECLOSURE UPDATE
### May 12, 2011

The rate at which a foreclosure happens is lengthening..Over periods of time the amount of foreclosed properties is decreasing. That does not mean the economy is getting better. It means somebody goofed and broke the law while doing a repossession. Those houses hitting the market are at reduced values 25% and give the impression that housing sales are rebounding when they are not.

Christopher Thornberg Principle of Beacon Economics stated: "The banks had to slow down and get more lawyers involved because all the fuss over the Robo Signing Scandle."From March to April 34%.In the year 2010 during this time 219,258 properties were filed on. The foreclosure filings in April 2010 were 239,795 in all. In California during this time 55,869 properties were filed on. In 2011 the California rate was down 19% from the year 2010.

Houston Smith a` Hermosa Beach real-Estate Agent stated: "Lenders are under increased pressure and encouragement to make every effort to do loan modification or a short sale and it has been a dramatic change. It does not mean there are fewer properties in trouble."There has been a rise in consumer advocacy on the behalf those who applied for mortgages. At this point with the distinct possibility of seeming simplistic I offer this idea. What if the banks could take the negative balances as a loss and the Feds let them write it off their books and put all those underwater properties on a even playing field so we can get this economy moving.

Alys Cohen Staff Attorney for the Constitutional Law Center: "Paper work needs to be proper, but the real question is whether home owners will get modifications when they qualify for them."

To show the progression of the slowdown we will start in 2007 it took 151 days to foreclose a property. It took 340 days in 2010 to do the same. It takes 400 days to do the same thing as of the date of this article. In California foreclosure occurs outside the court system. In 2007 it took 134 days to foreclose. In 2010 it took 262 days to do the same thing. In 2011 it takes 330 days to foreclose on a property. Nationally the court ordered foreclosures such as new York and New Jersey in 2011 are in excess of 900 days.

Today's environment has the Federal regulators investigating bank practices looking for ways to compensate those financially injured in this mortgage melt down. Those who took out mortgages are being more proactive in their defense. It was said a long time ago that a banker cannot take a loss and most economic theory supports this fact, but it May be time to reconsider that position.

## 426. THE CRISIS DEPARTMENT

We had a housing crisis in 2007. We had a Banking crisis in 2008. We had a unemployment crisis in 2009. We had the European debt crisis in2010. In 2011 it is going to be the crisis of the weakened dollar.

This does not mean that the economy falls flat on its face. In many respects a cheaper dollar allows the world to buy more American goods. Conversely we pay more for their goods. Our institutions will not collapse but adjust. In the last two weeks our bond market yields on Treasury securities have moved lower over the past two weeks. The same goes for Corporate and municipal bonds. A selling binge would bring higher not lower yields. This seems like a sublime contradiction but it May explain why our business sector is doing what it is doing.

## 427. MEXICAN CRAFT BEER
### April 18, 2011

The Mexican economy operates from the top down Which is probably why we have our immigration problem for we are entrepreneurs and encourage new ideas. We don't try to snuff them out at their roots. We just buy them out after they make it.

Back to the point Mexican Micro Beer brewers have to import all ingredients. That increases their cost. Restaurant's have signed agreements with the two main beer firms in Mexico and agree not to sell these small upstart companies. This means their beers lack the quality of other U.S. Micro brewing companies. Despite these obstacles or Maybe because of it some have captured a small market share of their homeland.

The two giants in the Mexican Beer industry are Grupo Modelo and Cauhtemoc Moctezuma. They offer equipment and discounts provided you don't use the other guys product.

The Guadalajara based Manerva Brewery Jesus Briseno is its owner. He presently produces three basic ales Amber Toned pale, Belgian inspired red and carmel hinted Porter, His beers have made it into some specialty shops and small business locations. He stated: "Basically we're working against the system. We have all the odds of dying in battle."

He got the idea for his company when he came up to the U.S. and fell in love with our Micro brewery industry. He shipped equipment down to Mexico to start his business. I can only wish him luck.

## 428. THE LENDERS TWO TRACK FORECLOSURE
### April 15, 2011

When properties get underwater and are about to enter the foreclosure process the borrower often tries to renegotiate the loan. They submit the papers for modification but it is hard to have the banks look at their application. Meanwhile the banks start the foreclosure procedure. The people are lulled into thinking the foreclosure process has stopped when it is continuing along to its conclusion. Geoff Greenwood a spokesman for the Iowa Attorney General Tom Miller stated: "We don't think that the home owner who is making a good faith effort to work through their troubled mortgage should have the roof ripped out from over them, while they are negotiating or try to negotiate."

The regulators are trying to initiate a halt to the process While the mortgage is being renegotiated. The Attorneys General submitted a 27 page report essentially urging the elimination of the practice known as Dual Tracking. It was also put forth that that the foreclosure stop during negotiation. The banks position is that dual tracking is necessary because of the lengthily time it takes to foreclose on a property. Alys Cohen Attorney for the National Consumer Law Center stated: "The settlement policy on Dual tracking completely misses the point. You have to obtain the loan modification before they stop the foreclosure."

Here is a case in point. Shirley Robertson had a property and a rental Her catering business was doing badly. She had fallen behind in her mortgage. She learned it was scheduled to be sold. She submitted two proposals and they postponed the sale. The bank said information was missing. This is according to a lawsuit that Robertson filed against the bank along with copies of a letter shared with the *L.A. Times*. She stated that she filed her third set of papers on August 23, 2010 which was a day before the deadline that was set By Chase Bank. That same day the house was sold at a foreclosure auction. Robertson stated that she still had equity in the home, meaning the amount owed to the bank was less than the price the house could have brought. Again I say this is according to the *L.A. Times*.

Robertson stated: "They have stolen equity . If I had known they were going to do this, I would have sold the damn house myself. And not be penniless."Chase did grant a loan modification on the former rental home.

Under proposed changes according to the Attorneys General concerning Dual Tracking The mortgage servicer provides home owners a written list of any missing documents from their modification package within ten days of submission. Mortgage servicers would immediately be required to notify the home owner in writing of any new sale date if the foreclosure clock has already begun. When the borrower reaches out for the modification.

In the event that the loan modification was denied then the mortgage servicer would be required to submit an affidavit in court summarizing all the efforts to work with the borrower and the basis for denying the modification. Unfortunately the State of California handles foreclosure in a non –judicial way. The sworn statement would instead have to be sent to the borrower.

President Obama did sign the Foreclosure Relief Initiative program to deal with this issue. It is unfortunate that the great majority of mortgage work-outs occur through the banks. Does that mean that the above has very limited context.

In the year 2010 1.24 million modifications were carried out. 513,000 of those modifications were courtesy of the governments Home Affordability Modification Program.

Peter Swire a former economic adviser to President Obama stated: "The biggest problem is that the majority of modifications are proprietary. The banks are not on the hook for their non HAMP modifications."Lost paper work and communication with the lender seems to be one of the major problems that the person with the mortgage has with the bank. He continued: "They have their foreclosure people and then somewhere else their modification people. They often are in different cities."

## 429. FEDERAL CUTS
### April 12, 2011

How do you deal with a deficit that won't go away. The debt ceiling has to be raised. To avoid a government shutdown. The pruning shears were coming out $250,000 a year was taken from the Pentagon. There was an argument that 5.8 trillion had to be cut from the budget over the next decade.

Congressman Ryan put out a plan from the republican side that the Democrats called unbalanced. $700,000,000,000 would be cut from Medicare and Medicaid over the next decade. Some of President Obama's cherished programs are at stake. These programs are Health care, Wall Street overhauls, His education program called race to the Top. Four of the policy czars get the ax. Thirty domestic programs were severely reduced. There were 18 billion in cuts from departments five billion from Crime victims, four hundred million from the Treasury Forfeiture account. Take another three billion from transportation and the wet lands fund.

Freshman Representative Republican Michigan, stated: "A Historic Cut? The side of big government got 97% of what they want. Senator Ron Paul stated: "I prefer to be on the other side.."A quote from the Congressional record stated: "There's no way a debt limit increase could pass the House unless accompanied by cuts and reforms. A vote on a clean debt limit increase would fail.... Period... then what would happen to world markets?"

White House Press Secretary J. Carney stated: "We strongly disagree with the lack of balance in Congressman Ryan's approach. It simply is not appropriate and it will not be supported by the American people. We have a fiscal plan that relies on dramatic restructuring reform of the kind of programs that provide security and health security to seniors and to the poor people and the disabled people, and at the same time gives enormous tax` relief cuts to the wealthiest Americans."

House Majority Leader Eric Cantor Republican, Virginia stated: "We all agree that we have to address our fiscal crisis but taxing families and business people is not the answer. We need to cut spending, address our insolvent entitlements programs and tighten our belt by doing more with less."

## 430. MORE ACQUISITIONS

Remember all my talk about Level Three and the Tec bubble and how in the late 90s companies did not at times see the sense of buying market share that only raised the water table a bit. The Fiber optic firm Global Crossing is being acquired by guess who Level Three for 1.9 billion dollars. The agreed upon price per share was $23.04. At the news of the acquisition its stock rose to $24.97 a share. Level Threes shares went up 18% to $1,70. This firm had its day in the sun with lavish offices. Those that worked for the firm lived well but now this west coast Los Angeles firm will become part of a larger firm hopefully to live on.

## 431. CONCERNING BEYOND PETROLEUM
### March 4, 2010

California is environmentally sensitive and passed Assembly Bill 32 which regulates industries that pollute or are energy related. Valero Energy Corporation and the Tesoro Corporation had pledged, 2 million dollars in a campaign to suspend A B 32 until the unemployment rate drops to 5.5%. Governor Schwarzenegger urged businesses not to support the campaign.

The Federal climate bill passed by the House was stalled in the Senate. The Tesoro Corporation was lobbying to block the Environmental protection Agency from regulating potential green House gasses. Valero was attempting to educate the public on cap and trade legislation. Meanwhile a great unseen tragedy was just over the horizon and that makes a bad pun.

## 432. THE STERILIZATION
### February 26, 2010

As a dozen power plants nuclear and otherwise, ocean water is drawn in sometimes for a one time use and re-released into the ocean supply. Two things happen fish and larvae are trapped and the larvae along with most of the fish die. The water was and is sterilized and won't support life.

Standards have been drawn up to put filters to prevent the fish from being drawn in. This is expensive and the industry was and is fighting it.

As to the actual loss of species, growth rates can rise and fall, some sharply. The bottom line is when you sterilize the water you lower the oxygen content and that affects the shoreline to some degree.

## 433. DEEP WATER HORIZON
### April 30, 2010

On about April 20, 2010 the Deep Water Horizon Oil Rig burst into flames and sank into the Atlantic. 11 of the 126 crew members perished. Those surviving had to sign wavers that they were able to later disavow because it was (Duress) The rig was in deep water off the Louisiana coast. Governor Buddy Jindel declared a state of emergency. President Obama immediately declared Federal Emergency Aid. The ecosystem on the east coast was in the balance.

President Obama stated: "Every single available resource at our disposal including potentially the department of Defense. Home Land Security Secretary Janet Napolitano stated: "This is a spill of national significance."That term had meaning for it meant that the Mississippi Delta would also be covered. To protect the estuaries and wild life. The area was and is still suffering from the affects of Hurricane

Katrina. They said the oil had been leaking at 5,000 barrels a day. The truth later was told at the figure of 200,000 gallons a day. The initial statement was that it would take 90 days to drill a relief well and start to cap the spill.

## 434. THE WILDLIFE EFFECT

In the beginning there is organization and with the uncontrolled convulsions coming from just off our continental shelf we were looking at a threat to our economy as well as our eco-system. This article details the formation of that fight as well as our own short sightedness.

Nancy Rablais, who was the Executive Director of the Louisiana Universities Marine Consortium, stated: "Everybody is really worried about the potential ecological disaster. The oil is going to move somewhere. It's not as likely to move off shore."

The materials of war were assembled to fight this belching oil slick. Here was the arsenal for the job: 76 boats and 17 water craft. Included in the fleet there were skimmers and tug boats. There was a robotic submarine to survey the damage. Add to that 175,000 feet of booms that had been laid. In reserve there was 1,243,000 feet of boom available. Under Coastguard Personnel: 1,178 oil slick fighters that were coming in from California. An official stated: "Our official goal still remains, permanently securing the well."Rear Admiral Mary Landry stated that the spill was 5,000 feet down beyond human exploration. They had to rely on a robotic sub to get a clear picture of the conditions. A oil dispersement was waiting to be used below the surface going down that distance. They would later wonder the wisdom of this because the chemicals were extremely toxic, and no-one knew what affect there would be on Marine life. (Duh) It was argued it was better to use this cocktail more on the open sea as opposed to close to shore.

Doug Suttles who was the Head Coordinator for B P stated: "Nobody absolutely nobody wants this oil stopped more than I do."

Here is the crux of the situation at this date. There was a storm coming in and they would have to suspend operations. On top of everything it was the worst time of the year to have a disaster of this kind. The reason 70% of the migrating foul including song birds, cranes, to the Brown Pelican who have their nesting season here this time of year.

Karen Westfall Wet Lands Expert of the Louisiana Auto-Bon Society stated: "It is very important that is sensitive to any changes in any piece of it. Our marshes are not a wall. This spill is not going to stay on the outer edge. Our marshes are a Sieve."

To complicate matters it is shrimp season and the Krill that feed the food supply for those fish and mammals higher on the chain could be contaminated. That would affect the commercial fishing industry. By the way it did have a chilling effect of the economic life of the entire east coast not based on reality, but perception.

The total coordination of forces, from smaller boats to thirty foot vessels controlled lengths of boom connected to one-another made of life vest foam painted bright orange. The Spots fishermen were pulling their boats out of the water and putting them in dry-dock. To prevent oil damage.

## 435. WASHINGTON DEBATED HOW BAD IT WAS

There was a split as to the appropriate course of action, on the oil leases to be issued for oil exploration in the gulf. Most considered it an isolated incident, and were planning hearings calling the five oil companies before the committee in the coming months to find the depth of the problem. I don't get the joke.

To understand the full depth of the Washington think syndrome I have to use the language of the paragraph as stated.: (Last month Obama unveiled a draft plan designed to open the water way for new drilling in the Atlantic off Alaska, the gulf of Mexico. But on Thursday the White House Press Secretary Robert Gibbs and other administration officials including the top energy and climate advisor Carol Browner said the plan was for entering a public comment phase, and could undergo modification as a result of the oil spill and possible public reaction to it.)

On the hill at this time was a Senate bill if left in its present form would expand the nation's oil drilling program, under the guise of a climate bill. The expanded drilling provision was added to gain Republican support... The problem was the Eastern Coastal States and their Democratic Governors felt invaded and compromised.

The White house Press Secretary Robert Gibbs told a cautionary tale on how the planned drilling leases would be handled based on those proposed Senate investigations.

There would be a similar reaction this time in the Northern States in 2011 through 2012 as to the route of a pipeline carrying oil from Canadian Oil Sands over the various states to Texas refineries. There have been breaks in the Alaskan pipeline with unintended consequences. The only reason there was not an outcry is people are basically greedy and the land has taken second place. They gave the native tribes a share of the revenues.

## 436. OIL DISPERSANTS
### May 4, 2010

The oil firms have explained the logic of dispersant use. Think of it in our terms when we wash clothes and our detergents are poison just have some for lunch. The argument goes like this according to the times. Again in some cases they say it so much better than me.

(The key ingredient in dispersants is a Surfactant or in laymen's terms detergent. It is mixed with organic solvent or an alcohol to help it mix thoroughly with the oil. Just like detergent in your washing machine. It binds with both the oil and the water reducing the surface tension that causes petroleum to form to form a sheen on the water's surface allowing it to form fine particles. These particles dissolve in water allowing the spill to disperse downward rather than shoreward. They also make it much easier for Microorganisms to attack and destroy the oil.)

The oil that is left untreated according to the industry can persist for years or decades. Thor Hyderdol wrote a book called Konticki and in that book through his adventure traveling as the Phoenicians did He told of pollution that just floats on the sea. The bad part is that it could hurt some of the larger animals as they migrate. These are things of the unknown.

In order for these dispersants to work they must be injected into the oil plume within 24 hours to be affective. If the weather is really bad they also don't work.

### 437. TOURISMS WET BLANKET

The economic impact on the economy of the East coast was severe. Governor Charles Crist in his State of Florida had declared 19 counties disaster areas. That covered from the Panhandle to the S W part of the state. In Louisiana the effects on fishing and tourism were devastating. They experienced a 757million dollar loss and ten thousand people lost their jobs. Quotes ran like this: "Every customer we've got on a boat now through July has called and wanted to cancel."(Josh Howard Owner of Deep South Charters Incorporated.)

The place was called Tiny Ship Island owned by Luis Scremetta This island attracts up to 1,200 visitors a day. With the situation they were folding up the umbrellas as the tourist season went poof. 70 school groups canceled what would have been money in his pocket."We are wiped out ... this could bankrupt me."

### 438. THE SCHEDULE

The war continued on many fronts down by the well head a valve was placed to hopefully slow the flow. In anticipation of the control box to capture the oil at the source. This device had never been used before. The sub was putting dispersants into the oil. On the surface planes were dropping dispersants on the surface oil. The weather was not good.

### 439. THE BIG BOX

We are talking about a big metal building being carefully lowered to the broken pipe that now had a control valve attached. The pipe was broken in three places. The plan was to pipe warm water down to the site. The reason was so that the natural Gas would not freeze and meld with the water forming gas cycles. That would clog the tube that was designed to take up the oil and natural gas. The gas would be separated from the water and the oil. The pumped up oil could be stored in the tanker up to 200,000 gallons. The spill itself was the size of Texas.

On Parallel points back in California pressure was building to re-establish the embargo on drilling from California to Washington State. Alaska was added to the list out of fear that another Exxon Valdese incident could happen. The Embargo had just been lifted in 2008 due to energy price hikes.

## 440. ALASKA

The argument that there could be a major blow-out in the Arctic is implausible because we are not dealing with deep water drilling. The distance would be 150-200 feet as opposed to 5,000 feet.

The George W. Bush Administration. Had initially set to sell leases to companies Like Dutch Shell Petroleum and compared to B P they do have a better safety record. They spend more on maintenance than Beyond Petroleum which has taken more risks for greater wealth. The courts put a stop to that.

Then President Obama looked into drilling in the Arctic for scientific reasons. He did not trust the Bush methodology. As I said earlier the Courts were of the same opinion but granted conditional drilling to the Gulf of Mexico.

The big downfall with the arctic is location resources and equipment.. The situation boils down to this:(Leslie Pearson) stated: "Based on my experience and the likelihood of being able to contain and clean up and control a well blow-out in the Arctic is slim. A lot of that is just the location of infrastructure in that part of Alaska where the equipment would have to come from to actually get to the scene and get mobilized and operational. There aren't even ant ports in that part of the world.

There was such a great concern that the National Oceanic and Atmospheric Administration advised the Minerals Management Service in 2009 to hold off oil and gas development from off the Alaska Coast, until research is done on oil spill risks. President Obama took into account the drilling leases when he drew up his plan. The NOAA organization stated: "The challenges exposed by Arctic conditions are greatly understood. The barriers and contingencies we have in place and the significantly different Characteristics of the wells we plan to drill here gives us tremendous confidence that the chances of a similar event taking place in Alaska off shore is extremely remote."

What would Shell do in-case there was a blow-out? The answer had a one hour cap on it. It would be a three tier system of an on-site oil spill response team. A fleet of near shore barges with additional vessels and response teams, staged across the Northern slope.

The proposed drilling on the Chukehi Sea had a 40% chance of a blow-out once drilling started. It was said that a full study was not deemed necessary. The same thing was said of the Gulf Of Mexico. Attention was paid to a blow-out preventer device that was judged to be the apparent cause of the deep Horizon Disaster. It had failed in tests and the rig owners did not want to incur the expense of replacing it. That is why the rig blew. It came to light later in disputed cost over-runs and shortcuts that many of the crew had complained about. That was the reason the company had the workers sign the affidavits or risk losing compensation.

According to NOAA: "If a spill were to happen off the coast of the North slope in 500 miles or so in light broken ice conditions, it could realistically be days or weeks before anyone could get to the source of the spill."

The other problem is that the Arctic is such a new environment for oil spill operations, we're kind of relying on equipment that was in warm water use. There's not been a lot of study done on how to use the same equipment will operate under Arctic conditions."

There is some good news in all of this Ron Moris General Manager of Clean Alaska Seas stated: "Ice is a blessing and a curse. It's hard to get around in it, but it also does not allow oil to expand. It keeps it kind of like a boom, captured and it keeps the oil layer thicker."

It is a pity that we did not have candor during the Bush Administration. Truth has a tendency to go along way.

### 441. May 7, 2010

Toney Hayward Beyond Petroleum's spokesman stated that the corporation would handle all legitimate costs relating to the oil spill. At the same time their teams of lawyers are busy at work. As we know Lawyers are good at least 12 feet deep. All we have to do is look at the Exxon Valdese oil spill to get the point. In 1989 a Jury awarded 5 billion dollars in punitive damages the case was appealed. The Supreme court heard the case and the amount was reduced to 508 million for 30,000 Alaskans that made their living off of the arctic seas.

### 442. A SMALL BOX

The big building failed and Beyond Petroleum had a backup plan. It was a smaller structure easier to handle with the same principle. An alternate plan would be to stop up the pipe with a fibrous rubber substance, PUT A CORK IN IT.

### 443. COAST INVADED

The oil had reached critical areas. The no fishing zone had been extended to the Atchafalfalyia wild life reserve and it was being threatened. The oil plume was menacing the Eastern shore. A State emergency was declared in La Fourcha Perish that is located next to the Mississippi River. A slick had entered Chandeleur and Bretan Sounds. This was just East of New Or liens that had just gotten through Katrina.

Meanwhile a sucking instrument seems to be collecting 1,000 gallons of crude and putting it in the Enterprise a oil Cargo ship. Beyond Petroleum had succeeded on controlling the spill.

## 444. TOP KILL
### May 25, 2010

Remember the Dispersant issue I was talking about and the fear of toxicity, well the Congress had the same fear and were urging they use something less toxic. Oil was washing up on Louisiana beaches and wild birds and mammals not to mention fish were being caught in the grimy ooze. Florida though not affected yet was testing water quality. What started out as B P s problem was becoming Obama's problem.

The technique known as Top Kill or burning the oil on the surface contained with-in booms was the next step. This is being applied amid threats from the Federal Government that were largely coming out of frustration for the Federal Government did not have the technology to deal with the chocolate smelly goo.

Thad Allen U.S. Commandant made the following statement: "I know that to work down there right now you need remotely operated vehicles. You need very technical work at 5,000 feet you need equipment and expertise that's not generally within the Federal Government, in terms of competency, capacity, or capability."

Hayward the B P Representative stated his horror at the affect on the coast and stated that a 500 million dollar research study was being launched in how to solve the problem. The top kill solution had never been tried at this depth. He added it had been tried in other cases with 60% to 70% success. The second part of the operation was pumping a special kind of mud to seal the wells. This done in conjunction with two relief wells was hoped to stabilize the situation. If the mud got into the gas pipe the flow would increase.

The political damage was matching the ecological damage. For now it was clear to everyone that the Obama Administration didn't create the spill and that it was aggressively pressing B P to do its best to clean it up. The problem was the more the oil oozed around the Gulf the more B Ps problem becomes Obama's problem. The states affected at this stage of the game were Alabama, Mississippi, and Louisiana where it all started.

There is a disconnect in thinking. A 50 million dollar subsidy for research on the part of the oil industry, when their profits are already excessive. This was the thinking of Congress, but at the same time key Senators and Representatives defend those subsidies. Bear in mind subsidies do have strings and as in farming subsidies that are now needed as of the drought facing a good part of the nation in the year 2012 can almost make it revenue neutral.

## 445. THE OIL ILLNESS
### May 26, 2010

Initially B P assured the Federal Government that those working on the spill would have the appropriate gear to deal with the oil contamination. That in practice did not happen. Fishermen and those in the industry who took jobs with B P because their livelihood went south were not provided with protective clothing as promised but did their jobs regardless.

Representative Charles Melancon Democrat Louisiana stated that he expected B P to fund medical treatment clinics. As of that date they had not. Placer mines Perish is where the fishing community lives. George Jackson was 53 years old and had been in the fishing industry since he was 12. He took the job of clean-up when the fishing industry collapsed. According to the *L.A. Times* (He was laying containment booms Sunday. He said a dark substance floating on the water made his eyes burn.) He stated: "I ain't never run on anything like this."What happened next was his head hurt and he got nauseated. He did attend the briefings but was not given protective gear as promised. He wore leather boots and regular clothing. He added: "They told us if we ran into oil it wasn't supposed to bother us. As far as gloves we haven't been wearing any gloves."

Now here comes the government to the rescue. The U.S. Assistant Secretary of labor David Michael's (Occupational Safety and Health) pledged as of the date of this article to review conditions for cleanup workers. He promised to ensure a safe work environment even in these toxic situations.

It was not that the matter had not been addressed. In the state of Louisiana the department of Environmental Quality, Dept of Health, and Hospitals according to the *L.A. Times* stated (Warned that oil clean-up workers: "Should avoid skin contact and oral cavity or nasal passage exposure to oil spill products by using appropriate clothing.(Respiratory protection, gloves and boots.) This was clearly not the case in practice. Later B P would say they complied and we did see video of workers in has mat suits doing beach cleanup but how universal the dispersion of equipment was I don't know.

### 446. MORE DATA

There is an old saying you deal with the situation even if it's to the detriment of your health. The *L.A. Times* put it another way. (You have unemployed shrimpers and oystermen grateful for the clean-up jobs."It is an unwritten rule. You don't Bite the hand that feeds you."Stated George Barisch President of the United Fisherman's Association of Saint Barnard Perish.) He had told the Press about the fishermen feeling ill.

Meanwhile back at Beyond Petroleum central Graham McEwen stated: "Some of those chemicals May cause short lived affects, like headache, eye, and throat irritation or nausea."He added that B P had taken (Hundreds of samples of so-called volatile organic carbons such as Benzene and all levels were with-in Federal Safety Standards. He added that those working for B P laying booms or skimming are protected with coveralls and gloves.)

Experts conflict Riki Ott, a Marine Toxicologist that studied the 1989 Exxon

Valdese Spill called it a (Déjà vu) he stated: "What we saw with Exxon Valdez was a parallel track, sick animals and sick people. Harbor Seals were looking like they were drunk and dying ... and autopsies showed brain lesions... What are we exposing these poor fishermen to."

One of the ascribed quotes according to the *L.A. Times* (Barisch) stated: he would not be going out to the Chandeleur Islands where the oil slick had hit."All the birds were walking around like a bunch of Zombies."

He added: "If they give us that type of equipment then they admit there are health hazards."He added that those fishermen that went to work for B P were having difficulty connecting their ailments to the job."It becomes a matter of honor. You left in the morning you were ok. Out on the water you got a pounding headache, throwing up."Doctors had been administering antibiotics and ant-inflammatory. His wife added My husband never had a breathing problem in his life."

Add to this local resentment of locals to outsiders adding their 3 cents in and you get resentment to the outside world. They have always worked with and for big oil and now they feared that their livelihood was being endangered.

## 447. THE TRUTH COMES OUT

All this time a drama has been building. It has been a drama of man, machine and nature. The script could not be more suspenseful. Do we save the East coast or do we just plain flat lose it. That is how the marquee would read were this a movie. The ultimate betrayal mixed with the ultimate promise.

According to the hearings there was trouble on Deep Water Horizon hours before she blew her stack. It was surmised that the ceiling cement failure was a preliminary cause. There were fundamental mistakes in reading the integrity of the well. They were behind schedule and over budget. Five hours before the explosion fluid was disappearing from the riser tube. This was the line that connected the rig to the well. A valve on the sea floor was leaking. There was conversation as to the cause and talk of retesting. Their final test was look at as satisfactory. Eighteen minutes before the rig went sky high they knew that things were amiss. A struggle ensued to contain what was essentially a gas bomb. There is a switch on the well that automatically separates the rig from the well. This device is used in case of storms. The switches did not work. essentially a spark due to resistance went from the well to the rig and luckily 126 survived and unfortunately 11 were incinerated.

## 448. TOP KILL CONTINUED
### May 27, 2010

It was just hours before anyone knew what worked and what didn't. B P Officials stated: "We will not be rushed. It's too early to know if it will be successful. We've ridden a roller coaster and I think we just need to take the next 24 hours and see what the results are."There was a major slip as to the wells depth originally stated at 5,000 feet. The true depth was 13,000 feet.

Another revelation was that the mud that had held the well stable was being withdrawn and replaced with sea water.(You see they reuse the mud in other wells) The clamps on the sea-floor did not hold.

The Robots on the sea floor had the job of connecting the lines from the two vessels on the surface to the now repaired blow-out preventer at the well-head. The whole job was extremely sensitive. Suttle stated: "You can't touch it you can't feel it. You can't get down there yourself."

## 449. IT DIDN'T WORK
### June 4, 2010

Twenty-four hours came and went and the Top Kill did not work. The pipe kinked and those brave robots had to cut away the damaged pipe. The well was releasing 500,000 to 800,000 gallons of crude a day.

As the oil now off the shore of five states, and the wild life affected had risen from 100 to 820 birds. 597 of that number were found dead. 223 were found in a oil soaked condition. The state of Texas for the first time reported oil soaked water fowl. The spill itself had split into several virtual islands of oil. Florida's Governor Charly Crist stated that had no complaints as to his equipment requests and the war against the ooze. He was setting up a battery of lawyer in the virtual possibility of expected lawsuits.

## 450. REVIEWING THE BAN
### June 6, 2010

The failure of the top kill to do its job caused the operation to take a turn. They cut the kinked pipe and that caused an increase in the oil flow. The pipe was cut to fit the new smaller contraption and hopefully close off the well. The increase in the amount of oil entering the Gulf increased an estimated 20 to 45%. The container ship Enterprise was recovering 15,000 gallons a day. B P stated that in the week that would follow that amount of recovered oil would jump to 28,000 gallons a day.

The East Coast States interest groups were arguing for a lifting on the ban. Ken Salazar the Interior Secretary was reviewing the issue. He was looking at new technology that would prevent a repeat of the Deep Water Horizon catastrophe. He stated: "If it can be done before six months then there's a possibility that we could take a look at it then. It was the Presidents directive that we press the pause button ... not the stop button, so that we can make sure that if we move forward with... drilling on our continental shelf, that it can be done in a safe way. That is protective of people and protective of the environment as well.."

Meanwhile our law makers in the Senate passed a bill lifting the ceiling of 100 million dollars on the amount that can come from the liability fund to deal with the situation in the Gulf. The fund currently sits at 1.6 Billion.

It was argued that the new equipment according to the Clean Up Commanders would burn off oil and gas that exceeded what could be gathered and (Shuttled to shore) New video equipment to replace the old images we had been viewing to that time. These images would more accurately figure out the flow of the oil. Believe me these images were a gushing success. The new estimates according to the government stood at 12,000 to 19,000 gallons of crude. The riser tube was cut to fit the temporary container cap that had been placed on June 3rd.

David Hayes the Government spokesman stated: "I'm not going to declare victory or anything until I have absolute numbers. I think we all have had estimates and some people had been disappointed. When they were changed so show me the numbers."Louisiana's Governor Bobby Jindel stated: "What I want to know is how much oil they think is out there in the water. How much oil is continuing to be released.? It's very frustrating that over 50 days into this they still don't have a reliable estimate."The Governor added concerning a Federal disaster declaration he stated: "They shouldn't do anything that puts the American tax payer on the hook for B Ps spill."

The Coast Guard on scene Commander Admiral James A. Watson stated: "Now that the so-called top hat containment system has begun to capture and recover some of the oil escaping from the well-head it is imperative that you put equipment systems and processes in place to ensure that the remaining oil and gas flowing can be recovered. Which means we could take the leakage down to almost zero."

## 451. THE BRITS REACT
June 12, 2010

The company known today as Beyond Petroleum has its roots in oil exploration in Saudi Arabia and came to be known as British Petroleum and became a cultural icon. It helped the British economy at home in the social services much the way the Soviets used their oil industry to maintain their system and each had the equivalent of the Dutch Affect. The Brits survived better than the Russians but the their pension fund became dependent on B Ps support of that system. With B P losing 50% of its stock price the people in Britain became concerned.

When President Obama criticized B P on its handling of the oil spill and stated that he would have fired Hayward for it the British became unglued. He had just attacked their Icon. The British press referred to Obama's comments as unfair Castration. That does sound like a British criticism. The quote was made by Malcolm Rifkind: "The president should make it clear that he has no desire to destroy a great global company."

There is a unrelated parallel to all of this going to Candidate Mitt Romney when he was in Britain for the Olympic games and said he was concerned about a few details on the running of the Games of the Olympiad. The British Press was all over him and Prime Minister Cameron was short with Romney on the subject. His points were justified but diplomatically it was not the correct thing to do. This reflects back to the Obama comment.

## 452. LOOSE FIGURES
### June 16, 2010

The Washington Establishment became angry with Beyond Petroleum when it was learned that they had only been guesstimating in all of their testimony. The newest estimates were between 35,000 barrels and 60 barrels a day. That was a far cry from what they were saying earlier which was 20,000 to 40,000 barrels a day being released into the Gulf. The total spillage for the Exxon Valdese was 257,000 barrels. Earlier estimates according to the Government were 12,000 to 19,000 barrels of oil a day which was up from 1,000 barrels of oil a day. The newest guesstimating based on the oil that was escaping the tube was 60,000 to 80,000 barrels of oil a day.

B Ps spokesman stated on the collection of the oil from the well: "Yeh, absolutely. We've always said we will build capacity to deal with what-ever the volume of oil flowing." There was almost another fire when lightning struck the vessel that was collecting 16,000 barrels. Nobody was hurt and the fire put out..

The Democratic Representative from Massachusetts Edward J. Markey symbolized the attitude on Capitol Hill when he said: "B Ps low balling was either deliberate deception or gross incompetence."McKay B P spokesman stated: " We are sorry for everything the Gulf is going through."He distanced himself from the earlier estimates even though they came from them.

## 453. THE PUSH FOR ALTERNATIVE ENERGY

Our President is one of the most glib of recent history. He has a way of turning things around to suit his interests.(Cooptation) At any rate, he used this situation to stress the need to develop alternative energy programs. The President stated: "The tragedy unfolding on our coast is the most painful and powerful reminder yet that the time to embrace clean energy future is now."

He made no references to global warming, but the Republicans thought it was an opportunity he was using to promote his carbon Tax initiative. He made his speech from the Oval Office as did president bush after the twin Towers attack in New York or President Clinton when he faced potential impeachment. It was that kind of importance.

Maryland Democratic Senator Benjamin L. Cardin stated: "The reliance on B P for information has been a big mistake. But that's spilt milk, spilt oil B P is responsible but the governments in control. We can't be confused about who's calling the shots. It's going to be our call not B Ps"

Senate Minority Leader Kentucky Republican Mitch McConnel: stated: "I can't think of anything more inappropriate than to suggest that a national energy tax is an appropriate reaction to this environmental disaster in the gulf."

The Senate Assistant Majority leader Democrat Richard J Durban stated: He was open to the ideas that were in Obama's speech and felt positive about a potential momentum in regards to the climate change issue in terms of congressional legislation. He did observe it would be a difficult task.

Durban stated: "If he is successful at linking the disaster in the gulf to the broader energy issue we May spark a new debate. It is important, it's timely but it is a tough political issue."

### 454. SB 1070

In the midst of this oil crisis we have another crisis. It was and is a contest of wills between the States and the federal government on the illegal immigration issue. A Federal suit had been filed against Arizona for trumping Federal enforcement. The trouble is the feds don't seem to be up to the task and lack the political will to act. There is an election coming and the democrats in particular are wooing the Latin vote. Motor Voter had been lax in its standards and charges of undocumented workers voting has become an issue. Only citizens are supposed to vote. I believe that is the underlying reason for this action at this time. Yes there should be a path to citizenship for the children of illegal immigrants for they were educated in our system and would not fit into Mexican culture. At any rate the suit has been brought and there was a resolution. But the law did survive as to checking for citizenship. Beyond that there was no authority as it was in the Florida case on voting.

At any rate this was a side issue at this time. The voting and immigration issue are here with us in the year 2012.

### 455. THE STORM

In the midst of gathering the oil into the tankers a tropical storm was moving in. It was at this time in the Grand Cayman Islands. The storm was expected to hit the Louisiana Texas cost and disperse the oil towards the shore. The tankers let alone the skimmers could not work in such an environment.

Here was the prognosis for a category 2, 3, or 4: "Our overall goal in this whole thing is safety of our personnel." Senator Democrat of Florida Bill Nelson added: "Figure several days of down time as the storm approaches a few more days as the storm passes a couple more days to get things into place. Your facing up to ten days of the well gushing some 60,000 barrels of oil a day unchecked."

That's 600,000 barrels we'd have to collect quickly after the storm passed and before it could hit parts of the Gulf Coast."

Allen stated: "I understand the need to skim the oil as soon as we can, but it's going to be after the storm passes. I don't think anybody wants vessels out there trying to skim oil with weather building beyond gale force winds." Just another day on the oil slick.

### 456. THE POLITICAL OIL STORM
### July 21, 2010

There's an election coming and despite the trouble on the East coast and Maybe because of it there is a combination of intransigence and new alliance. The Governor of Florida Chary Crist was running for the Senate as an independent on an environmentalist ticket. The Republicans are in the pro-oil position a hard thing to be at this time. The Democrats while pitted against the Obama Administration on the handling of the B P issue have set their sights on Beyond petroleum as opposed to the president and his handling of the matter. You see up to this point Obama has been pushing big business as a means of stimulating the economy. His post script is green industry but he is not thinking grass roots on the matter.

### 457. B.P. SELLS ASSETS
### July 21, 2010

The strain on any company that has taken a drubbing in the press and in the value of its profits as measured by the value of its stocks, has to get lean. The Apache Oil Corporation (AOC) a Houston based firm that specializes in older wells saw this as an opportunity to expand their assets. So for 7 Billion dollars they purchased the following from Beyond Petroleum assets.
In the sale was included the premium oil fields in Texas and New Mexico, the Los Angeles based ARCO concession as well as property owned in Canada and Egypt. B Ps Alaskan assets were deemed to be potentially a separate deal.
The bottom line in Beyond Petroleum's mind was that these assets were not central to their Corporation and would free up capital. B P had suspended dividends on their stock for the rest of the year. This was so 20 billion dollars could be used to pay restitution for the oil spill that affected five states. There would have been 10 billion dollars in assets in those dividends.

### 458. THE WELL WAS CAPPED

With the cap placed on the Well Head holding, concerns shifted to potential leaks elsewhere in the pipe. B P was planning to put heavy mud in the cap to force the oil back further. The Relief well was being drilled and would not be completed till August.
Halliburton's name was raised as an issue on the 18th. It was Halliburton that had contracted to cement the Deep Horizon Well Site and argued that the B P design

on the wellhead casings were putting the rig in danger of Sevier gas flow problems.. This was according to Sepulveda a specialist.

Donald Vidrine and Robert Kaluza (B P Managers) were scheduled as witnesses but neither appealed for varying reasons. The panel wanted to know why specific diagnostic tests were not done. It had been alleged that certain short cuts due to cost had not been done..

The Bush Administration was at this point dragged into this kettle of fish. Two Interior Department Deputies defended the decisions of the administration before the Senate Committee. It centered on the promotion under the Bush Administration of off shore drilling. Gale Norton stated: "If regulations on the books and industry best practices had been followed properly there May not have been a blow out."In a way that is what previous offered facts have suggested. Remember Beyond petroleum had the reputation of a risk taker. They also in the past had maintenance issues. They were successful in finding new oil when others were not.

## 459. THE HUNDRED DAY MARK
July 29, 2010

This is characteristic of Washington. The spill had been capped and the relief well was underway. Now that the damage wild-life and all was being addressed we had to find a villain. They found two potential candidates The natural Resources minerals management which President Obama belatedly split into three divisions because the royalty collection was managed by the same folks that did the inspecting and defining of standards. The second was the nature of the industry and inherent cost cutting mechanisms tied to the bottom line.

Aside from the Government position and its quandary on writing new legislation concerning off shore drilling the new spokesman for Beyond Petroleum Chief executive Robert Dudley put forth the position of the industry when he stated."I think, no guarantees- but I believe there will be no more oil flowing into the Gulf after July 15th."This was in reference to the mechanical cap that held the well in check.

According to the time table by August 10th (The crews will attempt to intersect the well far undersea with a relief bore that they will use to jam mud and cement into the bottom of the renegade well.) It was estimated that the whole process could take days to weeks. This is according to the *L.A. Times*.

The head of the Coast Guard relief effort General Allen stated: "We are optimistic that we will get this thing done."He added concerning the fishermen turned oil clean-up crew with no fishing industry to support them."How we transition from response posture and once the well is killed what needs to be done."

## 460. THE MOMENT ARRIVES
July 30, 2010

As explained by Peter E. Clark Engineering Professor at the University of Alabama (The cap is not bolted to the well, but sealed with a hydraulic ring)"I mean you just couldn't walk away from that, but filling a hole with cement is forever."

What he lists as the first step was the static kill operation. What was involved was sending(dense specifically formulated drilling mud., weighing 13 pounds per gallon. That is 1.5 times the weight of a gallon of Sea Water.- from ships down a mile long drill pipe eventually into the well through a valve. This will re-establish control over the high pressure oil .

## 461. PRESIDENT BARAK H.OBAMA
June 16, 2009

The Obama Administration was supposed to be one of the most innovative in the 21$^{st}$ Century but something went wrong. They started out on the right foot somehow things went back to the status quo.

The procedures were set in place to potentially seize conglomerates like AIG where prior authority was limited only to banks. A wide range of products from derivatives to bonds to Hedge funds specifically to reign in what is known as Securities that are called complex Derivatives. The goal was to reduce the incentive of companies to take excessive risks. Green Span called it Irrational exuberance. The Modern Banking Reform Act 1999. that replaced the Glass Siegel act which dated to the depression had grown cumbersome and outdated.(To bad in 2012 Banks are engaging in risky corporate debt under the guise of the Modern Banking Reform act. This new legislation dating to the Clinton Administration in anticipation of the Y2K crisis and the projected new economy allowed banks to engage in insurance and conglomerates/ Holding Companies and Insurance and conglomerates to engage in banking. So it sounds like the Obama Administration for all its rhetoric after saving the big corporations neglected the Small Business sector till lately and now the economy is flat in the year 2012.

The Treasury Secretary Timothy F. Geithner stated as of the time of this article: "We had a system that proved too unstable too fragile. The Administration had proposed an agency to regulate financial products marketed to consumers used to hedge risky investments. These include new reporting and disclosure requirements, required to retain 5% of the credit risks when those loans are changed into Securities. It would be the Congress that would institute the reforms by 2010. In a way you can put it to his influence in Washington but Larry Summers, Chairman of the White House Economic Council and Financial Advisor, had a lot to do with where we are today.

The Business groups had concern that the Obama administration for all its rhetoric would go too far in its reforms.

There is an example, AIG being able to make the choice of the Office of Thrift Supervision, its non-insurance Commercial business when it bought the small savings and loan in the1990s.

That particular office had been viewed as a weaker office regulator and was extremely criticized in a government report that year for ignoring repeated warnings about INDI Corporation Mac Bancorp, Pasadena based before the thrifts failure that summer. Barbara Roper Director of Investor Protection for the Consumer Federation of America stated: "I'm concerned that people think we've stepped back from the brink of disaster and are not committed to seeing the real meaning of the reforms adopted.

The fear of the business community was that the administration would go too far in reforming the system.(I would wonder if these same business men were in favor of risky ventures like insuring banks using hedge funds as derivatives against bad corporate practices just because of greater economic return. This was the case as of 2011 through 2012. J P Morgan even had a two million dollar loss which they were called on the carpet for but nothing above a tongue lashing happened. The banks were holding back on the standard mortgage and business loans to small business due to the lack of profitable return.

Scott Talbot the chief lobbyist for the Financial Services Round Table, was optimistic at the time of this article and states: "This has moved at lightning speed. You're talking about a historic piece of reform. "Critics argued that the administration had waited till the end of the crisis before taking action." Laurence H. Summers Chairman of the White house Economic Council stated: "There are people who believe that the wrong time to organize the fire department is while the fire is still burning. The president has concluded very strongly that, that view is wrong. Experience tells us that once a crisis has passed, the will to reform will pass as well."

Hear May lie the answer to the earlier question on bank behavior. Douglas J. Elliott an economics fellow at the Brookings Institute and former Investment banker stated the following according to the *L.A. Times*. (There is still enough political momentum to pass major reforms but as the financial crisis has eased there is less ability to tackle the difficult turf battles involved in merging regulatory agencies.) Because of the difficulty of the task this newly elected President settled on changing the rules of engagement along with the principles.(Than blowing up Government regulatory structure.)

The quote went like this: "As far as I can tell the administration doesn't think it's as important to get that structure right as to get the rules right and make sure people are focused on acting the right way."I can only suggest that the slippage of time, some risky behavior habits re-enforced by the old structure could have taken hold. The only other explanation is that the Builder-bergs did it, and I doubt that.

## 462. FOREIGN POLICY /IRAN
June 23, 2009

As you well know at this time we are engaged to one degree or another in Iraq and Afghanistan at this time. It is not possible to take our forces over there and solve the problem militarily. That leaves diplomacy and economic sanctions. Speaking from the year 2012 you can see potential distortions of fact when President Obama initially acted on the Iranian crisis and on a two level solution. If the forces for reform were successful there would be no need to act. If the revolting forces were subdued which they were acting on the issue would also be pointless. Initially because of Iran's Nuclear program the president saw no difference between Mir Hussein Mousavi and Ahmaddinajad . People were dying in the streets and were being shot and clubbed to death. He only reacted in condemnation after the world's leaders and the Congress condemned it. That was why in 2012 and earlier Mitt Romney said the things he did. At the time there was not much he could have done so we are looking through a distorted historical perspective looked at through the Republican prism. I really don't think then or now we would have been in favor of a Libyan style involvement in that country. As we saw it the Egyptians solved their problem on their own. Syria was starting to erupt and we didn't want to go there. The world did not want to go there. We were engaged in our Pelepaneasion War and could not have taken on another conflict.

According to the administration Laura Rozen stated: "Obama is dedicated to diplomacy in a matter that is almost ideological. He wants to do some stuff in the Middle East with a two step in the next eight years. He May not be able to achieve half of them unless he gets this huge piece of the puzzle right. It was perceived that president Obama was using the Iranian stance as a means of settling the Israeli Palestinian Issue. It would be the Medusa Head approach to the problem. Fast forwarding to the year 2012 Iran is testing short range and intermediate range missiles making it a force to be dealt with. I do hope if we have any clandestine SDI like HARP we can use them as a deterrent. It is also possible that the drone force has something to do with the strategy, just guessing.

Here is another angel as to the Obama Administration on Iran. In 1953 we helped to overthrow the Mohammed Mousadine Regime. The Anti American stance could go back to this matter. That is why every time people were butchered we were blamed for inciting it. It was a bias built into the culture based on history. When President bush invades Iraq in 2003 the whole issue comes up again. This is especially true when it was proven that there were no weapons of mass destruction. That is why the world only gave us lip service and we had to go it alone with only the Brits To join us. Thank God NATO got involved in Afghanistan. With a host of allies.

## 463. THE CLIMATE BILL
### June 29, 2009

In 2012 we are hearing about coal burning plants being padlocked and jobs lost. That goes back to this piece of legislation. House Speaker Nancy Pelosy used all her favors to get this vote. There were defections on both sides. Forty –four Democrats voted no and eight Republicans voted yes. The vote was 219-212 This bill put in place a new Carbon or right to pollute tax for those who did not change with the times. It was argued that this bill which the President expected in modified Senate form would usher in a new era of Green industry, wind, solar, and atomic. Coal was a major casualty and that has been reflected in the political commercials of 2012. This is the bill that introduced the carbon tax. Industries pay taxes for the privilege of doing business in a polluting way. One criticism was nations other than our own that we do business with were not affected and given a technical advantage. I am referring to China. That's the price we paid for them buying our debt. If it is any comfort, in 2011 the Chinese were having trouble with their labor force and were improving their act and raising prices because of labor costs. In the end all things are relative.

The Democratic representative from Montana House Majority Leader Steny H. Hoyer stated: "This is a transformative moment to build a clean energy future for our country. This is a moment to create jobs. This is a moment to take on at long last a defining challenge of our time global warming."We have had direction change and an error in direction simultaneously. All our solar eggs were put in one basket and they took over half a billion from the stimulus package and went bankrupt. This experiment left our citizens holding the bag. If that money from the stimulus package were given to small and medium sized business it would have created jobs and been a success. It is small business that creates jobs not large corporations. Be they green jobs or not. We should make our own turbines not the Chinese. More U.S. companies are starting to get into the business and I realize President Obama was after a quick start but at what cost to the U.S. industrial complex. We could build something like a wid generator. The important thing is as of 2012 green industry is growing in fuel/Ethanol, solar panels and not so much in the nuclear end thanks to disasters like the tsunami that hit northern Japan.

## 464. THE SUPREME COURT
### July 12, 2009

The concerns on who dominates the court are a concern of the Congress and the President. Sonia SotoMayor was a judge from the 9th circuit Court of Appeals. Her opinions number 400. Her big controversy concerns social values. Her Latin heritage was of concern as to how her empathy would play in certain cases. Her most controversial remark was one concerning the wise Latina looking at all sides and coming to a decision better than a white male judge.

Those that have appeared before her or know her have varying points of view Michael R. Bloomberg the Mayor of new York City was familiar with her history. David Cone was a former Major League Pitcher was a labor Union representative during the baseball strike. Frank Ricci was the lead plaintiff in the white Fire Fighters Discrimination suit against the city of New Haven Connecticut. Sandra S Froman is the former president of the National Rifle and pistol Association. Luis J. Freeh was the former Director of the FBI. He was also a New York Federal Judge on the 9th circuit at the time she was on the bench. These people were called to give their impressions of her.

The Gentlemen on the panel that would be reviewing her were: Representative Jeffry Sessions Senate Republican from Alabama He was concerned about the wise Latina concept. Senator John Cornyn Republican from Texas. He was concerned about bias and race. He also was concerned about judicial restraint. Patrick J. Leahy the Democratic Senator from Vermont. His concern as Chairman was that the nomination move swiftly through the hearings and to the floor for consideration. Arlin Spector a five term Senator who recently switched parties. He was the question mark. Al Frankin the Democratic Senator from Minnesota. He is the most recent addition to the chamber. His concern was the influence of foreign law on the U.S. System.

The historical dimension of her appointment would make her the second woman on the court among nine judges. She is the third Democratic Appointee, and the sixth Roman Catholic to serve on the court. She was confirmed by the Senate.

### 465. THE IRANIAN PROTEST IN WASHINGTON

Approximately 200 protestors made their voices heard on June 12, Ahmadinajad stole the election from Mousavi who was organizing mass demonstrations in Tehran(Peaceful). Many were beaten and killed. Among the Martyrs a young girl by the name of Neda who at her death became a symbol of resistance. In the end Ahmadinajad Succeeded the Good prince won. What these protests did was raise the peoples conscience and the long term battle is not over.

### 466. GOVERNMENT LIFTS OIL DRILLING BAN
July 17, 2009

On July 17, 2008 the Bush Administration lifted the ban on drilling in the gulf of Mexico and Alaska. The U.S. Court of Appeals of the District of Columbia (vacated) the 2007 through 2012 leasing program that was developed under George W. Bush. Officials from the Minerals Management Service which was part of the Department of Interior gave notice that 18 million acres were being opened to drilling off the continental shelf from Texas to Louisiana. The variances were as close as nine miles and as far as 250 miles.

The drilling in Alaska was forbidden because of the lack of environmental studies. A funny thing happened in 2012 those leases were ok'd. We along with the world are now drilling in Antarctica largely because of the global warming affect. The case in the Gulf of Mexico was not as clear. The Interior Secretary under President Obama, Ken Salazar stated the Interior Department would proceed with leasing sites. On the gulf.

Kendra Barkof spokes person for the Department of Interior would proceed with the leasing of the sites on the Gulf.

The Republicans were upset that the leasing had not started sooner. The criticism centered on the Obama Administrations lack of plan for drilling in the Gulf. When the leases were granted a faint praise was visited on the Obama Administration. Blame also followed when the Deep Water horizon Rig exploded.

Representative Doc Hastings of Washington stated: "While I appreciate any decision to expand American planned domestic energy production, today's announcement simply continues the Obama Administration policy. Instead of putting all our eggs in one basket, the Department of Interior should offer other parts of America's Continental Shelf so we can reduce our dependence on foreign oil. The importance of growing our economy and creating new jobs for the 9.5 million unemployed Americans.

The reality check would be you have to know wildcatting and drill operations in order to get employed in this field.

### 467. NAACP

Here is an interesting fact. The National Association of Colored People was formed in 1909. President Obama spoke to them on their centennial. The President stated: "I understand that there May be a temptation among some to think that discrimination is no longer a problem in 2009. But make no mistake the pain of discrimination is still felt in 2009 America. The symbolism of a Black President on the lectern 100 years to the date of the NAACPs birth is historical."

In citing the historical barrier he noted that African Americans were more likely to be hit by unemployment, spiraling health care costs and AIDS. He also took note that those conditions were not limited by racial boundaries.

He attacked the views of Jeremy Wright Jr. and called his speech a (Profoundly distorted view) of this country. He went on: "That means putting away the X Box and putting our kids to bed at a reasonable hour. It means attending those parent teacher conferences. Reading to our kids and helping them with their home work."

Under the concepts of pain and inequality the President stated: "By African American Women paid less for doing the same work as colleagues of a different color and gender. By Latino's made to feel unwelcome in their own country. By Muslim Americans viewed with suspicion for simply kneeling down to pray. By our gay Brothers and sisters still taunted, still attacked, still denied their rights."

Under perception and ability: "They might think they got a pretty good jump shot or pretty good flow but our kids can't all aspire to be the next Le Bron or Lil' Wayne. I want them to aspiring to be scientists, and engineers, doctors and teachers, not just Ballers and Rappers. I want them aspiring to be a Supreme Court Justice. I want them to be aspiring to be President of the United States."

The President continued: "If three Civil Rights Workers in Mississippi Black and White Christian and Jew, city born and country bred could lay down their lives in freedoms cause, I know we can come together to face down the challenges of our time. We can fix our schools, heal our sick, and rescue our youth from violence and despair."

## 468. THE DETAINEES
July 21, 2009

President Obama in his campaign to become President pledged to close Guantanamo. He said he did not want to make the mistakes of the Bush Administration that ran into legal trouble. Among those questions what do you do with detainees you can't bring to trial but can't hold indefinitely. The other question can you hold a prisoner of war indefinitely without charge. He had projected January 22 as the closure date for Guantanamo. The Administration said there would be a six month extension to make sure the decision matched existing law.

In an effort to find the solution to find a solution on what to do with 240 prisoners the administration spokes man said: "We want to get this right and not have another multiple years of uncertainty."It was argued that during the Bush years that spot at the end of Cuba that has given us so much unfortunate history. Similar to Angel Island off of San Francisco bay that is now a tolerance museum. Civil Liberties groups had expressed their concern that a notion delayed is a notion denied.

The spokesman continued: "The Obama Administration must not slip into the same legal swamp that engulfed the Bush Administration with its failed Guantanamo policies."As far as the delayed time goes: "To meet the executive order-that is our goal."Concerning some of the cases: "Substantially more than 50 cases of detainees could be deferred overseas, as well as a significant number of others could face trial. In the U.S.. or federal Courts before a revamped system of military commissions."

There was talk of incorporating CIA, FBI and other agencies for the higher Al Qaeda suspects. In the year 2012 Guantanamo is still open for business.

## 469. HEALTH CARE BATTLE
July 22, 2009

President Obama was on a mission from God. He stated from the Rose Garden: "We can choose to follow that playbook again and then we'll never get over the goal line, or we can come together and insist that this time it will be different. We can choose action over inaction."This was all part of the Obama blitz to get his health care plan passed by August before the Legislative recess. At the time of great battles Presidents take their public stock, Poll numbers. As of this date Obama had a 44% approval rating and a 50% disapproval rating

Michael Steel Chairman of the Republican National Committee Did not wish to pass the president's plan by a certain date. His concern was the complicated nature and state of the economy. He stated: "Why this rush to get a health care bill signed or at least passed before the August recess. The way the Administration is going about it is not appropriate to me."Representative Henry A. Waxman was looking to committees to gain support for its passage and at the same exact moment The U.S. Chamber of commerce was launching a publicity campaign to defeat the measure.

Back in the Rose garden President Obama stated: "Make no mistake. We are closer than ever before to the reform that the American people need... Americans don't care who is up or down in Washington Politics. The American people understand the status quo is unacceptable."

## 470. THE TRANSPARENCY WARS

Under the bush Administration the log and the visitors to the White house were considered privileged information. When Candidate Obama was running for the White House Address he vowed transparency in his administration in his fight against McCain for the presidency. Now that he has won the job and the headaches and fights that go with it he has taken Bushes stance of executive privilege. What I am amazed about is the hording of knowledge by the White House that I believe has lead to the Republican candidates making uninformed statements in the year 2012.

A group called Citizens for Responsibility and Ethics has filed suit against the Obama Administration for failure to provide lists of visitors in contact with the President. There initial request was denied by the Secret service. At this moment it concerns health care and those related to it. Among those seen entering the White house: Billy Tauzin President of the Pharmaceuticals and Manufacturers of America, Karen Ignagni President of America's Health Insurance plans and Chief Executive of Johnson and Johnson James Bohak, The President would say if you want to know about something ask the experts and he'd be right. The critics would say these are lobbyists. He was listening to the special interest groups. I say he is just being the President.

## 471. PROFILING AND A TEACHABLE MOMENT
### July 31, 2009

On about the fifteenth of July Henry Luis Gates an African American Studies Scholar was arrested by a white police officer Sergeant James Crowley and a law suit happened The Massachusetts community got up in Arms. When the issue became a national matter the President said the officer acted stupidly. This escalated the thing further.

The solution was novel to say the least. Both the officer and the Professor were invited to the White house for a glass or two of beer. The Vice president was also there. They talked and agreed to talk further. Maybe the Palestinians and Israeli's can sit down and talk over a glass of wine.

## 472. THE MEDAL OF FREEDOM

Under the Bush Administration this award was given in the spirit of the Bush presidency and his selections to some seemed jaded. Former Prime Minister Tony Blair, Former representative Henry J. Hyde, Former CIA Director George Tenet, Paul Bremer III, General Tommy Franks, Doris Day, Arnold Palmer, B. B. King. Some of Georges picks reflected his interests.

Under the Obama Administration the Picks had a theme. In all there were 16 honorees some posthumous. San Francisco's Supervisor Harvey Milk, Former Senator Jack Kemp who was also a football star in his own right. Senator Edward M. Kennedy the Lion of the Senate, Reverend Joseph Lowery American civil Rights Activist, Desmond Tutu South Africa's Archbishop, Nobel Laureate, Billie Jean King, Justice Sandra day O'Connor. This was actually quite a difference in style and a sign of the times.

## 473. LIBERAL REVOLT

While President Obama was negotiating with the conservative democrats and republicans the liberals were feeling the chill. The AARP had gotten involved and were meeting with Pelosy. It was argued that the good was being held hostage to the perfect.

The Liberal wing of the Democratic Party favored a single payer system modeled on the Canadian and British Models. Most in the Party felt that in order to give birth to this health plan compromise was in order for this year. During the election it seemed that candidate Obama had accepted the single payer system in principle. It seemed that faith had been installed in the liberal leaders like Pelosy, and Henry A. Waxman Democrat of Beverly Hills. It was Waxman that brought up an amendment on the second vote. This was despite republican objections to the move. This was a plan similar to Edward M. Kennedy's plan for a Government run insurance plan as an alternative to private coverage.

Senator Barnie Sanders stated: "What the American people want very clearly is a Medic-care type public option in fifty states in this country which will give them a choice against private insurance companies."The objection that was raised to this was private insurers and employers would simply bow out and Mr. Joe public would be forced into a government program.

Will Marshal President of the Central progressive Policy Institute, stated: "It is the moderates that give Democrats their majority. The bigger the democratic majority grows, the more moderate it becomes. Democrats are a center left coalition, so big legislative initiatives need to be shaped accordingly."

What is plain is the vast bulk of both the Democratic and Republican Party are close to one another philosophically. The problem is the conservatives control the Republicans and the Liberals control the Democrats. The extremes are causing the middle to fight and dividing this country on this issue.

## 474. GEORGE H. W. BUSH HONORED
August 10, 2009

There was a book I read once called *Acres Of Diamonds*. It was a little book that told of a man who searched the world over for meaning in his life and soul and found it in his own back-yard.

President Obama I believe was having one of those moments when he honored George Herbert Walker Bush for his life time of achievement. The President stated: "President George H. W. Bush is an example of someone who eschewed a life of comfort and privilege and instead devoted himself to public service inside government and out. The R and D next to your name is irrelevant in challenging times."

Obama continued: "You might not know it from watching Cable news shows or listening to folks on the radio, but I think we're standing in one of those moments."

George H. W. Bush reflected on President Obama as a man of concern who at the time of hurricane Katrina showed great compassion for the evacuees and seemed to ignore the camera. Bush stated: "He came without fanfare. He was someone I could quickly see was genuinely concerned about helping others."

Robert M. Gates also appeared on stage. Gates had served the father and the son. In a way this was an odd moment for president Obama had rejected the policies of G W Bush. The reason for this promotion was the 20th anniversary of the founding of the Points of Light Institute.

The comments made concerning George W. Bush's handling of Katrina were passed by as simply politics, President George H. W. Bush stated: "Politics is politics. But some things are bigger than that, he like other American would like to see the President be successful." There were protests for they were in the heart of Republican country. The protests were over spending and the National debt. Those that were in the audience were both polite and enthusiastic.

## 475. COMMUNITY OUTREACH
August 10, 2009

In this phase we move from the left to the center. The activists are now being asked to coordinate to cooperation with the Republican side to get the health bill passed. This is the creation of grass roots support. The difficulty lies in the enthusiasm for ideas they are not that thrilled about.: "Now people are going to have to work on something that is not quite as slick or sexy." A big part of this had been the ad campaigns in several states.

The other side of the coin became that the Obama Administration was forcing national health care on what some viewed as a states' rights issue. At this point in time the health plan was still very much in flux. That feeling of the unwanted pill one takes has continued to this day in some sectors.

## 476. ON EDUCATION
### September 8, 2009

It is common for Presidents to speak at High-schools as a format for promoting education in this country. When President Obama was to speak in Arlington Virginia protests were raised over potential content that were unfounded. Here is the partial transcript of that address."I know that sometimes you get a sense from TV that you can get rich and successful without any hard work. That your ticket to success is through rapping or baseball, or being a reality TV star, when chances are you're not going to do any of those things.

But the truth is being successful is hard. You won't love every subject you study. You won't click with every teacher. Not every homework assignment will seem completely relevant to your life at this minute. And you won't necessarily succeed at everything the first time you try.

You'll need the knowledge and problem solving skills you learn in science and math….to develop new energy technologies and protect our environment."He emphasized battling for justice and fighting poverty. These were not the messages of creeping socialism to borrow a phrase and I do think accusations should be weighed against reality.

## 477. BATTLE OVER THE FEDERAL HEAITH PLAN

At this point in the process National Health Care was just an idea. The President had submitted no concrete proposals. He was relying on the legislative process for that. This would later be a criticism about the Affordable Federal Plan as raised by the republicans who were not crazy about the idea.

There was a House and Senate version emerging. The then democratically dominated House favored the idea of a public option. The Senate backed the idea of Private cooperatives backed by the Federal government at first till they got established. The Senate also backed the idea of State insurance pools. The initial cost 65 billion spread over 10 years. The Public option was favored over the private cooperative. Now I am just guessing but I think Candidate Romney would probably favor the state based private cooperative over the Federal Public option.

Under eligibility there was a difference in the House and senate. The House using the Public Option argued for an expanded eligibility through Medicaid. They advocated making regular medical insurance more reasonable in cost courtesy of the public option. The Senate argued the idea of expanding Medicaid or Medicare to not only the aged or infirmed. Medicaid expansion would cost 500 billion over five years. As to Medicare there was no cost estimate according to the *L.A. Times*.

It was agreed by both Legislative bodies that no one could be denied care for a pre-existing condition. The other point was the uninsured and the fear that those that were healthy would not buy insurance. And those that would be indigent would be a burden to the system. Without the pre-existing clause it would make insurance more expensive and hard to get.

On improving health care the argument is technology could lower the costs because it eliminates redundancy and creates a information cloud on the status of a patient and the financial connection of a doctor to a hospital. The down side argues that government control would lead to downsizing of care. A thing that was not mentioned in the article but is a factor is that 5% of those seeking care especially in poor neighborhoods can be up to 60% of the cost. CNN is the source on this one.

Remember the drug benefit that G W Bush put in that added to the national debt because it subsidized the drug companies. Well this idea to plug the donut hole which is an allusion to the gap that seniors pay for prescriptions. The idea of a universal rule would eliminate geographic variations. Would this not create an artificial cost to the bottom line on some drugs The total cost of the legislation is thought at this time to be 1.4 trillion dollars over 10 years.

## 478. September 11, 2009

Addressing the Congress the President proposed an overhaul of the nations proposed Federal Health plan and not add to the National debt. Reaction to the President's speech was split largely along party lines. Jim Cooper a democratic conservative representing Tennessee stated: "If the details live up to the quality of the speech then it's a good plan." Representative Barbara Lee of Oakland stated: "The President last night spoke to the conscience of America. He talked about this being a moral imperative, an issue of social justice.

On the republican side Arizona Senator Jon Kyl stated: "It sounded very much like Chicago Politics that I know he's familiar with. It appeared as if he were trying to ram something through."

On the Democratic side the House ways and means committee chairman Democratic Representative of New York Charley B. Randal stated: "I wouldn't spend a lot of time on what the Senate is thinking. They are not thinking quite frankly. One thing we don't have responsibility for is the check with the other body." The Republicans aside the President still had hid divide in the Democratic Party. The split between the conservative and liberal wing was still quite wide. The major bone of contention concerned the public option. An example would be the Blue Dog Democrats in the House nearly blocked an important Committee that was advancing the Health Care Bill. The liberal wing of the party was fuming at the efforts of the Senate Finance Committee Chairman Democratic Senator from Montana who was putting together a bill conservative enough to gain republican support.

President Obama took a balanced approach on the development of the Health Care Bill. A member of the House Democratic Representative from Virginia Rick Boucher stated: "He clearly and proportionately opened the door to negotiations with Republican members." I want to note the give and take that is not and the accommodation that is actually cooptation. You can come and play in the sand box but we have a few rules.

### 479. THE ABORTION ISSUE

All things boil down to a matter of language. Under this current evolving health bill as it was at this time the language went like this (The logic goes like this: Most of the proposals for expanding coverage include provisions for people who can't afford private health insurance. They could receive federal subsidies to help them buy insurance. Abortion foes say that if a private plan offers abortion coverage and a federal subsidy is used to purchase it, this would mean taxpayers are subsidizing abortion.)

Now let's look at the Abortion Rights Supporters side. Representative Lois Capps Democrat Santa Barbara stated: "The President made clear that no federal funding would be used for abortion" To support this the House Energy and Commerce Commission passed narrowly a provision that would ensure that no federal dollars were used for abortions. Planned Parenthood stated: "It's time to stop spreading misinformation and creating confusion and distractions to undermine health reform."

The argument boils down to what are the barriers we are talking about.(Accounts would be created to keep federal dollars from comingling with an individual's contributions so in essence federal dollars will not support abortion.) This is according to the *L.A. Times*.

What I have just said the fractured mirror syndrome. That is despite the facts we are going to go ahead anyway. What I don't like about that idea is that dictators use that concept all the time to maintain control of their flock. Both sides launched a massive campaign putting forth partial arguments to substantiate their reality but the truth is federal funds under this construct would not go to abortions
.

### 480. THE SPECTOR EXPERIMENT
September 12, 2009

Senator Arlen Specter was a lifelong republican senator turned by the force of a powerful Jedi Barak Obama and his Padwa Vice president Joe Biden. Senator Specter was challenged by a now fellow Democrat Representative Joe Sestak of Pennsylvania. The President feeling honor bound to support Spector for he and Biden were instrumental in his conversion were risking their parties alienation should Sestak win the primary which he did by a narrow margin. The Great Senator Specter was defeated but he will be remembered in history.

481. THE DOCTORS
September 15, 2009

In any reform the main affected group. The American Medical Association after 60 years of resisting the federal bureaucracy finally found a bill they liked. It is argued as of this date that that according to the *L.A. Times* (A proposal that promises hundreds of billions of dollars for Americas doctors) The agreement essentially (guarantees that there will be no Medicare payment cuts over the 10 year span) Their support is a basic guaranty that their bill will be paid.

482. THE RACE ISSUE

In my long diatribes on the Obama Administration both praise and blame this concept had not come up. It took a Peanut farmer turned president to turn the soil on the issue. The republicans who were in attack mode to begin with. It was what the Obama Administration had proposed so far that inspired that now famous outburst (You Lie) by Republican Representative of South Carolina Joe Wilson when the President spoke to a Joint Session of the Congress. This out-burst was not a racial Epithet but an outburst of personal rage that never should have happened.

What former president Carter did by tying that statement to prejudice did was far more dangerous. Here is what carter said: "An overwhelming portion of the intensity demonstrated animosity toward president Barak Obama is based on the fact that he is a Black man. Racism still exists. And I think it was bubbled up to the surface because of a belief among many white people and not just in the south, but around the country that African Americans are not qualified to lead this great country."Blazing Saddles aside change comes with acceptance and the president was on solid ground there. The Carter statement stirred up what was not there before.

What I just got through saying though my words were stated differently By press Secretary Robert Gibbs in more diplomatic language."The President does not believe that the criticism comes based on the color of his skin."

What happened after that statement on September 9th was an increase in diatribes not based on reason but also not based on race. Whenever you apply power expect resistance. A protest was held in Washington. The placards (We come unarmed this time and Hitler gave good speeches to.) I wasn't aware that Hitler was black. What we were seeing was a reaction to Chicago style politics approaching an election year in a bad economy by displaced people.

The Manager of Hillary Clintons bid Phill Singer stated: " The more the White House communicates with regular Americans- not the people who spend 24 hours a day listening to talk radio and cable TV, but those who are trying to raise families and make ends meet the better off they'll be in the long run"

## 483. ON CONSUMER PROTECTION
### October 4, 2009

Freedom of choice is a two sided sword. The Obama Administration at this point in time sought to protect the public from themselves which in a way is admirable. When we are in a corner we do tend to make financial mistakes that haunt us for years. I have done that.

The Chamber of Commerce and other affiliated business groups have fought financial reform. They call it restraint of trade, interfering with personal liberties. Business men are not supposed to be street thugs. The proposed agency the CFPA would make it compulsory to stipulate the charges put on financial instruments. And limit the interest rates that credit card companies could charge.

It was argued that it was the people who irresponsibly entered into agreements that they could not afford that landed the economy in the mess that it was. Greenspan coined the term irrational exuberance. That as I said earlier was when speculative thinking exceeded the rational. An example flipping houses causing the market to inflate and collapse. The reason salaries and job losses were not compatible with the expected mortgage payments which put Properties under water financially. Corporations who over invested in technology at the expense of their work forces. All things have a balance. Again I refer you to Allen Tofflers Future Shock and the concept of managed technology.

As to the President's plan, the Consumer Financial Protection Agency would attempt to remedy flawed economic business policies that affect the consumer. Referring to the Chamber of Commerce. President Obama said: "They are doing what they always do, descending on Congress, using every bit of influence they have to maintain the status quo, that has maximized their profits at the expense of the American consumers, despite the fact that recently a whole bunch of those American consumers bailed them out as a consequence of bad decisions that they made."(Irrational exuberance)

The Republican side took up the cross of the bankers and business men who called the proposal undue regulation and (An intrusion of Government into business operation.) Of concern were large bank overdraft fees, high interest loan payments (Remember my reference to street thugs) An example was given in the *L.A. Times* where a $550 loan caused a charge of $2,700 in interest with not a penny going towards the principle.

President Obama continued: "It is true that the crisis we faced was caused in part by people who took on too much debt and took out loans they couldn't afford. But my concern is with the millions of American who behaved responsibly, yet still found themselves in jeopardy because of predatory practices of some in the financial industry. These are the folks who signed contracts they didn't always understand, offered by lenders who didn't always tell the truth. They are lured by promises of low payments and never made aware of the fine print and hidden fees."

Those who opposed the new agency again emphasized the limits put on consumer choice. Like in Stalin in his defense of his definition of democracy there is something lacking in the content. David Hirschmann the President of the Chamber of Commerce stated: "The proposed CFPA will exacerbate the weaknesses of the current system that clearly failed, restrict access to credit and make it more costly for consumers and businesses."I do believe they call that element greed. May be we should talk to the character in the movie "Wall Street" Mr. Gecko.

### 484. ON FOREIGN WARS
#### October 10, 2009

The war in Afghanistan is at a cross roads at this time. General McChrystal said reducing troops was a bad idea and increasing them to 60,000 was not necessarily a guarantee of success. It is an irony that on this very day he was planning an acceleration in troop levels, President Obama had won the Nobel Peace Prize for his efforts at brokering international peace and understanding. Also his stand on Human Rights. His critics called the award premature. State department spokesman P J Crowly stated: "We think that gives us a sense of momentum when the United States has accolades tossed its way rather than shoes"

This mixed blessing in a time of decision put the oneness on the administration to tackle the sour job market. The administration did over time do this to a certain extent. Democratic Stratagist Joe Tripi stated: " He got a Nobel Prize what did you get a pink slip. Either the economy is going and this won't matter, or this will be another tool in the republicans arsenal of accusing the President of not doing enough. Maybe if he won the Nobel Prize for economic recovery and created hundreds of thousands of new jobs this would be a good thing for him politically."To stress the positive he noted the return of Multi lateral Diplomacy as a renewed balance in the international arena.

The Obama Administration ended an age old policy of a missile defense system in Europe. At one point it was the right thing to do as a weapon against the Soviets large tank divisions. There was also the threat of the neutron bomb that in the end was declared illegal. With the fall of the Soviet Union and the rise of Democratic Russia the missiles had become obsolete and Russia still considered those missiles a threat, when Russia was no longer a threat. The argument of keeping the missiles for the sake of Iran did not satisfy Russia who regards Iran as a trading partner.

Remember the argument is really economic. It is Europe that is dependent on the Straits of Hormuse that is the artery for the Persian Gulf and the cause of two wars. We only use 20% of Arabian oil. The rest of our oil supply comes from Canada and Mexico not to mention our own reserves. This is why the hike in gas prices seems so obscene.

The Republicans had at this time not taken the same view that I just stated. They see it as appeasement of an old adversary that has tanks ready to roll. But as to the award congratulations are offered. Again we must remember it is the President who usurped the Republican positions so they had to oppose their own ideas and now we have Alice in wonderland.

Further into the clouds you have the Norwegian Nobel Prize Committee. They saw our entry into Iraq and Afghanistan as an abomination and a violation of international standards. 9/11 did not rise to our reaction to what we did in those two countries. President Bush was a cavalier abomination to European Idealism. For the Europeans they must not forget the fact that they have their own terrorist related problems especially Russia. The Obama approach to world problems was a breath of fresh air. That is why he got the Nobel Prize.

### 485. THE CLEAN ENERGY ARGUMENT
October 28, 2009

You have established interests and developing interests. On one hand you have the Coal industry that at this time is being squeezed and the solar/ wind industries that are being encouraged along with natural gas. The oil industry is also being pushed along with exploration on and off the continental shelf and in our national parks, not to mention Alaska and the arctic. There is still that nuclear push but I think mother nature has other ideas on that front.

The following is a break-down on our dependence on the various fuels. Renewable energy like ethanol, solar is only 7%. Our nuclear plants contribute 9%. Coal stand at 23%, but is being litigated out of existence. Natural Gas is at 24% and fracking is being used to extract more in conjunction with oil drilling which is 37%. Aside from the tooth-fairy that's where it stood as of this date.

The emerging idea of capping carbon emissions in the form of cap and trade that provides a safety valve in the transition was and does run into the concept of job loss. The other side to that is job creation in the form of creative destruction. That is key in a capitalistic system that keeps it from being static. Capitalism is not a clean transference system. It does create a unemployed underclass. There is no way around it you will have job destruction with job creation and things will not always be equal.

President Obama stated: "The closer we get to this new energy future, the harder the opposition is going to fight. The more we're going to hear from special interests and lobbyists in Washington. Those interests are contrary to the interests of the American people. It is a debate between looking backward and looking forward." The timing came when the Obama Administration was proposing investing 3.4 billion in the nation's energy grid. By the way they did invest in a solar plant and it declared bankrupts'. What they did wrong was support a big company that took the money and ran as opposed to a series of smaller companies that would have succeeded. That became the flaw in early Obama economic policy. It is small business that grows into a market that creates jobs and direction.

Remember there is resistance to change and representatives must represent their constituencies. These Senators and representatives are elected from sauterne states that have industry's in them that have been there for a long time and they won't disappear overnight. Representative Connie Mack Republican of Florida stated: "He's on what appears to be a PR swing to try to boost up his own popularity. To move legislation and policies that the American people don't want, don't need."That is the stand of a populist and populism tends to be antigrowth. Senator John McCain stood up for President Obama when he stated: "The President has done more to promote renewable energy than anyone."President Obama standing in front of a Solar Energy Plant in Arcadia stated: "Building this 21$^{st}$ century infrastructure will help us lay a foundation for lasting growth and prosperity." Remember Mr. President, growth is cyclical and at times the punch bowl must be taken away.

## 486. HOW TO BRIEF A PRESIDENT
### October 31, 2009

On the 28$^{th}$ an article appeared in the *L.A. Times* on the difference between George W. Bush who had a personal relationship with General Petraeus and President Obama who has a lack of relationship relying on the chain of command in the War in Afghanistan. The issue of adding 40,000 more troops is in debate in the way the war is now being fought. The President has met twice with the general and one of those meetings was not congenial.

Robert Gates and Mullen brief the President on the war in Afghanistan and it is argued that they in a (forceful) way put forth the views of general McChrystle. Staff comment went as follows: "There is no division between Obama and McChrystle. It's just an absence of a relationship."The relationship works well with the pentagon and its apparatus. They don't want any embarrassments in front of Congress.

## 487. A MILLION JOBS CREATED OR PRESERVED

How affective the stimulus has been to this point. Using 100,000 businesses as a base along with state and local governments the administration estimated that approximately 1 million jobs were either created or saved as a result of the stimulus money. This seems similar to a WPA program of the 1930s artificially extending services beyond the tax base. This in terms of government is a short term fix in hopes that future revenues will support this level of public employment.

The businesses saw the creation of 640,000 jobs. There were 80,000 in construction and 325,000 were in education. The remainder would be classified as hard to substantiate for we do not know if these folks would have been laid off. This could be called manipulated use of raw data.

Br that as it May like George W. Bush declaring an end to the Iraq war this grandstanding by Vice President Joe Biden with Governor Schwarzenegger and Governor martin O'Malley will only show its true colors in the fold of time.

### 488. 30,000 MORE TROOPS

It was judged to be in the interest of the united States to build up before we withdraw in 18 months. Critics say all the Taliban will do is wait us out and reassert control over time. The reality check come from the Taliban itself that has dictated what is to be taught in the schools to the boys in order for the girls to be allowed a limited education. How affective we will be as a partner in the new Afghanistan when it comes about remains an open question.

The net result of this action would mean an increase of four brigades country wide as the Al Qaeda/ Taliban elements are dealt with. It is meant to extend the control of the central government to the tribal areas of Afghanistan. The concept of the Clan still controls much of Afghan life. That in itself could inhibit the expansion of a woman's civil rights in that country. That goes back to the issue of culture and religion.

Ay home we have a different issue fractured families, delayed veterans benefits, the rise in spousal abuse, and other social disorders not to mention employment. Comparisons to the Vietnam war have risen along with that level of skepticism.

Here is another parallel Richard Nixon invaded Cambodia to disrupt the North Vietnamese supply lines and stunt the Tet Offensive. He also temporarily raised troop levels at this time to insure our forces could exit Vietnam. Just do a little thinking though the situation is far more orderly and the degree of control is greater. Remember in later years we could call Iraq a success.

### 489. JOBS
December 10, 2009

Depending on where you live the ability to get a job can differ greatly There are also certain ethnic lines that affect the outcome. Sometimes a built-in bias assumes it will get greater deference. This was exactly what happened when president Obama introduced a new job package. The study in what is perceived to be right is quite interesting:

Nationally at this time the unemployment rate stood at 10.0% if you counted all as equal. It also does not address the long term unemployed that are not listed in the unemployment statistics. Caucasians were listed at 9.3% as of November. African Americans were listed at 15.6% for the same period. Latin's in general were listed at 12.7%. Again remember in all these groups the numbers are larger than they seem.

Within this argument comes another. We have a African American President that is projecting equal opportunity for all groups. This means statistically some groups are going to benefit more than others. The Congressional black caucus stated that the Obama Administration had not done enough to raise employment opportunities in the inner cities where a good number of Black Americans live.

Bear in mind to this point his concentration had been on the health care issue and the new Afghanistan strategy. Now his eyes were turning to the employment issue. In all this time political snipers have been working counter to his goals. Earlier I explained why. I leave it to the American electorate to determine if the Republican behavior in this time frame was constructive or destructive,

We know that the Obama job plan centers on Creative destruction which is the best model to follow. The trouble was that he was not creating an environment for the rise of small business White, Black or otherwise. As I have said it is small business that creates jobs not major corporations that are concerned with the bottom line and the margin of profit.

## 490. THE MORE THINGS CHANG THE THEY STAY THE SAME
### December 21, 2010

Wall street was still being Wall Street and Mr. Gecko was still very much in charge. It was argued that the change in direction on limiting corporate greed came too late. The corporations we had bailed out were using that money though they argued differently to pay their CEOs and executives huge bonuses for their blunders. To make matters worse they would say it was a matter of contract. To some it was enough to make you turn Populist or some other extreme form.

It became apparent at the start of December that the Obama White House in its rush to organize the administration and its direction that the average Joe citizen was not satisfied with the health care pitch or the Stimulus package which were supposed to act like a kick start To the economy. The Afghan War did not help the issue either. What the people wanted was job creation and those 1 million jobs either saved or created did not seem to have the intended impact. With this atmosphere hanging over their collective heads, White House Strategist David Axelrod and his compatriots initiated what they called: "A hard pivot." It started with imposing (tougher) regulations on Wall Street a place where the banking world was at this time about to collect big bonuses for a failed performance after receiving a Federal Bail-out. It was argued the money was from other funds set aside. Should not they have used those funds to solve their problem instead of lining their pockets. The result of this was a Tea Party type swing in the 2010 election in the House. Candidate Scott Brown won the Massachusetts Senate seat from his Democratic incumbent.

## 491. GOING IT ALONE
### February 26, 2010

I can honestly say Senator John McCain helped set the tone for what was to follow. We all know the Obama Administration operates on the East Coast style of cooptation. He is a really good influential dramatic/informative speaker. McCain one year after the election between Him and Obama pointed out that the Presidents administration had cut a back room deal with Nebraskans and promised 100 million dollars as a sweetener to support his health care plan. He called it the Cornhusker Kick-back. Obama's response to this was: "We're not campaigning anymore… the election is over… we're supposed to be talking about Health care insurance."You notice he did not deny the point but told McCain to accept it as fact.

Now this brings me to the second point of the argument and a power grab on the Health Care Bill by the controlling Democratic Party that was acting in advance of the elections because they could. After the legislation was passed they could use the presidential "bully pulpit" to win the hearts and minds of the people.

There was a seven and half hour meeting in closed session so members could speak frankly. At the end of that session Senate Assistant Minority leader Jon Kyl of Arizona stated: "There are some fundamental differences that we can-not paper over."Senate Majority Leader Richerd J. Durben Democrat Illinois stated: "If nothing comes of this we're going to press forward, "And they did.

## 492. ON EDUCATION
### March 2, 2010

In 1997 Retired Army general Colin Powel formed an organization called the American Promise Alliance. It was basically biblical in its concept in the First should be last and the Last should be first. The Obama Administration in collaboration with the APA now at this time under the control of Mrs. Powel evaluated failing schools and reopened them as Charter Schools with matching federal funding. This was a good idea and a bad one simultaneously. The State of Oregon went broke to the point of part time janitors for their schools because of the Federal requirements.

900 million dollars was set aside for the year 2011 for the education program. In 2009 3 billion dollars was set aside from the stimulus money for education. These were issued in the form of grants or entitlements. This by the way will be a another bone of contention in 2012 for the conservative end of the republican Party is opposed to the concept of entitlements.

President Barak H Obama put forth his views on the subject."Not long ago you could drop out of school and reasonably expect to find a blue collar job that would pay the bills and help support your family. That's not the case anymore. Graduating from High school is an economic imperative."Talking about what failing schools would qualify for the program he put them at the bottom 5% of high school graduates below 60%. The winners would be chosen at the state level. The primary target of this program was the inner city schools. Failing schools could be closed and reopened as Carter schools. To add to this 50 million dollars was to be set aside for drop-out prevention. He is following his platform.

### 493. HEALTH CARE GROUND ZERO

It all comes down to this: there is no moderate ground. The politics of cooptation for the moment is the law of the land. Moderate democrats cannot vote no on the health bill for it would be an act of betrayal for your base support and if you vote yes on the compromise legislation everyone else would be upset.

I described the imagined issue of abortion funding and insurance policies. The issue of undocumented immigrants and the denying of coverage has drawn fire. I call your attention to the Motor voter controversy and how non-citizens had registered to vote for the democratic side in the 2004 and 2008 election.

The Republican minority Leader of the senate Mich McConnel stated: "They think they are smarter than the American people. They think they're going to give this to you whether you want it or not. There is an overwhelming likelihood that every Republican candidate will be campaigning to repeal it."(In truth today in 2012 that is what is happening. The question is what is the will of the American people.)

### 494. March 9, 2010

With the usual eloquence of a master speaker President Obama fired back: "They need to hear your voices right now. The Washington echo chamber is in full throttle. It is as deafening as it has ever been and as we come to the final vote that echo chamber is telling members of Congress, wait… think about the politics…instead of thinking about doing the right thing."

Senator Arlen Spector who had recently joined the Democratic side flew back to Washington to defend the president. He stated: "That is the most fiery I have seen him since the early campaign, when I was listening to him. I wish he had given that at the State of the union. "The president is treating this issue as of this date as when he was campaigning for office.

### 495. March 11, 2010

The negotiations were proceeding and centering on the fraud aspect of health care. It was flatly stated that the estimated 54 billion in wrongfully spent money needed to be corrected. Instead of stonewalling Human services secretary Kathleen Sebelius stated: "There's another choice, instead of spending energy attacking the parts of the proposal that you don't like come to the table with proposals strengthening the parts that are there....the second choice really May give up some short term profits but we May also working together could create a sustainable health insurance. Market where Americans will still be able to buy coverage."The statement was followed with more detailed information.

The battles in the mix center in several areas. One judicial decision allowing corporations to freely spend to influence the public under the freedom of expression clause had and has dramatically shifted the war of ideas. Certain issues like Immigration have lost steam and the congress has no stomach for it. Health care legislation was nearly in its complete state, And they were lining up the final vote tally. On the economic issues the specter was raised that you don't want to face the voters saying you were fighting for the banks. Populism is alive and well in the year 2010.

## 496. ON ISRAEL
### March 24, 2010

There has been a declining Israeli population compared to the growth of the Palestinian population. That lead the Arab population to dominate East Jerusalem. The building of Israeli dwellings in east Jerusalem has consequently rang the alarm bell in a increasingly balanced approach to the Middle East.

Vice President Joe Biden visited Jerusalem and had a disagreement with its leaders over Palestinian rights. The Israeli position was that Washington has not appreciated the compromise on the part of Israel on the two state solution. There is a yearning to make Jerusalem the capital of Israel as opposed to Televiv.

Prime Minister Netanyehu Met with President Obama and put a friendly face on serious disagreements of national sovereignty. The Prime Minister showed why the zoning laws were not applicable to putting a freeze on settlements in east Jerusalem which would be part of Israel even with a settlement. In the end they agreed to disagree.

## 497. OBAMA'S CORPORATE CZAR

President Obama used a series of autonomous appointees he called czars to reign in the various programs. Kenneth R Feinberg was the Pay Czar. When Corporations that took bailout funds started their old behavior and rewarded bad behavior this agency kicked in.

He sent letters to TARP recipients as to the compensation they paid their upper management(419 firms) He reduced the compensation of executives in 25 firms by 50% for the period covering November and December of 2009. His objective is to curtail risky behavior and as the Fed has put it irrational exuberance. Some of the firms affected were AIG, GMAC, GM, Chrysler Financial, to name a few.

## 498. HE DID IT
### March 28, 2010

March 26, 2010 was the date the Health Care Legislation became law. And it triggered a threat to repeal the legislation. President Obama's response was: "My attitude is go for it. If these Congressmen in Washington want to come to Iowa and tell small business owners that they plan to take away their tax credits and essentially raise their taxes be my guest."When a protester raised the point on the Public option, president Obama said that was not part of the deal. You see even at this point the public was misinformed. He accused the republicans of fear mongering.

## 499. ON AFGHANISTAN
### March 31, 2010

Total force from our NATO Alliance number 44,000 in addition to U.S. troop strength. Another 30,000 troops are part of our exit strategy in 2014. France has committed 4,000 troops the effort, Canada has 2,800 troops in troubled Kandahar province. The Canadians were asked to leave a presence after the departure of U.S. troops but declined saying there involvement would be civilian based. The Canadians had suffered 140 deaths this year and there was pressure building at home.

Secretary of state Clinton stated: "There all kinds of things that are possible. We would obviously like to see some forms of support continue because the Canadian forces have a great reputation."

The Netherlands have at this time 2,000 troops in place. They were planning to pull out in this year of 2010. The U.S. troop strength at this point was 87,000.

A short note on Iran Frances Sarcozy had agreed with President Obama on more sanctions aimed at deterring Iran from its nuclear ambitions.

## 500. THE NUCLEAR AGENDA
### April 5, 2010

There was a Summit proposed on the reduction in nuclear arms. Discussions were being held with the Russian in Prague on the reduction in nuclear forces by 30%. Critics were saying the number was closer to 13%. Iran is a signatory to the pact as is North Korea. We are all familiar with the problems with these respective countries. There is a new proposed START Treaty (Strategic Arms Reduction Treaty). Reagan's 1990 Treaty is regarded as obsolete.

At issue is how do you verify a country's Arms Claims? Iran and its stance with North Korea added to the mix add a touch of potential cyanide. The verification aspect of the treaty was regarded as (Murky) There are 67 votes for the verification but thorn in the side of the issue is the Republican question: would the treaty deter U.S. Missile Defense plans?

The Pentagon is an issue in all of this. Some issues related to defense would cause the preservation of the status Quo. This is despite the Nuclear posture review that urges fewer nuclear weapons for limited use. The never land issue would be the pledge to not do the first strike. That no nation agrees to and that is the rub.

## 501. NEW ECONOMY VERSES OLD ECONOMY
### April 8, 2010

This talk of having taxes rise to before the bush era tax cuts is more complex than you think. We have new financial instruments based on nothing but previous financial deals (Derivatives/Hedge funds) This is nothing more than a paper game. The Fed through the sale of treasury bonds is essentially printing money to create jobs largely in the public sector. The argument that small business would be impacted by austerity measure as is being done in Europe is being debated in this country. The argument is that austerity equals job loss and Europe's case is being sited. The facts dictate a reduction in U.S. debt and cut backs/ austerity are in are real world. Obama's expanded borrowing is not. He's selling Ice-cream. What flavor do you want.

## 502. ARMS REDUCTION
### April 9, 2010

Washington and Moscow have signed a Arms reduction treaty. As part of a joint statement with Russian President Demetry Medvedrev. The joint statement said: "Together we have stopped the drift and proven the benefits of cooperation. When the United state and Russia are not able to work together on big issues it is not good for either of our nations nor is it good for the world."

President Medvedev stated: "Open a new page in Russian American relations. Both parties have won."

We together with Russia account for 90% of the Nuclear missiles that have been incurred through history. The new limit in long range nuclear warheads with this treaty stands at 1,550. This is a reduction of 650 long range missiles that can be deployed by each side. This treaty does not impact those missiles that are in storage..

The bond between these two men is great. During the negotiation Medvedev called President Obama: "Have a very good personal chemistry."President Obama stated: "Friend and partner."

The relations between Russia and the United states still have their limits. One of those limits is Iran who has been butchering its citizens as result of a disputed election. The resistance to the government has been massive to say the least. The U.S. is trying to reign in Iran's perceived nuclear ambitions and is asking Russia to go counter to its old business partner and support increased U N sanctions. Russia though dissatisfied with Iran wants a tempered response.

## 503. THE KARZAI ISSUE
### April 10, 2010

More than the war is the issue of the nation's leader who has been called the Mayor of Kabul by his critics. The Obama administration appeared to doubt the leadership of Karzai. The Obama White House corrected this with an invitation of President Karzai to the United States. The United States security advisor James L. Jones stated: "We ought to calm the rhetoric as strategic partners intent on bringing about peace and security, not only to Afghanistan and Pakistan but the region as well."The background for this statement had its roots in statements made by the Obama Administration that seemed on the surface to embarrass President Karzai.

## 504. FEDERAL REACTION TO THE ARIZONA LAW

Attorney General Eric Holder at this point in time hinted a law-suit against the State of Arizona over its perceived anti immigration law. The argument is that having to show proof of citizenship was leading to profiling of citizens and non-citizens of Latin descent. The argument was if you spoke with an accent you could be targeted. The Department of Home-land security was being brought into this.

## 505. DISASTER ON THE GULF
### May 3, 2010

On May 20, 2010 Americas East Coast was plunged into yet another disaster but this one was manmade. An oil slick the size of Texas loomed off the Louisiana, Mississippi, Alabama, and Florida. President Barak H Obama made his first trip to the devastated zone on this date and promised swift Federal assistance. The President stated: "We're going to do everything in our power to protect our natural resources, to compensate those who have been harmed, to build what has been damaged and help this region persevere like it has done so many times before."

There was a reason the President was here on the gulf coast A good bulk of what we consume as a nation comes from this are. Would you believe 75% of the shrimp that graces our tables comes from the gulf coast. 20% of all our Sea food stocks come from the east coast. That's why when they airfreight them they become flying fish.

Now back to a serious reality over 5,00 feet down at this time in history a unknown amount of oil and gas were escaping from a ruptured pipe fouling the water and killing animal life.

Fishermen were being turned into oil skimmers and a detergent like formula was being used to break up the oil..There were company cover-ups to match a mystery novel and government perceived conspiracies to match the best of them. If you want to read about this in detail check my section on the B P Oil Disaster.

# 506. CALDERON, OBAMA, AND THE ARIZONA LAW
## May 20, 2010

There are certain false assumptions on the decline of illegal immigration to the United states. It is the fact that employment at the lower level of the economy is stagnant. No work for day laborers. The farm industry is fairly well regulated and agri-business employers are doing a better job on the status of their workers. Because of the stagnant job situation villages in Mexico are coming to life again. Mexico's economy is improving.

Now for President Obama's position and how he is presenting the matter. He now advertizes that his immigration policy is working and that the number of illegal immigrant arrested crossing the border is down. Using 2007 as a base when the economy at the lower end was hiring 859,000 were apprehended at the border. In 2009 those apprehended had dropped to 541,000. That was a crummy year for employment in the United States and it even affected the ability of day workers to get work. President Obama credited his efforts in the following statement: "Illegal Immigration is down not up is down not up, and we'll continue to do what is necessary to secured our shared border."

Now looked at this way Felipe Calderon the who was at this time president of Mexico was on a three day conference with President Obama. Mexico had put out an advisory on Mexican citizens traveling in the United States. it said they could harassed while traveling in the United States. I go to Mexico I must have a passport beyond the border towns. Mexican citizens have the inherent right to cross the border with no identification or in some cases forged and it is all-right.

President Obama has heard the complaint from the Mexican president and promised immigration reform. He is moving against Arizona's A B 1070 law. He is on the same page with the Mexican President Calderon on the immigration issue Obama stated concerning the Arizona bill that it was exceeding its authority in stopping and questioning potential illegal immigrants. This practice could lead to profiling and discrimination. That is my take on it. The President stated: "As a potential of being applied in a discriminatory fashion. A fair reading of the language of the statute suggests that those who appear to be illegal immigrants could be harassed or arrested. In the United states of America no law abiding person, be they an American citizen or legal immigrant, or a visitor or tourist from Mexico should ever be subjected to suspicion simply because of what they look like."

This posturing is just that posturing and it is the language used between heads of State on delicate matters like this, but the position and the angle will have to addressed at a later date.

### 507. May 26, 2010

The issue was addressed in a way. President Obama did order an increase in forces following the Mexican presidents visit. He made available $500,000,000 to support law enforcement efforts on our Southern border and boosted boots on the ground by 1,200 additional National Guard.

These troops are not here to stem the flow immigration but to target people trafficking drug and arms sales. There is a Russian funny part to this that would occur later. This was according to the National security Advisor James L. Jones and counter terrorism advisor John Brennon. According to Senator Carl Levin Democrat Michigan. There were 300 troops at this time on duty. They would not arrest or directly intervene directly. They were observers.

### 508. THE POLITICS OF OIL
May 27, 2010

I have given you a series of issues that have at this point in time take a toll on president Obama. As the oil disaster in the gulf disrupts the lives of the people there and the unemployment stats hold steady at just under 10% the president had plans to reset the agenda.

President Obama stated: "I know it's been 18 tough months and I have got a few more grey hairs. I know some folks say he's not as cool as he was when they had all the posters around everything. Now I've got a Hitler mustache on the posters, that's quite a change."There was criticism that there was not enough White house involvement at the initial phases of the disaster. He only had a 35% approval rating. A full 45% thought he handled the whole thing wrong. It is tough to be President.

James Carville the same guy we now see on CNN was an advisor to Clinton at his white house stated of President Obama: "These people are crying. They're begging for something down here and it just looks like he's not involved in this

## NATIONAL POLITICS 2010

The year of 2012 was still far away but already the political Parties were staking out their ground. The President was in the process of passing his programs. Mitt Romney son of George Romney was running for the nomination of his party as his father did before him. At this time he was battling an array of ideologues mostly to the right. Everyone was courting the Tea Party and being Republican meant painting yourself into a corner regardless of your record.
February 26, 2010

The contenders to the throne stated their strategy: "We all kind of know how to beat an incumbent: The country has to decide if it wants to unelected the incumbent and then has to decide the other guy is acceptable. We are breaking down that safety factor. We are giving the democrats what they want which is to make this into a choice, not a referendum."President Obama's approval rating sits at this time at 44% with a 60 % disapproval rating.

Whitney Ayres a pollster for the National journal stated: "Let's keep an eye on the big picture. Three quarters of the country thinks we're on the wrong track Sixty one Percent think the economy is worse. That is an incredibly difficult hill for an incumbent president to climb to win re-election."This all breaks down to the unicorn theory. Noah was loading all the animals by two's into the Arc. Two magnificent unicorns were standing by watching. Noah pleaded with them for they were the last of their kind. They responded this will pass and you are wasting your time and they wished Noah a good day and left. That's why there are no unicorns. Our economic realities seem to be following this principle.

Of the two candidates Senator Michael Bachmann put the bite on Former house of representatives Newt Gingrich for his lobbying for Freddie Mac and stated he received 1.6 million in consulting fees. She charged that colored his reasoning. Newt the ever present professor of all things political stated that the compensation did not influence his judgment. He Stated: "I have never once changed my position because of any kind of payment."He accused Bachmann of twisting the fact and she exploded: "I think it's outrageous to continue to say over and over through the debates, that I don't have my facts right, when as a matter of fact I do. I'm a serious candidate for president of the United States."She also had a word or two with Governor Rick Perry and Ron Paul.

Though not a candidate Sarah Palen was speaking on the circuit. She declared herself a feminist redefining it to the right. She put it as being akin to a mother Grizzly Bear."Momma grizzly's they rise up. Can give their child life in addition to perusing career and education and avocations. Society wants to tell these young women otherwise. These feminist groups want to tell these women that: Your not capable of doing both."She pushes candidates for the tea party and her own agenda.

## 509. THE BLOOD LIBEL ISSUE
### January 13, 2011

When Representative Gabrielle Giffords was shot in a Tucson public appearance point blank in the head by a crazed gun-man the nation was put into shock. She was loved by both Parties in the House. When Palin spoke mentioning that the shooting in Arizona was a great tragedy but should not be a rush to judgment in Passing new gun laws. Remember we already had the Brady Bill. This was just the act of a disturbed man. Fortunately Gabrielle lived and is recovering at home after a lengthily stay in the hospital.

The major candidates for President made statements but they were all but ignored but when Sarah Palin spoke on the tragedy and used the term Blood libel the Jewish community rose in alarm. The term blood libel refers to the Jews killing of Jesus and was used as a form of slander against the Jewish community of the time.

Palin in 2010 spoke on Gifford's District among others with cross hairs aimed at those districts. The Immigration law was paramount at the time and she was drawing attention to the problem. It was after that, the tragedy happened and Party lines vanished. Palin's statement was: "After this shocking tragedy I listened at first puzzled. Then with concern and now with sadness to irresponsible statements from people attempting to apportion blame for this terrible event. Blood Libel serves only to incite the hatred and violence they purport to condemn. That is reprehensible.

As I stated the Jewish community instead of taking the term in context made the following statement.(Palin's comments either show a complete ignorance of history or blatant anti-Semitism.)Politics is not a forgiving business and often small minded. I refer to both sides of the isle on that one. The reaction was not all negative 30,000 supporters that used face book applauded her. The attorney Dershowitz stated: "There is nothing improper and certainly nothing anti-Semitic in Sarah Palin using the term to characterize what she reasonably believes are false accusations that her words and images have caused a mentally disturbed individual to kill and maim."The feelings were all over the park.

## 510. BEFORE IT WAS OFFICIAL
### April 15, 2011

The financial men and women behind the candidates out of self interest, corporate greed, or the general economic good of the country. You have people like John Woodson involved with the New York Jets who is eager and you have people like Ashner who has to taste what a candidate is about before he jumps in. He stated: "I'm sort of hiding under my desk when the calls come in. I don't see a dynamic candidate out there yet. A number of them have interesting credentials, but they just strike me as a little lack luster." Former Massachusetts Governor Mitt Romney seemed first in line. Governor Tim Pawlenty was considering as was Governor Haley Barbour. Fred Malek the national Finance Co-Chairman for Mc Cain added: "I think many people feel the field is not yet complete and are holding back a bit to see how the prospective candidates themselves are taking much longer to reach a decision point and therefore it would be expected that major donors would be holding back as well."

Al Hoffman the former Republican National Committee Finance Chairman who had been sought after by every declared candidate felt: "For me to be involved in a Presidential Election I have to have my heart in it. I have to be emotionally involved and feel the world will come to an end if this person is not elected and I just don't feel that way."

I now take you inside the feelings as to why it is this way. July 15, 2011 was the drop dead date for entering the 2011-2012 race for the white house and in all fairness on the world stage many leaders I do believe will be departing and a new cast of characters will be dealing with each other France, Spain, Greece, China,and there are even signs of change in Germany so it become a bit like a fortune tellers tail.

At this point in history Romney and his team were the best organized Wayne Berman, and Lew Eisenberg had planned a massive fundraiser in las Vegas to raise fifty million for the Romney Camp. They stated: "One of the great things about the Romney finance team is so much of it was together the last time and has stuck with him this time."Eisenberg added: "There is no-one I know of at the moment who has anything as strong or well organized as Governor Romney if and when he decides to run."

Larry Finder a Houston Lawyer who was a Pawlenty supporter basically because of his blue collar Back-ground stated: "Governor Romney is formidable in the Primary process. It just means we have to work harder."He added concerning President Barak Obama."The donor base is going to be very, very, careful this time around as compared to the last cycle."

Gordon Sondland a Portland, Oregon Real-estate Investor stated: "A lot of people have a very skeptical wait and see attitude to see who is a really serious candidate and who is using the presidential race as potential publicity for themselves. When people make their investments, they want to know the candidate is all in."

This is a glimpse at the behind the scenes thinking process in one of our most cherished rituals especially when you have a sitting President as resourceful as president Obama.

### 511. ROMNEY'S HEALTH PLAN
May 12,2011

The reason there is a controversy over President Obama's National Health Care Plan is that he borrowed a Republican idea and gave it a twist. It also ironic that most of the Obama programs and accomplishment are republican ideas in new packaging forcing your opponent the republicans to change their colors seemingly in contradiction of themselves. It also makes for nasty divisive politics and it has.

A case in point is The Massachusetts Health Care Plan that only leaves 2%uninsured. It was enacted in April 12 2006 by governor Romney as a state based health plan. It was called the first of its kind in the nation. Not all saw it as a good thing Arkansas Governor Mike Huckabee who would later enter the race for president contended the Massachusetts experiment would blow up in the Governors face.. He was obviously wrong.

Romney calls his system a meeting of the minds and as of 2011 it was heralded as a success in the State. Michael Wildmer President of the Massachusetts Tax payers Association stated: "It is quite an irony. You will find nearly universal pride in the state of these reforms and a salute to Romney for his contribution. He has a pivotal role in health reform but he is clearly taking less credit than he deserves."It was never Romney's intent that his system would be tweaked into a National insurance program that expands the power of eminent domain through taxation and curbs states rights. That is the path of Rome.

To dwell on the details of the Massachusetts plan we first visit the concept of limiting Malpractice suits along with loosening the regulations concerning on private insurance companies. There was an expansion of tax benefits for those that are privately insured.

Here's where the fog roles in. Though Romney called the Obama Health Care Plan a major departure point from his Massachusetts plan (Affordable Health Care Act 2006) The same people that helped draft the state plan helped write the Federal legislation.(Federal Affordable Health Care Act 2010)According to Mc Donough the former Democratic State Law maker: "Massachusetts was the model for the federal Affordable Health Care Act. Romney is given credit for establishing the basic frame work for the health care plan even by his critics. The personal responsibility principle was the foundation of the Massachusetts plan based on private enterprise. I think that is the sticking point. It is the federal subsidized plan with the catch 22 on taxation and the extension of eminent domain laws that affect property rights that further limit state power.

The insurance market place (Regulated) was created. Those in the private sector who did not have insurance could shop for affordable policies on their terms. Government subsidies were made available to offset the costs of insurance. The mechanisms in the Romney plan to regulate cost were used in the national plan. The Bush Administration made it possible through federal aid that made it possible that the uninsured had their needs met in the hospital system. It was a private insurance framed structure not a welfare structure. The deficiencies were that you still had full emergency room and there was a lack of primary care doctors. It is those short falls where the nation's conservative critics linked Romney Care and Obama care. I think they missed the boat it was taxes on property and eminent domain in the federal plan that is the defining difference.

## 512. THE ISRAELI POLICY
### May 22, 2011

Candidates have this affinity of the support of Israel. Some statements have proven to be illusory and others factual. Some are even conditional historical. President Carter backed the 1967 border issue but never backed away from the State of Israel. He was never challenged on his position. When President Obama essentially takes the same position on the secure borders issue it seems to be another day.

Michelle Bachmann Senator and Presidential candidate up for nomination in the Republican Party for President go on the attack on this position it draws all sorts of attention. Her goal to break the 78% support of the Jewish vote that goes to President Obama but that won't happen. The other the Christian Right and its Pro Israeli stance to shore up votes for the Republican Party/Tea Party on a potentially illusory position, but that's politics.

Penny Pritzker who held the position of National Finance Chairwoman for President Obama in 2008 stated: "What's happening right now is people are trying to understand what the President is suggesting, and it's very positive what he's suggesting. He is saying we need direct negotiations to recommence and here are some ideas about how to approach that."

The organization ALPAC referred to as the Zionist Organization of America took the position that: "You can't unilaterally tell Israel you have to go back to 1967."(Ira Silverstein spokesman) He wasn't elected president of Israel. He was elected president of the United States."President Obama had met with the Israeli Prime Minister Benjamin Netanyahu who stated that was impossible because the 1967 borders were not defendable. The American Jewish community seemed more in support of his statements.

The President of the New York based Foundation of Ethnic Understanding Rabi Marc Schneier stated: "There has been a understanding for years that what was to be negotiated was a treaty based on the 1967 borders with land swaps. So I wasn't surprised by his statement, though he is the first U.S. President to spell it out."

As you can see the Bachmann statement was not targeted to Jewish voters but the Christian Right that occasionally lives on its own planet discounting the positions of others more directly involved. This is an election year and she and the other republican candidates would love to impact the jewish vote as well as the Bible Belt Christian Right.

## 513. THE INTELLECTUAL TWINGE
May 29, 2011

In a way Newt Gingrich is the Addlie Stevenson of the 21$^{st}$ century. He has been by far the most outspoken and articulate of the candidates. I could consider Ron Paul his equal. The trouble with intellectual candidates is that they don't capture the imagination let alone the attention of the average voter.

To give you a taste of the Gingrich style, he has been called a provocateur or polemicist. The Ryan Health Care reform Act was called by Gingrich (Right wing social engineering) This statement got a negative reaction from the Republican Party. They contended it gave ammunition to the Democrats.

Gingrich has written of the Democratic Party that it is (dominated by a secular socialist machine that represents as great a threat to America as Nazi Germany or the soviet Union did.) This was an obvious reference to President Obama's National Socialist melding of private enterprise and government services.

He once referred to President Obama as one who possessed a "Kenyan Ant colonial mentality."He refers to himself as the candidate of ideas and defiantly not of

Washington, Though he has in excess of 30 years of history there. To him his legacy would not be to rust away but go out with a bang. The problem seems to be his fuse though repeatedly lit has tendency to go out before reaching the main charge. In all fairness he has had an influence on this election.

### 514. PALIN AS A DISTRACTION
### May 29, 2011

Michelle Bachmann is a credible candidate Vying for President Obama's Position. The trouble is Sarah Palin and her bus tour seems to attract more attention than the candidates themselves. When she bought a house in Arizona it was rumored that Palin was going to launch her campaign from that state. She did not.

Even those who like what she says seem unwilling to back her. Carla Sam's a cashier stated: "I like what Bachmann has to say but I think we need a very strong male candidate in order to defeat him." She added: "I wouldn't mind having a woman President but I don't think this is the election. After what happened to Sarah Palin, I don't think the country is ready."

Bachmann said of herself: "I think people see that I'm a substantive person and a serious person." She listed as her accomplishments raising funds for Kindergarten through 12 years Charter Schools and taking on 23 foster children. She added: "People see that I've been very successful in the endeavors that I've done and I think more than anything they know I'm a fighter and have done exactly what I said I was going to do, and they can count on me."

The trouble is the souls occupy the same space and it was not until Sarah bowed out that Bachmann could begin to excel.

### 515. ON ROMNEY AND HUNTSMAN
### June 4, 2011

The former Governor of Utah Jon Huntsman has as his background being an ambassador to China Under the Obama Administration. This you would think would give him insight into our relations with that country. It was instead regarded as a negative (Collaborator) He was having trouble gaining traction. He was not regarded as a true Republican. He cooperated with the other side.

This was Jon Huntsman's position in his own words: "The encroachment on liberty here at home, the new Health care law, the seemingly unstoppable growth of Government, the resulting mass of regulation and debt. The list goes on and on. Americans are not buying a freer and more prosperous nation, we are buying national investment for future generations. No what we are buying is serfdom. What so many in the establishment do not get in this fight over the extension of the debt ceiling is it's not just about debt. It is not just about spending cuts. It is not just about confidence in our bonds and our debt. It is about the size of government in our society and our lives."

Former Governor Romney of Massachusetts put forth his ideas as follows: "Today three years into his term we have more news that unemployment has ticked up again (9.1 unemployment Rate) We have 16 million people out of work or who just stopped looking for work. Millions more are in jobs well beneath their capabilities. We have home values continuing to decline three years later. Three years later we have a record number of foreclosures. Three years later higher gasoline prices. People are feeling more squeezed."Romney praised the House of Representatives in Washington for refusing to raise the debt ceiling without the cutting of programs to lower the National debt. (Just a note what about repealing the Bush tax cuts completely. Greenspan had indicated that the tax cut had become a drag on the economy.) Romney continued: "We've got our colleagues in the House that are doing a heroic job. Their using every source of their strength to fight the excessive spending of this administration and I applaud them on that. They say they're not going to raise the debt limit unless they see commensurate reductions in spending and plans to hold down our spending in the future. Congratulations to them on keeping the battle going on."

Romney continued: "This President has failed. Look he's a nice guy. He's well spoken. He could talk a dog off a meat wagon and yet he hasn't delivered. We can't keep blaming George Bush. This is now his economy and what he has done has failed the American people, and the borrowing and spending and 1.6 trillion dollar deficit. These numbers are his. There on his back and that's why he's going to lose."He was asked about the concept of pre-existing conditions and he stated that insurer would should be obligated to provide insurance under certain conditions.

### 516. SANITORUM
#### June 7, 2011

Rick Santorum had been a two term Senator from Pennsylvania. He was defeated in 2006. He stood in front of the court house where he started. He is the son of an Italian immigrant who fled fascist Italy and settled in this coal mining town. Santorum is from the Religious Right.

This is how Rick Santorum entered the race: "I'm ready to lead. I'm ready to do what has to be done for the next generation, with the courage to fight for freedom, with the courage to fight for America." Santorum is a social conservative that like the Blues brothers before him was on a mission from God. When Santorum speaks you feel his emotion . He campaigned like an evangelist and in time his fuse was lit and the powder in the gun did go off but like the old Stanley steamer he ran out of umph. This was the beginning and he was like a fireball.

### 517. HERMAN CAIN

This gentleman was and is a Social conservative. He is a business man like

Romney. His call was for common sense government starting with his 999 tax structure. He argued for limited Government. At one point in the race he was a front runner with his simplified tax plan which he would later go into great detail on. He withdrew early in the race due to charges by former employees of sexual harassment which he denied. He withdrew from the race to save his marriage. He did not want his family dragged through the dirt.

### 518. THE FIRST REPUBLICAN PRESIDENTIAL DEBATE
### June 14, 2011

There were seven dwarfs the night of the first Republican presidential Debate. Mitt Romney had been considered the front runner to this point and lead the others out on stage. Here is there order on stage: Rick Santorum, Michele Bachmann, Newt Gingrich, Mitt Romney, Tim Pawlenty Ron Paul and Herman Cain. Not all candidates had agreed to this particular debate among them Jon Huntsman and Texas Governor Rick Perry. This first debate was dubbed the debate that wasn't. It largely framed the future attack on President Barak H. Obama.

Civility did reign Tim Pawlenty who had earlier made the charge that that Romney's Massachusetts health care plan was skewed and identified it as Obamney Care did not raise that gauntlet the night of the debate. The rules actually followed Ronald Reagan's 11 Commandment. It was more like a platform committee. Pawlenty went a step further this night when asked in reference to his quote he stated: "President Obama is the person who I quoted in saying he looked to the Massachusetts for designing his program. He's the one who said it's a blue-print and that he merged two programs."

The question came up as to the change in Romney's stand on Abortion (Pro) in his 2008 run for the White-House to his Anti abortion stance in the 2011-12 election. The question was it genuine or a matter of political expediency. The narrator opened up the question to each of the group. Herman Cain chose to speak for them. His answer was simple, "case closed."

Aside from making it official Michele Bachmann stated: "We need everybody to come together because we're going to win. Just make no mistake about it I want to announce tonight: President Obama is a one term President."It was resolved that: we need to cut taxes, set ambitious economic growth targets, make it more difficult for labor to organize, and repeal the Obama Health Care Law. On the same sex and marriage only Cain and Texas Representative Ron Paul dissented from the position of favoring a ban on what has been branded Gay Marriage.

Governor Romney in his oratory stated: "Why isn't the President leading. He's failed the American People on both job creation and the scale of government."He asserted that that a more slower paced withdrawal would have been better. Ron Paul differed and stated that our presence there was not making friends. Gingrich wanted U.S. troop reductions at a faster clip through-out the middle East.

From the White-House Press Secretary Robert Gibs stated that Pawlenty and Romney wanted to: "Return to the failed Republican policies of the last decade that put our economy on the brink of a second great depression."This was a obvious reference to the concept of letting unsuccessful businesses fail as part of the cycle instead of what happened propping up the brokerage houses and over extended corporations. A pity he had no such inklings when it came to those people with mortgages that were and are underwater. In all fairness in2012 President Obama has put forth such a plan but it is too late and restricted in nature.

Governor Huntsman who as of this date was not a declared candidate chose other means to announce the launching of his campaign for the following week.

### 519. JON HUNTSMAN BEGINS

With New Hampshire looming Jon Huntsman chose the Statue of Liberty to declare his candidacy for the Republican nomination as a candidate for President. Huntsman is to the left of the field with extensive foreign policy and executive experience. He favors the equality in marriage Act which puts him squarely on the side of Gay Rights.

He talked of reforming taxes and government regulation, ending what he called U.S. Combat deployment overseas. That put his position very similar to Ron Paul's. He added to his statement: "Without repeating past mistakes, "that lengthen military engagements. Specifically he supported the concept of Civil Unions. He as Governor of Utah extended Drivers licenses to undocumented immigrants. They differed from the standard license. Remember the uproar in New York over that very same issue. Huntsman's service in the Obama administration as Ambassador to China I consider a plus but those in the Republican Party don't. He stated: "I respect the President. He and I have a different opinion on how to help this country we both love, but the question each of us wants the voters to answer, who will be a better President, not who is the better American."

Huntsman had actually started his Presidential bid thirty days earlier. He is on record of serving three Republican Administrations. He did his Mission as a youth in Taiwan and served as Ambassador to Singapore under President George H. W. Bush and he was the Deputy U.S. Trade Representative under George W. Bush. He is fluent in mandarin.

His fund raising efforts center on three legs initially: Mormon diners which both he and Romney are competing for. The supporters of Senator John McCain and the Bush family. His campaign manager there are difficulties in raising campaign funds due to his late start.

## 520. BACHMANN/FEDERAL AID
June 26, 2011

Senator Bachmann Republican representative of the State of A thousand lakes has criticized federal farm aid and other transportation issues. She opposed the Obama Stimulus program. She saw no inconsistency in taking aid in the form of Grants to aid her husband's counseling clinic. The department of human resources was the source of twenty-four thousand 41hundred dollars in aid for staff training in their Minnesota based clinic that specializes in mental illness. Her Father-in-law who passed in 2009 got subsidies from the federal Government. The farm received two hundred and sixty thousand dollars from the Federal government to the year 2009. She stated she got 0 benefits from the farm but records indicated two transactions: $32,503 and $105,000 between 2006 and 2009.

She voted against the 2008 Farm Bill. The Bill was a 307 billion dollar package spread over five years. Her quote: "It was loaded with unbelievably outrageous pork and subsidies for agricultural business and ethanol growers."Times change and so do opinions for one year later she wrote the agriculture Secretary Tom Vilsack praising the federal program. Her praise was strong in the supporting of pig products and commodities as she put it in a time of need. She added: "I would encourage you to take additional steps necessary to prevent further deterioration of these critical industries, such as making additional commodity purchases She wrote this in October 5 2009. In that year there was an increase in purchases of pork for school lunches.

Now we start to see modern controversy Bachmann (Strongly Opposed) President Obama's 830 billion Stimulus Package. She stated: "I cannot support this new direction for the American Economy."After 6 months she wrote six letters to the secretary of Transportation Ray LaHood asking for Stimulus financed Grants.. These requests were for infrastructure projects centering in her district. After review none of the projects received funding according to Minnesota's Department of transportation.

In January of 2010 in her rebuttal to Obama's State Of The Union she stated: "The Presidents strategy for recovery is to spend a trillion dollars on a failed stimulus program fueled by borrowed money."

The strategist for the Republican Party Steve Grubbs had A rather off the cuff attitude on the subject: "Just because your against government spending doesn't mean you shouldn't get any funds your legally entitled to."Grubbs was the former chairman of the Iowa Republican party.

It was Bachmann's contention that funding a bridge over a water-way should not be considered pork as opposed to her analogy of a Tea Pot Museum. Her critics regarded her analysis as full of holes with exceptions built in.

## 521. MIXED MESSAGES
### July 5, 2011

    You have to go back to June and the new Hampshire when Romney commented on Obama: "President Obama didn't create the recession, but he made it worse and longer."Later on NBC he stated: "The States voters want to see an economy that's growing again and the presidents failed. He did not cause this recession but he made it worse."He was asked to clarify the statement which he made in front of a closed factory in Allentown Pennsylvania he appeared to take a few steps back: "I didn't say things are worse."

    Now let's fast-forward to the *L.A. Times* article on July5,2011. On a Monday in Southern new Hampshire. He stated: "Don't forget what this is all about. We love this country, It's the greatest country in the history of the Earth, and we face extraordinary challenges right now. Our president has failed us. The recession is deeper because our President has failed us.. The recession is deeper because of our president: It's seen as an anemic recovery because of our President.(Note Nixon, Ford, had anemic and volatile economies. Nixon's idea failed and Ford had moderate success.) The people who want the status –quo can vote for him. But people who want real change and jobs for Americans are going to vote for us."(Again in my opinion Obama's big mistake was propping up the fat cat conglomerates. Remember the process of creative destruction resulting from irrational exuberance. Helping the Green Industry's was a good idea it showed innovation. Helping small business was a good idea for those companies are our future. Instead of giving approximately 900 million to a Solar Energy Systems firm, if that same sum had been given to medium and small companies the competition between them would have been a success story.)

    I know the reality of the sound bite statements and campaigns have no room for the detail that I have attempted to convey and when this book is published it will give the electorate and the business community wisdom.

## 522. ARIZONA'S CLEAN ELECTION LAW

    The first step in this argument is to give you the election l law and then its unintended consequences. Followed by what the Supreme Court ruled on the issue. And of course my opinion on the matter.

    To boil the Clean Election Law to its simplest terms, it. Arizona's newly elected Senator Steve Smith who prior to his election was a Talent manager in the city of Exurban a subdivision of Phoenix. He had no prior political experience was able to raise the equivalent of $36,000 in public support and received the same in matching funds from the state with his pledge to seek no further contributions. If the person he was running against had not agreed to abide by the clean election act the state would match those funds which in this case would go to Smith that were raised by his opponent. Smith defeated his better known Democratic competitor. Smith stated: "Turns out all I needed was the Clean Election Act money and the grace of God."

The conservatives in the state of Arizona don't like this law that was initially a reaction to several scandals that hit the state. They have drafted a law to repeal what is left of the Clean Elections law  putting things back to the status –quo. You see moderate republicans are not appreciated in today's Republican Party.

The Supreme Court in a 5 to 4 decision struck down the provision of the Arizona Law that matched the funds raised by ones competitor with State funds. In essence reinforcing the old system with a twist. I guess they wanted professional politicians to run for office as opposed to those from the private sector.

The partial  lobotomy of this law creates an imperfect hybrid that established interest groups view as counter to their purpose and will bring potential corruption back.

## 523. RICK PERRY'S RISE
### August 4, 2011

The world of who supports who was just forming Governor Mitt Romney and Representative Michele Bachmann had only roughly 25% of the committed support so far in this race. Sarah Palin was conducting her bus tour and taking the lime light from both Romney and Bachmann. Rick Perry had an informal organization in Iowa. The governor of Texas is viewed as a candidate that could solidify both the business community and the Tea Party Activists.

The Ames Straw Poll was getting input to the affect that supporters should write in his name because he had been denied a place on the ballot due to the fact he was not a declared candidate. Craug Schoenfield Executive Director of the groups Iowa operation stated: "You get that sense when you talk to those folks, yeah the field is nice but their looking for leadership. Looking for energy, looking for charisma, looking for someone they can get behind." In the background we still have Palin thumping her drums. Remember she took the air out of the room when she arrived when both Romney and Bachmann announced their candidacies. It was speculated that this horse and pony show was to maintain her position as leader of the Tea Party and in a sense play the role of king maker.

Others were thinking  of joining the Frey  New York City's Mayor Ruldolf Giuliani and New York's Governor Pataki  were thinking of  throwing their hats into the ring. In the end they did not but they temporarily added some excitement to the race.

Governor Christi of New Jersey has been hounded to run but has flatly stated he has no interest all he wants to be is governor. He stated: "In the end it's something you've got to believe in your heart is necessary for you to do in your life. As I said before, I don't feel that at the moment. Here is what I have to say about politics. Two months is a long time, let alone five years.  I'm not out here to lay any groundwork at all about any kind of future aspirations. 2016 is a long way away."

Among others Senator Marco Rubio have been mentioned as one of those who could draw strong support. In all reality these names could mean something in the future. As for today they are names for some future slot of history.

### 524. A STRAW POLL DINNER
#### August 15, 2011

The location is Waterloo Iowa, Bachmann had just won the Straw Poll and Perry had made his official announcement that he was in the race for president. Pawlenty had just been beaten badly and had withdrawn from the race.

Governor Rick Perry in his opening statement stated: "I happen to think the biggest issue facing this country is that we are facing economic turmoil, and if we don't have a President that doesn't get this country working we're in trouble."

Representative Bachmann talked of her experience reflecting the evangelical religious right and business savvy: "We started our own successful small company. We know how to build from scratch, putting capital together and starting a business from scratch and building it up so that we can actually offer jobs to people."It is this segment of the Party that finds it hard to warm up to Romney because he was just to big

### 525. THE THREE WAY RACE
#### August 16, 2011.

Though Romney had been the front runner two others were rapidly catching up. It seemed the religious right was saying anyone but Romney and they were looking for a savior. It was not going to be an easy run for Perry and Bachmann for they were fighting hard for the social conservative vote. The interesting thing is that all this battling for the support of the right could in the end cost the election that operates off the middle. The moderate republicans were actually the cornerstones not the far right. The stage had been set for South Carolina and the soul of the South.

### 526. TEXAS

Perry's Texas brands itself the miracle state. Its economy did not begin to decline till after 2008. Affordable housing was a draw for retirees along with the warm climate.

It is argued the approach of conservative economic policies combined with a built in oil industry revenue, helped to carry the state through the Great Depression and helped the economy not feel the 9/11 effect until the last half of 2008. The states strict mortgage lending policies spared it the mortgage crisis that hit the rest of the nation. The unemployment rate in 2011 was 8.2 % lower than the other states like Florida and California. The Texas unemployment rate was slightly higher than that of New York. One out of four Texans is without health insurance. This rate is the best in the nation in terms of coverage due to local/ state response programs and of course their oil revenues. In a way they are a victim of their own success in terms of the Dutch affect or disease (Artificial expansion of health and or other services using oil revenues as opposed to investing in expansion. If there were not oil these programs would be over extended ones.)

The myth of the Texas Miracle comes from its rapidly expanding population from both Mexico and the Snow Birds in search of a warmer climate reasonable rents and land prices, combined with a lower cost of living.

Governor Rick Perry thinks he can solve the nation's ills by employing the Texas solution on a universal basis. His argument is that influx of middle class Mexicans in search of a safer environment combined with low wages combined with those who have retired adding their income to the economy has stimulated job growth and of course don't forget that illusive element oil. Add a touch of bible belt faith and you have the Perry Plan(Even in Texas as of the time of this article job growth has not reached its potential. It has reached or approaching a Plato. The point is his solution would not work as a national model.) To Perry's credit his state created 40% of new job creation largely due to the above formula but that would mean destroying the new middle class. This oddly puts him on the outsourcing page that he has accused Romney of being on with his corporate business solution. It also puts him at odds with Labor.

### 527. August 29, 2011

The strength of Romney lies in his organization and persistent discipline. The State of new Hampshire has been his primary focus and President Obama has been his primary target. The other candidates have targeted Romney and gotten name recognition. An example would be Perry 30%, Bachmann 23% and Romney for all his effort 12%. As I said this is the anything but Romney club. Not lacking funds the Romney camp waits and see how long these new front runners can maintain their lead. South Carolina has been a battle ground and Romney lacks a cohesive southern strategy.

### 528. September 1, 2011

Michele Bachmann could be regarded as a stranger in her own house.(The Capital) Her bid for the Presidency was done without the party's blessing. She has not paid her dues as Romney and even Gingrich have. Her legislative record is noncontroversial and she has sought funds from the vary programs she argues need to be cut. She has company President Obama as a Senator did not have that impressive of a record so who's to say. If you have a history it's bad. If you don't have a history it's bad take your pick.

## 529. THE DEMOCRATS
### September 2, 2011

To date President Obama's strategy has been to seek accommodation with the other side. Granted he took the other side's ideas and flipped them. I think things have gotten lost in translation. House Speaker John Boehner who I have nicknamed tearful John has called the Presidents accommodations unacceptable. He has tried to stall if not defeat the presidents initiatives. The Democrats have urged ideological attack on the republican positions and on Mitt Romney who actually after a long struggle did come out on top and is scheduled to become the nominee.

Here is a tale of the give and take President Obama and the republican agenda. President Obama had scheduled his speech for Wednesday the same day rough time frame as the second GOP Presidential debate. Boehner wanted the president to move his speech to Thursday to a time before the opening salvo of the football season. The President did agree to this and this was an act of compromise. Among the issues at hand the Red Ink totaling 1.3Trillian that was in the budget for the year 2012. The other thing is the 1.7 growth rate of the GDP in the year of 2012. You need a 2.0% growth rate to stimulate jobs. Below that line the jobs don't match the population growth and the economy remains basically at a plateau. The jobless recovery is making democrats nervous.

## 530. THE SECOND DEBATE
### September 8, 2011

This was the first time that Rick Perry was part of the Panel there were basically barbs between Perry and Mitt over jobs and Social Security which Perry called a Ponzi scheme. The border issue was also raised and Perry essentially called the president a liar or out of touch with the condition on the Texas Mexico border. He stated: "Either he has some of the poorest Intel. of a President in the history of this country. Or he's an abject liar to the American people."

Now here's an interesting point. The state of Florida wanted to require identification as a requirement for voting. In this case it would be a drivers license. The reason illegal immigrants were voting and did vote under Motor Voter in 2008 it was part of the controversy in several states including Florida. The Federal Government was going to sew the state of Florida for implementing that practice as it was against federal election law. The state was going to countersue. This is as of July 2012. I have not heard this raised as an issue in the year of 2012 so far.

What Perry's response on social security in his own words: "Let's find out what the science truly is before you put the American economy in Jeopardy."

Jon Huntsman played the role of the teacher correcting a student with wrong information. He stated: "Listen when you make comments that fly in the face of what 98 out of 100 climate scientists have said. When you call into question the science of

Evolution- all I'm saying is that, in order for the Republican Party to win, we can't run from science."

Texas Representative Ron Paul questioned the wisdom of Perry's proposal to force teenage girls to receive vaccinations against sexually transmitted diseases. Paul said: "This is not good medicine...It's not good Social Policy.

## 531. THE IMMIGRATION ISSUE
### September 27, 2011

Governor Perry stands in opposition to the fence being built from San Diego California to the Gulf of Mexico. He states that he has beefed up Border Patrol efforts in an active way. On the flip side his stance on below average tuition for children of Illegal immigrants. His reasoning so they can become good citizens. Those who say this should not be in his mind are heartless. When confronting the issues in Iowa this issue has been brought up to him. The location was Council Bluffs on the Missouri River. He was met by group of protestors the signs read(Gov. Perry No In-State Tuition for Illegal Aliens) In the state of Iowa the growth of undocumented workers from Mexico has grown from 1.2% Latino population in 1990 to 5.0% in 2010. Let's be fair the Black population has grown from 1.7% in 1990 to 2.9% in 2010. Under the classification of other that was 1.2% in 1990 growing to 3.4% in2010. The generic white population in 1990 was 95.9% by the time 2010 comes along it is 88.7%.

Michele Bachmann while in Franklin county hammered the governor on the border issue. She state: "I do not believe that the American people should be subsidizing benefits for people who are in this country illegally or their children and I hear all that across Iowa from people."

The Perry position as I look at it is one of geographic pragmatism. That is the position he must take to survive politically. All the Governors of California had to take that position except Wilson and his legislation that was declared unconstitutional. George W. Bush and John McCain took a similar stance.

Perry sited at the Presidential Debate: "There's nobody on this stage who has spent more time working on border security than I have."He cited the 400,000,000 in state money spent on border security that according to Perry included patrols and Texas Ranger Teams.

## 532. CAIN'S TROUBLES
### November 3, 2011

Herman Cain was a Executive Director of the National Restaurant Association. His claim to fame was his 999 tax plan that caught the imagination of business conservatives. It was then that a fire storm caught up with him and two women brought sexual harassment charges against him. He stood his ground and vowed to fight. Compensation was paid to the women on the condition that they let the issue go. In the end they did not let the issue be. The official statement went: "At the time she was a very low staffer Maybe two years out of college. This all occurred at a restaurant in Chrystal city an where everybody was aware of it."Cain at this point Cain was still in the race but as you can see his campaign had ceased.

### 533. THE OCCUPY WALL STREET MOVEMENT
### October 7, 2011

Here is a curious counter culture movement where there is no left or right. They are people that were disenfranchised. Move-On.org helped to organize the group that literally was able to fill the streets of New York and other cities like Los Angeles. This was a protest against greed and for jobs. It had teachers and bricklayers. It is viewed as the alter-ego to the Tea Party movement that has morphed into a political entity

Vice President Joe Biden was in the Big Apple speaking at a forum for Atlantic Magazine. He observed the movement to be something that had its roots in a system that had lost its way. Little did he realize he was talking about his own system. He stated: "We are bailing out the big guys in the financial community, while failing to fix the problems of hard pressed ordinary Americans."

He was asked about the Tea Party. His response was that they were a mixed blessing to the Republicans. He added that they did help to defeat democratic candidates in 2010. The side effect of pulling the republican Party to the right according to the *L.A. Times* (May prove problematic in next year's general election)

When you hit the street level argument the rules change. A mouse sitting in the corner is not heard but if that same mouse along with other mice interfere with the cat by taking his food the cat will pay attention. As a matter of fact will do his best to devour and disrupt this mouse movement.

The location New York on Wall Street a massive sit-in and mobile demonstration occurred. Thousands gathered to protest the greed of wall street. They argued for fair banking practices. The end to the housing market crisis from their point of view was jobs and the stopping of the foreclosure process. They were for all practical purposes arguing for what Japan did in the 1990s. Greenspan had urged the liquidation of the bad debts and the cleaning-resale of the properties to new owners. Who was this massive mob Teachers, Factory workers with no factories to go to. The long term unemployed and here's the rub the criminals that slip into these situations. This in turn brings the police backlash.

Steve Rosenthal Liberal Strategist stated: "You don't have to be a genius to see that you can overlay what is going on with Occupy Wall-Street to energize and mobilize a Democratic base, so it has enormous potential. How big it gets and where it goes I think is anybody's guess "They referred to themselves as the 99% referring to the 1% rich. This movement does prove one thing Polemics is alive and well.

Robert Weisman who is the President Public Citizen Anti –Corporate Advocacy

Group stated: "It is quite possible that the Occupy Wall Street Movement could evolve into a political movement along the lines of the Tea Party." He talked about Union involvement an financial support for this divers movement. He also argued that too much involvement could stunt the organization.

In a sense it did evolve from its outdoor encampment to actual rented offices and today acts as a advocacy group to stop foreclosures through isolated sit-ins to save the homes of disabled vets so that they would be able to keep their property.

## 534. ON FOREIGN POLICY
### October 8, 2011

The candidates at this point in time decided to concentrate on foreign policy. In a way they reinvented Never land for they ignore the changing insurrection in Afghanistan and the growth and creation of the Drone wars. In a way using Drones to kill Al Qaeda is an abrogation of personal responsibility reducing war to a video game. I'm not the first to say this and I won't be the last.

Mitt Romney lead the way with his calling Obama Foreign policy feckless. He stated: "If you do not want America to be the strongest nation on earth, I am not your president. You have that president today."Romney continued to press for unspecified reductions in administrative positions and he said there would be cost savings from procurement reforms, this according to the *L.A. Times*. A note of caution Carter tried reordering the military and Reagan had to correct his mistakes. Rumsfeld tried reorganizing the military and you had infraclass warfare in the reorganization period. His position as stated before the Citadel though on the hawkish side differed little from positions taken by previous Presidents. His most telling point was that the reforms would offset the increases in cost.(What would he do with the Drone Program, that is now very far advanced to the point of mini-drones used for smaller specific targets.)(Accidents and friendly fire as would occur killing 24 Pakistani Border Troops in the Pushkin Tribal areas. The question would be strength or diplomacy here.) Romney talked of deepening our involvement in the United Nations, NATO, ASEAN, what he called the unilateral organizations. To my knowledge all presidents to date have stressed this. The difference would be a fresh face after a time of war. Remember Winston Churchill lost his job as Prime Minister after WW2.

## 535. NEVADA
### October 17, 2011

Here is a State rated number one for the wrong reason and worse the candidates running for the Republican nomination are seemingly running away from the issue. Only Mitt Romney has thoroughly canvassed the state and stands a reasonable chance of success. Texas Senator Ron Paul has not helped but has commented on the situation in the state of Nevada. His recommendation is to stop attempting to prop up the home owners and let the market take its course. There are neighborhoods that are 80% empty with the houses red tagged. Shirley Ayala a resident 77 years old stated: "They're not really talking about it nobody is." The rebound in the economy is according to the experts tied to a rebirth of the construction industry in the state and there is no sign of that happening even into 2012.

The emphasis on job creation does not resonate in this state. John Restepo who manages the Las Vegas consulting firm stated: " Job creation is not in of itself the answer you have to deal with the housing market, since that is the biggest asset most people have."The candidates are not paying attention to business let alone the people in the state of Nevada. Beyond knocking the President for handling the issue they have little that is concrete to say about it. Restepo added: "The Free market will work over an extended period of time. The question is how long do you let the pain and suffering go on."Only Rick Perry has the support of Nevada's Governor Bryan Sandoval. As I stated Ron Paul has support in the Tea Party in the State. It is obvious that President Obama has been unable to help. I ask the question? Is this a State without a country.

Here are the standings of the states in the degree they are in trouble. 1 Nevada at 60%. 2 Arizona with an underwater rate of 49%. 3 Florida with mortgages under water at 45%. 4 Michigan with a 36% underwater mortgage rate. 5 California with 30% of its mortgages under water. 6 Georgia with a 30% rate of underwater mortgages. On the national curve a full 23% of properties are under water. Nationally property values in the United states are down and employment has plateau's.

### 536. HEALTH CARE WAR
October 18, 2011

Since this article came to be the Supreme Court has upheld the Constitutionality of President Obama's Affordable Health Plan on the basis of the power to tax and Justice Roberts following his conservative line held that the government does indeed have the power to tax. However the court also pointed out that the legislature could modify that ruling by changing or even eliminating the law itself as if it never existed.

Now back to the time of this article and what was happening. There is a tactic in Roberts Rules of Order as it would relate to an institution of the Congress. By a simple majority of the house they could negate parts of the law. The process is called Budget Reconciliation. Tom Miller a Senior Fellow At the American Enterprise Institute stated: "The window for action comes and goes. We need to be ready. None of the Presidential candidates has offered a health plan (There was initially the Paul Ryan Plan but that lost to the Obama plan.) and conservative experts think the GOP needs a strategy to quickly dismantle the current law. And replace it before all Americans are guaranteed insurance coverage under the law.."This follows the Supreme Court ruling to a tee.

Michael Needham who heads Heritage Action for America affiliated with the Heritage Foundation stated: "This needs to be a threshold for both Presidential and Senate candidates."The Paul Ryan Affordable Health bill under consideration in 2009 had a cost of 61 billion spread over 10 years as opposed to president Obama's Affordable health plan of 900 billion in costs. Part of this plan involved freeing insurers from government requirements according to the times.

## 537. THE 999 TAX PLAN
October 19, 2011

Herman Cain had a simple platform and he was a states right advocate. He was defiantly conservative. The other fact that must be mentioned he is African American of the older generation. His 999 tax plan is described as follows Snake oil for reasons to be explained does not work. It was argued by Cain it would replace the Income tax, Payroll tax, and the Sales tax

The income tax would be 27%.(wage earners would pay 9% income tax and 9% sales tax and a 9% tax from the first dollar to the last. That last 9% would affectively be a tax increase on the worker. There would be no such thing as a tax deduction on labor. Kleinbard the source of expertise as designated by the times stated that a family with a 120,000 income would see a reduction of $541 in disposable income. A family having a 50,000 income would see a reduction of $4,848. Here comes the rub. An employer could lower his tax burden by paying himself and others in dividends. This is something Allan Greenspan called stealing from yourself by lumping expenses and profit together.

Herman Cain obviously disagrees and states that his plan would increase the gross domestic product by 2 trillion dollars and that translates to 14% and raise wages 10%. According to the *L.A. Times* the 999 system has no economic model to work off of. The projections are merely illusory.

## 538. THE VEGAS DEBATE
October 19, 2011

This particular debate was a vendetta in the making. Perry attacked Romney on the hiring of a landscaping firm that employed Illegal aliens in 2008 when he last ran for President. Perry stated: "The idea that you stand here before us and talk that your strong on immigration on its face is the height of hypocrisy. After arguing several minutes and denying the assertion Romney stated: "This has been a tough couple of debates for Rick and I. I understand that you're going to get testy."Perry entered into a diatribe and Romney stated: "You have a problem with allowing someone to finish and I suggest if you want to become President of the United States you've got to let both people speak."

When Perry knocked Romney's job creation record on Massachusetts when he was Governor. Romney raised a debating point in saying that Perry in 1988 supported Al Gore for president. The technical point was that Perry only recently became a Republican and was a Democrat when he supported Gore. Romney stated: " There was a fellow Texan named George Bush running. So if we're looking at the past, I think we know where you were."Romney made a counter point that half of the jobs created by Governor Perry at that time he was Governor went to Illegal Aliens. Perry countered "That is an absolute falsehood on its face. You failed as the Governor of Massachusetts.

Herman Cain came under attack for his 999 tax system that I described earlier. The point was re-enforced the negative aspects of the impact on the average family. His idea did resonate with the people foe he was at or near the top of the polls of recent date. Cain disputed the point: "The reason that our plan is being attacked so much is because lobbyists, accountants, politicians, they don't want to throw out the current tax code. And put something that's simple and fair."

Governor Perry was vicious and suggested that Cain's plan layered new taxes on the existing system of taxes. He was referring to State and local taxes and a double redundant affect. Perry stated: "Go to New Hampshire where they don't have sales tax and your giving them one. They're not interested in 999.

Governor Romney joined the ruckus of the mixing of federal and state taxes. He stated: "I'm going to get a bushel basket that has apples and oranges in it because I've got to pay both taxes."

The exchange between former senator Santorum and Romney was also brutal. Romney stated: " Why don't you let me speak."Santorum replied: "Your allowed to speak. You can't change the facts."

Gingrich befriended and attacked Romney stating that the others were over reacting and over stating the similarities but he did regard what Romney put together as a big government bureaucratic program that was high cost.

Representative Michele Bachmann who was buried in all of this mishmash finally was able to put her opinion in on the concept of a double fence. Senator Ron Paul opposed the fence. That was the gist of the 2011 Vegas debate. Note the housing mortgage problem was not addressed.

### 539. THE IOWA TRAIL
October 21, 2011

The bible belt is important here. The states rightists dominate here. The Iowa Caucus is part of the process. One of the key questions was as in Kennedy's day concerning Catholics and the Pope. Now transplant the Mormon faith and the preconceived notions that surround it. The issue of the concept of a cult arose. Many consider Mormons a cult. The reason this issue was so important this time around was when in 2008 Romney campaigned in Iowa he went in full force and alienated the state. This time it was with a small staff and they were better received. Still the question came up and this was Romney's reply: "The great majority of the American people want to select the person most capable of getting our country going again with strong values and a strong economy and a strong military. Among the things that are unique and exceptional about our country is the fact that in America we recognize and appreciate differences in faith we expect religious differences."

He continued: "I am shaped by Judeo Christian values which I have, and I hope those will hold me in good stead as they have so far."

The back-ground to all of this started earlier in the morning the Pastor Robert Jeffress introduced Texas governor Rick Perry and the purpose was a religious summit meeting. He urged those in attendance to support Perry because he was a born again Christian. He later told the press later that it was his belief that Mormonism was a cult. Being that the state clings to what we call a small town atmosphere you can see how fast such things spread. Jon Huntsman was probably having a similar problem. As for the others they share a splintered vote pattern and as long as it stayed that way Romney had a chance.

## 540. CALIFORNIA
October 28, 2011

As you know California has a deficit and a third term Governor is trying to get the consensus on what kind of taxation would pass in the November 2012 election. The Governor has stated the people don't know what they want. The legislature is as usual divided. Groups as diverse as the teachers association to community activists. We know that you can't increase the sales tax or license fees. Dog licenses you could Maybe get away with or tolls on certain freeways. We know you can't raise money from fines on red light cameras that has already proven to be ineffective. Add to that the mortgage issue and you have a lovely bunch of coconuts.

## 541. CAIN ECLIPSED

Herman Cain the nonpolitician and business man (CEO of God Fathers Pizza)was operating just under the radar and speaking off the cuff and catching non-critical attention. He made a couple fumbles concerning Uzbekistan calling it Ubeki Stan-stan. He said it was a joke. Some people don't have a sense of humor.
The language tight rope for a front runner is like the politically correct rhetoric of the PTA. His 999 tax plan that has been discussed earlier was dissected lambasted and supported by idealists. There is nothing wrong with that. He rose above the Radar when he won the Ames Straw Poll in August. It was Carle Rowe who pin-pointed it his eclipse happened between October 6 and 10 of this election year and according to Rowe he has been in decline ever since. As of this month he still is in first place and raised 3 million dollars this month. The argument was and is as of this date (Let

Herman be Herman) His stand on abortion(It ultimately gets down to a choice that, that family or that Mother has to make. His argument would later be that his words were taken out of context. Remember the Israeli Swap of one Israeli for 1,000 Palestinians. He thought it the equivalent of trading those in Guantanamo for those held by Al Qaeda. By this issue is largely gone and there are few prisoners left and the attorneys are gone. So the issue on the closing of Guantanamo has been rendered mute. We still control this piece of Cuban soil.

### 542. THE FLORIDA VOTING ISSUE

It was argued that in the year 2008 some 400,000 fraudulent voters usurped a rite reserved for Us Citizens. The new law requiring the showing of your photo ID and the shortening of the voter registration period were acts similar to the Jim Crow laws. It was stated: "These laws will have an effect on the margin on who votes and in a state like Florida a small difference matters. It could easily decide the outcome. The Bush Gore contest was used as an example. State senator Nan Rich Democrat from the Miami area stated: "I have to wonder if the only problem that can be found with our electoral process is that some people don't like the outcome of the last Presidential election."On the other side a representative from Ocala Denis Baxly stated: "We are going to have a very tight election here next year and we need to protect the integrity of the election. When we looked around we saw the need for some tightening."I might add this is a states' rights issue and each state stands on its own and yet together with the Union. The state decisions must independently hold the higher card when measured against other state in an election. That's why we have the Electoral College.

### 543. THE CAIN EXPLANATION
November 1, 2011

Coins argument centered on the idea that items settled are like water under a bridge you tend to forget the details and move on. I think all of us can agree with that concept. The trouble is in a political year the irrational becomes the norm.

The two undisclosed employees that filed the suit and later went public with news conferences made it seem that Herman Cain was shifting his story from denial to limited knowledge and emerging memory of specifics lost in time. Cain stated: "I just started remembering more. In twelve years a lot of stuff can go through your head."As stated the two accusers did come forward and affectively ended the Cain candidacy much like what happened to Senator Gary Hart in his bid for the presidency.

## 544. THE FORUM

The two front runners at this time Romney and Cain for their own respective reasons side stepped the forum sponsored by the National Association of Manufacturers and the Iowa's Governor Terry Branford who was also cosponsoring the event. The Governor stated: "It is unfortunate that Governor Romney and Herman Cain weren't here because they missed a great opportunity today. They missed out on the opportunity to address the number one issue in this campaign and that is creating jobs...It was not a situation where there were a lot of gotcha questions but it was really an open ended opportunity to talk about reducing regulatory and tax burdens revitalizing the American economy."

The candidates involved: Santorum, Rick Perry, Ron Paul, Michelle Bachman, Newt Gingrich were all in basic agreement on a list of issues that included eliminating Federal Agencies, Reducing tax Rates, and the common thread repealing President Obama's health plan.

Governor Perry was made to look giddy on a video. He countered with this statement."This was a great crowd, good response and I guess you can do anything you want with a video and make it look the way you want but I felt good, I felt great.

The Governor made other appearances in Des Moines at the University of phoenix. He was introduced by the Chief Executive of the university's Corporate owner Greg Cappelli who stated: "We are going to use our time to talk about our nations needs and a more highly educated and skilled work force not to deliver a political message."

Governor Perry stated: "You'll find out pretty quick I'm not much of a status quo person. The establishment is not real fond of me and that's OK. As a matter of fact one of my opponents has a 59 point plan, to preserve the current progressive tax system...Some think we can fix Washington with a pair of tweezers. Nibbling around the edges if you will. I happen to think we need to take a sledge hammer to it."Machiavelli once stated when you invade a country the one thing you don't mess with is the tax structure in a radical way. I do believe Machiavelli was right in this instance.

## 545. ROMNEY ON CUTS
### November 5, 2011

The target for Romney's cuts would be in entitlement programs. He was not specific as to which programs would be cut. He set the figure for those cuts at 500 billion dollars. He was addressing a Tea Party oriented group. Entitlements are the bread and butter of most Senators and representatives at the national level, occasionally they are referred to as pork, They can be education, the arts, Health related issues, and infrastructure that badly needs attention these days. Such cuts could be unpopular. It is a Social Darwinist solution that could put the brakes on economic growth done the wrong way.

## 546. CAIN ON RACE
### November 8, 2011

Herman Cain is of the generation of Martin Luther King. His way of standing up was succeeding in business and leading by example. His conservative roots would seem a contradiction to the generally liberal democratic movement.

Here are some of Mr. Cain's thoughts."I have been called Uncle Tom, sellout, Oreo, shameless."As he spoke to his largely Caucasian audiences in his seeking of the Republican nomination: "In the words of my Grandfather: I does not care, I does not care."

Amid criticisms from his fellow piers Harry Belafonte who called him a bad apple, his reaction was resilience. Cain remembered the circumstance of the charge related to the fact stating: "Was referring to the fact that I wouldn't stay on the Democratic platform because I ran away and I ain't going back."

With his campaign troubles mounting he has played the race card. He has compared himself to Clarence Thomas who was in his quest for the Supreme Court accused of sexual harassment. Thomas referred to it as a High Tech Lynching. The funny thing is that his accusers are black. The left wing media was targeted by Cain's super PAC. Cain stated: "Liberals are trying to attack me to intimidate other black conservatives to not go public or to not think about looking at other ideas on the other side of the spectrum."Cain did acknowledge that he never deliberately set out to sexually harass anyone but his language might have been (Misconstrued.) Niger Innes who happens to be one of the head figures of the Congress of Racial Equality stated: "The oversexed black-man is one of the most powerful negative charges. It has had a traumatic affect on the American Psyche for 200 years."

In brief Herman Coins view of life comes from the fact that he is the son of a Chauffeur and domestic who rose through the ranks of the food industry stating at Pillsbury and Burger king to become the chief executive of God Father Pizza. He is a cancer survivor that beat the odds. Invitations have been extended to him to sit on many Corporate Boards. I have thought, when you rise as Herman did with an independent spirit defying what had become the rational norm you will be misunderstood.

## 547. CAIN'S FALL
### November 9, 2011

Initially on the first of November three women brought to light allegations of sexual harassment and the settlements that were arrived at by the National Restaurant association. The sexual harassments occurred between 1996 and 1999. Cain stated: "In all my forty years of business experience. I have never sexually harassed anyone. When talking to the FOX channel he denied any knowledge of a settlement and added: "I hope they didn't pay much."

Here's a lesson for the guy's. If you're in business young astute and with an eye for the ladies keep your hands off and fantasize in your mind. A Karen Kraushaar charged that 14 years earlier Cain had groped her. A Sharon Blalek also came forward. Cain predicted that more accusers would be popping up in the coming days. He added: "The charges and accusations I totally reject. They simply didn't happen."At this point he acknowledged the damage to his Presidential bid and the possibility of suspending his campaign to deal with the issue.

### 548. QUANDARIES
### November 10, 2011

I call this the oops factor and any candidate can be its victim. Governor Rick Perry said he would cut three Federal Agencies. He listed two Education and Commerce but he could not name the third. Ron Paul and others on stage even tried to help him out. I have one the Federal Reserve that regulates interest rates and takes away the candy before the economy potentially over heats and bails out troubled corporations and countries. It thrives on debt and sells securities to make money to sustain itself. The treasury department could assume those duties. At any rate after the debate Perry did a rare post event news conference and stated: "I stepped in it. Yeah it was embarrassing of course it was.

The Cain Campaign was assaulted over the sexual harassment charges and he responded: "The American people deserve better than somebody being tried in the Court of public opinion. Based on unfounded accusations."He went on to declare his innocence and talked about his family.

### 549. CHANGING STATUS
### November 17, 2011

The fortunes of political war are round and circulating and sometimes spiteful. It does not matter whether we are talking about intra- party politics or inter- party politics. The base they are appealing to determine their vocabulary and volume of ideas. Those that engage in this game are bound by rules and those rules limit their options.

The standings of the candidates on the republican side are as follows: Romney 27%, Cain 20%, Gingrich 14%, Texas Representative Ron Paul 6%, Perry 3%, Bachman 2%, Jon Huntsman 1% and Santorum 1%. Jesse M Unruh and his USC institute of Politics stated: "For the last year we've seen a steady stream of conservative alternatives to Romney emerge, audition and fade away."Romney is basically a centrist like Huntsman. It is just that Romney took off and huntsman didn't. Those challenges from the right are the restrictor plate that could cause the Republicans to lose. The reason would be that they as a whole do not reflect the spirit of the majority no matter how slim.

Remembering that California is a barometer for the nation if you average the votes out we get some amazing contradictory results. As of this date in California President Obama despite the 12% unemployment rate in California is preferred over Romney on a on a 48 to 40 percent margin. Stats vary from state to state but the overall sentiment could lead to controversy.

## 550. ON CHILD LABOR
November 26, 2011

Newt Gingrich was widely criticized for his idea on loosening the child labor laws Mike Gal lager a writer for the *L.A. Times* stated: "I can only assume that the editor did not work as a child, unlike the children for most small business owners. I've never known a working kid who didn't have time for homework so-long as there wasn't a long transportation requirement.

"The idea that a kid might spend a limited number of hours working at the local school, if they wished to do so would not be a homework burden as you naively suggest. A persons first job positively reinforces more work habits than I can list here. Which also has positive economic benefits.

Gingrich's proposal isn't about exploiting children. It is about opportunity and positive reinforcement for kids who choose to work part time."

If I were to inject my experience of a paper route for what we referred to as a green sheet throw away paper. The collecting of the price of the paper and the satisfying of the customer does create a basis for a responsible attitude.

# NATIONAL ELECTION PRIMARY 2011

## 551. BANK OF AMERICA
November 2, 2011

You might think bank stocks are a great deal. This is not necessarily the case due to some bad judgments that I have outlined earlier. Their stocks fell 6.3% to $6.40 a share. They decided to use the debt card as a means of making up the difference. There was a revolt, ADC customer by the name of Molly Katch started the concept of Bank transfer day. Bank of America withdrew the fee they were going to charge. They defended their actions by stating they had to make a profit. What is wrong is that if you sting your customer with user fees for less they will deposit less in your bank to begin with and you as a bank will lose. This was an election year and if business wanted to reinforce populist anti-corporate feeling in the people they the banking industry should have stuck

Here is the rub, if you conduct multiple transactions say 3 you will be charged $10 for each transaction at Wells Fargo if you don't use the Visa Debit Card. If you have such a card it's one dollar per transaction up to $10 or ten uses if you are under a certain amount in your account. That happened to me. The only other way is to have $2,000 in your account. So you see B of A was not the only one. They wonder why the savings rate in America is low. Maybe I have just given one of the reasons.

Mr. Romney I wonder what your attitude would have been on banking practices had you been elected. The same question would have applied to the field of candidates.

Back to B of A: they are in the process of downsizing to improve their bottom line. J P Morgan Chase benefit from this, in the process they are laying off 30,000 employees. The argument is to reduce expenses.

On Capitol Hill a Mock Shock was being displayed. Senator Dick Durban introduced a Bill to limit the amount of fees a bank can charge on their Visa Debit Cards. Unfortunately he left a hole that I just described above. Now I have a debit visa card and they can only charge me one dollar from my checking account but I must use the card 10 times in a month. Isn't this progress wonderful. Durban's statement was: "For years big banks have been rigging the rules with a lot of fees and charges we were not aware of, "Hog wash. He continued: "Through a combination of reasonable regulations and customers voting with their feet we are bringing transparency and competition back to the financial service industry."

Vice president Joe Biden was less euphoric in his welcoming of this perceived change.. He stated: "It certainly stands to reason that these customers did not react well to it."According to the *L.A. Times* these reforms would: See more clearly what they're paying for."I'm trying to figure out who's side he is on.

## 552. CANDIDATES SKIP IOWA FORUM

Meanwhile where the corn grows, along with some humor, only the less popular republican field participated in an economic forum to air their views on the direction of the economy. This gathering was sponsored by the National Association of Manufacturers. Governor Terry Bradstad stated: "It is unfortunate that Governor Romney and Herman Cain weren't here because they missed a great opportunity today. They missed out on the opportunity to address the number one issue in this campaign and that is creating jobs. It was not a situation where there were a lot of gotcha questions, but it was really an open ended opportunity to talk about reducing regulatory and tax burdens revitalizing the American economy.

Just who did show up for this avant-garde affair: Rick Perry, Michelle Bachmann, Ron Paul, Rick Santorum. There was a unanimity in what they expressed from reducing taxes, eliminating agencies, and of course the repeal of president Obama's Affordable Health Care Plan.

If you feel good about yourself and what you're saying you could be interpreted as giddy and that was the perception of Governor Perry in the previous debate. He was countering that image in this forum, he stated: "This was a great crowd, good response, and I guess you can do anything you want with a video and make it look anyway you want, but I felt good-great."

One of the sponsors Gregg Cappelli stated: "We're going to use our time to talk about our nations need for a more highly educated and skilled work force not to deliver a political message.

Both Cain and Romney were too busy strategizing at this point.

## 553. THE EUROPEAN EFFECT
November 3, 2011

The austerity measures and bail out loans were indirectly affecting our stock market and speculators were having a field day. Note they were not reacting to factual situations but projected economic models. The result was a drop of 275.5 points or 2.5% (1,657,000). It was relinquishing all the previous weeks surge. You might call it an adjustment. The point is that it was an artificial manipulation of numbers with no bearing on actual events.

## 554. CAIN LINKS ISSUE TO RACE
November 5, 2011

Herman Cain linked himself to Justice Clarence Thomas and the sexual harassment charges that were leveled against him at that time. He talked of being accused of being a traitor to his race because he was of his conservative ideology. Cain stated: "Liberals are trying to attack me, to intimidate other black conservatives to not go public or not think about looking at other ideas on the other side of the spectrum."

The historical stereotypes May be playing into all of this. The Head of the Congress for Racial Equality: Nigger Innes stated: "The over-sexed Blackman is one of the most powerful negative charges. It has had a traumatic affect on the American Psyche for 200 years.

The long made short is this argument is that we have not escaped history and the three charged sexual harassment cases to someone who represents black conservatism and argued liberal bias that elements especially given in the present political environment.

## 555. ROMNEY IN IOWA
### November 5, 2011

There are two sides to this story, one of refusal to attack a competitor who was at this point in time facing charges of sexual harassment and his goal to displace Barak Obama at the end of this political season.. We call it an election. Romney stated: "This is a critical time for us. I don't want to wake up a year from now and turn on my TV and have it say President Obama re-elected. Because I know what that means. I mean a weaker America."What I have just put to you is a sample of campaign rhetoric and trust me the same but slanted statement was being said from the Obama campaign.

We were looking at hooking the Religious Right slash Bible Belt Ethic for the general Election. The block of middle ground states were deemed critical in light of the liberal leanings of the states like California, New York, Florida and as a swing state Massachusetts. This was part of other Eastern and western border states that tend to vote Democratic and have the bulk of the Electoral votes, needed as opposed to the predominantly agricultural middle that has less population.. Since it is the state tally that determines each victory and not necessarily the averaged gross population. The candidates were paying attention to the middle.

The concept of loose money to stimulate the economy as fostered by the Fed at present in the year 2012, candidate Romney poses a contrast. He stated: "Unlike a lot of people in Washington, I believe that deficits matter. I believe one of the reasons we've had such a hard time getting the economy going again is because of the huge deficits being racked up by this president and politicians in Washington. I will slay the deficit beast. It's killing jobs. (I ask you to refer to Greenspan's arguments in assessing Romney's words and judge for yourself where the true balance stands.) It's shadowing our future and keeping our kids from having the prospects they deserve."This middle section of states was hit hardest going back to 2001, and is having trouble recovering so their tempo is important.

## 556. ROMNEY CUTS /CHANGES
### November 5, 2011

The idea of entitlement is central to Romney's theology. He opposes them at least at the federal level. It is a bit like reinventing the Lapher Curve that we had under Reagan. He would link any aid (Food Stamps) to a work program. Social Security would face changes as in the age of eligibility. Medicare would see more privatization and seniors would purchase benefits. This would affect 47 million of the older generation such as myself. It sounds as though he wants to return the initiative to the states and financial power of choice of the states. That would again make the people choose their governor and legislator. That would be very important and there could be no intransigence. He outlined a plan to cut 500 billion from the federal budget.

This could be smoke and mirrors to some extent for the people. He was talking to Tea Party advocates with their politics on the right. He would later in 2012 start back-peddling for the new Governor Rick Perry stated on the Sean Hamilton Radio Show: "I have never felt better and I think you saw a glimpse of what you can expect out of me as we go forward in the latest debate we had in Iowa."At this point in time Perry's poll numbers were single digit.

## 557. THE TIDE WAS TURNING

As of November 30, the political scenarios had changed . Herman Cain was being confronted by the third accusation, this time in front of camera's and had told his staff he was reassessing his campaign for the Presidency . His supporters were considering supporting Gingrich.

Governor Rick Perry got his boost from Arizona's favorite Sherriff Arpaio: "He doesn't just talk about it. he does something about it. He's an honorable ethical person. A Governor Rick Perry had a part in his state's budget put 400 million into securing the borders of Texas over the past decade.

Rick Perry was battling Romney who had heavily invested in New Ham-shire Primary. His views click more with the Tea Party than the views of Romney. Again these candidates seem to be battling for the House of Mirrors, while invading armies are Marching on their door step.

In this Gingrich camp this icon of political history was living up to his reputation Gingrich stated: "I wouldn't lie to the American people. I wouldn't switch my positions for political reasons. I don't claim to be the perfect candidate. I just claim to be a lot more conservative than Mitt Romney and a lot more electable than anybody else.. He has risen to what is called the top of the heap as the newest conservative alternative to Romney. Bear in mind Romney is not a conservative. He is just playing to a conservative audience.

## 558. ON ROMNEY
### December 3, 2011

The location was the Annenberg Public Policy center in Pennsylvania and the question before the group: What emotion / impression do candidates pictures evoke. Santorum didn't rate at all and Newt Gingrich for his three marriages and his affairs still rated at the top. The way he carries himself say's leader. Romney was in the seventh position and people thought of him as a preacher, salesman, TV Pitchman,, Actor, you see people think quite shallow and have a ten second attention span in which they make they're judgments. This is despite the fact that he has the best organization and had run for the presidency previously. His image is the perfect family man and husband loving wife and people weirdly embraced Gingrich and his reputation. Herman Cain was slaughtered but he was viewed as an alternative to Romney. Romney did secure the nomination but what is it that the Republicans are thinking these days.

It all boils down to a question of intent. When Gingrich and Romney campaign they clash with salvos usually intended for their democratic rival. Here is an example of such attacks.

Newt stated: "I would say if Governor Romney were to give back all the money he's earned from bankrupting companies and laying off employees over his years at Bain Capital I would be glad to listen to him. I bet you 10 dollars not 10 thousand he won't take that offer."

## 559. ROMNEY'S CAMPAIGN
### December 17, 2011

The Romney campaign was split between two states: Iowa and South Carolina. Mean while the other candidates were shooting rhetorically at him. He was setting his sights on President Obama Romney stated: "I watched our President over the last three years, I shake my head and say he's over his head. He doesn't understand."His remarks were being aimed at a steel mill in Iowa and the Obama Affordable Health Care Bill along with the bank regulations that were killing small business. He added: "I want to keep America the most attractive place in the world for every kind of innovation, investment and growth."

In the state of South Carolina he secured the endorsement of Governor Nikki Haley who won office in 2010 courtesy of the Tea Party. Romney stated to an audience: "I'm planning that as you take a closer look at all the presidential contenders and give them a kick in the leg, and get to know who they are, that you're going to end up supporting me for the next president of the United States."

Romney continued: "I respect your Governor ... A lot of us stood in line at her door, hoping for her endorsement. I could not be more proud."The great challenge in places like South Carolina is that they are not keen on prospects of a Romney presidential candidacy. In 2008 Romney tried and failed in this state, so this time around he was low key.

Attacks by Ron Paul and Romney on Gingrich have given the campaign pause Michael Krull stated: "The 9 million in negative advertizing by Ron Paul, Mitt Romney and their supporters against Speaker Gingrich is starting to have an impact and we need the sources necessary to respond on the air in Iowa. Iowa holds the first caucus in the nation on January 3, 2012.

### 560. A SYRIA REFLECTION

I have been giving you all the pertinent information on various U.S. interests domestically. Briefly I turn my attention to the killing of innocents that has continued into October 2012. Here is an account from the *L.A. Times*.

First I have to give you a word Shabiha that translates in Arabic to Ghost. The Alawites are a minority sect clan supporting the Assad Regime which is Sunni based. The Shiites are essentially disenfranchised and must work abroad to improve their lives on their farms and wish to be left alone. With the birth of the Arab Spring these villages gained a sense of courage and started to protest. These protests have been met with death squads. This created the Free Syrian Army and a exodus to the Turkish border of civilians. The Government planted mines that continue to kill and maim. Assad is the house guest that just won't leave. Coptic Christians are remaining neutral so far for fear of annihilation. That is how Islam rose in the first place in this once Christian nation. Now cell phones film and the truth leaks out, but what will the west do nothing.

### 561. THE RON PAUL AFFECT

It is December 20, 2011 and it appears that the edge in Iowa was going to the Libertarian Ron Paul. This would and did hurt Newt Gingrich. The Ron Paul movement also served to block Perry, Bachmann and Cain who was in deep trouble. Paul is a populist on the right while Barak Obama could be considered an emerging populist on the left. Paul apposes intervention in world affairs and is a state's rightist. The people are in that kind of mood. So it was that Ron Paul's star was shining in Iowa.

The candidacies of Perry, Santorum and Bachmann were to test their fate this year. Rick Santorum made the following statement: "We still have a chance to send a message if the results of Iowa are inconclusive, we've failed to send the message, we've wasted our time."

The article in the *L.A. Times* on Super Pac's (Dec. 21, 2011) has Romney and Gingrich on the same yet different sides of the fence. Super-Pac's have the ability to raise unlimited amounts of money, but must not be connected to any Presidential campaign. This was the decision of the Supreme Court as a civil right of free speech.

Newt felt the Pac's attacking him were connected in some way to the Romney campaign. Romney denied this and urged the reigning in of Super Pac's . In general Gingrich stated: "It would be nice if the candidates were held responsible for the things done by people who know them, personally who are trying to help them get elected. It is very disappointing to see some of my friends who are running putting out negative junk.

Romney did have a reply to this statement and it was brief: "My goodness if we cooperate in any way we go to the big house. Campaign Finance Law has made a mockery of our political campaign season. We really ought to let campaigns raise the money and get rid of these Super Pac's

A supporter of Gingrich, Rick Tyler was joining two Gingrich based Super Pac's. Gingrich commented: "I don't object to being outspent. I object to lies. If Rick Tyler wants to do positive adds within the current law, I would encourage people to give money to his Pac. If Rick Tyler runs negative adds, I will discourage anyone from giving him a penny."

## 562. THE LATIN VOTE
### January 30, 2012

When we talk about the Latin Vote it is not a unified subject. California's Hispanic population is largely democratic and to be a republican in the state and win you must be in the middle. All those to the right usually get defeated. Florida is another world. It has a general split. The younger generation vote democratic.

In 2008 a Kennedyesk Senator Obama captured the younger generation but that dream soured for some. The Romney stand on Immigration was ironically helped by Democrats with the Latin Cuban Vote. Here is a sample attitude from Dade County: "Obama had at least a chance to make some inroads for democrats about younger Cuban Voters, but the persistent bad economy. If his presidency had been more successful those Cuban American people who voted for him in 2008 would have stuck with him."Thus stated Dario Moreno Professor at Florida International University.

The demographics of the 1.2 Million Latin /Cuban young American voting block is largely Republican by tradition in Miami –Dada County. (74% Registered Republican.) The political route usually follows the Versailles Restaurant with an Anti- Castro Speech and a visit to the Freedom Tower. Mitt Romney did not do his homework when he associated an Anti- Castro with Castro himself. This was a self-inflicted wound that opened the way for Obama. From the time of 2004 to 2008 there was a shift of 20% of the younger Cuban voters regarded themselves as liberal and support was not tied to the unsuccessful embargo that has increased Cuban trade with Europe and Asia. Their issues go straight, to the domestic U.S. economy. What holds the Cuban vote in the Republican column is the older generation and here was another gaff. When Romney as of September 2012 stated that 47% of the population in general were essentially addicted to entitlements. He was offending those older voters that made up his base of support. How their judgment on his words pared out helped swing the election.

Benjamin Bishin Professor at U C Riverside noted: "The community is moderating very slowly. That's in part because 50 years after the Bay of Pigs the Cuban community is becoming more diverse. It's made up more from young immigrants from Cuba and a second generation of Cuban American, for whom economic issues trump arguments about the embargo or regime change. Recent immigrants think that the embargo hasn't worked. Younger generations are more open to voting for a different party, but often register as independent."

Intransigence and fundamentalism could make the Republican Party a relic of history. Governor Romney tried to moderate his positions to the general election and was accused of flip flopping. He was trying to go back to his centrist positions in order to get elected in the general election. When I initially wrote this section I projected that if he won it would be by no more than 2% to 3% . I stated if Obama won it would be by3% to 4%. This proved to be President Elects Obama's percentage of victory. What limited Romney was the Tea Party Affect. That same affect has given President Obama some major head-aches.

Back to the battle that was going on at this time: Governor Romney had been bogged down by Gingrich over his saturation bombing of his campaign that increased after Gingrich bested Romney in South Carolina. Remember Romney lacked a southern strategy. Romney stated: "Mr. speaker remember your trouble in Florida not because the debate audience is too quiet or too loud or because you have opponents that are tough. Your problem in Florida was that you worked for Freddie Mac at a time when Freddie Mac was not doing the right thing for the American people and that your selling influence in Washington at a time when we need people who will stand up for the truth."

I can understand the position of the House Speaker Gingrich who regarded what he was doing as legitimately representing the interests of his client, the same way I sold tickets for various causes that were not doing the right thing and misrepresenting their product. Remember he had financial obligations too. That part did not diminish the historian part of his legacy.

The Gingrich take on president Obama was linked to his policies with European style socialism and the Romanization of America. This could be considered partly true in that the powers of the States have diminished since 2008. I refer to the various Marijuana initiatives from California and other states of the Union. The fight over immigration, and perceived states rights, and the disputed border areas. Arizona in particular could be cited. However the switch away from socialism on the European continent starting with Sweden in the 70s Germany and France though the French dumped Sarkozi in favor of a socialist. Spain and Greece had their economies on the ropes at this time. As you can see the picture is not all that black and white.

### 563. TO BE A EXECUTIVE AND A PRESIDENT THAT IS THE QUESTION

Since 9/11 happened and the new economy decided to visit us the argument has been made that the President should have private sector experience. In a way this May be true for Americans seem to have redefined themselves in this post apocalyptic period. But it has not always been the case.

If Romney would have succeeded in capturing the presidency he would have been the first true executive to do so. Historically of the 21 presidents that served this country only four not counting President Carter and his peanut farm who remotely had any business experience. They are Theodore Roosevelt, Woodrow Wilson, Harry Truman, and Ronald Reagan.

Roosevelt operated a cattle ranch in North Dakota. Woodrow Wilson was president of Princeton University. Harry Truman owned a haberdashery and went bankrupt for a few years in Kansas City. Ronald Reagan was president of the Screen actors Guild and spokesman for General Electric.

There were a few with experience exclusively in the public sector. Franklin D Roosevelt, Dwight D Eisenhower, John F Kennedy, and Lyndon B Johnson.

Under writing Warren Harding was a newspaper publisher. Herbert Hoover was an engineer who managed mining operations. As I said Jimmy Carter was a Peanut Farmer. George H. W. Bush and his son George W. Bush were oil men and G W was partners in a baseball franchise.

Note of those with the most business experience Harding, Hoover, and George W. Bush are rated at the bottom. To compound this the business man with his goal being primarily profit and bottom line contrasts, with a multifaceted approach of the non-business oriented president who employs business men and corporate types who give their collective judgment on how to manage the government and the people's business. All this has an ebb and flow of the public will.

### 564. THE CONCEPT OF WEALTH
February 1, 2012

All industries have their brokers and backers. This includes the political industry. As of this time republicans were out raising democrats. Here are some examples: Harold Summers a Dallas billionaire gave $500,000 to Rick Perry's campaign. A man by the name of Adelson is being pursued for he is regarded as a major donor according to the Simmons group. An organization called Cross Roads organized by Karl Rowe was lining up potential donors. There was 18.4 million from the Simmon's group with 5 million coming from Simmon's himself. $500,000 came from Crow Holdings that is operated by Harlan Crow and Kenny Troutt who is a communications billionaire in Dallas There is also support by such corporations like A T and T. You get the gist. For more detailed information see the *L.A. Times* article (REPORTS UNDERSCORE ROLE OF WEALTHY INDIVIDUALS) February 1, 2012

### 565. REGIONAL VICTORIES
February 1, 2012

Here's a real question: can a candidate win outside his sphere of influence. House speaker Gingrich is popular in the south not in the North or West. Governor Mitt Romney is popular in the north and middle ground states and not in the south.

The concepts that make up the consideration: Mississippi holds its primary on February 7, but no delegates go with this victory. Michigan and Arizona are the only primaries that count in terms of delegates. Those that Romney won last round: Nevada, Colorado, Minnesota and Maine are caucus states. Very few delegates are derived from those contests. Newt was counting on victories in Georgia, Tennessee, Oklahoma, Alabama, and Mississippi.

The main factor was this sustained three person race was rich in donors supporting a cause, despite flagging support. The candidates like the donors are out to make a statement and both Newt and Santorum fight on at this point.

### 566. THE RON PAUL EFFECT

There were two candidates with an organization as wide spread as Romney and Ron Paul. His followers are called Paulists. It is almost biblical. In 2008 Ron Paul got 14% second to Mitt Romney. Those that trailed were John McCain, Rudolf Guliani, and Fred Thompson the fellow who now sells reverse mortgages.

This is a silly but important point, but in 2008 the brothels in Nevada supported President Obama. But when he allowed horse meat to be sold for consumption as it is in Europe, the animal rights people got up in arms and in this election supported Ron Paul.

Nevada is an independent states rights State. The two candidates that were an easy fit were Romney and Paul. Paul is a 12 term congressman from the state of Nevada. His almost Libertarian views put him at odds with the party. A senior Romney advisor Ryan Erwin stated: "Ron Paul and Mitt Romney are always going to outperform polling because of the strength of their organizations. The Paul organization is strong. You'll witness that on Saturday. We like to think of ourselves as just as strong or stronger. "He continued: "Sure the campaign has a lot of Mormon supporters and volunteers, but four years ago, we had enough self-identified Catholics to win the caucuses. The election goes on.

### 567. THE RACE NARROWS

Having won Florida Romney was starting to urge others to coalesce behind his candidacy. He stated: "Leadership is about taking responsibility not making excuses. Mr. President you were elected to lead. You chose to follow and now it's time to get out of the way.

Newt Gingrich was not as congratulatory, towards Romney. He stated: "This will be a two person race between the conservative leader Newt Gingrich and the Massachusetts moderate. We have 46 states to go. We are going to contest every place and we are going to win and we will win in Tampa as the nominee in August."

Aside from the rhetoric coming from the Gingrich camp, the race was made lively by the sweeping victory of Romney in Florida over all age and class categories. The fact that the religious right was not strong in Florida added to the Romney momentum. The Gingrich camp accused Romney of having a casual relationship with the truth and the Romney camp wanted Newt to look in the mirror.

### 568. THE BATTLE FOR MICHIGAN
February 21, 2012

Former senator Rick Santorum this being his natural battle ground hoped to deal Romney a blow. He stated: "What could be a sound heard round the world, here in Michigan next week."He went on to attack Obama and what he called the elite society.(Radical Environmental Ideology) He went on to argue that what president Obama offered was essentially a stone or false choice between protecting the environment and stimulating the economy. He stated: "It is a choice that wants to limit your productivity. Limit your ability to rise in society. Limit your quality of life, so they can control the resources that you can get."He stated that, that was what cap and trade was all about.

For Romney Michigan was important for it was his birth place and the state where his father George Romney was Governor and ran for the Presidency and was top executive in the auto industry. Since his moving to Massachusetts many had lost attachment to the Romney name. In 2008 Romney did take Michigan by 9% in that primary. He considered Detroit his family home town.

The Santorum camp was playing a risky game spending so much time in this rust belt state, for contests in Georgia, Ohio, Tennessee, Oklahoma, North Dakota, and Massachusetts could be put in jeopardy.

Romney's attack on Santorum was vicious and went like this: "Senator Santorum goes to Washington and calls himself a budget hawk. Then after he has been there a while, he says he is no longer a budget hawk. I don't want to spend more money than we take in."Romney criticized the vote by Santorum to raise the debt ceiling five times as opposed to handling the issue. Romney continued: "We have in Washington a malady that affects so many that their not your Senator but many others, who somehow think it's ok to spend money borrowed from China and others to pay for it, and pass that burden onto your families and to your kids."

Santorum while he was campaigning in Ohio stated: "We need someone who understands, who comes from the coal fields, who comes from the steel mills, who understands what ordinary working people in America need to provide for themselves and their families."That is the populist stand that has a self limiting affect counter to the world economy.

### 569. THE BATTLE FOR DELEGATES
### March 26, 2012

When is the battle over? The other question is when does, the floor fight begin. The last time there was such a thing was the Ford for President Campaign against Ronald Reagan in 1976. After that both parties developed the concept of super delegates as tie breakers. This was to head off a fight before the convention. This to me was a way of rigging the convention. When senator Obama fought Hillary Clinton for the nomination he pulled in my mind's eye a dirty trick. He got the backing of the super delegates to offset the fact that Hillary almost had it tied up. In the 2008 race Hillary should have been the nominee. After the delegate fix her organization fell apart. The convention concept is the battle ground of ideas not a side show.

With much effort Romney accumulated 478 delegates far more than the others. The other candidates retained their delegates in hopes of influencing the platform or were hoping for a dark-horse nomination. Some did indeed set delegates free. The number of delegates needed to win the nomination is 1,144. Josh Putnam who is a political science professor at Davidson College North Carolina stated: "By all accounts if things stay as they are, now though the end of the primary process then we're probably talking about June before Romney can get to 1,144. The percentage of delegates needed to secure the nomination is 45%. He currently has 55% of the delegates. This number also probably includes super delegates.

It was speculated that Rick Santorum could run a nuisance campaign, if his funding keeps up. Republican strategist Mike Murphy stated: "The problem for the Party is that it keeps the narrative of the campaign about division within the party rather than focusing on the fall. There comes a point where the campaign becomes more about helping Obama than his own principles."Santorum's advisor Jon Yob stated according to the *L.A. Times* (Santorum actually had piled 300 delegates already- more than any independent tally gave him, and Romney's lead was much smaller than others were assuming) It was guessed that one in five would go to the convention as free agents. This was the factor that was giving Santorum hope.

### 570. TACTICS

Field operations differed from mobile to massive stationary ones. The later requires much more money. Senator Obama blitzed Hillary Clinton's campaign in 2008 and in conjunction with the available Super Delegates secured the nomination.

The Romney camp did not hire get out the vote organizers around the country.

They instead used the leap-frog approach. Teams jumped in and out of various primary states. In the important states staff was increased. This kept costs down. It also tells something about a Romney White House. Campaign Director Richard Beeson for the Romney campaign stated: "It has the infrastructure in place. We're taking care of business in the Primary. We're setting up infrastructure in states that make sense in general. But at the end of the day, I'm not losing sleep over having a general field operation. I know it's being taken care of.

When you drift to the Obama camp the tempo shifts. David Plouffe and David Axelrod as they did in 2008 election now preserving then arresting the nomination from a broad range of candidates at massive fund raising lifted the former community of fund raiser to national status in 2008 and preserve his populist image in 2011 through 2012. This early get out the vote effort in 2012 has made it difficult to find staff to fill the positions because of interest in the campaign is not ramped up. The concept of on-line advertizing has taken the bulk of the budget 15.1 million. High tech volunteers are being utilized to reach a broader more informed group.

The Romney camp seems outpaced with this Doug Gross a veteran GOP activist stated: "You won't be able to compete with the Obama ground game. For the republicans what's going to drive turnout is not going to be Mitt Romney, it's Barak Obama. The Romney camp was relying on Super Pac's, something they have no control over. To stimulate their message. That's why those funky adds along with the controversy.

### 571. THE LATIN VOTE
#### April 27, 2012

President Obama had his Dream Act which would allow sons and daughters of illegal immigrants to obtain citizenship by serving in the armed forces or attend college. To me this would be the simplest route. We educated them and in this way we assure their loyalty to this country. That to some is appeasement.

Earlier Mitt Romney managed to alienate the Latin vote that has married itself to this new immigrant based movement. Florida Senator Marco Rubio proposed different legislation. It does not guarantee citizenship through what I just mentioned but it grants a permanent worker visa to those children and they can apply for citizenship through regularly established channels.

Governor Mitt Romney has as of this time not backed the Rubio Bill but his vision does should Romney get elected provide a possible way to make peace with the Latin community. That community is not solid and support from U.S. Citizens of Hispanic descent who despise the flood of labor from their former countries costing them wages, just might vote republican. That was the hope.

### 572. CALIFORNIA'S OPEN PRIMARY
#### May 14, 2012

The name of the game has changed at least to some degree. That relates to all state level races. The 21% of the electorate that now count themselves as independent can vote across party lines for all state level offices in the June 5th election. In the general election the standard rules apply. The only exception to this would be Presidential and Senatorial Representative levels representing us in Washington DC.

This new found power at the state level forces candidates to spend more money to influence a broader base of the electorate not based on party structure. Democratic strategist Richie Ross stated: "What the open primary has done is shuffle the strategic deck. The timing and manner of which you communicate have to be adjusted."This idea of negative advertizing the way this law has been rewritten ca come back to haunt a candidate. You are no longer assured victory by catering to members of your own party.

Richard Temple a GOP consultant stated: "It's very complicated, very new and everybody is going to learn a lot about how this is going to work. South Bay 66th district would be an example for it was considered a swing district not safe to either party. Two republicans and democrats were running in this district. Craig Huey Republican had sent out advertisements to Democrats in this evenly divided district knocking his democratic opponent, Al Meratsuchi. Mseratsuchi was viewed as the probable winner of the run-off spot. California has always been a innovator.

# OBAMA 2011

## 573. THE SHIFT TO THE CENTER
### January 7, 2011

With the loss of the House of Representatives to the Republicans President Obama had to rethink his strategy. He shuffled his cabinet to reflect this new direction. William Daily was appointed Chief of Staff. He was formerly the Commerce Secretary. He had warned Obama about straying too far to the liberal side alienating the moderate voters. Gene Sperling was nominated to the position of Chief Economic Advisor. He like Bill Daily came from the Clinton Administration. Both men are centrists. Laurence H. Summers had held the post of Chief Economic Advisor and was returning to Harvard. David Plouffe who served as Obama's campaign manager in 2008 was appointed Chief White House Advisor.

President Obama as a result of the loss of the House in the 2010 election was forced to compromise with the Republicans on the Bush Tax Cuts which I think should be repealed for they were one of the causes for this economic mess. The other mistake was the senior drug plan and the Subprime mortgage issue that speculators took off on. This and a sinking economy at the time was the reason for our slump.

Economies are cyclical and this one is on the verge of recovery. I will say it again not all will benefit. Those over 50 are at disadvantage and those long term unemployed though they restart their work search are not desirable because of gaps in their employment some up to a year or so. That's just the way it is.

## 574. A TIME OF UNITY
### January 26, 2011

The Nation had almost lost Arizona's Democratic member of the House Gabriel Gifferd to a mad-mans bullet and there was a profound sentiment this day including the empty chair in honor of Gifferd. Democrats and republicans sat side by side. For this State Of The Union. President Obama stated: "We are part of the American family and perhaps like a family the slights arguments and habits were not easy to abandon."As you might guess the Democrats were quick to rise on some cues and republicans hesitant to follow.

Even in this time of unity minds were not changed and in post scripted comments members of the legislature made their views known. Representative Paul Broun Republican of Georgia was tweeting some 40 separate moments, "Mr. President you don't believe in the Constitution, you believe in Socialism." A more unfortunate remark was yelled from the floor by Representative Joe Wilson Republican, from South Carolina when he unceremoniously yelled: "You Lie." This moment fortunately quickly passed. You could tell we were approaching an election year and the republican TEA Party right were gearing up their guns.

Senator Mark Udall Democrat from Colorado spoke of the backdrop of the shooting that that almost killed Representative Gifferd and killed 6 souls and wounding 13 in Tucson stated: "If we can continue to build on this symbolic gesture by emphasizing unity over division. I know that can have a real affect on the way we work together."

Here are some excerpts from President Obama's State Of The Union."There is no secret those of us here tonight have had our differences over the past two years. But Tucson reminded us that no matter who we are or where we come from, each of us is part of something greater. We are part of the American family. We believe that in a country where every race and faith and point of view can be found, we are still bound together as a people, that we share common hopes and a common creed, that the dreams of a little girl in Tucson are not so different than those of our children and they all deserve the chance to be fulfilled.

At stake right now is not who wins the next election, it's whether we sustain the leadership that has made America not just a place on a map, but a light to the world. Two years after the worst recession most of us have ever known the stock market has come roaring back. Corporate profits are up. The economy is growing again."(By the way this has always been the case just to remind the reader The economy started in 2003 under G W over heated as I said earlier due to speculators, crashed, rebooted by the later part of 2006 and just started growing in 2007 so Barak is the recipient of a newly emerging cycle of the post Y2K economy that is stingy with jobs and generous to investors. The stimulus helped but again I point out it only helped holding companies and did not fuel initially small business. Back to the President's speech.)"But we never measured progress by these yard-sticks alone. We measure success by the success of our people. That's the project that the American people want us to work on.

Half a century ago when the soviets beat us into space with the launch of a satellite called Sputnik, we had no idea how we'd beat them to the moon. The science wasn't there yet. NASA didn't even exist, but after investing in better research and education, we didn't just surpass the Soviets we unleashed a weapon of innovation that created new industries and millions of jobs. This is our generations Sputnik moment.

With more research and incentives we can break our dependence on oil with Biofuels and be the first country to have 1million electric vehicles on the road by 2015. We need to get behind this innovation and to help pay for it, I'm asking the Congress to eliminate the billions of tax payer dollars we currently give to the oil company's, that I don't know if you've noticed they're doing just fine on they're own.

We need to teach our kids that it's not just the winner of the Super bowl who deserves to be celebrated but the winner of the Science Fair. That success is not just a function of fame or PR but of hard work and discipline. Of course the education race doesn't end with High-School diploma. To compete higher education must be in reach of every American. This year I ask Congress to make permanent our tuition tax credit, worth $10,000 for four years of College.

The last point about education today, there are hundreds of thousands of students excelling in our schools who are not American citizens. Some are the children of the undocumented workers who had nothing to do with the actions of their parents. They grew up as Americans and the pledge of Allegiance to our flag, and yet every day live with the threat of deportation.

Now I strongly believe we should take on once and for all the issue of illegal immigration. I am prepared to work with the Republicans and Democrats, to protect our borders, enforce our laws and address the millions of undocumented workers who are now living in the shadows."(Only one point here, if these undocumented workers have taken on someone else's identity I know of a couple victims of this practice they should be prosecuted and deported.)

Over the years a parade of lobbyists has rigged the tax code to benefit particular companies and industries. Tonight I'm asking Democrats and Republicans to simplify the system. Get rid of loop holes, level the playing field, and use the savings to lower corporate tax rates for the first time in 25 years without adding to our deficit.

I've ordered a review of Government regulations. When we find rules that put an unnecessary burden on businesses, we will fix them, but I will not hesitate to enforce common sense safe guards to protect the American people. That's what we've done in this country for more than a century.. It's why our food is safe to eat, our water safe to drink, and our air safe to breathe.(Just a note in China, their advancement has come at the expense of their quality of life. An example would be pollution and the quality of food each class eats.)

Now I have heard a few of you have some concerns about the new health care law so let me be the first to say that anything can be improved. If you have ideas on how to improve this law of making care better and more affordable, I am eager to work with you. What I am not willing to do is go back to the days when insurance companies could deny someone coverage because of a preexisting condition... instead of fighting. Instead of refighting the battles of the last two years. Let's fix what needs fixing and move forward."(The interesting note was at the first presidential debate between Romney and Obama. On Romney's part there was no talk of scrapping the act but tweaking it.)

President Obama continued: "Now the final step- A critical step- in winning the future is to make sure we aren't buried under a mountain of debt... So tonight I am preparing to start this year, we freeze annual domestic spending for the next five years. This would reduce the deficit by more than 4 billion over the next decade, and will bring discretionary spending to the lowest share of our economy since Dwight Eisenhower was President....(In a way Obama was pre-empting Romney who would probably make a similar move. This of course means eliminating Pork from Congressional bills a Reagan experiment.) He Obama added: "And... before we take money away from our schools or scholarships away from our students we should ask millionaires to give up their tax breaks.

From the earliest days of our founding, America has been the story of ordinary people who dare to dream. That's how we win the future. We do big things.

The idea of America endures. Our destiny remains our choice. And tonight more than two centuries later, it is because of our people that our future is hopeful. Our journey goes forward and the State of our Union is strong."

## 575. THE REPUBLICAN RESPONSE

The Republican response was a diatribe with a twist. This is just as President Obama's first two years twisted Republican ideas as if they were in a mirror. Congressional Representative Paul Ryan who would later become Governor Mitt Romney's running mate delivered the Republican rebuttal. Essentially while accepting responsibility for past error in contributing to the deficit he pointed to the newly elected House of Representatives and the reduction in their budget to 2008 levels.

Representative Paul Ryan in characteristic Republican style put his spin on the State Of the Union when he stated: "Whether sold as a stimulus or repackaged as investment, they're actions show they want a Federal Government that controls too much and spends too much in order to do too much." (Just too keep both sides honest President Obama had proposed a freeze on Federal spending. Also remember he had spent a significant amount of money on the stimulus package that was starting to give some results. The criticism I think could be used against the Romney Ryan ticket in the General Election.)

Representative Michele Bachmann speaking for the TEA Party stated: "For two years President Obama made promises just like the ones we heard him make tonight. Yet we still have high unemployment (9.0%) devalued housing prices and the cost of gasoline is sky-rocketing."(As of October 2012 the unemployment rate is 7.8%, though there are less looking for work and the labor force has changed. 2 The price of commercial property is starting to rise. 3 Gas prices had been down but now are up again.)

Senator Mitch McConnell being the statesman he is stated: "I like the fact that he wants to do something about spending, however freezing government spending for five years at the increased levels of the last two years is really not enough. We need to reduce domestic spending substantially, and I hope the President will work with us to achieve that."(Note the maneuvering along with the praise with the door left ajar.)"He added: "It sounds to me like the President changed his tone and the rhetoric from the first two years, and I think that's an appropriate adjustment in the wake of last year's election when the American people said basically they want to go a different direction."

Representative Paul Ryan continued with is conjecture: "We are at a moment where if government growth is left unchecked and unchallenged Americas best century will be considered our last century. The last two years Obama's stimulus program cost too much and did nothing to reduce unemployment."(That is not entirely true for new public and private sector jobs were created. The only thing is that it took federal funds to create those jobs and that money came from treasury and Fed policies. That is what they do. They juggle Public Debt bonds and treasury notes to expand or slow the economy. That is part of the process of creative destruction.)Ryan did offer a plan of his own(A Road –map for America's Future. He has faced resistance from his own party on this plan. To date in 2012 Candidate Romney has not endorsed it.

### 576. HOW DO THINGS STACK UP
January 27, 2011

In the 2008 election the margin of victory in the end was 14 points over John McCain but this time around it seems we are on another planet. To date there is 4 points separating the then perceived nominee Governor Mitt Romney. Remember Romney at this point in time is having to ideologically look to the right for that is the current base of the Republican Party. The moderates seem to be out of it. So what will happen when Romney shifts to the center and he will for he is a centrist.

The critical states at this time were: Virginia, North Carolina, Ohio and Wisconsin. An analyst stated: "No matter how you slice the data Wisconsin is going to end up being one of those critical Mid Western swing states in 2012. If two years from now Obama is in danger of losing Wisconsin then he has horrible problems throughout the Mid west. The federal Deficit at this time rose to 1.5 Trillion from 1.4 Trillion. The Fed projected that the unemployment rate would drop to 8.2% by 2012. As it turned out it exceeded that by November of that year. That put the republicans in adjustment mode.

President Obama at this time stated: "We need to win the future. We've got to be more productive, more capable, more skilled than any workers on earth."President Obama is a sports fanatic and he played up that angle. He touted the Green bay packers over his team the Chicago Bears. You always use culture and the touch of the common man to make points with the public.

In the midst of this public euphoria is a ground swing to the side of the G O P. At the core of this swing is the concern that his Stimulus combined with his Affordable Health Care law will bankrupt the nation. The Obama plan is one based on the assumption of gradual continuous growth, which was the same hope George W. bush had prior to the 9/11 incident. Now for the year 2012 there is job creation in a flattening curve that will plateau.

### 577. SMALL BUSINESS
February 23, 2011

The President concentrated on Cleveland in his switch in emphasis from the corporate interests to the small business interests. His admission that 2 out of 3 jobs are created by small business. So this becomes a fact check. When he saved General Motors and he did he was preserving capital interests that are still down over saving those jobs that were preserved.

The President stated: "When it comes to our economy it is small business that packs the biggest punch. Small business creates two out of every three new jobs. Swe.re here again to seek your council, to talk how America can help you succeed. There is an inherent conflict of interest in all of this in Ohio just next door there was legislation afoot to limit the Power of Unions in collective bargaining and a demonstration had been slated for that Tuesday.

The outside world was also knocking in all of this for the events in Libya and Syria concerning what some called the emerging Arab Spring. Pressure to become involved due to the massive slaughter of civilians to maintain, power. By the way in 2012 top Assad advisors have defected including his propaganda minister. We have taken some limited action and turkey has become involved and NATO say it will back Turkey. We are still basically out of it. In Libya was a case where we let others lead. Kaddafi was later killed but the newly formed government would having trouble controlling the country. There are radical elements that reflect the fundamental elements of Islam that seem to be in control in some section like Benghazi. This is tugging on our domestic economy even as we exit the Iraq Afghanistan war situation. We know how that war tore down our economy. There are two terms that could describe this situation Fratricide which is one that murders his mother sister or countrymen. Or Genocide deliberate destruction of a racial group that could be your own to maintain power. Something new is forming down in that region and we should tread cautiously. A new empire could be rising.

Meanwhile back home business interests are reacting. John Grabner founder of Cardinal Fastener and Specialty Company location Bedford Heights stated: "He's doing the right thing by talking to us. The fact that he's talking to the business community tells me he's focused on the right things."Treasury Secretary Guithner and four cabinet level officers were present so high level direction. Physical notes as to the exact nature of the problem were noted. To reflect on the Romney campaign which has implied that The Obama solution is not a hands on operation is sort of blown away by this. If actual progress proves to be elusive this is just show.

Jen Psaki who is the spokes woman for Obama stated: "The President wants to hear from businesses that are doing things well. These are the kinds of things he might not hear in the bubble."This obviously refers to the White House Circle.

### 578. LIBYA AND U.S. PRESSURE
March 12, 2011

The slow as you go was the U.S. policy. There was backing for a no fly zone. Russia and China felt it was exploitation of the country. NATO was the military engine forcing Kadafi to resign which he was refusing to do. His troops were slaughtering Civilians and in a real sense creating the Free Libyan Army by their atrocities. The Obama Administration stated: "When it comes to military action, whether it's a no fly zone or other actions you've got to balance the costs verses the benefits."The President of the European Union Jose Manuel Barrusso stated: "The problem has a name Kadafi and he must go. Time is running out, we have to intensify our international pressure on the current regime to step down."

France was taking steps as the first nation to recognize the forming Libyan resistance as the legitimate government of Libya. This would pave the way for action on the part of NATO. What is behind this action was the total lack of action on the part of the world when Ahmadinajad illegally retained power slaughtering his own people and the world did nothing. This was also on the Presidents watch and the reason for Republican criticism. That is why President Obama was moving cautiously to military action.

The French President Nicolas Sarcozy was viewed as to far advanced in policy in recognizing the opposition by his European counter parts. The carrot and the stick was being applied, more sanctions with a caveat that reform brings goodies.

### 579. ACCOUNTABLE CARE ORGANISATIONS
April 1, 2011

One mechanism for managing the cost of care which the Obama Administrations says is not the same as H M Os would divide people into groups, the figure of 5,000 was mentioned. Primary Care Physicians would take responsibility with-in each group. The goal is to help patients stay healthier and therefore reduce costs. Health and Human Resources Secretary Kathleen Sebelius stated: "We've known for a long time that too many Americans fail to get the best care. It doesn't have to be this way.

Just how many of the older generation are out there. The figure stands at 45 million. It is their hope that at least 1.4 million of that figure will sign up by the year 2014. That it is said would generate 500 million in savings.

The big fear is that such a set-up would give a natural advantage to the larger data based organizations that would end up limiting the care available. This would be along the lines of the British system. In a way President Obama seems to be following the European examples and directions. The negative for Doctors is the risk of losing their money. This could well keep doctors from being a part of this. Vice President Chet Speed(American Medical Group Association) stated: "That is going to be a difficult pill to swallow for many providers."This system is in place in hospitals and has helped to lower costs on a local basis. It is the expansion of an idea.

In a way this is a corporate model, but the only hope is that there is not too much consolidation as occurred in the H M Os. That brings us back to the point that it could be a limiting factor in patient care. This brings to mind a question are we just repackaging the old H M Os. There is also the concern that medical hospitals and clinics won't give better services but administer more tests. To be successful there would have to be revenue sharing between this system and Medicare.

## 580. THE QUESTION OF LIBYA
### April 2, 2011

The President was launching his Latin American diplomatic initiative and at the same time crafting what would be his limited plan of action in Libya. He did not want to pull a G W Bush approach of massive propaganda and then an oval office call to war. It was in Brasilia that he held two news conferences. He stressed the targeting of government resources that were be used against the civilian population. He had not gotten to the point of assisting the Free Libyan Army. He also stressed the broad coalition under the NATO umbrella that was forming.

He did not want to follow the Bosnian approach that was followed by Clinton which was indeed genocide. His response was much more measured and limited. It would be the Libyan Army that defeated Kadafi not joint NATO forces.

These are Obama's words on the matter: "We wanted to make the point that this was not an Iraq like war engagement. The commitment was limited in duration and scope. And so the ways in which you deliver that message help convey it. It is not just what you say but how you say it."The president did not want to invent a new U.S. Doctrine. That is why we did not take the lead but left it to the NATO Commander.

Another concern was the Ivory Coast. There the president had refused to leave office and was using the military against the civilian population. President Obama emphasized a range of tools but it was stressed that among those tools was not the military option. The White House spokesman stated: "He's really attempting a blueprint for a new international way of dealing with humanitarian problems. Bush talked about promoting Democracy in the world, but Obama talked about it as a template as part of the selling job. He would be careful what kind of expectations he creates. Caution and prudence as opposed to braggadocio."We as a country are facing a new concept in this post Arab spring atmosphere where the youth of the world are looking at forging new institutions but they lack the knowledge on how to do it so they are subject to extremism.

## 581. OBAMA'S EDGE

As President Barak Obama for his first two years in his presidency has attempted to embrace the center while filling in the programs and economic designs of his administration. The republicans were feeling blindsided and were playing the part of the obstructionist or if you prefer the loyal opposition. Now that the election cycle is coming around again both the republican Romney and his opponent President Obama are ignoring the right and the left appealing to those central independent votes and party crossers.

Here is the analysis from Don Sipple who was the strategist for Bob Dole in 1996."From an ideological perspective it is a huge advantage to spend two years working on the middle of the electorate. While the President repositions... The Republicans are moving out of position as far as the task they'll face in the General Election."

Now on this talking point we see a conservative Romney softening his position on the Affordable Health Care law imperceptibly and the Obama Administration has not caught on yet. The conservative candidates are now standing in a field without a plow and a emerging Moderate Romney is just under the surface. Add to that the problem of Michigan, Pennsylvania, Wisconsin, and Iowa where the jobless rates are worrisome. His decision to keep Guantanamo open was a violation of a campaign pledge he made to the left and they are not happy about that.

David Axelrod the Presidents chief political advisor stated: "The notion that somehow he has shifted his thinking is belied by the things he said through –out the campaign. That's what he said then and that's what he believes now."

Sipple continued: "After the fiscal crisis the public was scolded for irresponsible spending and maxing out their cards., so they pulled in their belts and tried to reduce their debt. The watched as the government piled up more debt through prolific spending."

Matthew Dowd who ran President Bush's 2004 campaign stated: "Independents don't see Democrats as Socialists and Republicans as Corporate Ogres. They don't believe that principle trumps process. They get along with they're neighbors, have them over for dinner, sit around the table and while they May disagree they don't scream at each other. It isn't a Democratic or Republican idea. It's patriotism."It is just too bad that the defensive nature of the past has a habit of clouding the present and tainting the future.

Another part of that equation is high gas prices which are the result of the lack of gasoline refineries and the specks required by states like California. President Obama still looking at the economy and the affect of a specific thing on it does see the price of gas as part of the equation. President Obama stated: "It 's on the minds of a lot of people right now because you're paying more at the pump."People figure that the oil company's like B P, Shell oil, Chevron Standard are pocketing the difference. Please read my section on the oil industry for a fuller understanding.

Analysts have stated(Douglas Scheon): "The bottom line is unless prices go down it puts the President in mortal peril. Every American faces higher gas prices every day. So in a certain sense, it has the likelihood of being a more serious problem than the unemployment rate., because 9% are unemployed, but 100% of the American people have to deal with the impact directly and indirectly of rising fuel prices."As of this date gas prices were $3.59 a gallon. In October of 2012 the gas prices are 4.69 a gallon so things are worse especially in California.

## 582. THE DEFICIT
### April 12, 2011

There was a battle over raising the debt limit and the TEA Party was in favor of default as a means of making us face up to our problems. Our funding for our programs exceeds our ability to pay for them. We are also funding health care and education for the undocumented at a time when the economic reality does not match our expenses. The disadvantaged are being used in a co-optive way similar to what the Mexican government does to stay in power.

Despite what I just said there is the perceived argument of compromise with the republicans of the Bush tax cut being preserves as the price for raising the debt limit. It is argued that the debt limit is periodically raised relative to world debt verses domestic debt. This is so we can continue to buy from each other. In my opinion the bush tax cuts should have expired and were a mistake in the first place. Remember those tax cuts were a campaign promise that never should have been kept.

## 583. SB 1070

The 9th circuit court of Appeals upheld the injunction against the Arizona law after an appeal the Arizona's Governor Jan Brewer. The law was put on hold in July 29, 2010.. The U.S. Judge Susan Bolton is the presiding judge cited that the law potentially violates the Federal law enforcement of Immigration laws. The Obama Administration is after the Latin vote and Latin's as a block seem to be opposed to SB 1070 at least as the press puts it. I have heard quite a few sentiments from the Latin group leaning to the other side.

One of those objections is identity theft committed by the undocumented taking the identities and ruining the credit of those legally here. They're pissed. The other area is jobs and making life difficult for Americans of Mexican descent. So President Obama the issue is not all that black and white.

## 584. ENDING THE WAR IN IRAQ
### April 14, 2011

The target date of 2012 is the set date for ending US involvement on any kind of war footing.. The Government though elected is not in place and women's rights groups are expressing concern with the insurgency not defeated. Al Qaeda continues to prey on the minds of the Allies. Funding for the war effort has become an issue as it did in the Vietnam conflict. The Presidents own party 102 Senators and Representatives voted against the 59 billion funding bill for the Iraq Afghanistan War effort.

At the time President Obama entered the White House as our President there were 33,000 troops in Afghanistan. The President added to that level till as of September of 2010 there were 96,000 U.S. Troops in addition to our allies. Total troop commitment for both wars will see a decline in numbers from 177,000 to 146,000. The president stated: "If Afghanistan were to be engulfed by a wider insurgency, Al-Qaida and its affiliates would have even more space to plan their next attacks."Unfortunately in 2012 on the anniversary of the September 11 remembrance our Diplomatic Mission in Benghazi was attacked killing our Ambassador to that country. His death has become something of a political football as it relates to our foreign policy and readiness. The President continued: "Because in this region and beyond we will tolerate no safe haven for Al Qaida and their extremist allies."Unfortunately measured response has drawn criticism as being weak on foreign affairs. This is despite the killing on Osama Bin laden in Pakistan by our special forces.(May 2, 2011) The Pakistani government lodged a protest about violating their severity. I would call the Obama method a drone/black opts protocol system with a built in denial system. Where are you Mr. Phelps.

As for our oops shortcomings that is civilian death our figures are 535 the Iraqi figures are higher for July 2011. As for our goals a spokes man stated: "Iraqi's had hoped they would have a strong, independent government by now. But no-one expected it to drag on so song."So goes this snap shot of war.

## 585. AN UNPLANNED ROAD TRIP
### April 30, 2011

No matter how hard we try to put our lives together there is always that random factor. Whether it is talking to China's President Hu Jintao for nine times talking about trade and the value place on China's Currency. The affairs of the Arab spring on when and when not to be involved. This would include any other hot spot you could think of you need a experienced guiding hand. Donilon is Obama's Rasputin and he has as did Rasputin unlimited access to the President.

As National security Advisor knows his president and his need to create a process in a chaotic situation. President Obama is not so much about helping emerging movements as in Syria, Libya, Iran, Egypt as he is about balancing the interests of the U.S. in the region and keeping a balanced relationship with Israel. Where there is chaos he needs a process. Obama contrasts with Bush in that his vision is global while G W tended to concentrate on Iraq, Afghanistan and Iran's/ North Koreas nuclear proliferation issue. Donilon stated: "At the core of our foreign policy has been about restoring American prestige authority and power and influence in the world. We went through a significant period of diminution of American power and authority. And prestige in the world for lots of different reasons. There was a high cost to that war in Iraq to American capital. We spent a lot of capital on that. We spent a lot of policy band-width on that, understandably to the detriment of other problems we have in the world."

His back-ground originates in Rhode Island and helped to organize the Carter Campaign. For complete information check the *L.A. Times* article (ORDERLY PRO-

### 586. ON BIN LADEN
#### May 2, 2011

We had been searching for the elusive figure for ten years. The country of Pakistan was seen as a country of divided loyalties and sympathies. To some in the Pakistani tribal areas Bin laden was a folk hero fighting imperialism. The Pakistani government would take out aid, repackage it and give or sell it to the people because America was so hated. Our aid package to their military was and is significant. We have propped up their government. Abottabad was their equivalent of West Point. Where Bin Laden was hiding was a rented fortress that had been fortified. It was a Pakistani Doctor that helped us by a faked vaccination drive against Polio. Bin Laden's family DNA were obtained and the black box operation was carried out. We lost a helicopter in the process which the Pakistani government seized. They called the attack on the Bin laden compound an attack on Pakistani sovereignty and threatened to break off relations with us. We use Pakistan to supply our troops in Afghanistan and pay a fee per load for such shipments. The fees were hiked. The doctor was charged with treason for aiding the U.S.. We did get Bin laden and buried him at sea over the protest of all those involved. President Obama did act decisively but this tale is a reminder that even our friends are not necessarily our friends.

### 587. THE JOINT CHEIFS OF STAFF
#### May 29, 2011

Tasks shift and so do purposes but in the end the results are the same. The subject is the winding down of the of the Afghanistan conflict. Army general Martin Dempsy was under consideration to round out the Pentagon team. The outgoing head of the team Admiral Michael G Mullen. He was to quietly retire and it was deemed that no announcement was to be made. The previous month Leon Panetta was to be named head of the CIA was to make the move to the Defense Department replacing Robert M. Gates. General David H. Petraeus will become the new head of the CIA. Petraeus was head of the forces in Afghanistan in 2003 under G W Bush.

It seems to me that this mix of old and new talent, borrowing from both Clinton and Bush is a realization that the leaders of the past did not make all bad decisions or their surrogates would not be appointed for this new transition period.

### 588. THE SECOND EUROPEAN TOUR

At this time the president was in Europe. On his first trip he was official and there was strain in the Middle East. The trip lacked humor and was cordial. This time around he has paid his dues. He and David Cameron the British Prime minister were playing a doubles table tennis match against some teen age students and were on the losing end. The piece was aired with all good will.

The success of a President abroad has not proven as insulation against domestic criticism and no guaranty that you will survive. Just look at Nixon after his 1972 victory over McGovern and his opening of our relations with China. The storm clouds still gathered and he did pass into history.

Stephen Flanigan who holds the title of European Specialist and Senior Vice President of the Center for Strategic and International Studies, stated: "He's not the Junior person anymore. He has gained a lot of credibility for things he has done and for his general message about how he wants to engage the rest of the world."This was in reference to his balancing act between the Israeli's and the Palestinians. At issue the pressure for recognition at the U N of that Palestinian state.

Nile Guardner former advisor to Margaret Thatcher stated: "He received a particularly warm welcome in London despite a track record that has been viewed as anti-British by the U K Press and some politicians. However I think his tour will have limited impact domestically."The truth hurts and the gentleman was right for at home the House was fighting the Senate each disregarding the other. Cooperation or crossing the isle had become a dirty word. This was true nationally, just look at the governor's race in California where Steve Poizner was denied his party's nomination because he helped craft a compromise on the budget.

You can look at our Russian Relations and see a warming up. The talk of a new Strategic Arms Reduction treaty was forming. Russia's President Dmetry Medvedev were talking and laughing about people in their profession. Russia has and continues to support its business affiliations. It was stated: "The reason they can talk about the issues they're talking about now is because of the amount of time they've invested in that personal relationship."Between the U.S. and Russia there are 20 groups that were working on the problem. In the end we did get a new treaty.

### 589. NATIONAL SECURITY
#### May 31, 2011

Being Memorial Day we honor our dead and those that have served. This is also a day of change Army General Martin Dempsy became Secretary of defense. His selection came as a result of his two tours in Iraq and the planned drawdown of Afghanistan. The President joked that his appointment might well be the shortest appointment in history. The President stated: "We have much to do. Army general Martin E Dempsy is one of the nation's most respected combat tested veterans. He and the defense Department would oversee some difficult budget choices, while also keeping our military the finest in the world."

Army general Ray T. Odierno also a Iraq War Veteran became the new head of the Chairman of the joint chiefs of Staff. Odierno was an artillery officer who commanded the 4th infantry division. He handled the insurgency in Tecrit.

The President in closing comments stated: "The men and women of our Armed forces are the best in the nation has to offer. They deserve nothing but the absolute best in return and that includes leaders who will guide them and support their families with wisdom and strength and compassion."These are the duties of a President. This one has met his challenge, but the future is not assured.

## 590. THE ORWELLIAN HEALTH PLAN
June 3,2011

I do not believe we are ignorant of the directions we take. In writing this book I became less physical myself. The Government looks at us and the expanding waistlines and figures there ought to be guide lines and fees /taxes are attached to soda's. I prefer black coffee but I speak for others. The Center for Disease Control should be about controlling harmful products like the steroid medicine that caused fungal Meningitis in October 2012. Not regulating the fat content in hamburgers that everybody loves. They say they want us to live longer more productive lives, but should we succeed in this it would amount to deferred costs and a whole different set of circumstances. We all die of something Parkinson's, Alzheimer's would be ha horrible humiliating death, and that comes with age and it is expensive. It makes a heart attack look good.

The sum of 100 million dollars has been budgeted to help alter our habits, and a lot has been put to advertizing. Money in terms of Grants to support evidence based strategies working towards the elimination of deserts for example. Have an apple forget the ice-cream.: "will empower communities with resources, information and flexibility, to help make their residents healthier. This is the brain-child of the head of Health and Human Services Kathleen Sebelius.

It is argued that these are worthy goals in doubtful times of belt tightening. The program itself is called.(Communities Putting Prevention to Work) CPPW brought to a television set near you. It is argued that what-ever this social engineering is called it is still a federal welfare program whether fostering a community garden in Pima County or a program supporting healthier foods in Philadelphia. In fact in some cases evidence shows that projects don't work or in other cases that the program is affective. It is just another case of big brother with delayed alternate results.

## 591. THE ROUGH ROAD
June 4, 2011

The concept of a bail out first tried by George W. Bush and later by President Barak Obama is developing on a sliding scale adrift in a sea of turbulent political waters. When Chrysler was bailed out in 2009 it led to the political storm of 2010 and the Republican capture of the House of Representatives.

In 2011 what was once a negative became a positive and a selling point for the

2012 campaign. Loose language on the part of Governor Romney on the fact that Chrysler should have gone into bankruptcy and they actually technically did caused an uproar in the country ignited by Obama as to state Romney did not care about jobs and was willfully shipping jobs abroad. That was not true because for 8 years Romney's assets have been in a blind trust, as have President Obama's with investments in China. That is just part of this political reality.

The concept of the Bail-out of the big corporations among them Chrysler have paid back a majority of their loans only wing a small part of the balance all the while collecting dividends as shareholders. In a way it has been a good deal for the American public.

June 7, 2011

The Chrysler issue aside there is another argument that does have some merit. Remember the Stimulus money was borrowed money that increased our National debt. Even putting that aside the unemployment rate was 9.5% and as of June it was 9.1%. This displacement figure was well above the 8% cap that had been placed on the stimulus package. There was a White House memo that was composed by Economic advisors: Jared Bernstein, and Christina Romer in January 2009 that stated: even if the Stimulus package had not passed the unemployment rate would have been 8.8% in the last quarter of 2010. Again aside from bailing out the corporate interests what was the initial importance of the stimulus.

It is argued that since the stimulus deal we have gotten vital investment. Since this speech another 2.8 trillion in borrowed money has entered the public sector. In return we have acquired 3.7 trillion in debt.

President Obama has made his stand. After the loss of 2.8 million jobs and a debt increase if 3.7 Trillion. The President acts like he has it handled and the republicans don't have a clue. He promises services and needs but we don't have the sustained capacity for the programs we are looking at. If you don't have the money for the candy bar you don't get it. The President stated: "I will not sacrifice the core investments. We need to grow and create jobs. Mark Halpren President of MSNBC was asked about the political impact of the bad economy and he gave full assurance that President Obama was as he put it (Fully engaged) in job creation."The republicans though have the onus to come forward with some ideas. The President ideas are still up in the air."

The jobs that were created were basically food service jobs fully half of them and they came into existence because they got a waiver from the presidents Affordable health care law. Those 250,000 to 500,000 new jobs turned out to be a illusion.

June 14, 2011

The President is using the bully-pulpit to drive home his message."I want the pocket protector to be the new sex appeal." He was speaking at a company called Cree INC that builds LED lights. He always projects at how bad it could have been. The President continued: "I will not be satisfied that everyone who wants a job that offers some security has a good job that offers security. In economic theory employers offer less than the minimum wage in hopes of controlling cost leaving the upgrade to the next employer. That's just how it works He continued: "I will not be satisfied till empty store fronts in town are open for business again."Here is the quandary often the reason business store fronts are vacant is not for want of clients but the red tape, lag time and intransigence of hidden interests as in Ontario California's uptown area and the Granada Theater/ Emmons building in specific. This is a historic purposely neglected structure they would love to destroy. More on this example later. He continued: "I will not be satisfied until working families feel like they're moving forward again that they're progressing again."This is a periodic thing and we all have stages and episodes in our lives. The trouble with this new post Y2K economy is that the continuous employment concept is a thing of the past and employer demands will increase the burn-out potential of the new work-force through the multitasking demand being put on labor for the sake of the bottom line. It is important to note that people will fill this niche.

On the Republican side which is not that much better Representative John Boehner of Ohio stated: "Each of these events is a fresh reminder of the Presidents failure to deliver job creation he promised. Photo-ops with business leaders only reinforce that no —one in his administration has ideas to create private sector jobs our economy desperately needs."Not exactly true President Obama initiated a jobs bill but it was rejected by the House without amendment. I would say the President would not be entirely incorrect in labeling the Republicans Obstructionists.

### 592. MORE ON THE LATIN VOTE
June 15, 2011

Puerto Ricans are spread widely across the United States New York to Florida to the District of Columbia. In addition there are 4.6 million people in Puerto Rico who vote in the general election but not the Primary. President Obama in an effort to solidify the Latin vote at the expense of Romney made a stop in this American territory. The only other time a sitting president has visited was JFK. Their unemployment rate on the island is 16%.He met with the Governor Luis G. Fortuno. They talked about the economy and how it had been lagging behind the main-land.

Here are the key population areas where Puerto Rico's citizens have settled in the continental United States. New York: 1,192,000, Orlando: 248,000, Philadelphia: 210,000, Chicago: 177,000, Tampa/Saint Petersburg: 145,000, Boston: 104,000, Miami: 96,000, Fort Lauderdale Florida: 76,000, Washington DC: 55,000, Los Angeles: 48,000.

This group along with the Cuban, Mexican, Brazilian, Columbian, Venezuelan, Chilean, and other groups offer Barak quite a challenge to meet their needs.

## 593. THE DRAW-DOWN

Inside the Obama Administration they were debating the effectiveness of the Surge and the withdrawal of those troops. The arguments were drifting to the use of Drones a weapon we have used where no ground troops are present. Then the argument goes to the need for boots on the ground. The economic impact was found to be little and would be a savings of only a small portion of the 107 billion dollar cost of the war. Arguments over the Haqqani Network and the Taliban would unite with Al Qaida and undo all our efforts. It was countered that if we pulled out all our surge troops there would still be 70,000 troops from the U.S. in Afghanistan.

I now pose a question. If after all this time our policy has had so little affect on the general culture despite the organization of government and townships we have promoted how long do you think they would last when we officially end our military involvement as we have in Iraq which seems to be a success story. This is just one of those questions we have to think about along with our own financial existence.

## 594. CAMPAIGN MONEY
### June 25, 2011

We have just got through looking at the meat and potatoes of this administration and now we are going to take a peek at the cost and fund raising aspects of this election.

The program is called Presidential Partners and is asking wealthy donors to pledge $75,800 to the campaign. This buys you access to those running the campaign or at least their secretary. This opportunity is brought to you by the Democratic National Committee. Individual small donors can contribute up to $5,000. This group has made up about half of the contributions amounting to 745 million dollars that were raised in 2008.

At the lower upper end of the fund raising issue is the $35,800 a plate dinner rubber chicken of course. This applies to both parties. There is one difference and it is a big one the DNC seems to be doing better at getting the larger donations RNC. The DNC raised 11 million with donors contributing in excess of $30,000 compared to 3 million in that category from the efforts of the RNC. Over all the Democrats are doing better at this stage of the game but as issues clarify themselves and Romney moves more openly to the center you will see a shift in donations.

## 595. THE INOVATOR
### June 29, 2011

The idea of using federal funds to stimulate manufacturing is being used by the Obama Administration to the tune of 2 billion dollars. My guess is he will use the Federal Reserve to promote some derivative slash bond or tax break to light a fire under those manufacturers. But there must be a demand for the item and not the creation of a new Bacon Stretcher.

The President stated: "Right now there are people all across America with talent waiting to be tapped. Those people are sparks waiting to be lit and our job is to light them. The irony of the American economy is that a lot of people are looking for work, while many companies are looking for skilled workers. There's a mismatch that we can close."I think he is talking about retraining programs, but those programs will probably not benefit those over fifty unless there is a tax incentive to do so. If he satisfies the youth base, he will basically satisfy the concept of economic growth and job creation but not touch the problem of the long term unemployed who have fallen through the cracks. The economy is slowing and there at this time is a fear of a double dip recession. A figure of 60% now blame President Obama for the economy. The reality is that the econometric models are not working or falling short of their targets. Education seems to be the key to his program but will this education saddle the learner with more debt and no prospects.

The National Republican Committee Chairman Reince Priebus stated: "It's pretty clear what's happening. We know that unemployment s at a level that's staggering. We know that the debt and the deficit are going to crush future generations, and it's a message that average Americans understand is an unacceptable record that the President has accumulated on his watch."Again I remind the reader that Obama is not completely to blame for job creating legislation has been blocked in the past and this won't be the last time.

There are those who support raising the debt ceiling but only with deduced spending and unfortunately those infamous Bush Tax cuts. Representative Ben Quail of Arizona who came in on the TEA Party coat tails stated: "My top priority is reducing the size and scope of government. Those of us who are new to the Congress believe that's what we're doing here. That's what the 2010 election was all about."He stated flatly "I do not want to have a default."He did in fact say he would vote for a raising of the debt ceiling.

He reflected to an earlier era under President George H. W. Bush: "I'm reminded of 1991 when President George H. W. Bush agreed to a tax increase. The spending decreases never materialized."Dan Quail lobbied against the Tax increases. I see another dynasty in the works.

As of July 24, 2011 no compromise had been reached with Representative Boehner the Majority whip of the House on the needed economic reform and the raising of the debt limit. The Democrats were not happy either for they felt too many compromises had been made especially on the Bush Tax cut. At stake was Social Security Medicare and Medicaid. Matthew Dowd was also in attendance and had a conference with President Obama but would not release details. The bottom line was that there was little cooperation with the Republicans.

On August 3, 2011 a compromise was reached, but the cost was high. The Bush era tax cuts remained and cuts were made in the democrats' favorite programs. A panel was formed to potentially administer automatic across the board cuts should no agreement be reached through sequestration of funds and that time is drawing near in the year 2012. At least 2 trillion is to be cut from the budget at that time on an arbitrary basis.

On August 10 in the *L.A. Times* an editorial surmised the dilemma by pointing out we would not want the cure for it would be similar to Greece or Spain and the Euro Crisis and we aren't far off from that. Would we indeed elect a leader that would make us give up our goodies to save the nation, I think not. That money would be diverted, to stimulating industry and that would be National Socialism or Private industry could step up but they would do so only if they had a niche in the market. The banks would not step in unless they made a substantial profit for that is what banks do. We could even revert back to a form of mercantilism. Canada with its strong growing economy could absorb ours. The other options at least for now appear to be pure science fiction.

### 596. THE PENTAGON FACTOR
#### August 4, 2011

When sequestration hits a major target would be the military Defense Secretary Leon Panetta and a host of other senior officials suggested that the potential cutting of up to 400 billion from the defense Budget would be potentially disastrous. It would be better to raise taxes than touch that part of the budget. The idea of cutting a half trillion from the budget would be absolutely inappropriate according to the Defense Department. Amending proposed cuts in a bill with bipartisan backing it is argued would be difficult. There would be a natural down-sizing of the Armed Forces with the ending of the Iraq war and the proposed ending of the Afghan war in 2014. Panetta stated: "Properly done we will end up with a Defense department budget that is a trillion dollars down and still be a very capable force."

One little thing interferes with this logic. That is Turkey's request for assistance in the emerging Syrian conflict and the potential for violence in, Lebanon that just had a car bombing in the Coptic Christian section. The non-interference directive from the Obama Administration as it relates to the spreading violence in the region as a whole could change with the landscape. The Iraq and Afghanistan Wars though initially boost to the economy became a drag on it as did Vietnam before it. The bad thing was this one was done on a credit card. We can't engage in another conflict even one similar to the Libyan conflict because the fragile nature of our economy. We can play spoiler and sell weapons like Russia does but to be involved with boots on the ground would be a big mistake. Currently our cuts slated for next spring would be $50 billion to $60 billion in the base defense budget.

Now let's drift to 2012 and the election. Bearing in mind that Romney has accused Obama of cutting the defense Budget at the expense of national security and the pre-eminence of our military placement and active response to say the attack that occurred at the Benghazi U.S. Embassy where our Ambassador was killed along with three other Americans. Requests for additional security went unheeded because of the channel of requests for additional security. In this downsizing game how would that work?

August 4, 2011

The first step in this little argument goes to the use of credit and I would say even debit cards over cash. The fee charged in both credit and debit purchases add to the total cost in terms of hidden fees and add to the general cost of a product, be it a car or a stick of gum. The water level rises with uniformity because it is simpler to do it that way. If you pay cash you are paying a higher price as a simple matter of book keeping. It also makes you spend more because you are not physically handing over money. If there was a duel price structure as I have seen in some gas stations one for cash and one for credit card/Debit cards which in some instances are treated the same as cash with a dollar charge and merchant charge in some cases.

As the economy rebounds and it is, though it is starting at a special rate selectively defined, will the belt tightening on credit card use put us back in the whole or will it be part of an improving economy?

The clarity of our direction is the other part of the argument. While arguing over the deficit and what cuts to make in spending such as social welfare costs or general costs the President has let others take the lead to his detriment. Compromising with the republicans to secure a raising of the debt limit which is done periodically has cost him in the issue of clarity and substance. The Republicans have on the other hand brought too much of it to the table. When Speaker Boehner walked away from the negotiating table it temporarily put Obama in a quandary. Again the survival of the bush tax cuts hurt him with the liberals and centrists. The real deal makers were Vice President Joe Biden and harry Reed. The President was pretty much out of the picture according, to the article Obama's Clarity Gap(A15).

## 597. OUR CREDIT PROBLEM

Part of the problem of a consumer based society is, that it is dependent on deficit spending. This would be true if you were buying a house, purchasing a car or buying clothes at May Company with a credit card, some of which have guaranteed cash back. It is usually one dollar per hundred spent and that is no bargain. It also leads to higher prices because fees are passed on to the consumer. Add to that accumulated debt sometimes packaged as a derivative sold as a bond or hedge fund by those same credit corporations purchased by banks and resold as risk debt. The reason, high profitability on repayment to the bank, that does not exist with the average mortgage.

This illusory money has now become real and must be repaid. Foreign country's buy this debt in good faith from our institutions(banks) The same applies to mortgages and bad debt in general. This is called the loose money policy and the fed applies the brakes or stimulates activity to what it sees is the ultimate good. Do you see how things are connected and as other country's rise in their spending no matter what the product creating potential jobs and demand. Depending on where the economy is in its cycle, stocks, bonds, derivatives, treasury notes, circulate through the air at whatever price and people are laid off or hired. Now do you see how the events of 9/11 and the recessions that followed would have the affects that they had. Now think on who would be the best person to lead this country for the next four years.

The argument that education I of our citizens to make them employable in today's economy is a targeted crap shoot that will help only those in the niche leaving older workers discarded for various reasons and along with them the debt they have accumulated as part of this society.

Rick Perry attacked the direction the Obama administration had taken the nation when he said: "We know what the problem is. We're being over taxed and over regulated and over litigated"

President Obama stomping through the same but different political atmosphere stated: "It is going to be driven by folks here in Iowa. It's going to begin in the classrooms of community colleges like this one. It's going to start on their ranch lands and farms of the mid-west, the work-shops of basement inventor and store-fronts of small business owners."We can only see which rhetoric is superior to rural America.

## 598. ENOUGH NOT ENOUGH
### August 18, 2011

President Obama was in Illinois addressing the farming communities. In this case the citizens numbered 671. He stated: "We can't afford to do one or the other. We've got to do both. He was referring to the duel track of stimulating the economy and raising taxes on the upper end of society.

While we were in the middle of the debt ceiling argument in Congress members of his own party don't like his seeming compromise with the republican on the bush tax cuts. The president continued: "When Congress get back in September my basic argument to them is this: getting our fiscal house in order and jobs and growth."

Eric Cantor House majority leader, who I is republican representing Virginia stated: "We must put an end to the policy of uncertainty constantly being driven by this administration."Do you see the battle between econometric and social national models. He continued: "That means stopping discussions of new stimulus spending with money we simply don't have."In the pike there are proposals that go to payroll tax cuts and three free trade bills. The bottom line seems to be that there is no appetite for heavy federal spending but incentives should be applied to boost the economy. That to me means action by the Fed.

While traveling through Iowa in farm country where cows graze by solar panels a woman by the name of Emily asked President Obama: "So when you ran for office you built a tremendous amount of trust with the American people that you seemed like someone who wouldn't move the bar on us. And it seemed especially last year as if your negotiating tactics have sort of cut away that trust by compromising some key principles that we believed in, like repealing the tax cut, not fighting harder for single payer. Even Social security and Medicare seemed on the line when we were dealing with the debt ceiling. So I'm just curious moving forward what prevents you from taking a harder negotiating stance being that the republicans are taking a really hard stance.?"

The Presidents reply was this: "Now I know that people would like to say well just do something to get these guys under control. You don't want to reward unreasonableness. Look I get that but sometimes you've got to make choices in order to do the best for the country at that particular moment." He again reiterated to Emily's question: "A very specific plan to boost the economy, to create jobs and control the economy."

To this question I must go back to President Carter who tried to boost employment and control the deficit by conservation of resources and limiting of expectations through controlled econometric models of his day. There were too many variables for him to control and he went through five economic plans. Job creation does not necessarily equal reduction in the national debt. At time the principles are at odds with each other. So President Obama as you go forward with your ideas, don't pull a Carter.

## 599. August 19, 2011

There is a time to take a break even if you're the president and will be criticized for it. The first thing you have to do is conduct surface foreign policy. In this case President Obama called this day for President Assad to step down from his presidency. You must look at a stock market plunge and a global recession, not to mention restless voters demanding jobs. Having faced that down in your mind you can now retreat to Martha's Vineyard. For your Presidential vacation.

White House Spokesman Josh Earnest stated: "I don't think the American people begrudge the president spending a little time with his wife and daughters at the end of the summer before his daughters head back to school."

## 600. ENTERING THE RING

The President was in compromise mode in part out of a promise to work with the republicans across the aisle. The Republicans were in a way in no mood to compromise because the President had taken their ideas and gave them a twist. This is what made the word compromise a bad word.

Now that the election cycle is now upon us again the Presidential image has to give way to the old image of the campaigner who wants to be President, but in this case since Obama is the incumbent he can manipulate policy and therefore insure his re-election. This doubles with the old fashioned whistle stop.

On the republican side you at this time have many combatants though they be a dark horse candidate. As I have said in the end Romney did triumph but there was always that there must be an alternative to Mitt. You see though the right took over the party they can't control the center and any winning candidate must be able to move to the center. There were just three men in that category Romney, Johnson and Gingrich. The others were just too far to the right to make the adjustment. Having a purely conservative Republican Party could cause its extinction.

So it was that the old Obama would eventually meet the old Mitt Romney and the rightist that was necessary in the primary contests. Again this would be called flip-flopping in some circles. Should Obama win the ballgame stays basically the same, but should Mitt Romney win we potentially have an Eisenhower administration.

Since business is the main thrust of this election, those, thing that make it easier for business to run would be central to the point. These would be consolidating IRS paper work, simplifying hazard warnings, Expediting payment to government contractors. These actions were taken by the Obama administration. This is the power of the presidency to initiate reforms to steal your opponents thunder. The outsider is left with theory and promise based on past performance.

## 601. KATRINA: THE EFFECT
### August 29, 2011

Katrina devastated the East Coast and set the model for future federal response. Six years earlier when Katrina hit in the Bush Administration the local people dropped the ball and Washington did not act in a timely manner. When Irene hit it was Obama's opportunity to show the country especially the eastern sea-board that Federal assistance was indeed meaningful.

Brad Davidson who represented the business community and a self described libertarian stated: "The trend in our country is to call on the Feds or state foe any problem. But for most of the life of this country we have been rugged individualists relying on our wits in time of crisis."Note he did not say those affected were left on their own but he did not give credit to the federal response that was indeed massive.

Irene hit which hit in new jersey area caused massive flooding and 22 deaths. Insurance wise the losses were 1.5 billion to 3 billion. This was better than Katrina which was 50 billion. In a very real way the bush administration was not prepared for such a massive storm and Obama was lucky. In the Oakland quake damage in terms of uninsured losses 5 to 7 Billion. The Northridge Earthquake in 1994 cost 40 to 50 billion. Katrina cost 70 billion.

Mark Sandi the chief economist at the research firm Moody's Analytics stated: "We haven't gotten all the data yet on Irene, but I think the damage is much less severe than had been feared and the economic impact will therefore, be a lot smaller than people predicted."

Now President Obama got defensive during this time of crisis and blamed the lack of economic growth on a number of seemingly unrelated factors. Those situations were: The European debt Crisis, The Japanese Earth-quake and Tsunami, and Irene that caused him to cut his vacation short to deal with what was potentially considered similar to Katrina.

### 602. A TIME FOR ACTION
### August 30, 2011

There is a general shift in the economic team at the White House. Austin Goolsbee was exiting the Obama Team along with Treasury secretary Laurence H. Summers, Christina D. Romer and Fed Chairman Paul A. Volker who was replaced Bernecky. The newest appointment was Alan Krueger as chairman of the council of economic advisors. He has his roots in the treasury department and is expected to be swiftly appointed. His expertise is tax incentives that encourage employment. His efforts in the past sparked a rise in auto sales and building projects. He is considered to be part of a new emerging super economic team. The problem is that with current Congressional agreements there is very little wiggle room.

Krueger is an advocate of raising the minimum wage and contents it does not impact the bottom line that causes the rise in prices. The plan being put together would provide: job training, tax credits for employers who hire workers, and investment in the infrastructure as a jobs stimulus. The Romney camp contends it is the private sector that creates jobs not the federal government. The solution on the republican side stresses the lowering of corporate and small business taxes to encourage production and the hiring of employees in this country. Along with this the closing of loopholes that allow hiding profits in foreign accounts to avoid taxation. This is also favored by the Obama Administration. You see the two are not exactly that far apart.

### 603. September 1, 2011

There was one of those rare meetings of the mind When Representative John Boehner House majority leader met with President Obama over the presidents scheduling of a rare joint meeting of the Congress so as it would not conflict with a scheduled Republican Presidential Primary debate on Wednesday the seventh. The President and the Speaker concurred and the President moved the joint session to the eighth.

### 604. September 8, 2011

In his address to a Joint Session of Congress the President outlined his 245 Billion jobs stimulus program. In it was a mix of tax cuts, construction projects and unemployment relief. The President stated: "Every proposal I've laid out tonight will be paid for and every proposal is designed to meet the urgent needs of our people and our communities. You should pass this jobs plan right away."There was an internal debate on just how big to make the plan designed by Mark Zandi. It was argued that adoption of this program would add 2 million jobs in the year 2012. Zandi stated: "It's a bold effort to provide more support to the economy, certainly bigger than widely anticipated."The promise was made that the Bill would not increase the Federal deficit and a plan with all the details would be released on September 19th 2011. The president spoke of a Grand Bargain that would reduce the deficit over the long term according to the *L.A. Times*. There would be some raising of taxes and trimming the costs of Medicare, Medicaid and other programs that have a history of Democratic support. It was hinted that there might be what was referred to as sticker shock on the part of the Republicans in the Congress.

    The Republican response was tempered largely because of the presidents attempt in their eyes to have them labeled obstructionists. In truth Boehner himself stated that this president would be a one term President. Judge for yourself based on what I have described previously.

    Boihner stated that some of his ideas merited consideration. Renewal of the Payroll Tax cut could be part and parcel to the solution. That tax cut was the largest element of the plan. It would be expanded to 3.1 percentage points and be extended for the following year. It would amount to a $1,500 tax cut for the average American family.

    On the business side firms with 5 million or less in revenue would get the equivalent of a holiday on that tax obligation. That would be giving a break to half the businesses in this country. $140 billion would go directly to providing jobs (Again it is the private sector that hires and they do so on their own needs to projected sales.) $35 billion would go to infrastructure. Those with underwater property were not addressed at this time and the Foreclosure rate rolls on. The success of this package that remains in limbo in 2012 May well have to wait for the decision of the voters.

    On the Democratic side there is a quote in the *L.A. Times* that goes like this: "The president will present a meaningful responsible set of ideas to create jobs and grow the economy. The Republican Congress will have to choice whether they're going to work with the President to achieve those goal or play politics. The President will go to the country(And he did) and explain who's stopping the progress and why." The conjecture goes like this: the Obama Administration in its infinite wisdom has to prove the steps proposed will in-deed create a better job market and attack the deficit that could kill us as a nation must convince the people it's the right thing to do. As of this date the unemployment rate was 9.1%. To the chagrin of the republicans by October of 2012 it had dropped to 7.8% but remember the economy had not really improved and only had marginal growth. The reason for the data was seasonal employment and other people had fallen off the unemployment rolls or stopped looking for work. The President put the blame on the education gap in this new economy that is technology driven at the expense of labor. I'm just waiting for Sky Net to appear.

### 605. THE FAA
### September 17, 2011

As of this time in 2011 the debt ceiling issue had not been resolved and the Federal Aviation Administration was about to see the end of its funding period. President Obama made a last minute emergency bill to fund the agency into the new year. 80,000 aviation and construction workers would have been affected.

Other agencies potentially under the gun the Highway Trust Fund were due to expire in April. FEMA that agency that handles our disasters asked for 6.9 Billion. The original request was for 1.9 Billion. The republicans wanted to offset the increase with reductions in other programs. As a consequence the agency is mired in a funding battle as of this date. This position flies in the face of tradition according to the democratic side. Offsets have never been a condition in funding this agency. House Minority Leader Nancy Pelosi stated: "House republicans are setting a dangerous precedent by requiring that disaster aid be offset especially when Americans are struggling to rebuild their homes, businesses and communities."

As I said the Republicans had a different take. Their position according to House majority leader Eric Cantor of Virginia was that you cut expenses or cut in other areas like any family in crisis. You live within your means.(There was a filibuster going on and it was finally broken when six Republicans from disaster affected states crossed the line and supported the funding unconditionally of FEMA for the 6.9Billion figure.

### 606. THE SOLINDRA ISSUE

As you well know President Obama had and has been pushing alternate energy sources at the expense of the Coal Industry. Solindra was such a company. It was to start big to give it an immediate advantage in the market. It was funded under the Stimulus Program. T he Problem was they took the money and then declared bankruptcy This put the Obama agenda in a bad light. The congress was in the process of probing this irregularity that cost billions and saddled each of us with Solindra's debt. The President was correct when he stated all economic ventures have risks. My criticism is that the funds should have been split between several smaller companies and competition would have taken care of the rest.(Too big too fast with no established market.)

### 607. THE NEW PATENT LAW

The President signed into law the America Invents Act of 2011. This bill now law streamlines the process by which ideas are Patented and marketed creating opportunities that equate to new jobs and revenues for the public good. It had broad bipartisan support.. It will not immediately have an effect on the job market and it would mean new training programs for future worker's, but that is what America is all about. He did put one jab in though reminding the Congress and especially the republican side of the American Jobs Act that as of this date was stalled in the House. In a way the two pieces of legislation are interdependent on each other.

## 608. THE CONCEPT OF THE BEAR

A conservative and a Liberal look in a mirror. The conservative resembles a lumbering creature and the liberal a faster animal say an ocelot. If you let the bear sleep the ocelot can change his environment and even that of the bears. The problem comes when you attach an, individuals actions to a movement and blame the movement conservatism for the actions of say George W. Bush you are poking the bear in the stomach and you will get a reaction.

That in a nutshell is what Senator Obama did to Senator McCain in his search for the presidency. His reward was Republican intransigence and a dedicated effort to block even helpful programs that had Republican precepts with a twist. That is why the economy was so slow to recover. Add to that the Corporate self-serving mind be that liberal or conservative you have a readymade sand box where two children are fighting over the same space.

I guess what I am saying is don't paint your opponent with too broad a brush because you will get a fight over principle. Governor Romney is both right and wrong. If he can boost the GDP to 4% he can accomplish his goals of reviving the job market and demand for American goods and services.. The Presidents government stick in the stomach approach can work and has but the bear is saying enough!

## 609. BEING ROME

When we were attacked on September 11,2001 President Bush reacted with a series of measures that restricted our civil liberties and our rights when traveling on Planes Trains and Buses, not to mention various laws affecting Habeas Corpus. Along comes Senator Obama who attacks not only the war but the methods and reasons employed in the conflict. Once in office he not only upholds what George did but he expands on it. In all fairness he is bringing the troops home and one war has ended and the other is about to end in 2014. Guantanamo still exists as do the laws that could affect U.S. citizens. The same principles used on them could at some future time be used on us.

At present we are a Democratic republic and all republics have a right to defend themselves against aggressors and even descent with-in. Lincoln did it as did FDR when the Japanese were interred in California. We even have the example of Angel island off San Francisco bay. The big but is we have to move back to the protection of our civil liberties or we will fall as Rome did of our own weight.

## 610. ON EDUCATION
### September 29, 2011

When president Obama pushed his Stimulus Package 447 billion was designated for education. He was targeting the children to be better able to save the nation where their parents could not. He attacked the concept of standardized testing pushed by the No Child Left Behind Program as authored by George W. Bush as being non-workable and encouraging cheating which it did. He argued in favor of a math, science and literacy based program so we have more future adult citizens with the tools to compete in the global economy and make America number one again. He put it this way speaking to a group of middle school children: "We're working to make sure you have the most up-to date schools with the latest tools for learning, and we're working to get the best teachers into the class-room as well so they can help you prepare for college and a future career."Note his real target market is not the currently unemployed or the older set of workers but those that could be trained for the future one world economy.

## 611. WHAT IS JUSTICE

In 2001 then President George Bush on September 18 of that year made the following executive order: "The Justice Department is authorized to use all necessary and appropriate force against those nations, organizations, or persons he determines planned, authorized, committed or aided the terrorist attacks that occurred on September 11, 2001, or harbored such organizations or persons in order to prevent any future acts of terrorism against the United States by such nations, organizations or persons."In that declaration American citizens were not exempted. It is interesting that initially that fact was not initially caught.

What has brought this aspect of the argument to light is the assassination of a U.S. Citizen by the name of Awlaki who was number two or three in the Al Qaeda. The Civil Liberties Union stated he as a citizen had the right of trial. Initially President Obama was in agreement with that position but on reviewing the situation supported the bush position and went a bit further.

Awlaki was special because he was conducting his war against the United States from foreign soil and was very much a combatant and had he been captured alive would have been in Guantanamo. If I remember correctly Americans who fought on the communist side in Spain against general Franko were threatened with the loss of citizenship. Bearing this fact a person U.S. Citizen or not conducting war against the United States would be subject to Awlaki's fate.

## 612. JOBS ACT PRESSURE
October 7, 2011

Intransigence has become the name of the game and the bully-pulpit the presidents weapon of choice. He said he intended to remind the voting public of the obstructionist practices of the Republican minority in Congress. He was following the path of President Harry Truman in his battle for his Fair Deal Agenda where he labeled the Republican dominated Congress The Do Nothing Congress. The President said: "If the Congress does something, then I can't run against a Do Nothing Congress." To refresh your mind on the Republican position, it contends that the private sector creates jobs not the government. The best way to do that is to reduce targeted taxes and lessen regulations. I do not believe these Republican interests are talking about deregulation as Obama has inferred.

In a way this was pulling a Carter because President speaking before a forum of public defenders and prosecutors contended that the poor were not afforded adequate defense. The stunned group had to inform the President of recently passed Pro=bono legislation of their own addressing what the President was talking about.

Prior to his statement on the Jobs Act the Congress had passed three pieces of his legislation exactly as he wanted it. Those pieces of legislation were: Patent Reform Bill, High Way Construction Bill, and a Bill to Fund the Federal Aviation Administration. His last piece of legislation had not been acted on because it had only the previous week reached the legislature. That bill was the Trade Pact Bill that was and is designed to make us more competitive.

Senate Republican Mitch McConnell of Kentucky targeted a Democratic Bill that would impose a surtax on those earning in excess of one million on a yearly basis. That tax would be 5.9% of that figure and the funds would go to finance President Obama's agenda. He stated: "If the president is concerned about inaction he should set his sights on the democratic run senate." He called it an unwise tax hike.

President Obama stated: "The problems Europe is having today could have a very real affect on our economy at a time when it's already fragile. But this jobs bill can help guard against another down-turn if the situation in Europe gets any worse. It can boost economic growth. It will put people back to work."

## 613. FAST AND FURIOUS UNRESOLVED
October 7, 2011

The Congressional sub-committee on the Fast and Furious issue held under the auspicious of the department of Alcohol Tobacco and Firearms was contending because of previous testimony and internal memo's Eric H Holter was aware of the program that he is now denying he knew of as far as its intent was stated. Roughly 2,000 automatic Assault weapons were allowed to pass into the hands of the Mexican cartels. It was supposed to be a sting operation but they lost control of their merchandise. Sting operations are standard practice but this one went wrong and a Border patrol Officer was killed as a result.

President Obama has stood by Holter stating: "He's indicated he was not aware of what was happening in Fast and Furious. Certainly I was not and I think both he and I would have been very unhappy if somebody had suggested that guns were allowed to pass through that could have been prevented."It was noted that a 15 month program of surveillance be conducted by the Justice department of the Federal Bureau of Alcohol Tobacco and Firearms in the Phoenix office. The President continued: "I have complete confidence in him.."

## 614. SOLYNDRA
### October 8, 2011

To briefly recap the situation Solynra a solar panel products firm secured a loan backed by the Federal Government for 535 Million. It was supposed to be the crown jewel of President Obama's Energy independence Plan. Instead it became a thorn in his side. There was a 25 billion dollar program directed by Steven Spinner to select the firm to be used in the grand solar economic adventure. He was supposed to recues himself from making any decision on Solyndra because of his wife's connection to the firm, but he did not. After the loan was made the Fremont California Company went Bankrupt. Leaving the American tax payer with the bill. In all 1,100 employees lost their jobs. They came to work one morning and the Plant was closed.

In all fairness to the Obama administration events can go wrong and sometimes companies don't make it. I can also say that this deal stinks. The administration should have sponsored several smaller companies as I said earlier and let them fight for a share of the market.

## 615. LATINO VOTERS WANTED
### Oct. 19, 2011

Pundits on the Republican side have made so severely off color statements including electrifying the border fence. Mitt Romney while debating with Rick Perry thought it was wrong to have education grants for the children of illegal immigrants and a path to citizenship. Romney himself at this time preferred those kids get permanent legal status and a fair chance through regular channels to attain citizenship. President Obama was promoting his dream act that was ironically similar to Perry's position.

Here is one of my tasteless election jokes: What do you have when a fisherman is taking the bait off the hook? He's debating.

This is a serious issue as out lined by a statement made by New Mexico's State Senator Linda M. Lopez Democrat. Who stated: "People aren't illegal and they aren't aliens. Aliens are what my ten year old son watches on Transformers."

The Latin groups and individuals have indeed enhanced our culture. Their families go back three four five generations in California. What is wrong is those that come over and steal the identities of others if only to make a living. That is still wrong. Add to that the fact that only citizens have the right to vote and the controversy around this election and that issue. I could raise the point of the American citizen who is homeless and is denied his right to vote simply because he does not have an address. That to me should supersede a non citizen's right to vote.

## 616. TRANSPERANT GOVERNMENT?
### October 31, 2011

Remember the Patriot Act and the great howl on how unjust it was to those accused. Well President Obama is now our leader and he has not released his take on that act. Just how does the department of home-Land Security define itself these days. Should not we be restoring some of those rights we have sacrificed in the name of security?

I will give you an example for purely economic reasons. Ontario International Airport suffers from the lack of business because it is now managed as a stepchild of Los Angeles International Airport. The shops are gone where you could have a drink and see the planes take off and land The closest you can get is the ticket counter and the baggage pick-up. Business is down 40% and the place lacks any social services. The reason 9/11 , and security concerns.

Here is another in Laughlin Nevada Arthur Paul Davis has the largest natural earth and rock filled damn in the western U.S. just above that city in 2001 I was able to take a tour boat the USS Riverside up to the base of the damn and hear the history of the region and places of interest to visit. As recently as 2003 there has been a cable and a affective forbidden zone set up to prevent it from being blown up by terrorists in fishing boats. Today there is a trail you can take to a park at the site of the damn. That is an improvement. There used to helicopter rides that lasted 25 minutes I have all this on film and stills. Because of national Security that too no longer exists for others to enjoy. I can only do it as a ancient memory. The concept of 9/11 hurt us in so many ways.

On a more formal level information that can be secured under the Freedom of Information Act is now limited. Government can and does distort and hide what it perceives to sensitive facts as outlined by the Patriot Act. The courts now determine potential exemption related to that act. This is a mechanism by which the government can deceive its own people. In this Democratic Republican society we still can challenge the status Quo but as we cede more to the central government that could change. It is time to take some of the power back.

## 617. TRANSCANADA'S PIPE-LINE
### November 7, 2011

We keep on arguing about energy independence. Our Neighbor to the North Canada is a staunch ally and good business partner. The project that has ruffled so many feathers is the Key-Stone XL Permit that would if it had become reality stretched from Hardesty in Alberta to Houston Texas where the oil would have been refined. The other route going to the West coast was opposed by the Canadian side. It would have passed through Montana, North Dakota, South Dakota, Nebraska, Kansas where it would split and go to a refinery in Illinois (Patoka). The other end of the split would have gone through Oklahoma, to Houston Texas.

What went wrong was those states mentioned basically said not in my back yard. This put the plan back to zero. Environmental groups formed huge demonstrations opposed to the idea. There was talk on the Canadian side of selling that sand based oil to Asia for a greater profit if their southern neighbors were not interested.

Here is the horns of the dilemma. The Obama Administration was being blamed by the Romney camp of not vigorously pursuing energy independence through this pipeline. Remember this is an election year and even if the federal government had insisted on this path imagine the animosity of those states affected. So the Romney Camp was wrong on this one. Also remember that little oil spill on the east coast that I spoke of earlier and the criticism over that one. For more information check the chapter on beyond Petroleum.

## 618. THE LOW PROFILE
### November 9, 2011

The President would later shift into high gear, but at this time you see he had a lot on his plate. He was also observing the shifting political landscape. It revolved around the reaction to his Stimulus package that had not born its full fruit yet and his Affordable Health Plan that had come under fire for too much too soon.

In Arizona, Russel Peirce who was the States Senate President was defeated by fellow Republican Jerry Lewis. You see names do live on. He was the architect of SB 1070.

In Kentucky Governor Steve Bashear defeated his republican opponent David Williams who was the Senator of that state and president of the Senate. He also defeated the third party candidate Gatewood Galbraith. I wonder if there is any relation between him and the economist.

In the State of Mississippi voters elected Phil Briant the Leftenant Governor over Haley Barbour. Also defeated was a historic attempt by Johney Dupree to become the first African American Governor of that State.

In the State of Colorado the pro abortion forces had a bill that was defeated. Those defending a woman's right to an abortion(Row vs Wade) received a reprieve in one of this nation's most conservative states.

The State of Maine repealed a Republican backed piece of legislation passed the previous year that would have put to an end the long standing tradition of same day registration.

In Des Moines Iowa the State Senate saved a Democratic seat from being lost to the Republicans, preserving the democratic majority in that state.

Louisiana's Governor Bobby Jindel won re-election in his State.

West Virginia's Governor Earle Ray Tomblin was elected to fill out the term of his states Senate seat.

All across the political demographic there were subtle shifts in the nations landscape. But I think not enough to cause the president any real great worry. He was just taken aback by the conservative nature of this country to his progressive agenda.

## 619. ASIAN CONFERENCE
### November 12, 2011

The previous week the president had been at the G 20 in France and this week his preparations are the Asian Conference. He is due to Chair that conference. He was getting heat for doing his job. Again the republicans like Majority Leader of the House John Boihner were off base because this is what presidents do.

The other side to this argument goes to the spawning of new initiative that do not require legislation and build a buffer in the event of intransigence especially in an election year. The conference was held in Hawaii. He then conducted business in the region Australia and Indonesia. Both these regions are facing trouble from expanding Chinese influence and a solid backing of the nations in the region are needed when negotiating with the Chinese. So again for different reasons this trip is important.

## 620. THE PALESTINIAN STATEHOOD ISSUE

The Palestinian Authority and its Foreign Minister Riad Malki were accepted into UNESCO which is the social organization aiding the non-aligned movement in developing countries. It was applying for full membership at the U N as a state. They had lined up eight of the nine members of the Security Council. With the U.S. taking the position of a threatened veto and countries like France now taking the position of abstaining from the vote. The only country's that supported them were: China, Russia, Brazil, India, South Africa, Lebanon, and the country of Gabon. Those on the no side: Bosnia Herzegovina, Britain, Columbia, France, Germany, Portugal and of course the United States.

Faced with such overwhelming odds they are rethinking their position. They are however proud of the fact that they got eight of the nine members of the Security Council and there is always tomorrow. Remember when Taiwan was on the Security Council and it was voted off by the other members of that council in favor of mainland China.

### 621. THE CAMPAIN TRAIL

The Michigan Campaign is a case in point. There has been all this talk of job creation but no visible jobs. There was jaw-boning on the revival of Detroit but as of this date the industry had not really taken off.

The Political Analyst Charley Cook stated: "Things were pretty awful before President Obama was even sworn in. But by this point you own the economy. There's just not a state in the Union where he's better off today than he was a year ago and in some states, particularly the industrial mid-western states, like Michigan, Pennsylvania, and Wisconsin the erosion has been greater than others."These states in2008 were concerned with the Free Trade Agreement, gas prices, and health care. In that year we had several of these issues raised and I can only guess if they are happy in the area of health care.

The Analyst continued: "They rebelled against Bush in 2006 and 2008 against the lagging living standards and the economy, and then rebelled in the 2010 election. The republican candidate for Governor even swept Macomb County. They're still in rebellion. There's no evidence that the President or the Democrats have won them back all since 2010."

### 622. ASIAN CONFERENCE (continued)
November 14, 2011

There are 21 nations that compose this organization and the United States is a odd fit but being the leading power in the region we have to defend our ground. China's President is said to be moving his currency the Yuan more in line with the other currencies in the International monetary Fund. At issue is also the burgeoning military power of the Chinese navy challenging the U.S. presence in the yellow sea that separates Taiwan Indonesia and its neighbors from main land China. Australia actually has a more active relationship with China than it does with the United States and Great Britain. Add to that the growing Asian population in Australia itself you see a tug of war for its soul. That is why the president went there.

### 623. THE BALANCING ACT
November 30, 2011

While President Obama is looking for agreement with our Asian allies Secretary of State Hillary R. Clinton is in what was formerly known as Burma now called Myanmar coaxing a formerly secretive tyrannical regime into the light of day. Sanctions that have burdened this nations recent history will be lifted if certain things happen and their leaders seem so inclined.

She was in their Capital Naypyidaw talking with their President Thein Sein and their Foreign minister Wunna Maung Lwin.This recent change of heart has led to the freeing of Nobel Lauriat Prize Winner Suu Kyi who had been under house arrest for 15 years for leading a non-violent revolution that was brutally crushed by its military. She is now the new symbol of hope in this emerging changing culture that is of Buddhist Muslim mix. The National league For Democracy, which is the emerging party of change, in the country.

Tom Malinowski representing the Human Rights Watch stated: "This trip is a huge gamble that only pays off with substantial progress. The administration is very much aware of the risks."At issue is the release of some 1,600 political prisoners which, Hillary has promised to be very blunt about. Secretary of State Hillary Clinton commented: "We are not making any abrupt changes. We have to do more fact finding and that's part of my trip. The meeting is a real opportunity for both sides, even if reform and lifting of sanctions takes time."

The other major reason for even Hillary, to be where she is that a free Myanmar with good U.S. relations would counter the efforts of China in the rights to oil leases in the South China Sea. You see no matter what we do it still breaks down to oil and power. These things matter not only to us but to those 21 nations that make up ASEAN.

## 624. THE PAYROLL TAX CUT FIGHT

As has often been said what a president does overseas or as a balancing act to increase his own prestige can get lost in the translation. At issue is a 2% tax cut to stimulate employment by lowering the cost of hiring employees and stimulating demand.

The Republican side argues that if you give a 2% cut you affect revenues and because you affect revenues and you cannot assume that it will cause growth you have to offset it with cutting a program someplace else. There comes the rub.

As I have all too often stated: since this is an election season at this time Phil Musser a political consultant stated: "Whoever the Republicans nominate should make strong executive leadership part of the central thesis of the campaign to replace him."

From the perspective of the White House a spokesman for the White House stated: "He's going to put a lot of effort into making sure everyone in the country is aware that the payroll tax will expire at the end of the year unless Congress acts. We will travel. We will do interviews. We will do events."

Concerning the confrontation of ideas the White house stated: "They going to have to get out there (Referring to the republicans) it's just a question of whether they're going to do it the easy way or the hard way."

## 625. MEANWHILE BACK IN EUROPE

The European Union as of this date was considering a series of steps to help those nations of the Union that had fallen on hard times because of their economic policies. A Treasury Bond backed by the seventeen nations that compose the Union was under consideration.

Remember the concept of the prime rate, which is the rate the European Fed charges banks to do business with their customers the county's of the European Union that are in need of funds. Well that was set at 8%. For Italy to secure a loan to pay for its functioning was 8%. Now imagine what they charged their citizens. At present our Fed Prime rate as of this date in 2011 is zero. The reason is our economy has reached a plateau and the Fed is trying to stir growth ignoring the deficit. In Europe they are tackling their debt at the expense of social services and even the size of government. Italy is considered too big to rescue and its collapse into bankruptcy would trigger worldwide (Calamity) that would have an adverse affect on the investor themselves.(The whole of Europe and us) The reason would be we are trading partners and linked in this new Y2K economy.

This concept of bonds and the policies of nations like Greece, Portugal, Spain, Italy, Ireland have consequences. That would be the limiting of economic sovereignty of the nations involved and those nations administering the funds. This is why Germany has called the idea initially a non-starter. Germany and Austria have strong economies and would be imposing their will on others in economic social areas.

Should we be forced into a similar affair, we would not like it. The IMF would be dictating to us on our pensions, health care, size of public sector jobs. Add to that we would no longer hold the place in the world we have today.

## 626. THE JAW BONING AFFECT
December 1, 2011

President Obama in order to defend his agenda as of this date is reverting to candidate Obama. He spoke to the citizens of the State of Pennsylvania one of the key states linked to his re-election. He stated: "Send your Senators a message. Tell them, don't be a Grinch. Don't vote to raise taxes on working Americans during the holidays."

What the President was referring to the extension of the pay tax cut with enhancements expanding the amount the average family would save from 1 thousand dollars to 1 thousand five hundred dollars. Employers who hire would get a holiday from the 6.2% tax hike that is scheduled for 2012. The size of this econometric model is 240 billion. The Democratic Congress hopes to offset the cost by a 3.25% Surtax on private incomes starting at 1 million dollars for individuals and married couples in that income range.

The President put it succinctly stating: "So let's just be clear if they vote no your taxes go up. Vote yes you get a tax cut. Which way do you think the Congress should vote?"I have it all along President is similar to Reagan in one area he a great communicator. The trouble is economic realities could get in the way similar to what happened to George. That could happen if the economy flattens out.

## 627. ONE WAR ENDS
### December 13, 2011

The site is Washington D C and President Obama and Prime Minister Nouri Maliki stand side by side. In a joint declaration they declare the Iraq War over and the beginning of government to government relations. It is pointed out that the future is uncertain but both parties are committed. There is a vow to contain the influence of Iran that has been itching for this moment when they as a influential neighbor fill the void left by our departure.

President Obama stated: "We're here to mark the end of this war, and to begin a new chapter in the history between our countries, a normal relationship between sovereign nations."

Senator John McCain had a different take on this step. In affect call it election year jitters but the Senator felt that both men had failed in their responsibilities and the region at risk for wider violence. The Senator stated: "They failed the responsibilities to protect shared interests. All the progress that both Iraqi's and Americans have made at such painful and substantial cost has now been put at greater risk."

Again we can only guess how the domestic fronts in Iraq, be they Kurds, Sunni's, or Shiites not to mention the Coptic's and Jewish communities will deal with their fundamental differences. Add to this the insurgency and fringe Al Qaeda remnants you have quite a pot of stew to deal with. Prime Minister Maliki stated: "The relationship doesn't end with the departure of the last American soldier, "

## 628. MEANWHILE BACK IN BRITAIN

As of the date of this article there was in affect a coalition government between the Conservative Party and Liberal Democrats. The measure of linkage of economic policy of the 26 European nations as a means of propping up the Euro was rebuffed by Britain and the Prime Minister David Cameron. Deputy Prime Minister Nick Clegg was in open disagreement over the prime Ministers decision to not join this part of the economic pact.

Cameron minus Clegg at the House of Commons made the following statement: "We are in the European Union and we want to be. I am absolutely clear that it is possible to be both a full committed and influential member of the European Union but stay out of the arrangement where they do not protect our interests."

Nick Clegg of the Liberal Democrats stated: "It would have been a distraction if I was there. The prime Minister and I clearly do not agree on the outcome of the

Summit.... Isolation in Europe when we are one against 26 is potentially a bad thing and a bad thing for jobs, a bad thing for growth and a bad thing for the livelihood of millions of people in this country."

In France its President Nickolas Sarcozy had hailed the agreement as the birth of a new reality. He stated: "There are now clearly two Europe's one that wants more solidarity between members and regulation and the other that is only interested in the idea of a single market."

Other voices out of Europe Ollie Rehn an official of the European union stated: "I regret very much that the united kingdom was not willing to join the new fiscal compact. I regret it as much for the sake of Europe and its crisis response as for the sake of British citizens and their perspectives. We want a strong and constructive Britain in Europe and we want Britain to be at the center of Europe not on the sidelines."

Now I ask you to again think our reaction to the European situation as a whole and our partnered response to global trade and our respective GDPs which are shrinking. Our market share is still many times larger than that of our Chinese partners but there share is rising though at a slower rate. Is the world economic cycle about to head back to recession or are we still on the rising side of a bell curve.

### 629. THE CANNONS ARE SOUNDING OFF
#### January 24, 2012

Imaging a group of military strategists now whittled to four squaring off on stage looking for a common strategy. That is the GOP at this point in the game. They don't hear what is around them for they are seemingly consumed with their own matters. That was this last GOP candidates forum.

Governor Mitt Romney started: "So we have very different perspective on leadership and the kind of leadership our conservative movement needs. Not just to get elected but to get the country right."

Texas Representative Ron Paul stated as to his reasons for the Gingrich defeat in his 1998 election stated: "He didn't have the votes. That was what the problem was. So this idea that he voluntarily resigned and he was going to punish himself because he didn't do well in the election, That's just not the way it was."

The trouble is that Republicans have too much history. When Gingrich went to work for Freddie Mac as a consultant though he calls himself a historian, and he is that he inherited political baggage. That is the financial organization officially blamed for the mortgage melt-down.

Governor Romney stated: "They don't pay people 25,000 a month offering no explanation to the work that was done."Gingrich had a response that issues needed to be resolved.

On the issue of Romney's income it was reported that he made 21.7 million in the year 2010 and an estimated 20.9 million in 2011. This was according to the *L.A.*

*Times*. It was also reported that his tax rate was 14% for that period. This was because took advantage of the deductions available to him as we all do. Somehow this financial success has demonized him along with the nature of his business and his company Bain Capital when he was there CEO. They make money on the margin of the transaction and not the success or failure of a business. Job growth is the result of creative destruction and change. People do get hurt and misplaced.

Romney's response to his methods of creating income were as follows: "I will not apologize for having been successful. I did not inherit what my wife and I have, nor did she. What we have, what I have been able to build, I built the old fashioned way, by earning it by working hard."

It is unfortunate but the amount of people that have been displaced in this economy has set up a populist mentality that president Obama has been able to exploit. At the end of 2012 the projections of economic growth were still 9 million below where president Obama said we would be and people have fallen through the cracks though the unemployment level at this point in time is in 2012 is 7.8% but that is misleading.

Jumping to what is now November first we have had an odd event. Hurricane Sandy that ravaged New York, New Jersey and other cities on the East coast has turned a dead even contest into a 6% advantage for the President. This event and the human tragedy that has gone along with it has done what the President himself could not do. We will just have to wait for election day for the results.

### 630. THE STATE OF THE UNION
January 25, 2012

The Republicans had been rambling along attacking each other and proposing programs and directions they wanted to take the country. Barak Obama just as he had done with senator McCain took republican ideas and adopted them as his own. Rick Santorum of all the candidates gave Barak a gift the unfair trade practices of China and how President Obama would get tough with China. Among other things he referred to the price of labor and currency manipulation a theme Romney himself would use later in the campaign.

The emphasis on the common man, and the blue collar mentality. The struggling work force and having the rich pay their fair share all the while demonizing Romney without mentioning his name. The President said: "On the day I took office our auto industry was on the verge of collapse. Some even said we should let it die: Tonight the American Auto Industry is back.(He attacked the uneven distribution of wealth.) You can call this class warfare if you want, but asking a Billionaire to pay at least as much as his secretary in taxes. It's not because they envy the rich: it's because somebody else has to make up the difference."The President was using republican words with a twist to his advantage. That is just good debating.

Again this is just a snap-shot of the process we here on the continental United states call the election process. It is a game but it is a very deadly game that employs and draws in a lot of people. It is still the best system in the world but we are not alone in trying to occupy the same space.

On the theme of patriotism he looked or policy of limited duration missions and our drone air-force."Each time I look at the flag, I'm reminded that our destiny is stitched together like these 50 stars and thirteen stripes."His reference to his gotcha operation to get Bin Laden along with the other Al Qaeda leaders that have had their careers cut short with no loss of life at our end to some is the ultimate Orwellian Dream.

Gabrielle Gifferd was honored for her service in the three terms she has served the House. She survived an assassination by a man who is now in a mental institution. Six others died around her. Her resignation is so she can recover. The Presidents embrace of her brought true togetherness as a nation.

Indiana Governor Mich Daniels echoed the republican point of view: "We do not accept that ours will ever be a nation of haves and have knots. We must always be a nation of haves and soon to haves."

Those around the President know he has a certain proportion of the population behind him. In this case it is 44%. Here is an analysis: "Obama knows he has 44% of the electorate. 44% is a big number. I'm going to keep these people on board then we'll go after everyone else."I think I have presented the mindset of the period. You as the reader have to figure how you fit in.

### 631. HOUSING
### January 26, 2012

There is a difference between action and perceived action. The housing market and the mortgage crisis became the target for some degree of solution which could be in reality illusory.

The President has proposed aid to those who are current on their mortgage but their property is under water and I am not referring to Hurricane Sandy though it would be a good euphemism. Under the program the average loan holder could save $3,000 a year. New regulations and stricter enforcement could lead to the prosecution of larger banks. The catch 22 is that some of these investigations are ongoing and have been around for years. I do expect a fall guy or two but no real action. Thomas Gorman an attorney at Dorsey and Whitman a Washington based firm stated: "Frankly it's coming to the table somewhat late."

What we have here is pretty much a standard practice. Be it a President or a member of the legislature. You initiate action to late for it to have an authentic affect and brag on how much you helped the situation. That is how you defend your position be you Democrat or Republican.

## 632. ARIZONA'S GOVERNOR

Arizona's Governor Janet Brewer recently wrote a book that reflects the ill will between her state and the Federal Government. Her quote in the book is: "I felt a little bit like being lectured to and I was a little kid in a class room, if you will and he was this wise professor and I was this little kid and this little kid knows what the problem is and I felt minimized to say the least."She added about the 2010 visit to ASU."He did blow me off at ASU."

When he visited her state she handed him a hand written invitation to visit her state again and have lunch. She also wanted to give her a personal tour of the border problems."I said to him, you know I have always respected the office of the President and that the book is what the book is."When the President complained about her perceptions she stated: "I said that I was sorry that he felt that way. Anyway we're glad he's here and we'll regroup."

The White house version of this meeting was stated like this: "The Governor handed the President a letter and said she was inviting him to meet with her. The President said he'd be glad to meet with her again but did note that after the last meeting a cordial discussion in the Oval Office the Governor inaccurately described the meeting in her book."All I can say is at least President Obama read the book.

## 633. THE PRESIDENT'S MANUFACTURING PLAN

Again perception and size figure into this argument. On the surface it looks really good reflecting his new populist image. There would be a 20% tax credit for those companies that are currently abroad to relocate back into the United States. Deduction according to the proposal would be tailored to greener industries. This of course means ignoring the oil industry as the coal industry was ignored and called a major polluter. I have a problem those generations of coal miners that are now in a chronic state of unemployment and even if retrained would not fit the social profile for the Y2K economy and the creative destruction that goes with it. I understand that all of this might be as inevitable as the sun-rise, but the consequences are still worth pondering.

There would also be a 30% minimum tax on all those with incomes in excess of 1 million dollars. The president by this action intends to preserve the social net for the poor and disconnected. The problem is the corporate structure will see it as an excuse to promote one class above another. This will work hand in hand with the concept of open borders for the corporate class leaving the late 20th century class behind.

The President has optimistically stated: "There's no reason we can't restore the basic American promise that if you work hard you will do well."He added while on a whistle stop in cedar Rapids Michigan: "Americans are not about hand-outs. America is about earning everything you've got."

Analysts on the Republican side according to the *L.A. Times* stated: "The President was attempting to be a populist and generate the applause line. But if you really want to show your serious there would be focus on lowering the differential. You do that by lowering the Corporate tax rate."

Add to this foreign firms actively producing goods in the United States you would have to twist the tax codes to a greater extent. Some have argued that would be the tax code argument upside-down. Question do you allow Chinese firms that are indeed private with government interest to operate in the United States? Do we stick strictly to our historical allies?

This I have just mentioned is to some the hammer that hits the nail on the head. Elizabeth Jacobs a fellow of the Brookings Institution stated: "It seems a very neat pivot between this idea that we need to be the best educated, most innovative economy in the world and harking back to something we view as very American, build stuff that the rest of the world wants."

Other voices are heard in this potential boondoggle Dennis Hoffman Economist at W P Carey School of Business stated: "Economically we would face some clear unrelenting head-winds to try to bring low and medium tech manufacturing back to the states. We need to do research and development here and high-tech manufacturing and in that way seize the pockets of the competitive advantage."

# THE NATION 2012

## 634. SYRIA
### March 7, 2012

It never rains. It just pours and in this case the Arab Spring that saw violence in Iran, Libya, Egypt, and now Syria has shown how the fundamental brand of Islam seems to be setting up a emerging empire of some sort. The Coptic Christian communities and their Jewish counterparts seem to be in the position of odd man out.

President Obama as a representative of western influence has to take a moral stand. This country has to side with those getting the worst end of the deal. At the same time we can-not get involved in this conflict. We can impose sanctions freeze accounts that we control. We can put the angst on our trading partners to do the same. The President stated: "For us to take military action unilaterally as some have suggested or think that some-how there's a simple solution I think is a mistake."

Action by the United Nations is out of the question because of a guaranteed veto of such action. Both Russia and China are on the same page on this one. It is their belief that any revolution must be fought from with-in with no foreign influence. They happen to have contributed a few bombs bullets and airplanes but that's not interference. You see they have contracts and economic interests central to their economy and Assad is central to that point.

It is unfortunate that those seeking power did and do not comprehend the constraints we are in as we extricate ourselves from Afghanistan as we have from Iraq. Mattis a White House spokesman basically stated that our military involvement would intensify the conflict and increase casualties. I think Assad will survive this because the world cannot afford to get involved and it will be a catalyst for some alliance in what was the old Persian Empire. The building blocks are all there.

Earlier the President was defining the United States as a re-emerging economy coming out of a great depression. The progress is not what we want it to be but we are improving in all our sectors. He used the Federal help given to the Auto Industry in defiance of the pessimists. The use of TARP was actually one of Obama's better ideas. That program actually made money for the government. The only problem is that you could draw a reverse parallel between our efforts and the Chinese experiment with capitalism as a form of National Socialism.

You can even go to Ronald Reagan who stated: "An incumbent has to err on the side of realistic optimism. A challenger has to figure out a way to sell the need for change without terrifying the people."Our involvement in the world is a tenuous affair and being a leader plunging in with both feet. We have to protect our economy and our interests in the world. We do that through alliances and if your people don't want to go to war you don't go to war. You build your economy. Bring in manufacturing and stimulate both economic and job based growth.

David Axelrod was commenting on Romney and his middle ground attack position in relation to the other republican candidates and reflected on the Obama position stating: "Even in the worst of times no one wants a President who is grinding his teeth and cursing in the darkness."Obama's message of hope and his rhetorical talents coupled with incentives has served as a beacon of direction for a segment of the working force. It is unfortunate that not all will be able to take that train to opportunity.

### 635. MORE ON SYRIA

Those that oppose the Assad regime be they children or relatives of those that oppose this power grab are dealt with cruelly. A story from Amman Jordon from a woman Um Eddine her nick-name who fled with her 2 children after hiding in house after house being hunted by forces loyal to Assad. Her husband she thought was dead. She witnessed the beheading of the son of a neighbor and as a result of her husband and what she had seen decided to flee to the Jordanian border. They left only with the clothes on their backs so as to not slow down their journey. They were met by Jordanian border guards and offered tea after their escape. These are the stories of tyranny that are sparking debate in this country.

### 636. ON RUSSIA

As Russia continues to defend Syria and not necessarily Assad but the interests he represents comments made in what was supposed to be a private moment between President Obama and then President Dmetry Medvedev assuring the Russian leader of more flexibility on the missile defense treaty caused a hyperbole here at home. All of the candidates for president jumped on that bandwagon.

What should ring a bell though is something under consideration by the Russian Dumas expanding the meaning of high treason to mean any contact with a foreign news agency or foreign individual deemed to compromise the security of the state.

Now use your imagination on how such legislation could be used. Right now the measure is in a tie of sorts 139 to 138. The opposition is pleading with Putin who has now been re-elected President to veto the measure. It could and probably would bring on another Stalinist period.

Now look at the somewhat cozy relationship we have with the Kremlin. The argument is with good relations we get more done as opposed to the colder tone of stiffer relations. The Russians reminded us that the Cold War was over. If that is so why this new definition of Treason? Maybe Romney is right and we are the fool to be glossing over what happens in that country.

### 637. LAGOS NIGERIA

There was a peaceful transition of power in Senegal after the two term President

Aboulaye Wades was fighting his own two term limit law like Chaves did in Venezuela when compromised their electoral system. In the end Wades conceded defeat Macky Sall age 50 won the contest. This peaceful resolution in a nation known for military Coups showed their democracy had matured despite the demonstrations in the street. This to the administration under President Obama was in a sense showing by example showing what was copied by Senegal and is giving hope to Africa.

## 638. THE KOREAN SUMMIT
### March 24, 2012

Earlier I told you of that private moment Dmetry and Obama. There back drop was much more important keeping the Korean Peninsula nuclear free. China is on board on this one. The North Koreans had at this time planned the testing of a rocket capable of what they said was an endeavor to enter the space race. The US and its allies contended this test by Kim Jung Un would put at risk the food and social aid promised in exchange for the halting and potential dismantling of their nuclear fission reactors. That test which was held blew up so no harm no foul.

The President did also speak to the Chinese President Hu Jintao as he did with then President Dmitry Medvedev who he had that now famous slip of the tongue conversation.

Speaking of Russia we have been on a slippery slope with them. Last year a reporter was detained by the NKGB after speaking with a Russian citizen and taking a note from him. He was held for 30 days and then deported. Newspapers have been systematically shut down. The Billionaire that ran for the presidency was hassled by the Putin administration. Good or no it gives credence Governor Romney said was basically correct as to them being a geopolitical foe. And should this expanded definition of Treason become law you are looking you are defiantly looking at a cooling of U.S. Russian Relations. For now we are just fine and I hope what has transpired as recent history does not go any further. We need the Russians to help solve the problems we are having with Iran and they are an important ally.

Ben Rhodes the Deputy National Security advisor stated: "What the president's personal leadership and investment in the Nuclear agenda has done is allow the world to come together behind common approaches to apply pressure on country's that break the rules, and provide incentives for country's to do the right thing."This is a taste of what the conference was about and you can see we are still an important part of the mix.

## 639. HEALTH CARE ISSUE AS A TAX

When this grand idea was introduced we call the Affordable Health care Plan the penalty that would be charged to those without health care was not called a tax. it was only later when the Supreme Court took up the issue it ruled that the Federal

Government did have the right to tax for a service. That in the end justified the Obama health care bill.

It was a big deal at the time and it is argued that had an ace been called an ace the argument over the nature of the health care legislation would have been a better bill. Just Maybe we would not be fighting over the issue today. It was a bit like arguing whether a square was a rectangle.

The concept of struggling with social issues started in 1938 when the Department of Agriculture dictated the nations farmers all 1.5 Million of them. The issue was how many acres of grain they could grow. This grew into a doctrine of suppressing public evil. There was seemingly no distinction growing for public consumption and one's own need. It was a presumption that higher crop price levels would enrich our pocket books. You can't blame the thinking of the time we were coming out of a great depression. It was President Hoover who thought he could corner the worlds wheat market. That contributed to the Crash of 1929-30. We were back in business by 1933 to some degree. Price supports drove up American prices as we let our exports fall. This led to surpluses and the legislation of 1938. A man by the name of Filburn said: "The paradox of want amidst plenty by doing away with the plenty."The New dealers had what they called the Chinese Wall. The Canadian and Australian wheat famers suffered far less from the depression because they had less protectionist legislation. When Roosevelt brought the issue to the courts he neglected to describe the origin of the conflict and called the farmers orphans. He asked for mercy from the courts on price supports (Wickard vs Filburn) He related what was happening to an act of God. The U.S. D A Secretary that profits were not possible in a free flowing market. Now let's look at health insurance and cross reference. The question whether the Federal Government could compel a citizen to purchase health insurance. We look at subsidies and we see artificial price supports. Prices will always rise to the occasion. It was assumed by the supreme court that the government had an inherent right to regulate policies held to artificial standards like the wheat issue. They forgot in the medical profession the phrase first do no harm. They remembered the phrase "let's play golf."

## 640. IRAN'S PRESSURE
### February 29, 2012

The Israeli government had at this point in time been watching Iran with alarm as it was building what it called a plant of the peaceful use of the atom to provide power for its country. The problem was that the spent rods could be used as the centrifuge for a bomb.

The policies of the Obama administration of don't go beyond this line were being met with skepticism by its prime minister Benjamin Netenyahu. The Republican candidates including Governor Romney were accusing the president of abandoning our ally.. This tension was reflected in their meeting. Today we still have strong relations and we have not yet struck Iran.

## 641. THE KEYSTONE PROJECT
### March 23, 2012

Earlier state opposition to the Keystone Pipe-line because states said the resulting oil spills could potentially contaminate their aqua filter systems and crop lands. We are talking about the breadbasket of the nation. Environmental groups and those on the left and the right thought he would either abandon the plan or leave U.S. domestic production in the quagmire it has been in for some time.

The administration proposed building the pipeline known as Keystone XL, from Oklahoma to the refinery in Texas. This to both sides was a call to arms. The President went to the town of Cushing and stated: "Today I've come to Cushing an oil town because producing more oil and gas here at home has been and will continue to be a critical part of an all the above energy strategy. As I have stated above he was promoting the Trans-Canada project. This project would carry oil gathered from oil sand from Alberta Canada to a refinery in Houston Texas.

The Republican position is that Obama flipped his position to the Republican position of promote all energy measures solar, wind, coal, oil, and natural gas. House Speaker Boihner stated: "The President now says he supports the Republican all the above strategy for our country. But for three years his administration has made every effort to block delay and restrict new energy production in our country."

The Vice President of the Petroleum Institute Martin Durbin stated: "We now hope he will speed up the approval of the entire pipe-line.(Don't these people read. Key states over which the pipe-line was to travel were filing suit in federal court to stop the project.) Supply matters when it comes to the price of gasoline. Keystone X L would bring up 830,000 additional barrels of oil to the market every-day."

What the energy policy of this country will be actually does rest with the states and what they will or will not allow in their back yard. In a way what governor Romney says about energy independence using our most plentiful resource coal or the Obama plan to shift away from petroleum to natural gas and a solar / wind combination is going to go to land use. That requires the cooperation of the states.

## 642. THE TRAYVON MARTIN CASE
### March 24, 2012

Trayvon Martin case was one of social tension over the killing of a 16 year old boy wearing the hoody-style while walking home in the rain by a security guard who ignored the instructions of a 911 call to not pursue.

The President weighed in on this racially charged issue as any father would to his sons interest. The security guard Zimmerman was initially not charged with a crime. Florida has the right of self defense law and the security guard was claiming that he was the victim and had to kill the young man. The issue died. No one was convicted to my knowledge. The President got mixed reviews on this one.

## 643. THE PRESIDENTS TAX ISSUE
### April 14, 2012

It has been a long running gambit battle between Governor Romney and President Obama and it all started about this date. The President made jointly with Michelle his wife $789,674 and paid $162,074 in taxes. That was a rate of 20.5%. On average those making $532,000 pay 24%. The Obama's contributed heavily to charity so their rate was lower. Governor Romney paid 14% of his income. Households that make between 60 and $100,000 pay 8% at present. Most according to the *L.A. Times* pay their marginal rate as opposed to their average rate. The White House secretary who has a salary of $95,000 a year paid a slightly higher rate than Obama. This according to the President is why we need to reform the tax code. The President has proposed a tax rate of 30% for those who make 1 million or more.

In the Obama tax reform package you would see the repeal of the George W. Bush tax cut that for couples making over $250,000. The tax rate as he did three years earlier though he is making three times as much.

For the record President Obama donated $172,130 of their adjusted gross income. The largest group donated to was the Fisher Foundation($117,130,00). So you see the man has a heart and a direction. Romney has his charities also.

## 644. THE ELECTORAL COLLEGE

Here is my favorite pet peeve. It is true that nowhere in the constitution is it stated that a citizen has the right/privilege to vote. That came through various amendments, and is tied to the ownership or be it tentative control of property, and the concept of universal suffrage.

The states to which this power has been attached is the result of preservation of the Union. It was feared that that unless equal and proportional representation was built into each state of the Union we would over time become as fractured as the nation states of Europe. That was the reasoning behind the electoral College, to give Ohio as much power vote wise as New York or California. This was and is a device to keep the states in the union. It was not to give the universal U.S. Citizen of who he or she wants as President. The power utilized by the states must be preserved and only those powers for the universal good should lie with the Federal government(The power to tax, regulate commerce, today certain social programs, the national defense,) All else is the property of the state.

## 645. THE FINAL STATEMENT

We have been on a long journey and even as I write this conclusion we are deciding who will be our next President. From my earliest recollections of California politics to the world around me at that time draw direct parallels to our present situation. What I have in effect discussed with you in these pages with various time-lines are issues we must address if we are to survive as a nation. Please think about what I have said. Understand it is okay to disagree. The important thing is to know why.

www.ingramcontent.com/pod-product-compliance
Lightning Source LLC
Chambersburg PA
CBHW081057290526
45795CB00006B/1894